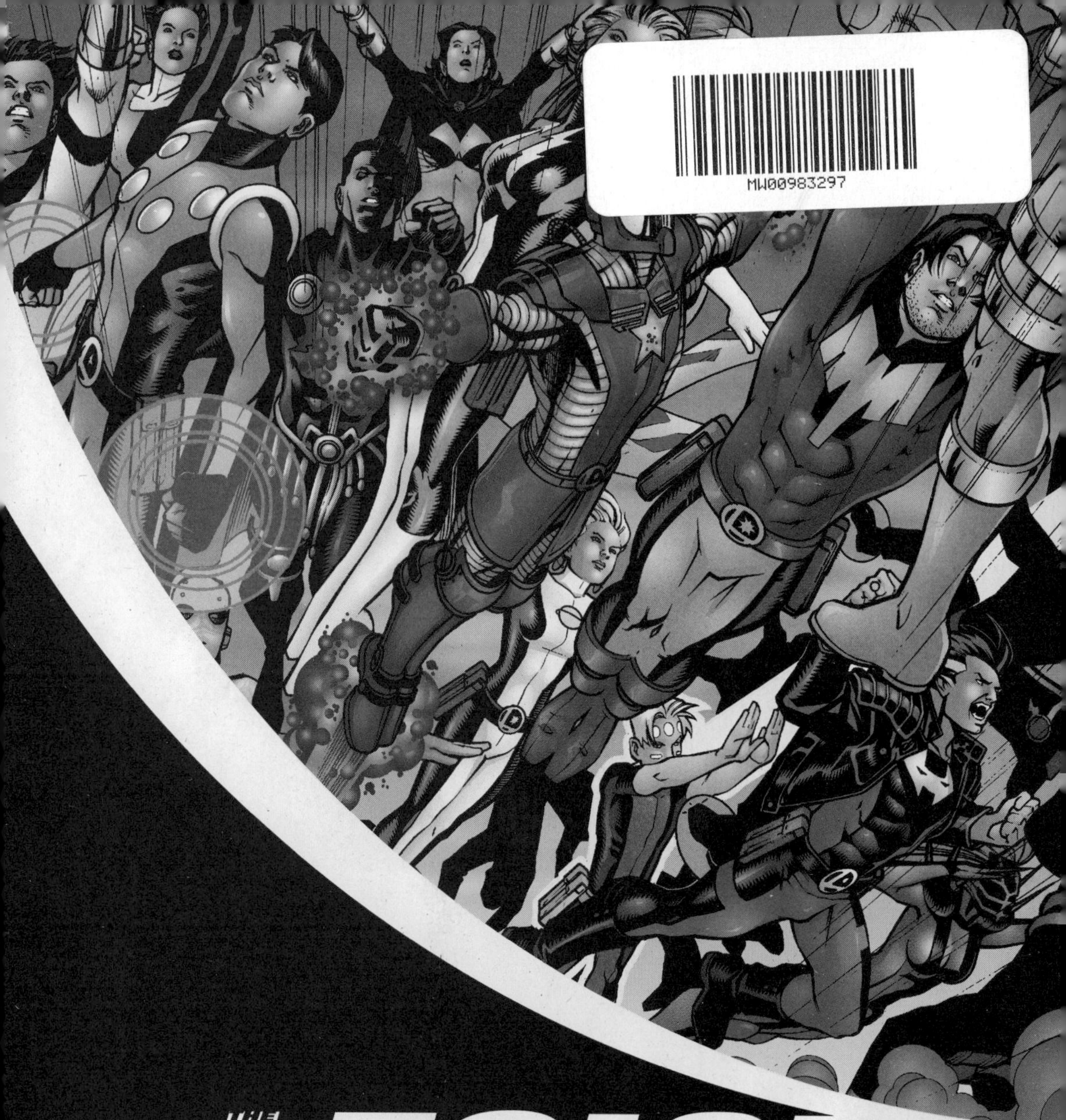

THE LEGION

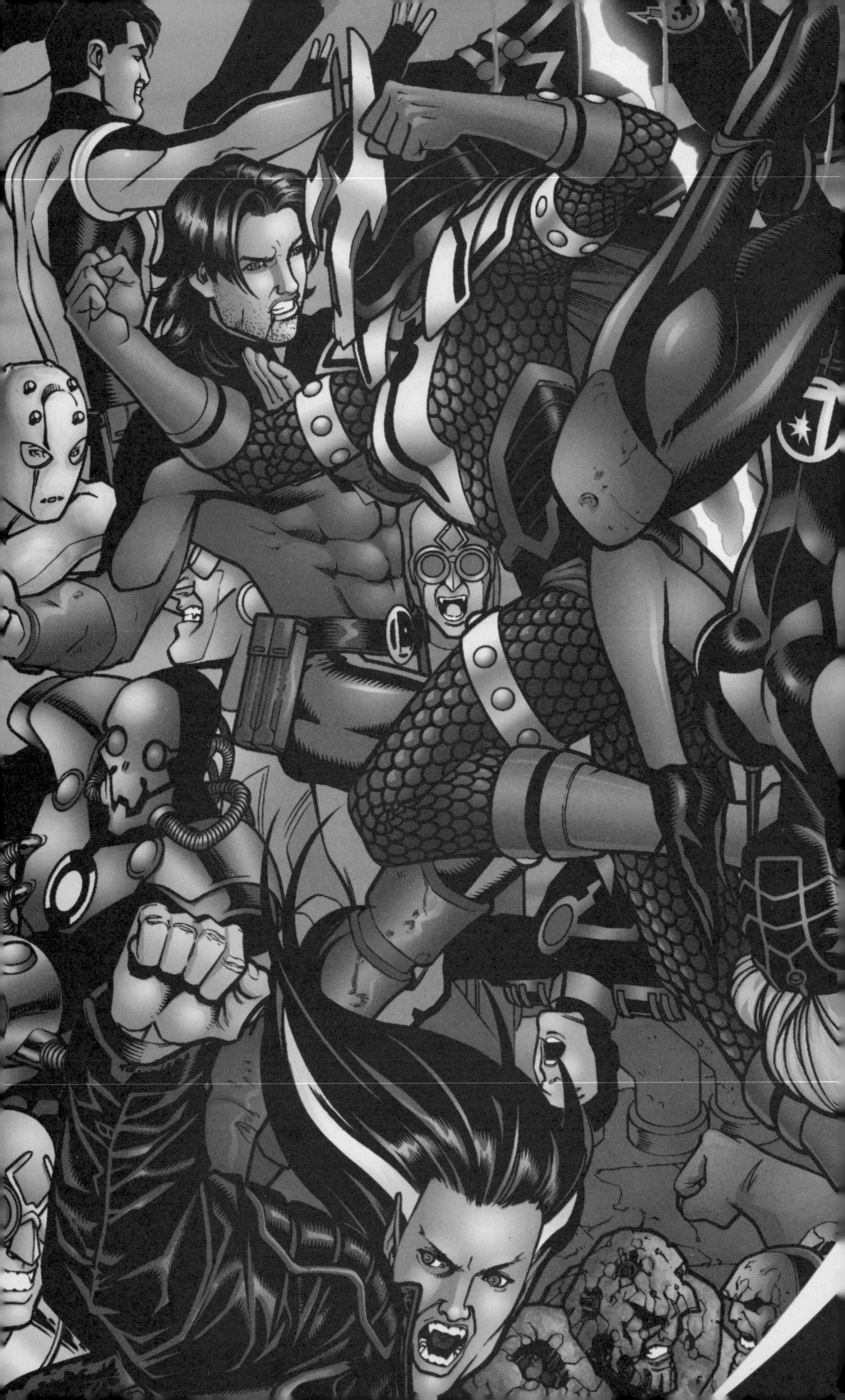

THE LEGION
FOUNDATIONS

WRITERS
DAN ABNETT &
ANDY LANNING

PENCILLERS
CHRIS BATISTA
TONY HARRIS
  & TOM FEISTER
LEONARD KIRK
PAUL RIVOCHE
ERIC WIGHT
DAVE COCKRUM

INKERS
CHIP WALLACE
ROBIN RIGGS
TONY HARRIS
  & TOM FEISTER
ANDY LANNING
DOUG HAZLEWOOD
PAUL RIVOCHE
ERIC WIGHT
AL MILGROM

COLORISTS
SNO CONE
TONY HARRIS
  & TOM FEISTER
PAUL RIVOCHE
ERIC WIGHT

LETTERERS
JARED FLETCHER
ROB LEIGH
KEN LOPEZ
NICK NAPOLITANO

ORIGINAL COVERS
TONY HARRIS
  & TOM FEISTER

THE LEGION: FOUNDATIONS

Published by DC Comics. Cover and
compilation copyright © 2004
DC Comics. All Rights Reserved.

Originally published in single magazine
form in THE LEGION #25-30 and THE
LEGION SECRET FILES 3003. Copyright
© 2003, 2004 DC Comics. All Rights
Reserved. All characters, their distinctive
likenesses and related elements featured
in this publication are trademarks of
DC Comics. The stories, characters and
incidents featured in this publication
are entirely fictional. DC Comics
does not read or accept unsolicited
submissions of ideas, stories
or artwork.

DC Comics,
1700 Broadway, New York, NY 10019.
A Warner Bros. Entertainment Company.
Printed in Canada. First Printing.
ISBN: 1-4012-0338-8
Cover art by Tony Harris
and Tom Feister.
Publication design by
John J. Hill.

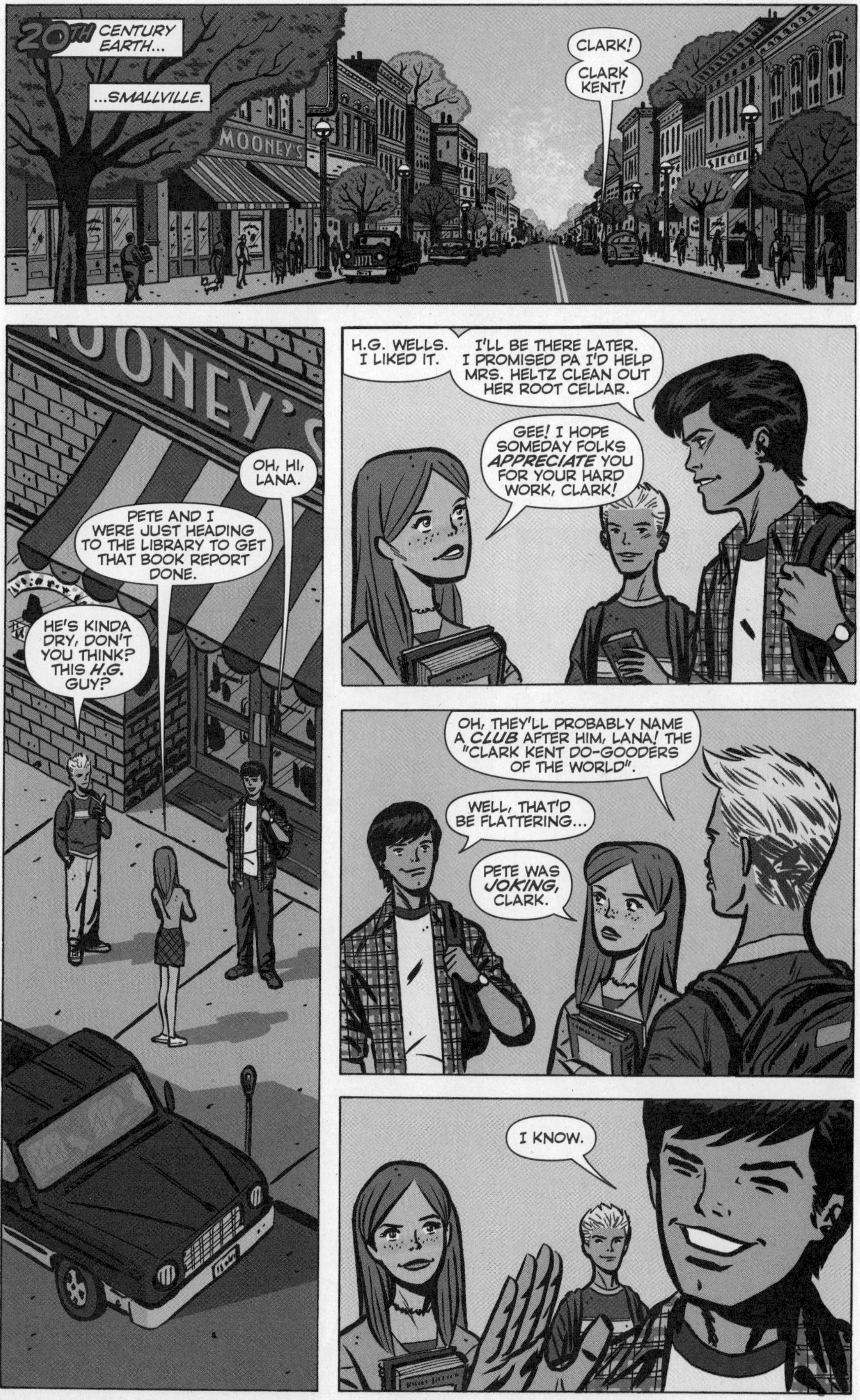
20TH CENTURY EARTH...
...SMALLVILLE.
MOONEY'S
CLARK!
CLARK KENT!
OH, HI, LANA.
PETE AND I WERE JUST HEADING TO THE LIBRARY TO GET THAT BOOK REPORT DONE.
HE'S KINDA DRY, DON'T YOU THINK? THIS *H.G.* GUY?
H.G. WELLS. I LIKED IT.
I'LL BE THERE LATER. I PROMISED PA I'D HELP MRS. HELTZ CLEAN OUT HER ROOT CELLAR.
GEE! I HOPE SOMEDAY FOLKS *APPRECIATE* YOU FOR YOUR HARD WORK, CLARK!
OH, THEY'LL PROBABLY NAME A *CLUB* AFTER HIM, LANA! THE "CLARK KENT DO-GOODERS OF THE WORLD".
WELL, THAT'D BE FLATTERING...
PETE WAS *JOKING*, CLARK.
I KNOW.

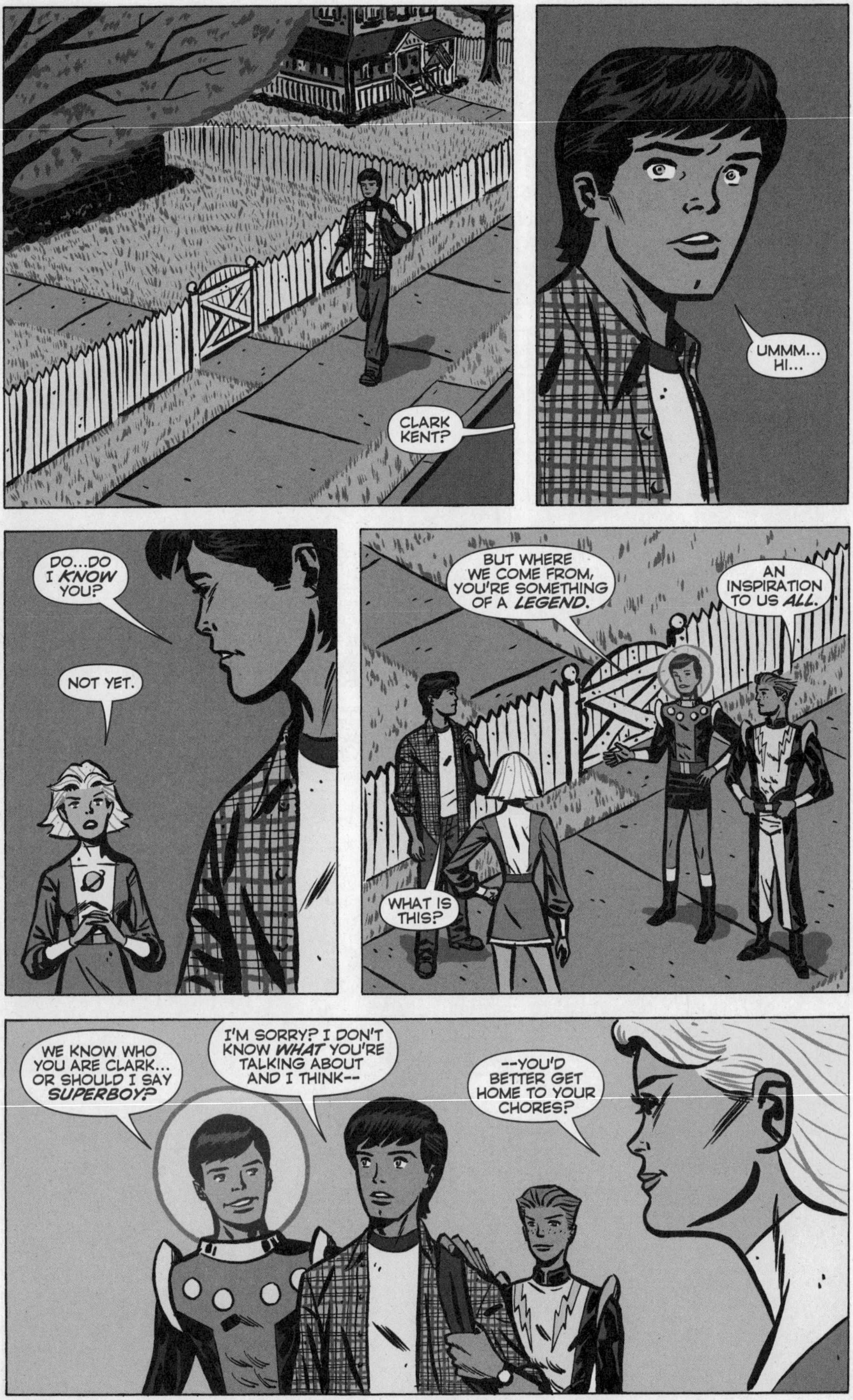
CLARK KENT?
UMMM... HI...
DO...DO I *KNOW* YOU?
NOT YET.
BUT WHERE WE COME FROM, YOU'RE SOMETHING OF A *LEGEND*.
AN INSPIRATION TO US *ALL*.
WHAT IS THIS?
WE KNOW WHO YOU ARE CLARK... OR SHOULD I SAY *SUPERBOY?*
I'M SORRY? I DON'T KNOW *WHAT* YOU'RE TALKING ABOUT AND I THINK--
--YOU'D BETTER GET HOME TO YOUR CHORES?

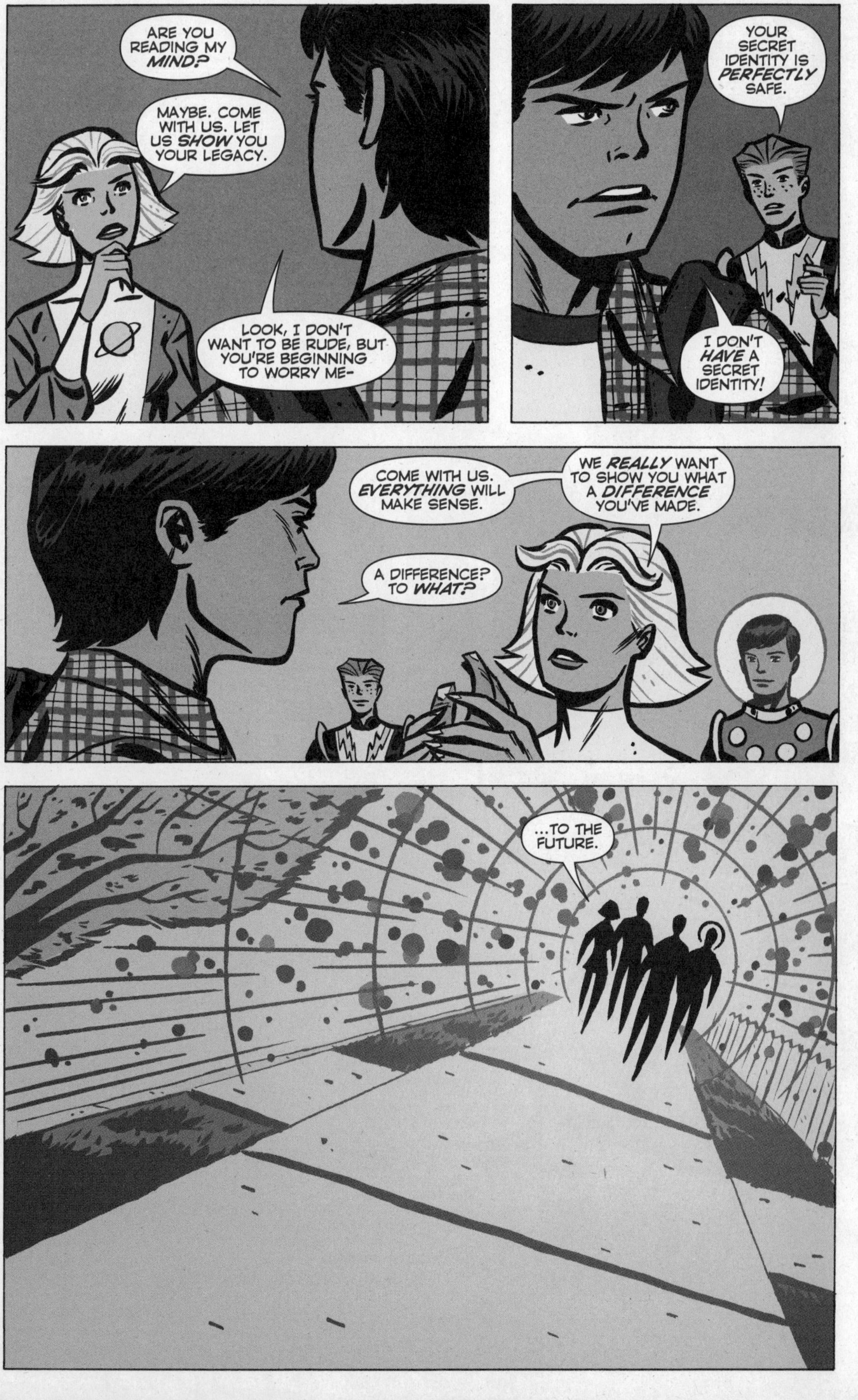

ARE YOU READING MY *MIND?*
MAYBE. COME WITH US. LET US *SHOW* YOU YOUR LEGACY.
LOOK, I DON'T WANT TO BE RUDE, BUT YOU'RE BEGINNING TO WORRY ME-
YOUR SECRET IDENTITY IS *PERFECTLY* SAFE.
I DON'T *HAVE* A SECRET IDENTITY!
COME WITH US. *EVERYTHING* WILL MAKE SENSE.
WE *REALLY* WANT TO SHOW YOU WHAT A *DIFFERENCE* YOU'VE MADE.
A DIFFERENCE? TO *WHAT?*
...TO THE FUTURE.

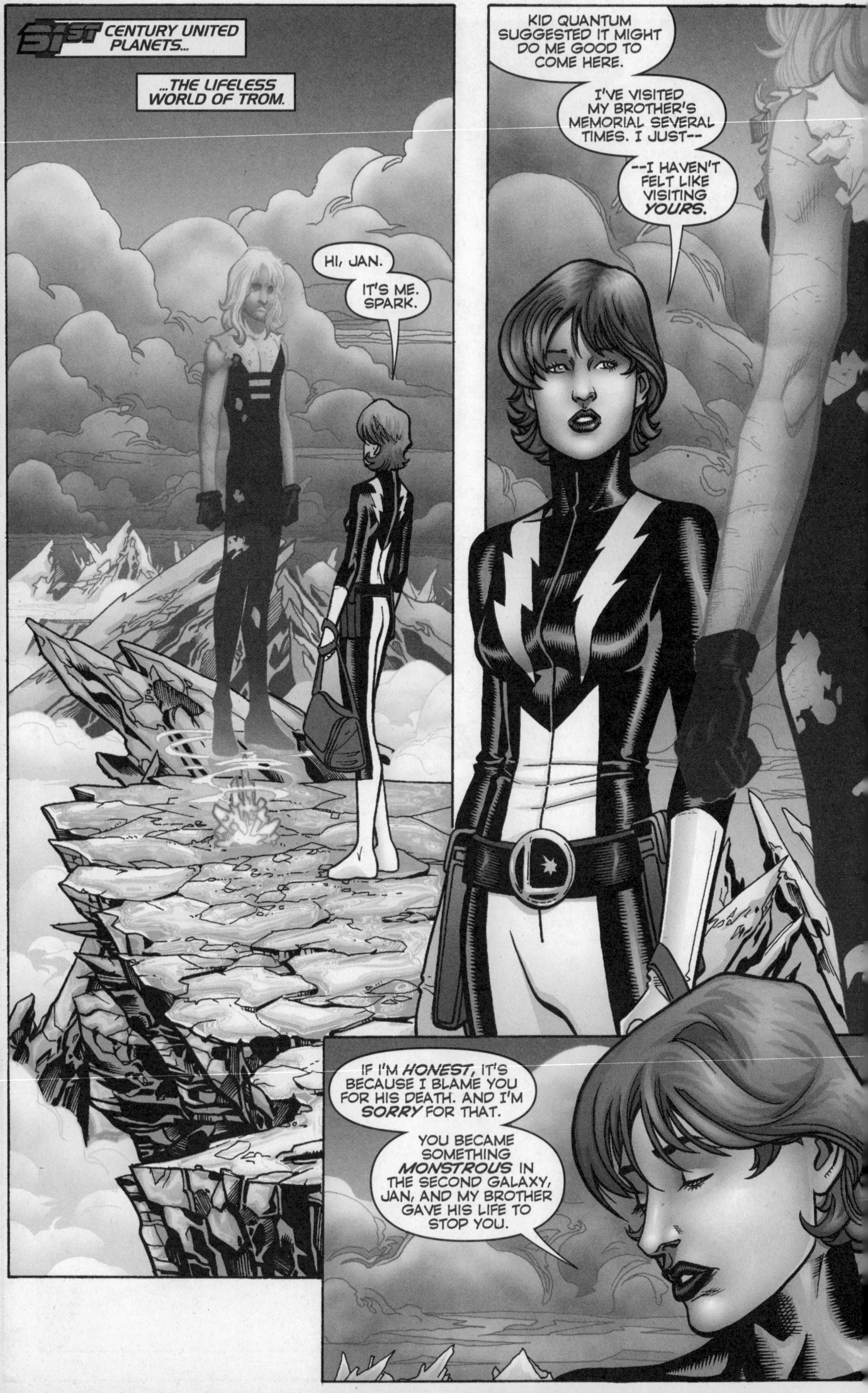
31ST CENTURY UNITED PLANETS...
...THE LIFELESS WORLD OF TROM.
HI, JAN.
IT'S ME. SPARK.
KID QUANTUM SUGGESTED IT MIGHT DO ME GOOD TO COME HERE.
I'VE VISITED MY BROTHER'S MEMORIAL SEVERAL TIMES. I JUST--
--I HAVEN'T FELT LIKE VISITING YOURS.
IF I'M HONEST, IT'S BECAUSE I BLAME YOU FOR HIS DEATH. AND I'M SORRY FOR THAT.
YOU BECAME SOMETHING MONSTROUS IN THE SECOND GALAXY, JAN, AND MY BROTHER GAVE HIS LIFE TO STOP YOU.

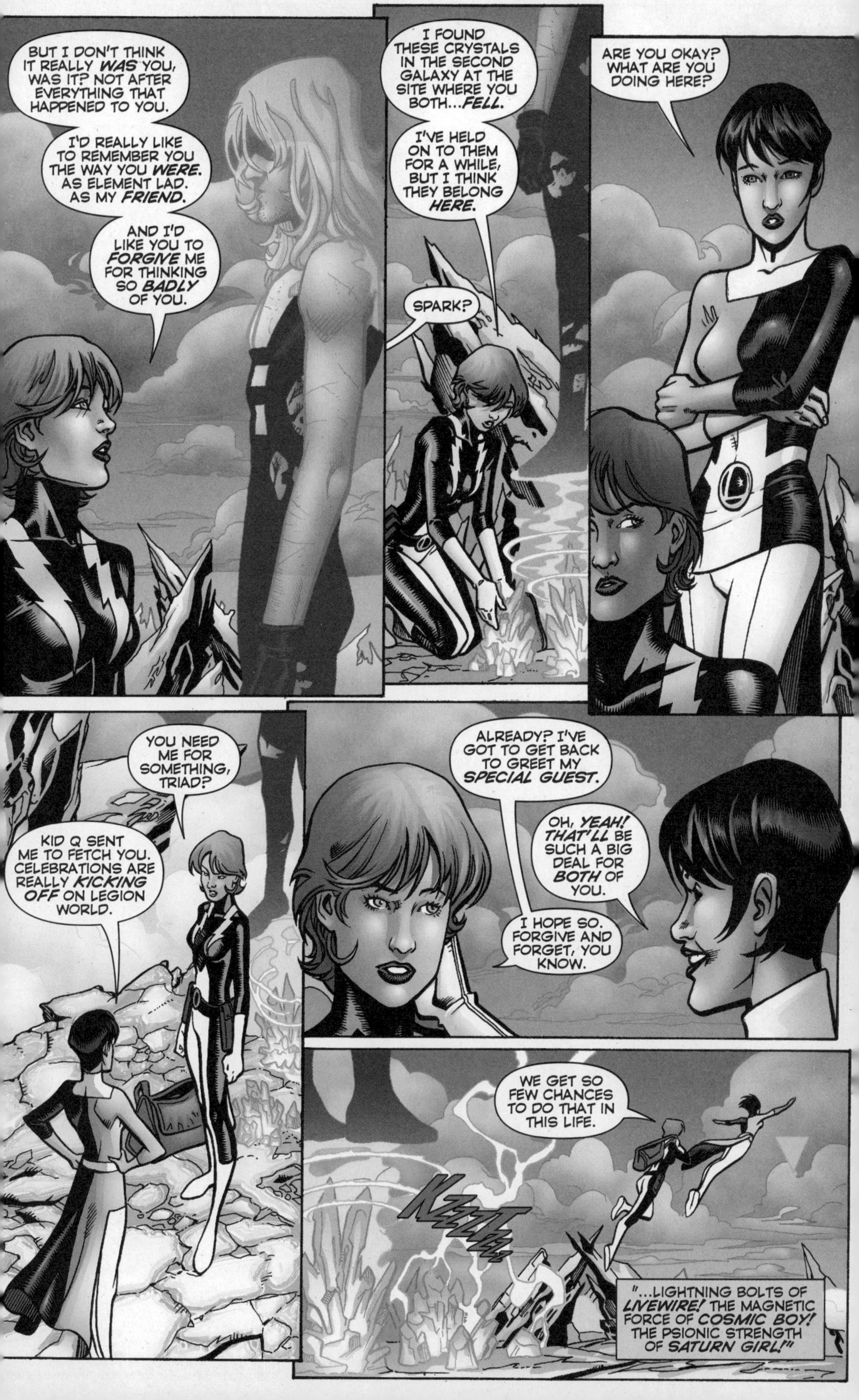
BUT I DON'T THINK IT REALLY WAS YOU, WAS IT? NOT AFTER EVERYTHING THAT HAPPENED TO YOU.
I'D REALLY LIKE TO REMEMBER YOU THE WAY YOU WERE. AS ELEMENT LAD. AS MY FRIEND.
AND I'D LIKE YOU TO FORGIVE ME FOR THINKING SO BADLY OF YOU.
I FOUND THESE CRYSTALS IN THE SECOND GALAXY AT THE SITE WHERE YOU BOTH...FELL.
I'VE HELD ON TO THEM FOR A WHILE, BUT I THINK THEY BELONG HERE.
SPARK?
ARE YOU OKAY? WHAT ARE YOU DOING HERE?
YOU NEED ME FOR SOMETHING, TRIAD?
KID Q SENT ME TO FETCH YOU. CELEBRATIONS ARE REALLY KICKING OFF ON LEGION WORLD.
ALREADY? I'VE GOT TO GET BACK TO GREET MY SPECIAL GUEST.
OH, YEAH! THAT'LL BE SUCH A BIG DEAL FOR BOTH OF YOU.
I HOPE SO. FORGIVE AND FORGET, YOU KNOW.
WE GET SO FEW CHANCES TO DO THAT IN THIS LIFE.
KZZZT
"...LIGHTNING BOLTS OF LIVEWIRE! THE MAGNETIC FORCE OF COSMIC BOY! THE PSIONIC STRENGTH OF SATURN GIRL!"

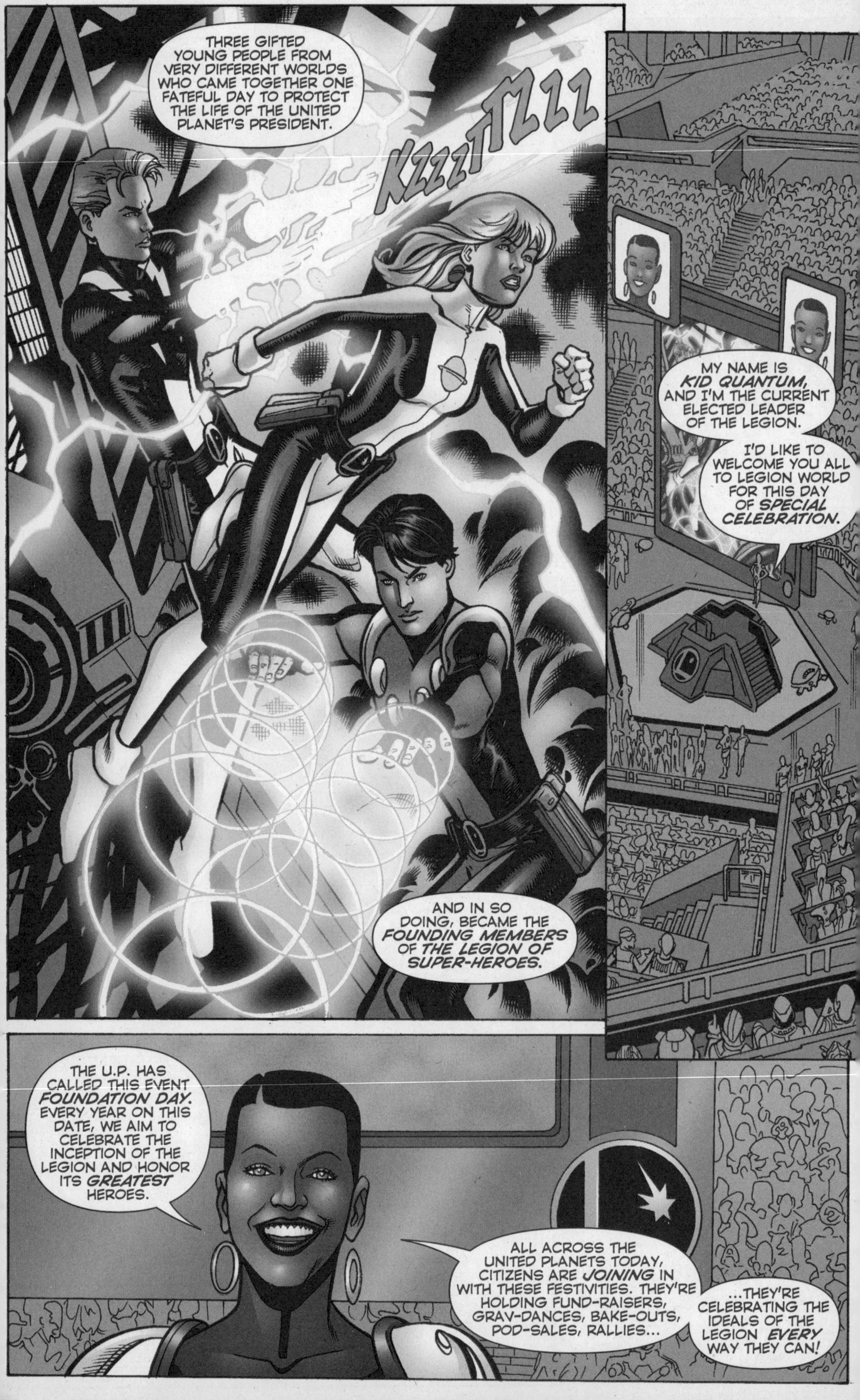

THREE GIFTED YOUNG PEOPLE FROM VERY DIFFERENT WORLDS WHO CAME TOGETHER ONE FATEFUL DAY TO PROTECT THE LIFE OF THE UNITED PLANET'S PRESIDENT.
KZZZTTZZZ
AND IN SO DOING, BECAME THE FOUNDING MEMBERS OF THE LEGION OF SUPER-HEROES.
MY NAME IS KID QUANTUM, AND I'M THE CURRENT ELECTED LEADER OF THE LEGION.
I'D LIKE TO WELCOME YOU ALL TO LEGION WORLD FOR THIS DAY OF SPECIAL CELEBRATION.
THE U.P. HAS CALLED THIS EVENT FOUNDATION DAY. EVERY YEAR ON THIS DATE, WE AIM TO CELEBRATE THE INCEPTION OF THE LEGION AND HONOR ITS GREATEST HEROES.
ALL ACROSS THE UNITED PLANETS TODAY, CITIZENS ARE JOINING IN WITH THESE FESTIVITIES. THEY'RE HOLDING FUND-RAISERS, GRAV-DANCES, BAKE-OUTS, POD-SALES, RALLIES...
...THEY'RE CELEBRATING THE IDEALS OF THE LEGION EVERY WAY THEY CAN!

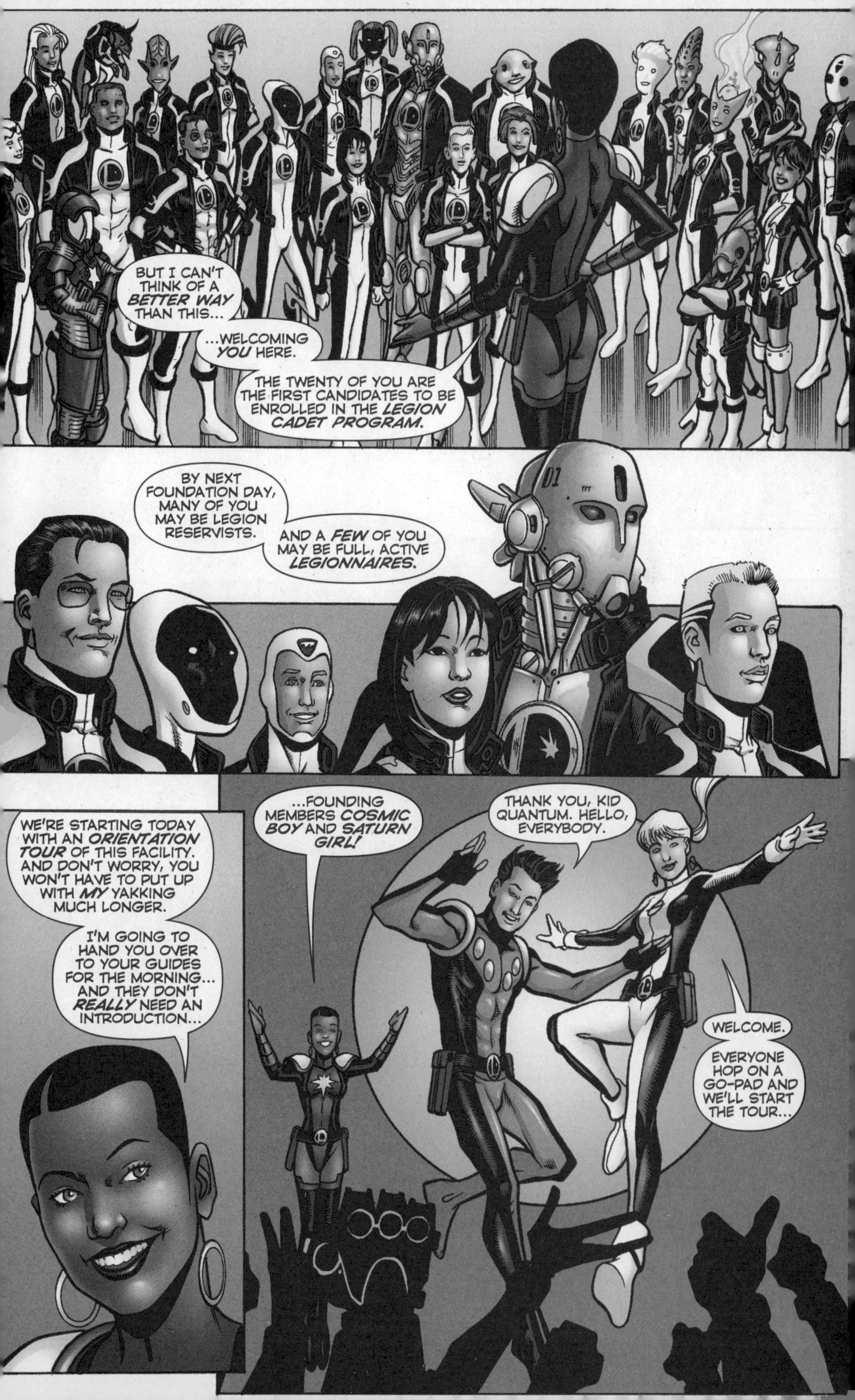
BUT I CAN'T THINK OF A *BETTER WAY* THAN THIS...
...WELCOMING *YOU* HERE.
THE TWENTY OF YOU ARE THE FIRST CANDIDATES TO BE ENROLLED IN THE *LEGION CADET PROGRAM.*
BY NEXT FOUNDATION DAY, MANY OF YOU MAY BE LEGION RESERVISTS.
AND A *FEW* OF YOU MAY BE FULL, ACTIVE *LEGIONNAIRES.*
WE'RE STARTING TODAY WITH AN *ORIENTATION TOUR* OF THIS FACILITY. AND DON'T WORRY, YOU WON'T HAVE TO PUT UP WITH *MY* YAKKING MUCH LONGER.
I'M GOING TO HAND YOU OVER TO YOUR GUIDES FOR THE MORNING... AND THEY DON'T *REALLY* NEED AN INTRODUCTION...
...FOUNDING MEMBERS *COSMIC BOY* AND *SATURN GIRL!*
THANK YOU, KID QUANTUM. HELLO, EVERYBODY.
WELCOME.
EVERYONE HOP ON A GO-PAD AND WE'LL START THE TOUR...

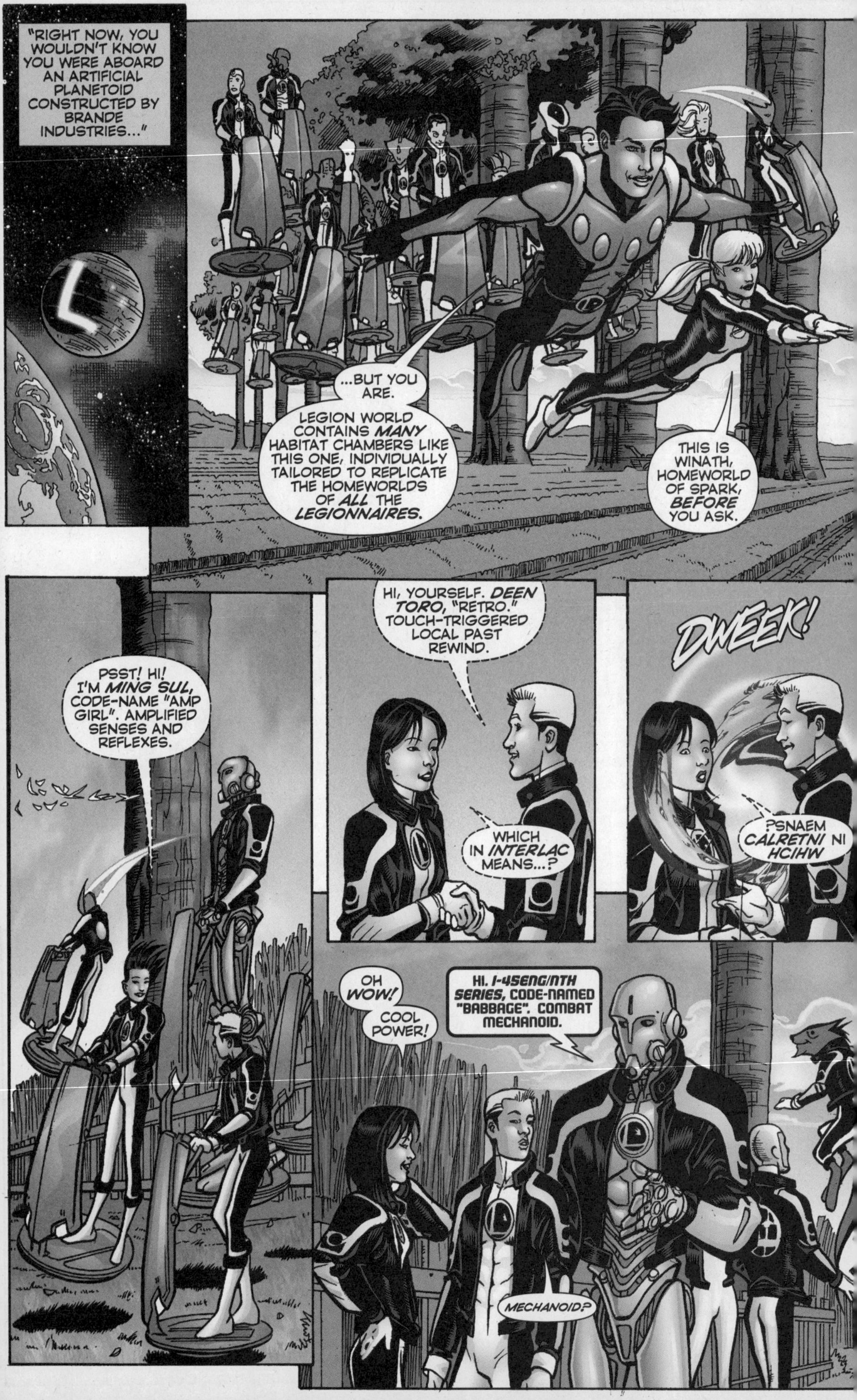
"RIGHT NOW, YOU WOULDN'T KNOW YOU WERE ABOARD AN ARTIFICIAL PLANETOID CONSTRUCTED BY BRANDE INDUSTRIES..."
...BUT YOU ARE.
LEGION WORLD CONTAINS MANY HABITAT CHAMBERS LIKE THIS ONE, INDIVIDUALLY TAILORED TO REPLICATE THE HOMEWORLDS OF ALL THE LEGIONNAIRES.
THIS IS WINATH, HOMEWORLD OF SPARK, BEFORE YOU ASK.
PSST! HI! I'M MING SUL, CODE-NAME "AMP GIRL". AMPLIFIED SENSES AND REFLEXES.
HI, YOURSELF. DEEN TORO, "RETRO." TOUCH-TRIGGERED LOCAL PAST REWIND.
WHICH IN INTERLAC MEANS...?
DWEEK!
?SNAEM CALRETNI NI HCIHW
OH WOW! COOL POWER!
HI. I-45ENG/NTH SERIES, CODE-NAMED "BABBAGE". COMBAT MECHANOID.
MECHANOID?

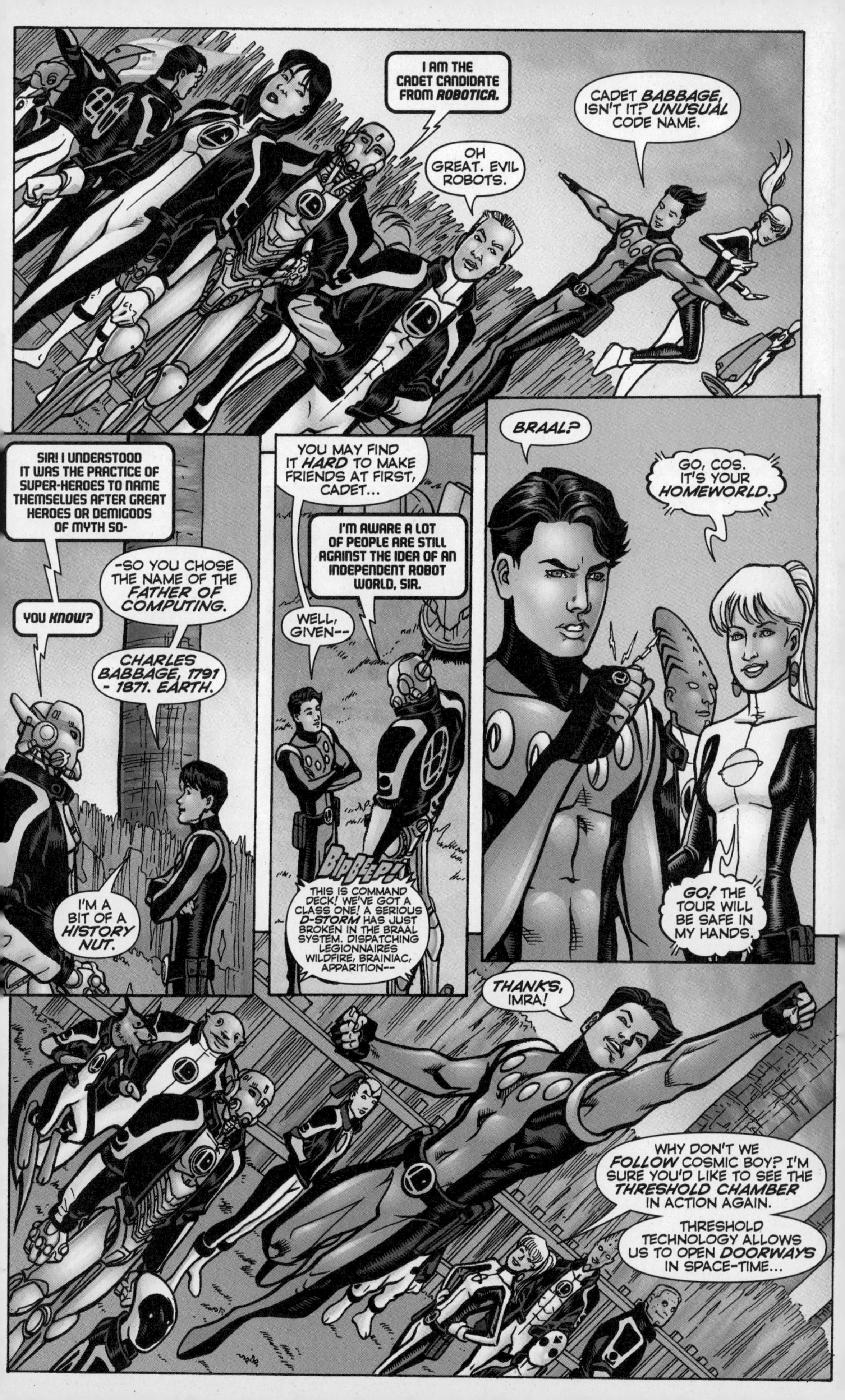

I AM THE CADET CANDIDATE FROM ROBOTICA.
OH GREAT. EVIL ROBOTS.
CADET BABBAGE, ISN'T IT? UNUSUAL CODE NAME.
SIR! I UNDERSTOOD IT WAS THE PRACTICE OF SUPER-HEROES TO NAME THEMSELVES AFTER GREAT HEROES OR DEMIGODS OF MYTH SO-
-SO YOU CHOSE THE NAME OF THE FATHER OF COMPUTING.
YOU KNOW?
CHARLES BABBAGE, 1791 - 1871. EARTH.
I'M A BIT OF A HISTORY NUT.
YOU MAY FIND IT HARD TO MAKE FRIENDS AT FIRST, CADET...
I'M AWARE A LOT OF PEOPLE ARE STILL AGAINST THE IDEA OF AN INDEPENDENT ROBOT WORLD, SIR.
WELL, GIVEN--
BIPBEEP!
THIS IS COMMAND DECK! WE'VE GOT A CLASS ONE! A SERIOUS D-STORM HAS JUST BROKEN IN THE BRAAL SYSTEM. DISPATCHING LEGIONNAIRES WILDFIRE, BRAINIAC, APPARITION--
BRAAL?
GO, COS. IT'S YOUR HOMEWORLD.
GO! THE TOUR WILL BE SAFE IN MY HANDS.
THANKS, IMRA!
WHY DON'T WE FOLLOW COSMIC BOY? I'M SURE YOU'D LIKE TO SEE THE THRESHOLD CHAMBER IN ACTION AGAIN.
THRESHOLD TECHNOLOGY ALLOWS US TO OPEN DOORWAYS IN SPACE-TIME...

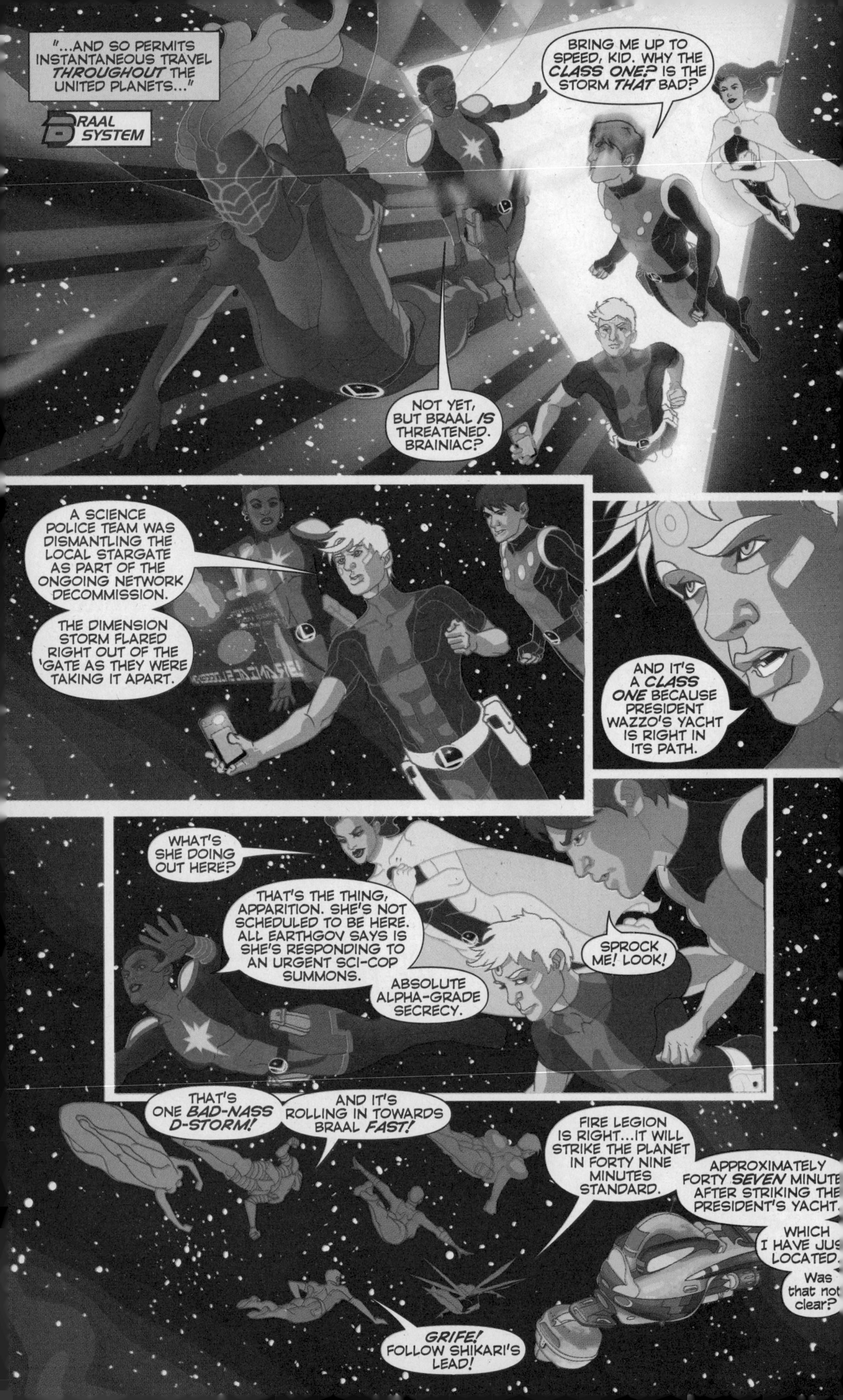
"...AND SO PERMITS INSTANTANEOUS TRAVEL THROUGHOUT THE UNITED PLANETS..."
BRAAL SYSTEM
BRING ME UP TO SPEED, KID. WHY THE CLASS ONE? IS THE STORM THAT BAD?
NOT YET, BUT BRAAL IS THREATENED. BRAINIAC?
A SCIENCE POLICE TEAM WAS DISMANTLING THE LOCAL STARGATE AS PART OF THE ONGOING NETWORK DECOMMISSION.
THE DIMENSION STORM FLARED RIGHT OUT OF THE 'GATE AS THEY WERE TAKING IT APART.
AND IT'S A CLASS ONE BECAUSE PRESIDENT WAZZO'S YACHT IS RIGHT IN ITS PATH.
WHAT'S SHE DOING OUT HERE?
THAT'S THE THING, APPARITION. SHE'S NOT SCHEDULED TO BE HERE. ALL EARTHGOV SAYS IS SHE'S RESPONDING TO AN URGENT SCI-COP SUMMONS.
ABSOLUTE ALPHA-GRADE SECRECY.
SPROCK ME! LOOK!
THAT'S ONE BAD-NASS D-STORM!
AND IT'S ROLLING IN TOWARDS BRAAL FAST!
FIRE LEGION IS RIGHT...IT WILL STRIKE THE PLANET IN FORTY NINE MINUTES STANDARD.
APPROXIMATELY FORTY SEVEN MINUTE AFTER STRIKING THE PRESIDENT'S YACHT.
WHICH I HAVE JUS LOCATED.
Was that not clear?
GRIFE! FOLLOW SHIKARI'S LEAD!

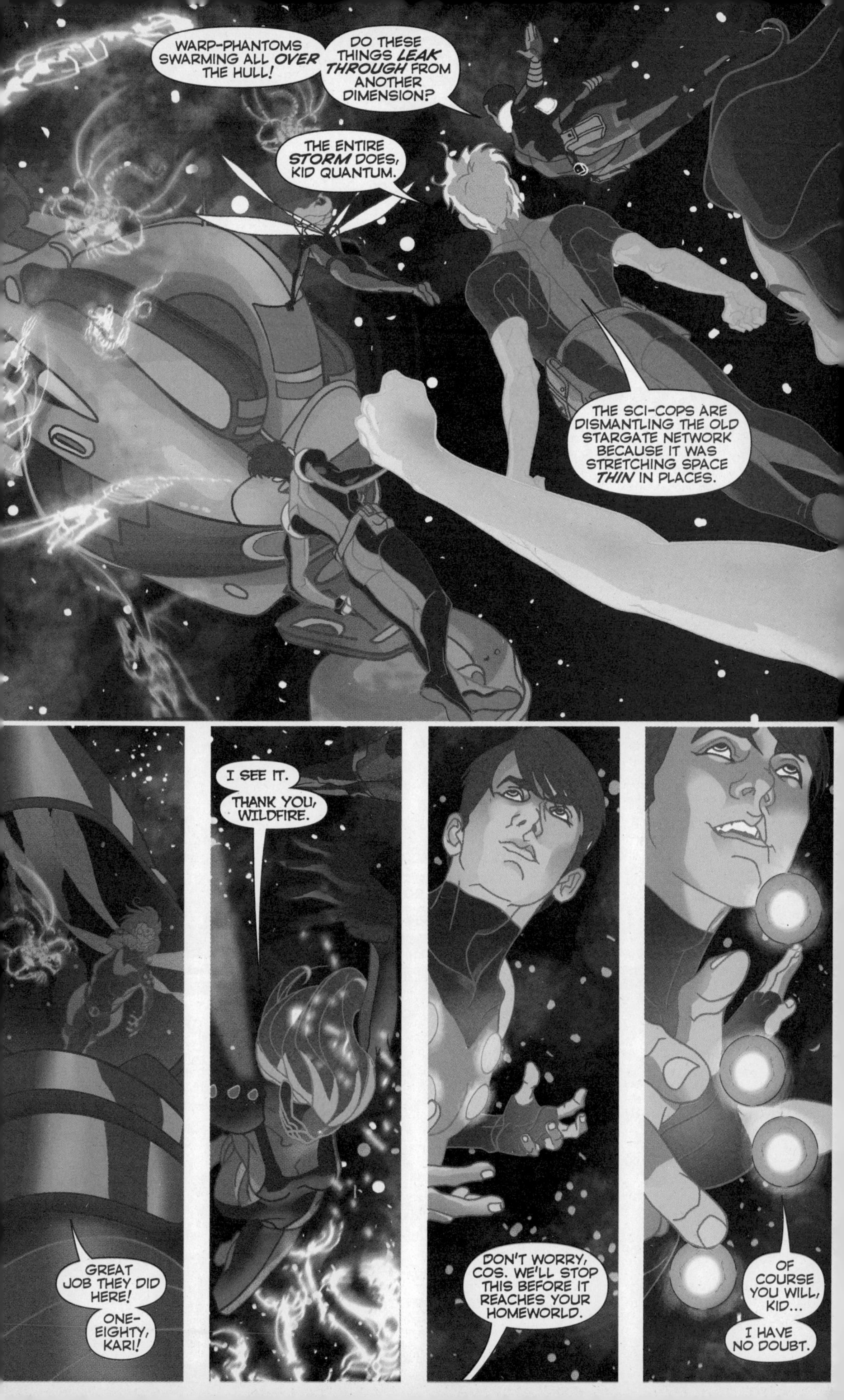
WARP-PHANTOMS SWARMING ALL *OVER* THE HULL!
DO THESE THINGS *LEAK THROUGH* FROM ANOTHER DIMENSION?
THE ENTIRE *STORM* DOES, KID QUANTUM.
THE SCI-COPS ARE DISMANTLING THE OLD STARGATE NETWORK BECAUSE IT WAS STRETCHING SPACE *THIN* IN PLACES.
GREAT JOB THEY DID HERE!
ONE-EIGHTY, KARI!
I SEE IT.
THANK YOU, WILDFIRE.
DON'T WORRY, COS. WE'LL STOP THIS BEFORE IT REACHES YOUR HOMEWORLD.
OF COURSE YOU WILL, KID...
I HAVE NO DOUBT.

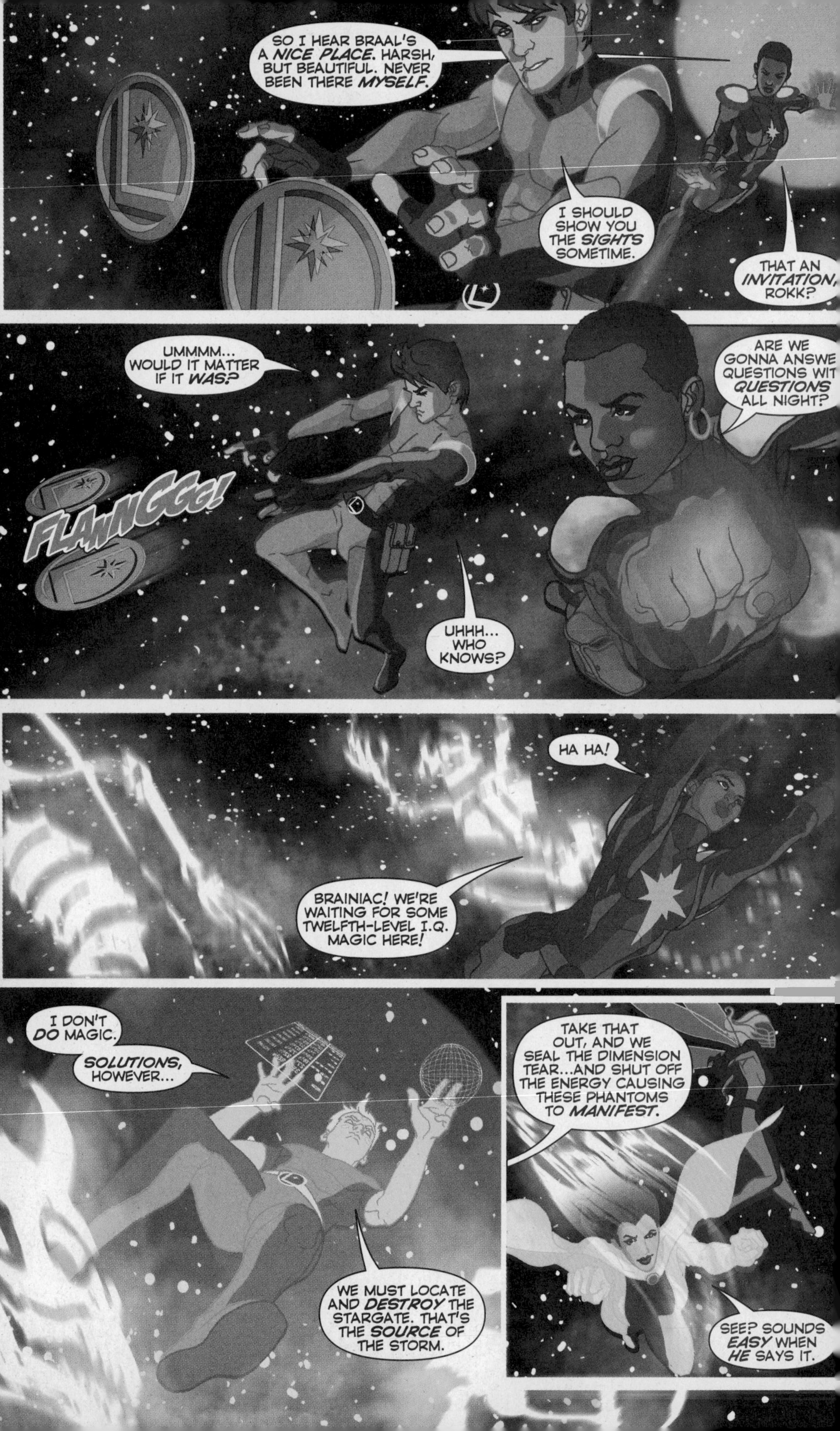
SO I HEAR BRAAL'S A NICE PLACE. HARSH, BUT BEAUTIFUL. NEVER BEEN THERE MYSELF.
I SHOULD SHOW YOU THE SIGHTS SOMETIME.
THAT AN INVITATION, ROKK?
UMMMM... WOULD IT MATTER IF IT WAS?
ARE WE GONNA ANSWE QUESTIONS WIT QUESTIONS ALL NIGHT?
FLANNGGG!
UHHH... WHO KNOWS?
HA HA!
BRAINIAC! WE'RE WAITING FOR SOME TWELFTH-LEVEL I.Q. MAGIC HERE!
I DON'T DO MAGIC.
SOLUTIONS, HOWEVER...
WE MUST LOCATE AND DESTROY THE STARGATE. THAT'S THE SOURCE OF THE STORM.
TAKE THAT OUT, AND WE SEAL THE DIMENSION TEAR...AND SHUT OFF THE ENERGY CAUSING THESE PHANTOMS TO MANIFEST.
SEE? SOUNDS EASY WHEN HE SAYS IT.

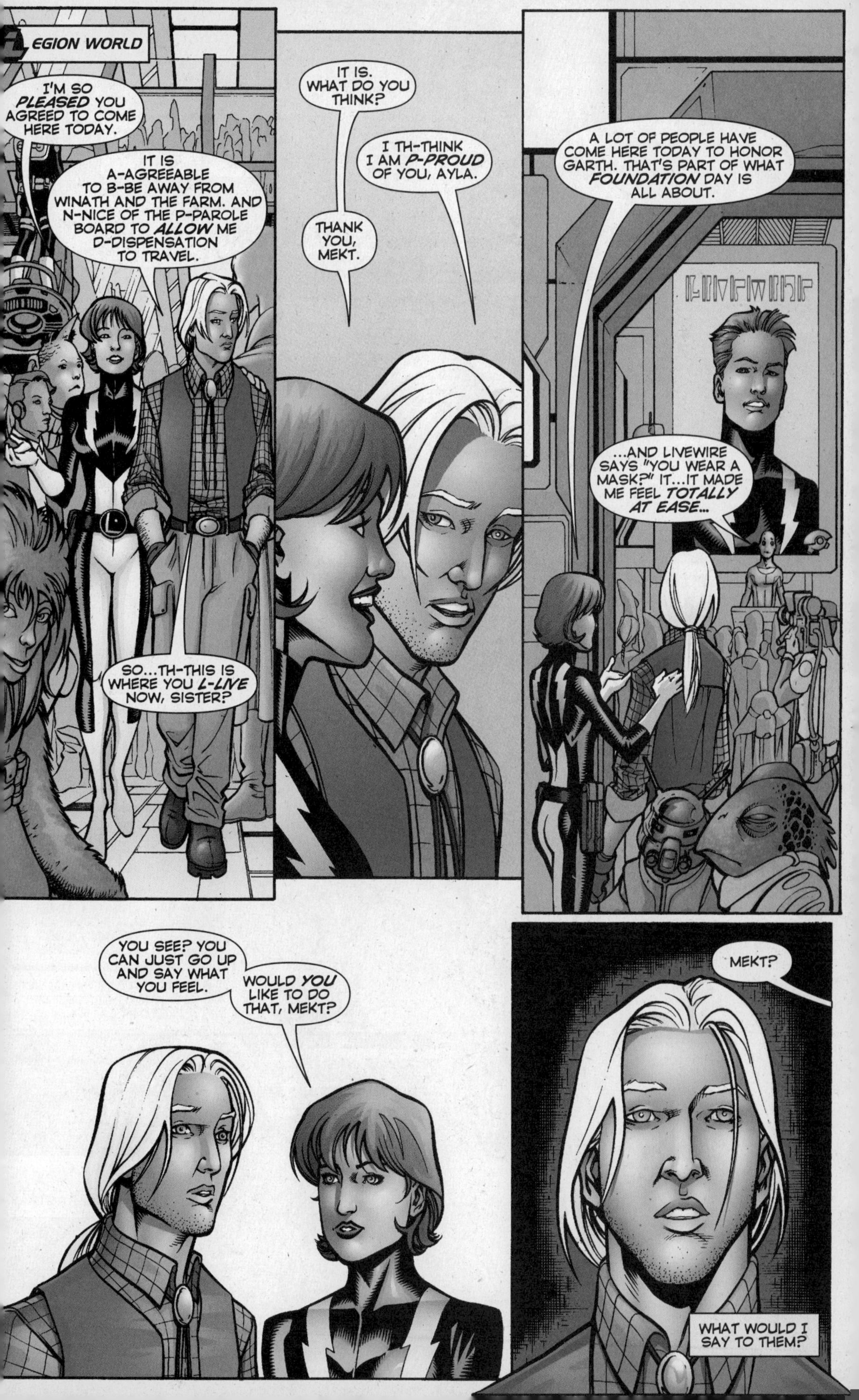
EGION WORLD
I'M SO PLEASED YOU AGREED TO COME HERE TODAY.
IT IS A-AGREEABLE TO B-BE AWAY FROM WINATH AND THE FARM. AND N-NICE OF THE P-PAROLE BOARD TO ALLOW ME D-DISPENSATION TO TRAVEL.
SO...TH-THIS IS WHERE YOU L-LIVE NOW, SISTER?
IT IS. WHAT DO YOU THINK?
I TH-THINK I AM P-PROUD OF YOU, AYLA.
THANK YOU, MEKT.
A LOT OF PEOPLE HAVE COME HERE TODAY TO HONOR GARTH. THAT'S PART OF WHAT FOUNDATION DAY IS ALL ABOUT.
...AND LIVEWIRE SAYS "YOU WEAR A MASK?" IT...IT MADE ME FEEL TOTALLY AT EASE...
YOU SEE? YOU CAN JUST GO UP AND SAY WHAT YOU FEEL.
WOULD YOU LIKE TO DO THAT, MEKT?
MEKT?
WHAT WOULD I SAY TO THEM?

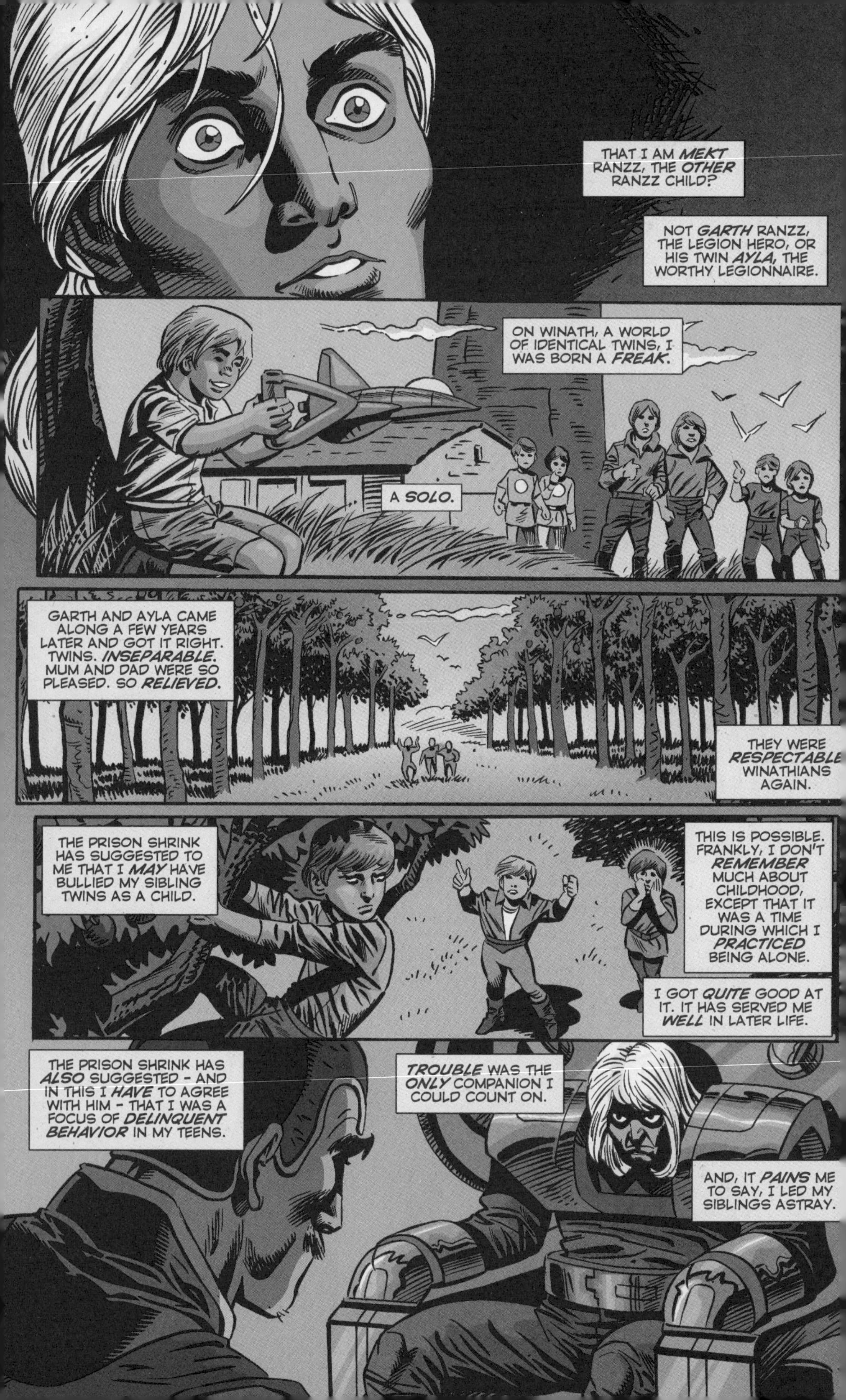
THAT I AM MEKT RANZZ, THE OTHER RANZZ CHILD?
NOT GARTH RANZZ, THE LEGION HERO, OR HIS TWIN AYLA, THE WORTHY LEGIONNAIRE.
ON WINATH, A WORLD OF IDENTICAL TWINS, I WAS BORN A FREAK.
A SOLO.
GARTH AND AYLA CAME ALONG A FEW YEARS LATER AND GOT IT RIGHT. TWINS. INSEPARABLE. MUM AND DAD WERE SO PLEASED. SO RELIEVED.
THEY WERE RESPECTABLE WINATHIANS AGAIN.
THE PRISON SHRINK HAS SUGGESTED TO ME THAT I MAY HAVE BULLIED MY SIBLING TWINS AS A CHILD.
THIS IS POSSIBLE. FRANKLY, I DON'T REMEMBER MUCH ABOUT CHILDHOOD, EXCEPT THAT IT WAS A TIME DURING WHICH I PRACTICED BEING ALONE.
I GOT QUITE GOOD AT IT. IT HAS SERVED ME WELL IN LATER LIFE.
THE PRISON SHRINK HAS ALSO SUGGESTED - AND IN THIS I HAVE TO AGREE WITH HIM - THAT I WAS A FOCUS OF DELINQUENT BEHAVIOR IN MY TEENS.
TROUBLE WAS THE ONLY COMPANION I COULD COUNT ON.
AND, IT PAINS ME TO SAY, I LED MY SIBLINGS ASTRAY.

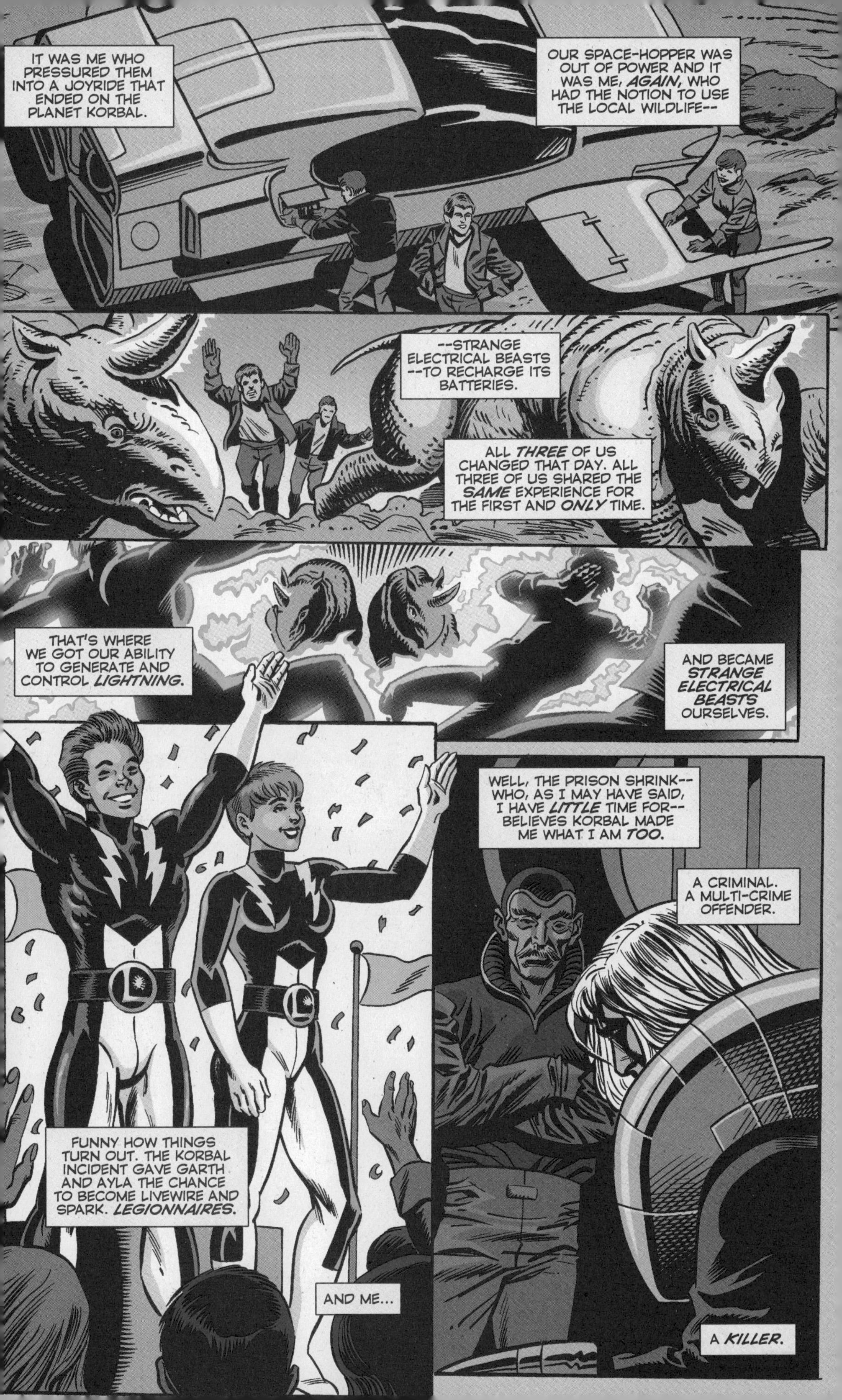
IT WAS ME WHO PRESSURED THEM INTO A JOYRIDE THAT ENDED ON THE PLANET KORBAL.
OUR SPACE-HOPPER WAS OUT OF POWER AND IT WAS ME, AGAIN, WHO HAD THE NOTION TO USE THE LOCAL WILDLIFE--
--STRANGE ELECTRICAL BEASTS --TO RECHARGE ITS BATTERIES.
ALL THREE OF US CHANGED THAT DAY. ALL THREE OF US SHARED THE SAME EXPERIENCE FOR THE FIRST AND ONLY TIME.
THAT'S WHERE WE GOT OUR ABILITY TO GENERATE AND CONTROL LIGHTNING.
AND BECAME STRANGE ELECTRICAL BEASTS OURSELVES.
FUNNY HOW THINGS TURN OUT. THE KORBAL INCIDENT GAVE GARTH AND AYLA THE CHANCE TO BECOME LIVEWIRE AND SPARK. LEGIONNAIRES.
AND ME...
WELL, THE PRISON SHRINK-- WHO, AS I MAY HAVE SAID, I HAVE LITTLE TIME FOR-- BELIEVES KORBAL MADE ME WHAT I AM TOO.
A CRIMINAL. A MULTI-CRIME OFFENDER.
A KILLER.

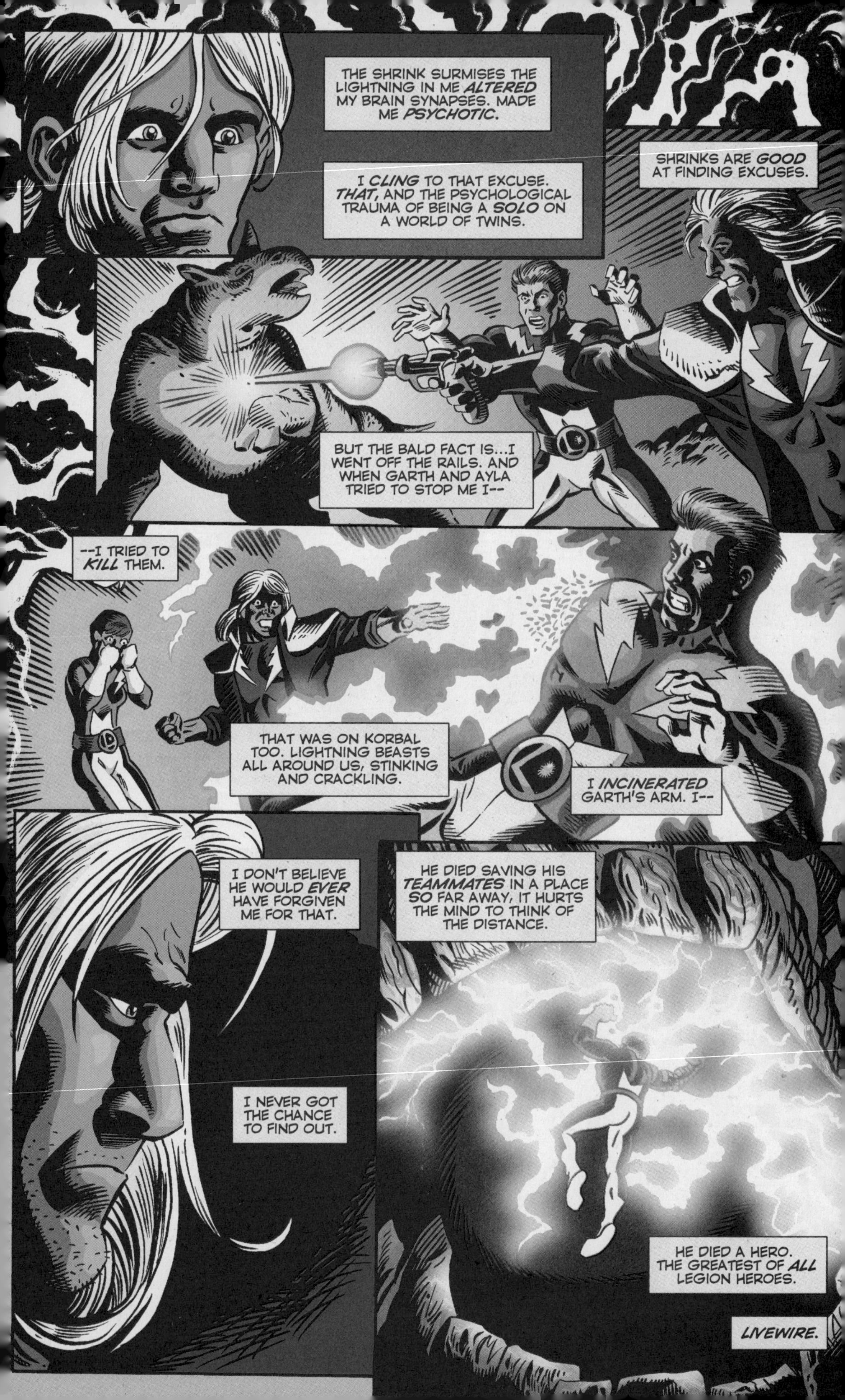
THE SHRINK SURMISES THE LIGHTNING IN ME ALTERED MY BRAIN SYNAPSES. MADE ME PSYCHOTIC.
I CLING TO THAT EXCUSE. THAT, AND THE PSYCHOLOGICAL TRAUMA OF BEING A SOLO ON A WORLD OF TWINS.
SHRINKS ARE GOOD AT FINDING EXCUSES.
BUT THE BALD FACT IS...I WENT OFF THE RAILS. AND WHEN GARTH AND AYLA TRIED TO STOP ME I--
--I TRIED TO KILL THEM.
THAT WAS ON KORBAL TOO. LIGHTNING BEASTS ALL AROUND US, STINKING AND CRACKLING.
I INCINERATED GARTH'S ARM. I--
I DON'T BELIEVE HE WOULD EVER HAVE FORGIVEN ME FOR THAT.
I NEVER GOT THE CHANCE TO FIND OUT.
HE DIED SAVING HIS TEAMMATES IN A PLACE SO FAR AWAY, IT HURTS THE MIND TO THINK OF THE DISTANCE.
HE DIED A HERO. THE GREATEST OF ALL LEGION HEROES.
LIVEWIRE.

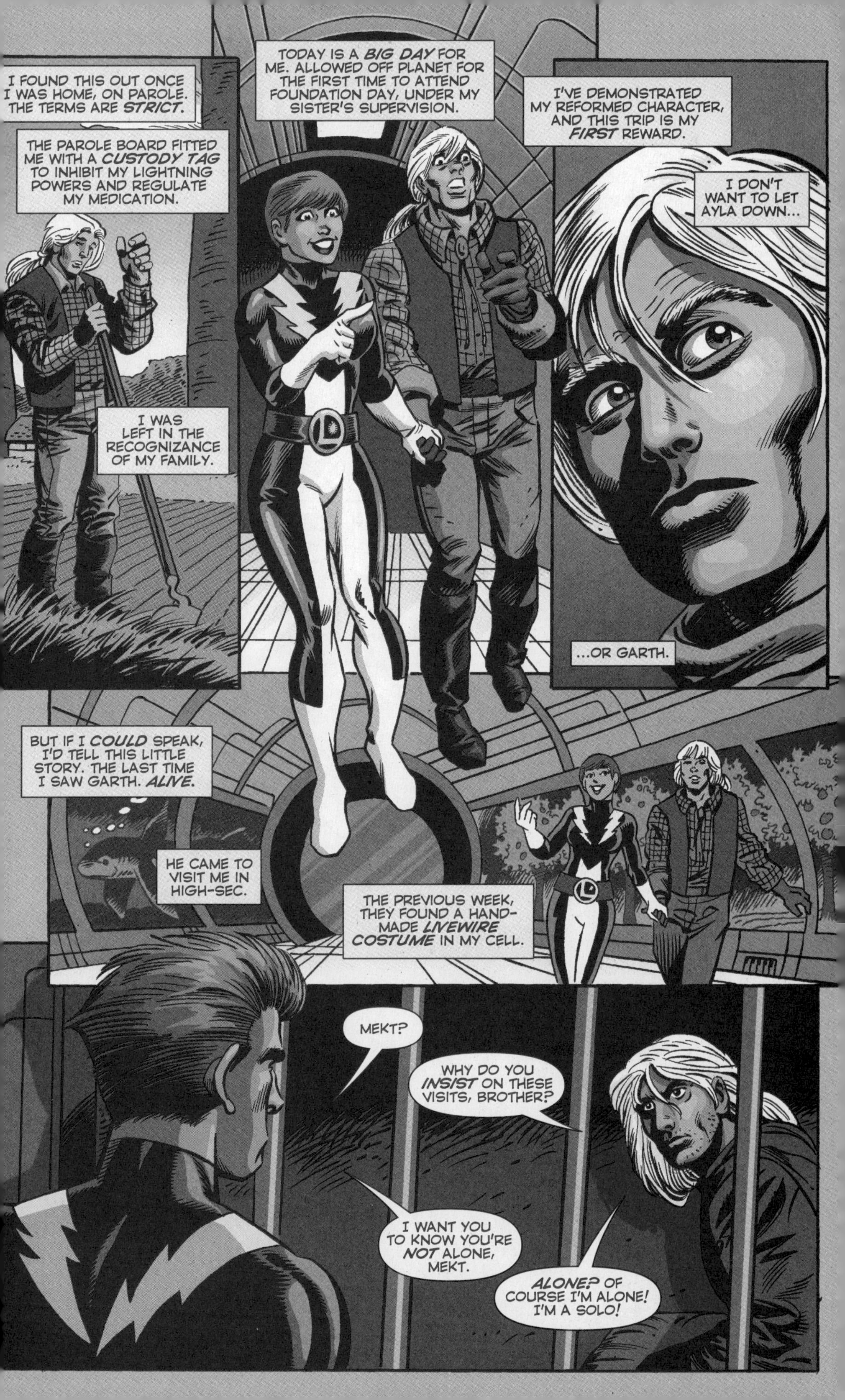

I FOUND THIS OUT ONCE I WAS HOME, ON PAROLE. THE TERMS ARE STRICT.
THE PAROLE BOARD FITTED ME WITH A CUSTODY TAG TO INHIBIT MY LIGHTNING POWERS AND REGULATE MY MEDICATION.
I WAS LEFT IN THE RECOGNIZANCE OF MY FAMILY.
TODAY IS A BIG DAY FOR ME. ALLOWED OFF PLANET FOR THE FIRST TIME TO ATTEND FOUNDATION DAY, UNDER MY SISTER'S SUPERVISION.
I'VE DEMONSTRATED MY REFORMED CHARACTER, AND THIS TRIP IS MY FIRST REWARD.
I DON'T WANT TO LET AYLA DOWN...
...OR GARTH.
BUT IF I COULD SPEAK, I'D TELL THIS LITTLE STORY. THE LAST TIME I SAW GARTH. ALIVE.
HE CAME TO VISIT ME IN HIGH-SEC.
THE PREVIOUS WEEK, THEY FOUND A HAND-MADE LIVEWIRE COSTUME IN MY CELL.
MEKT?
WHY DO YOU INSIST ON THESE VISITS, BROTHER?
I WANT YOU TO KNOW YOU'RE NOT ALONE, MEKT.
ALONE? OF COURSE I'M ALONE! I'M A SOLO!

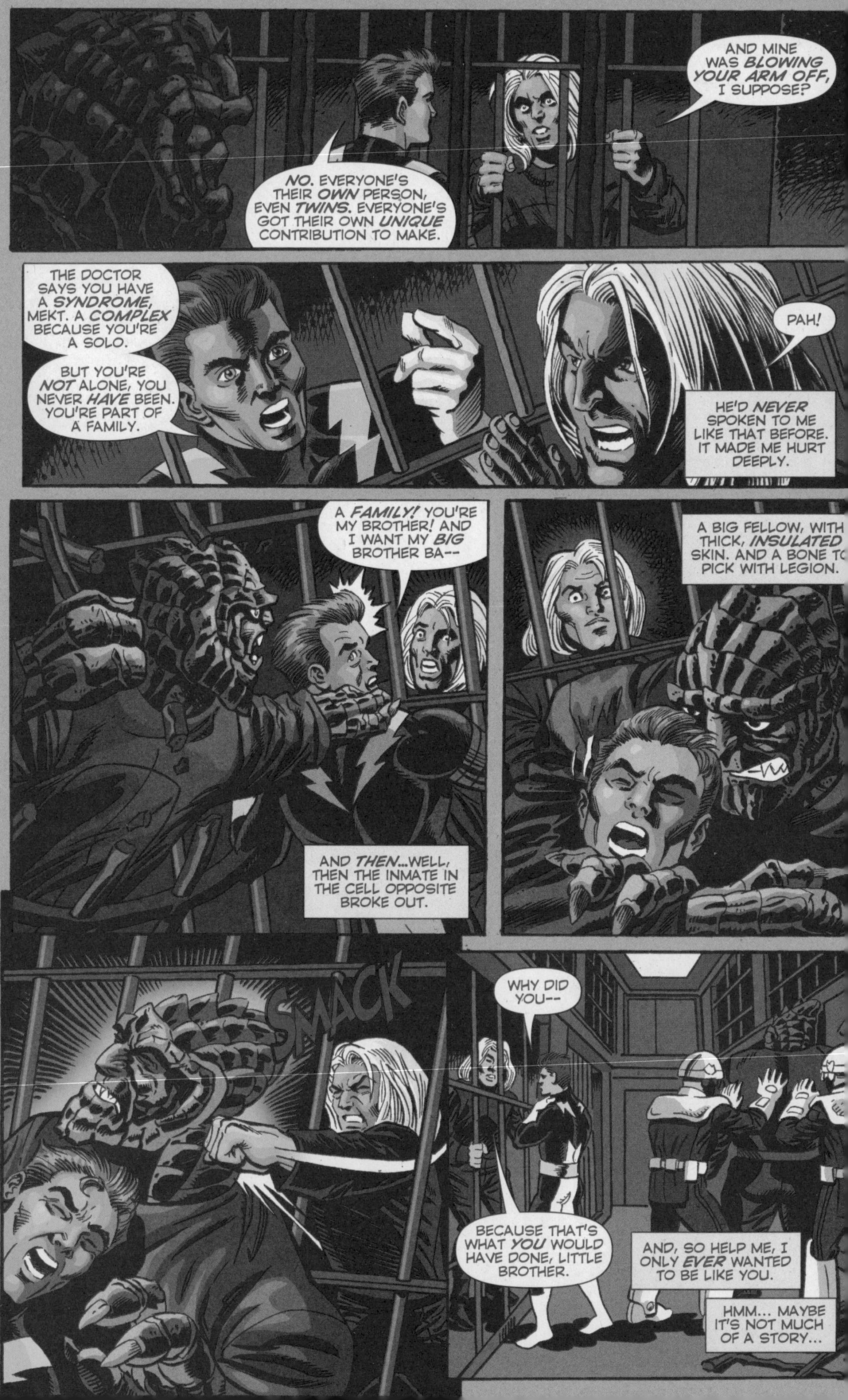
AND MINE WAS BLOWING YOUR ARM OFF, I SUPPOSE?
NO. EVERYONE'S THEIR OWN PERSON, EVEN TWINS. EVERYONE'S GOT THEIR OWN UNIQUE CONTRIBUTION TO MAKE.
THE DOCTOR SAYS YOU HAVE A SYNDROME, MEKT. A COMPLEX BECAUSE YOU'RE A SOLO.
BUT YOU'RE NOT ALONE, YOU NEVER HAVE BEEN. YOU'RE PART OF A FAMILY.
PAH!
HE'D NEVER SPOKEN TO ME LIKE THAT BEFORE. IT MADE ME HURT DEEPLY.
A FAMILY! YOU'RE MY BROTHER! AND I WANT MY BIG BROTHER BA--
AND THEN...WELL, THEN THE INMATE IN THE CELL OPPOSITE BROKE OUT.
A BIG FELLOW, WITH THICK, INSULATED SKIN. AND A BONE TO PICK WITH LEGION.
SMACK
WHY DID YOU--
BECAUSE THAT'S WHAT YOU WOULD HAVE DONE, LITTLE BROTHER.
AND, SO HELP ME, I ONLY EVER WANTED TO BE LIKE YOU.
HMM... MAYBE IT'S NOT MUCH OF A STORY...

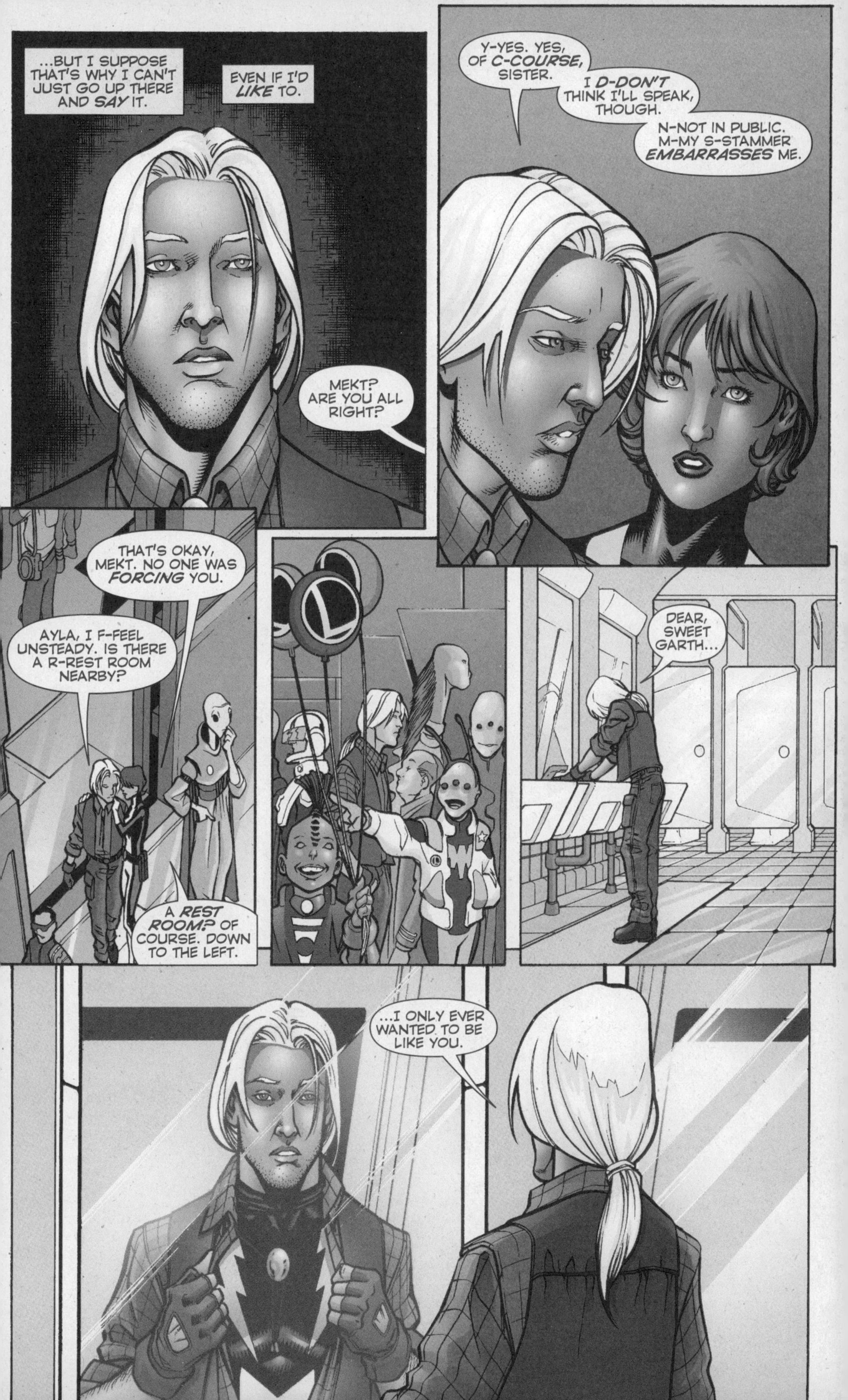

...BUT I SUPPOSE THAT'S WHY I CAN'T JUST GO UP THERE AND *SAY* IT.
EVEN IF I'D *LIKE* TO.
MEKT? ARE YOU ALL RIGHT?
Y-YES. YES, OF *C-COURSE,* SISTER.
I *D-DON'T* THINK I'LL SPEAK, THOUGH.
N-NOT IN PUBLIC. M-MY S-STAMMER *EMBARRASSES* ME.
THAT'S OKAY, MEKT. NO ONE WAS *FORCING* YOU.
AYLA, I F-FEEL UNSTEADY. IS THERE A R-REST ROOM NEARBY?
A *REST ROOM?* OF COURSE. DOWN TO THE LEFT.
DEAR, SWEET GARTH...
...I ONLY EVER WANTED TO BE LIKE YOU.

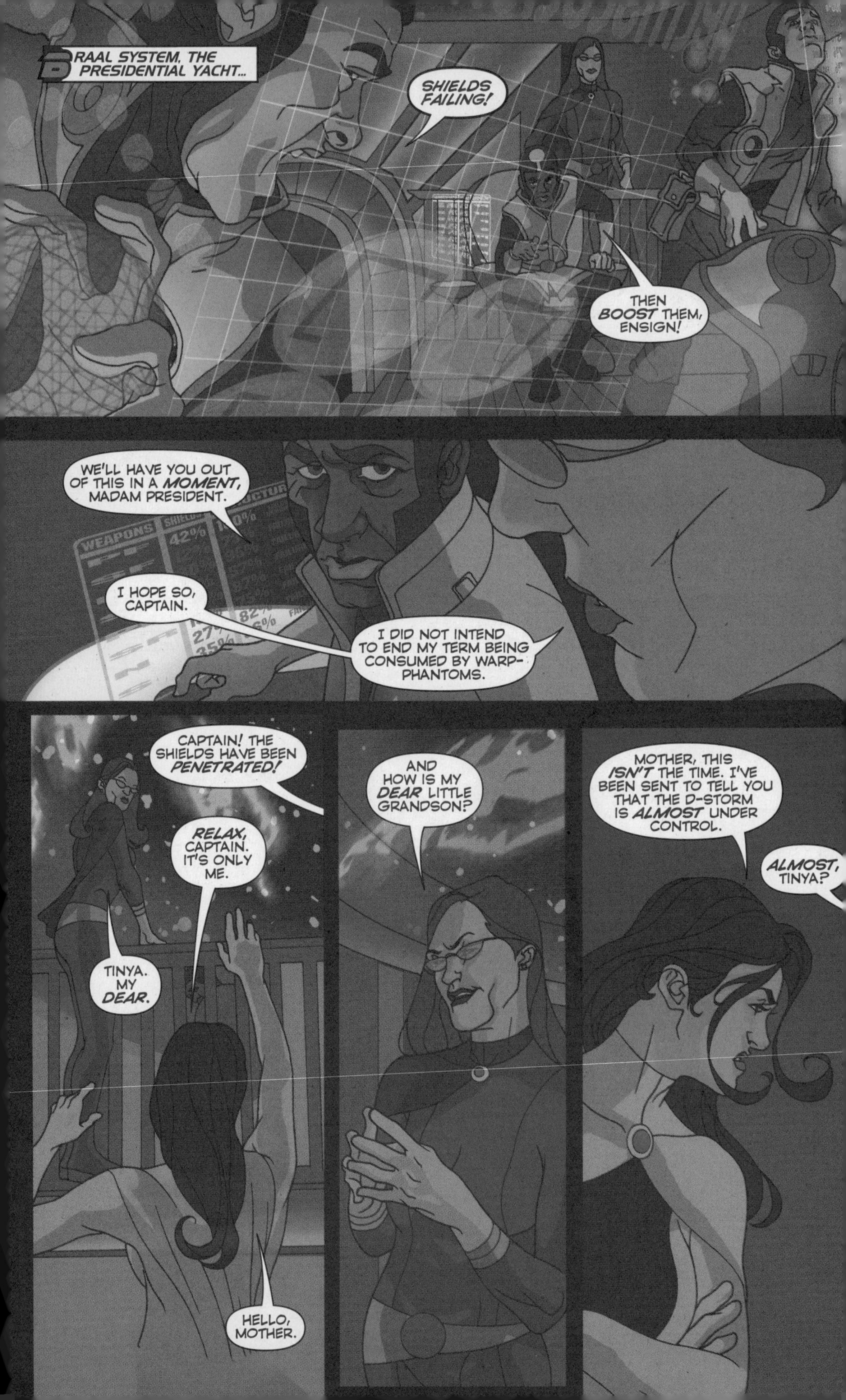
DRAAL SYSTEM, THE PRESIDENTIAL YACHT...
SHIELDS FAILING!
THEN BOOST THEM, ENSIGN!
WE'LL HAVE YOU OUT OF THIS IN A MOMENT, MADAM PRESIDENT.
I HOPE SO, CAPTAIN.
I DID NOT INTEND TO END MY TERM BEING CONSUMED BY WARP-PHANTOMS.
CAPTAIN! THE SHIELDS HAVE BEEN PENETRATED!
RELAX, CAPTAIN. IT'S ONLY ME.
TINYA. MY DEAR.
HELLO, MOTHER.
AND HOW IS MY DEAR LITTLE GRANDSON?
MOTHER, THIS ISN'T THE TIME. I'VE BEEN SENT TO TELL YOU THAT THE D-STORM IS ALMOST UNDER CONTROL.
ALMOST, TINYA?

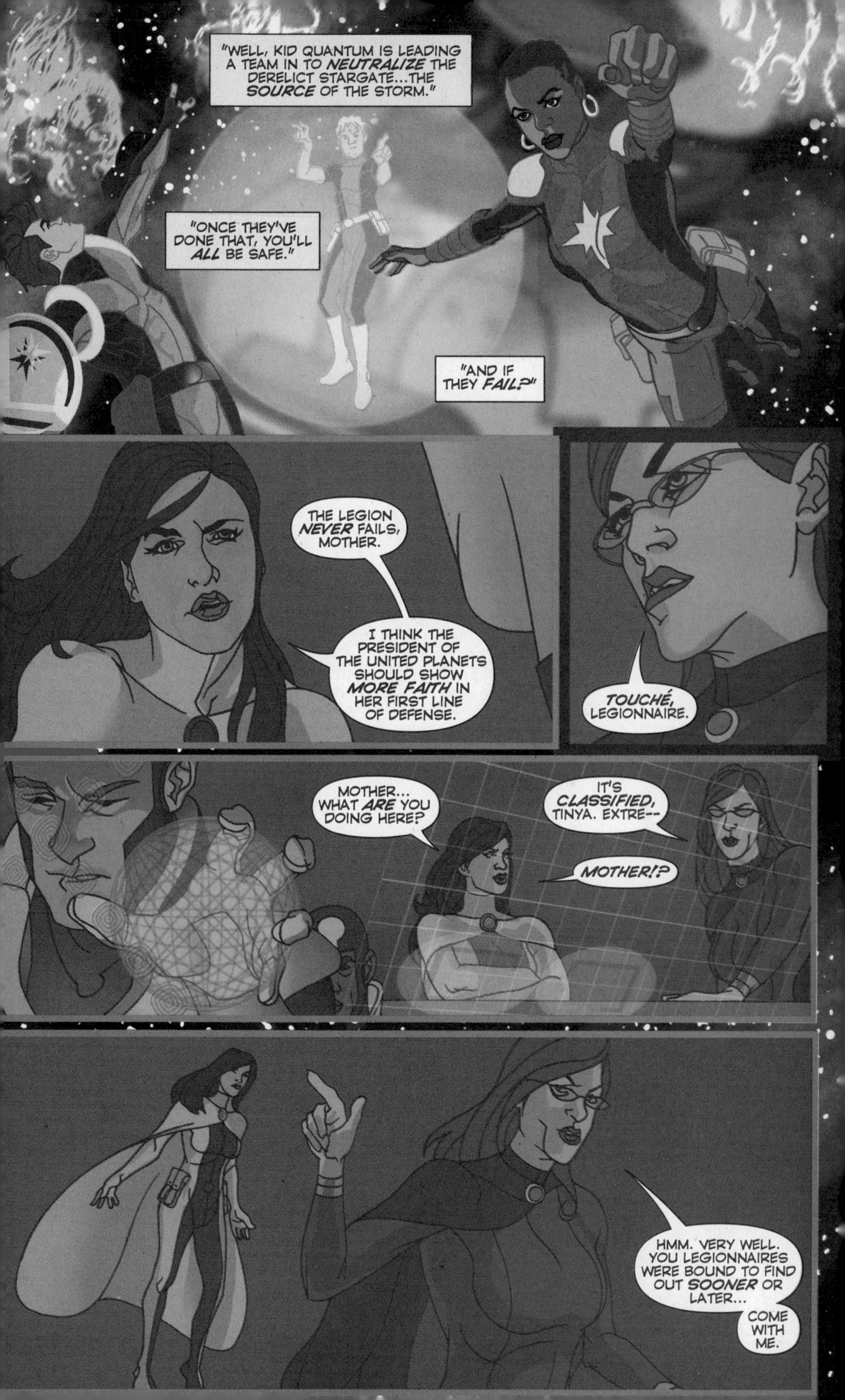
"WELL, KID QUANTUM IS LEADING A TEAM IN TO NEUTRALIZE THE DERELICT STARGATE...THE SOURCE OF THE STORM."
"ONCE THEY'VE DONE THAT, YOU'LL ALL BE SAFE."
"AND IF THEY FAIL?"
THE LEGION NEVER FAILS, MOTHER.
I THINK THE PRESIDENT OF THE UNITED PLANETS SHOULD SHOW MORE FAITH IN HER FIRST LINE OF DEFENSE.
TOUCHÉ, LEGIONNAIRE.
MOTHER... WHAT ARE YOU DOING HERE?
IT'S CLASSIFIED, TINYA. EXTRE--
MOTHER!?
HMM. VERY WELL. YOU LEGIONNAIRES WERE BOUND TO FIND OUT SOONER OR LATER...
COME WITH ME.

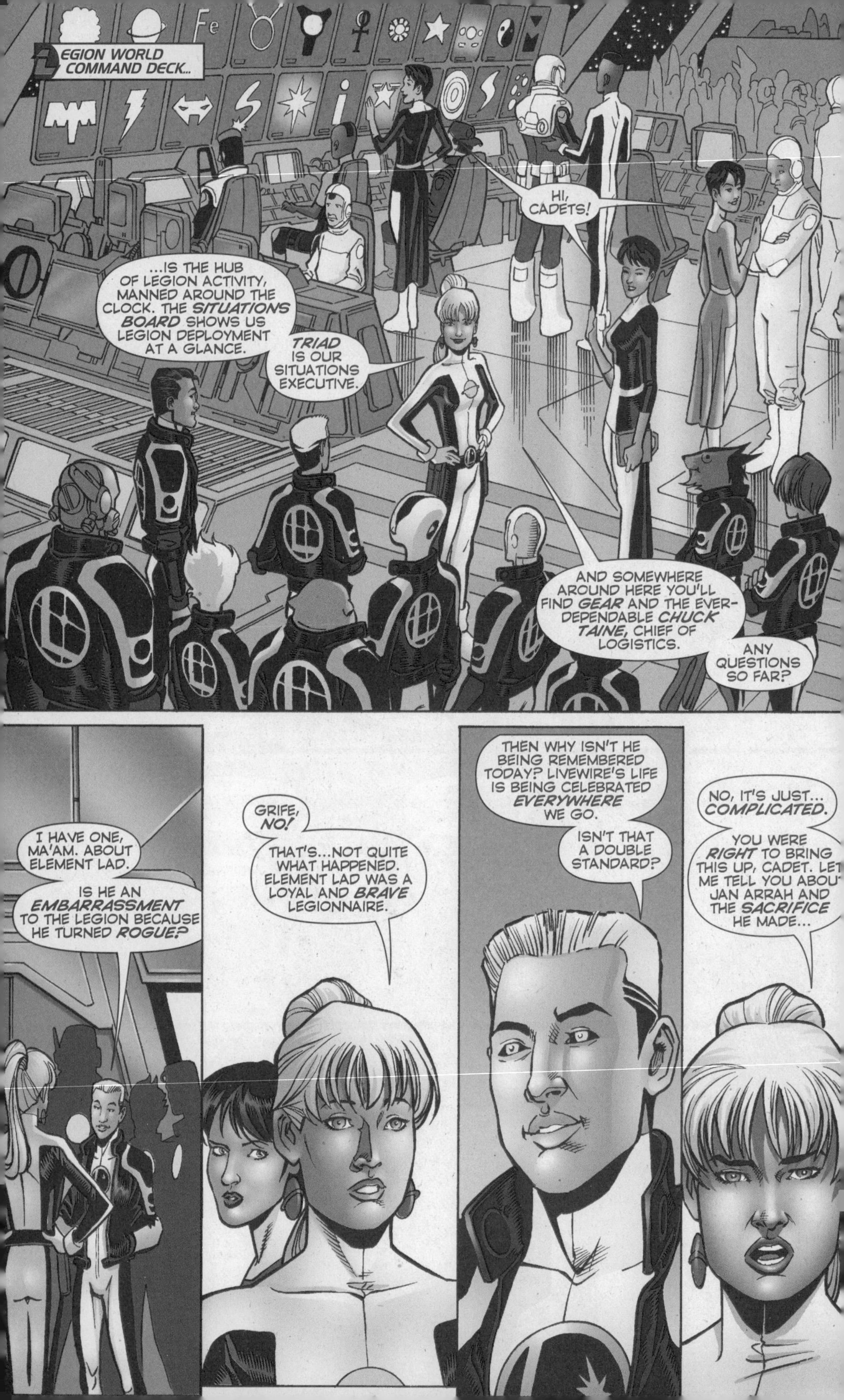

LEGION WORLD COMMAND DECK...
HI, CADETS!
...IS THE HUB OF LEGION ACTIVITY, MANNED AROUND THE CLOCK. THE SITUATIONS BOARD SHOWS US LEGION DEPLOYMENT AT A GLANCE.
TRIAD IS OUR SITUATIONS EXECUTIVE.
AND SOMEWHERE AROUND HERE YOU'LL FIND GEAR AND THE EVER-DEPENDABLE CHUCK TAINE, CHIEF OF LOGISTICS.
ANY QUESTIONS SO FAR?
I HAVE ONE, MA'AM. ABOUT ELEMENT LAD.
IS HE AN EMBARRASSMENT TO THE LEGION BECAUSE HE TURNED ROGUE?
GRIFE, NO!
THAT'S...NOT QUITE WHAT HAPPENED. ELEMENT LAD WAS A LOYAL AND BRAVE LEGIONNAIRE.
THEN WHY ISN'T HE BEING REMEMBERED TODAY? LIVEWIRE'S LIFE IS BEING CELEBRATED EVERYWHERE WE GO.
ISN'T THAT A DOUBLE STANDARD?
NO, IT'S JUST... COMPLICATED.
YOU WERE RIGHT TO BRING THIS UP, CADET. LET ME TELL YOU ABOUT JAN ARRAH AND THE SACRIFICE HE MADE...

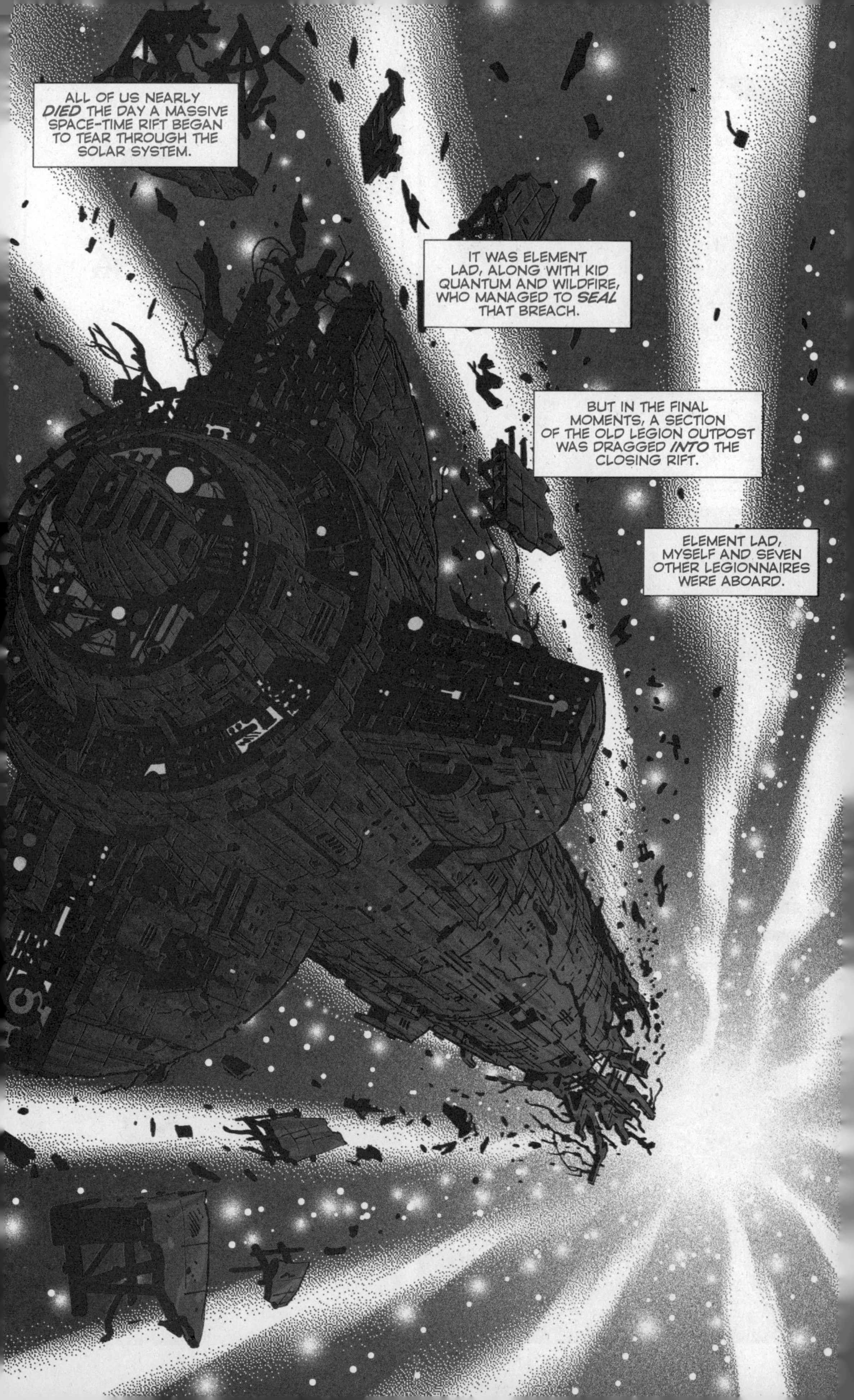
ALL OF US NEARLY DIED THE DAY A MASSIVE SPACE-TIME RIFT BEGAN TO TEAR THROUGH THE SOLAR SYSTEM.
IT WAS ELEMENT LAD, ALONG WITH KID QUANTUM AND WILDFIRE, WHO MANAGED TO SEAL THAT BREACH.
BUT IN THE FINAL MOMENTS, A SECTION OF THE OLD LEGION OUTPOST WAS DRAGGED INTO THE CLOSING RIFT.
ELEMENT LAD, MYSELF AND SEVEN OTHER LEGIONNAIRES WERE ABOARD.

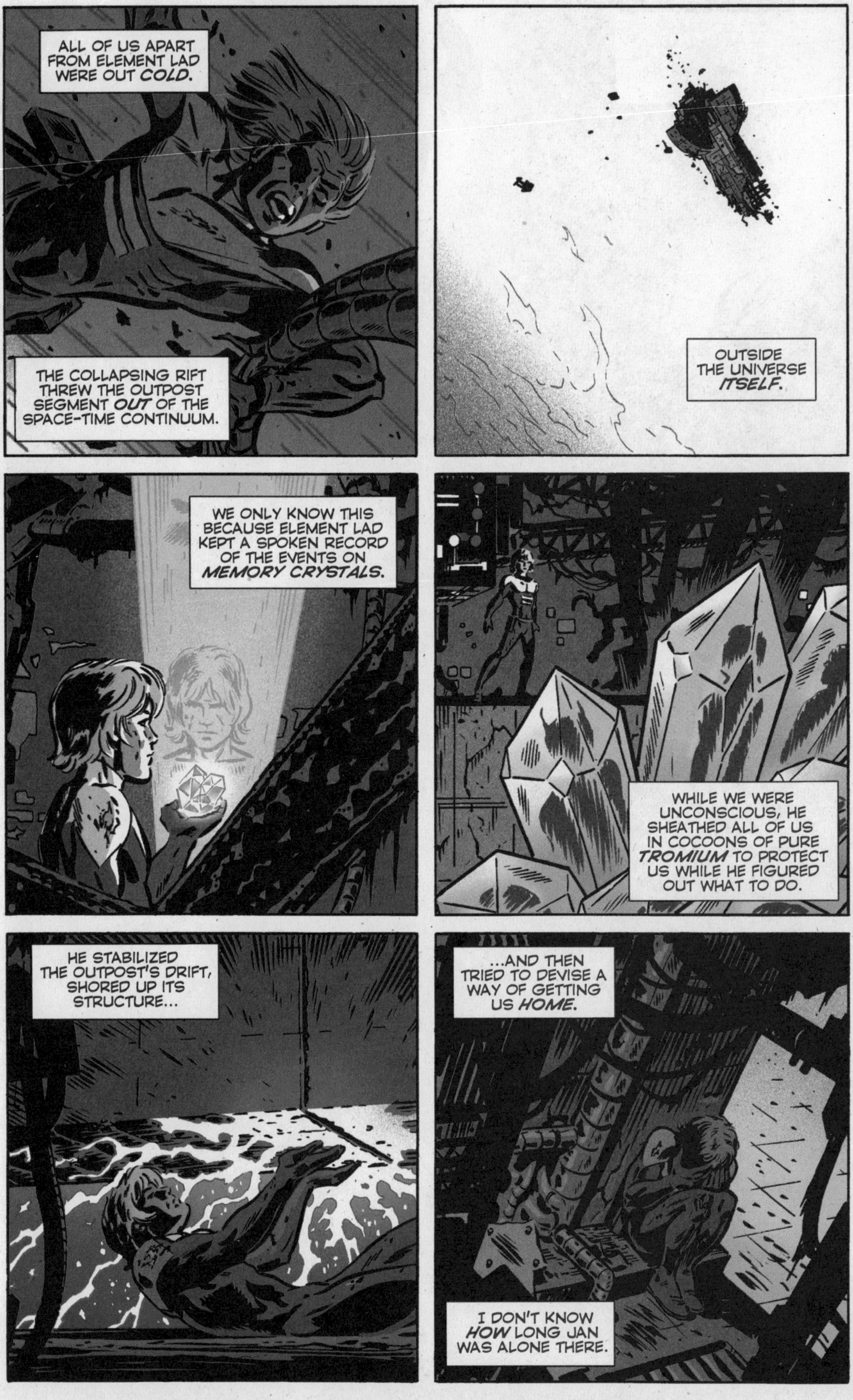

ALL OF US APART FROM ELEMENT LAD WERE OUT *COLD.*
THE COLLAPSING RIFT THREW THE OUTPOST SEGMENT *OUT* OF THE SPACE-TIME CONTINUUM.
OUTSIDE THE UNIVERSE *ITSELF.*
WE ONLY KNOW THIS BECAUSE ELEMENT LAD KEPT A SPOKEN RECORD OF THE EVENTS ON *MEMORY CRYSTALS.*
WHILE WE WERE UNCONSCIOUS, HE SHEATHED ALL OF US IN COCOONS OF PURE *TROMIUM* TO PROTECT US WHILE HE FIGURED OUT WHAT TO DO.
HE STABILIZED THE OUTPOST'S DRIFT, SHORED UP ITS STRUCTURE...
...AND THEN TRIED TO DEVISE A WAY OF GETTING US *HOME.*
I DON'T KNOW *HOW* LONG JAN WAS ALONE THERE.

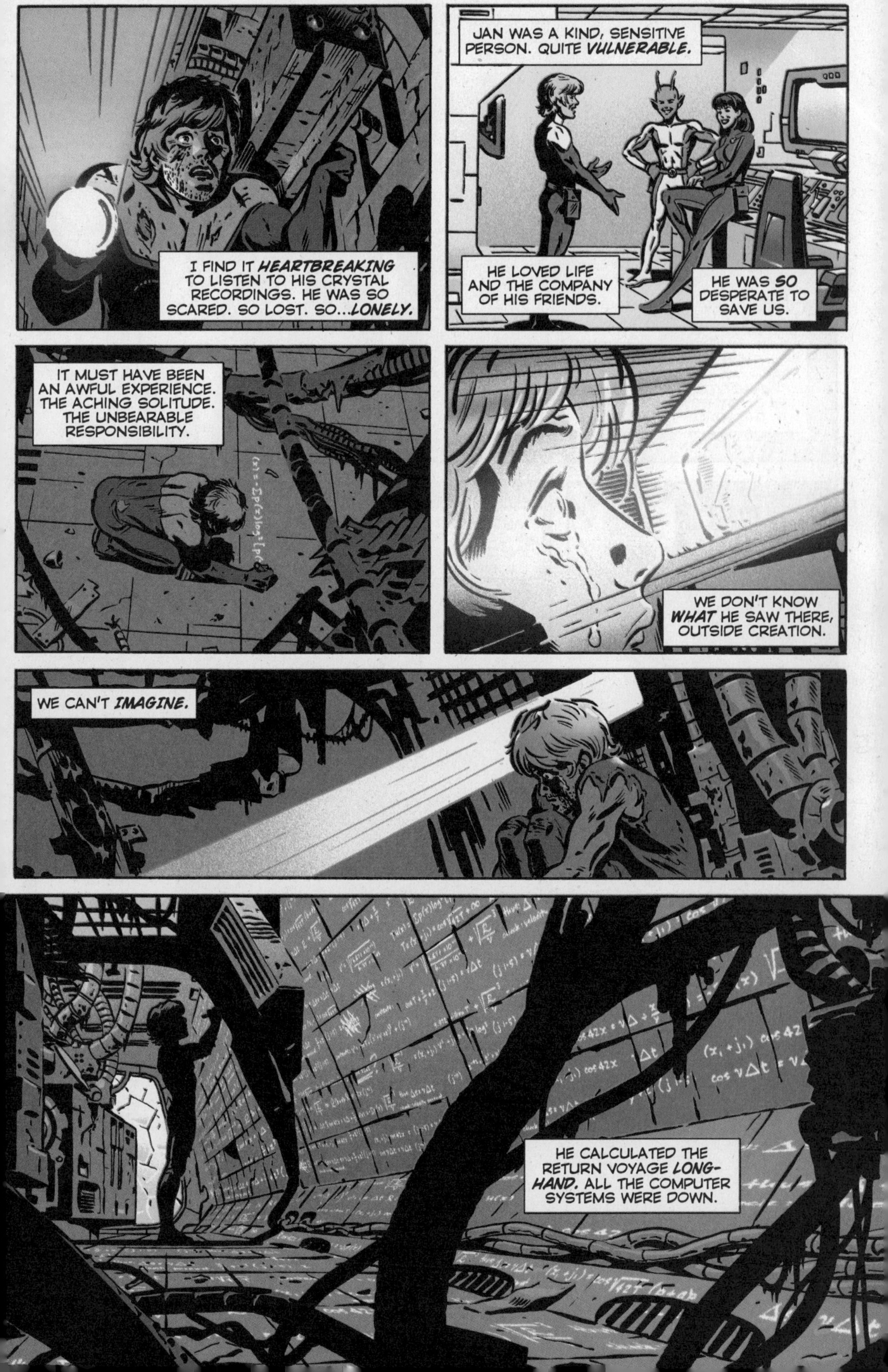

I FIND IT ***HEARTBREAKING*** TO LISTEN TO HIS CRYSTAL RECORDINGS. HE WAS SO SCARED. SO LOST. SO...***LONELY.***
JAN WAS A KIND, SENSITIVE PERSON. QUITE ***VULNERABLE.***
HE LOVED LIFE AND THE COMPANY OF HIS FRIENDS.
HE WAS ***SO*** DESPERATE TO SAVE US.
IT MUST HAVE BEEN AN AWFUL EXPERIENCE. THE ACHING SOLITUDE. THE UNBEARABLE RESPONSIBILITY.
WE DON'T KNOW ***WHAT*** HE SAW THERE, OUTSIDE CREATION.
WE CAN'T ***IMAGINE.***
HE CALCULATED THE RETURN VOYAGE ***LONG-HAND.*** ALL THE COMPUTER SYSTEMS WERE DOWN.

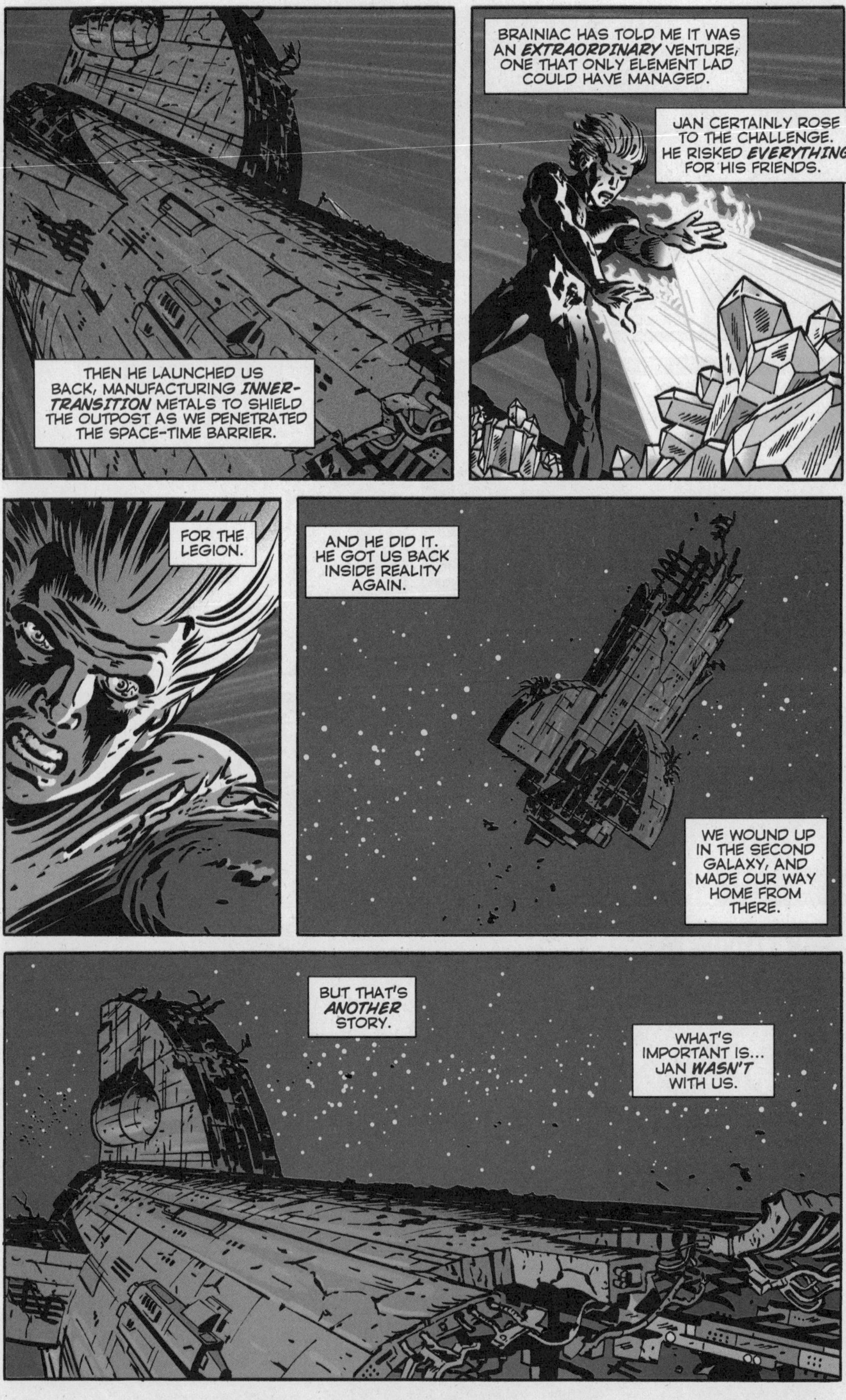
THEN HE LAUNCHED US BACK, MANUFACTURING *INNER-TRANSITION* METALS TO SHIELD THE OUTPOST AS WE PENETRATED THE SPACE-TIME BARRIER.
BRAINIAC HAS TOLD ME IT WAS AN *EXTRAORDINARY* VENTURE, ONE THAT ONLY ELEMENT LAD COULD HAVE MANAGED.
JAN CERTAINLY ROSE TO THE CHALLENGE. HE RISKED *EVERYTHING* FOR HIS FRIENDS.
FOR THE LEGION.
AND HE DID IT. HE GOT US BACK INSIDE REALITY AGAIN.
WE WOUND UP IN THE SECOND GALAXY, AND MADE OUR WAY HOME FROM THERE.
BUT THAT'S *ANOTHER* STORY.
WHAT'S IMPORTANT IS... JAN *WASN'T* WITH US.

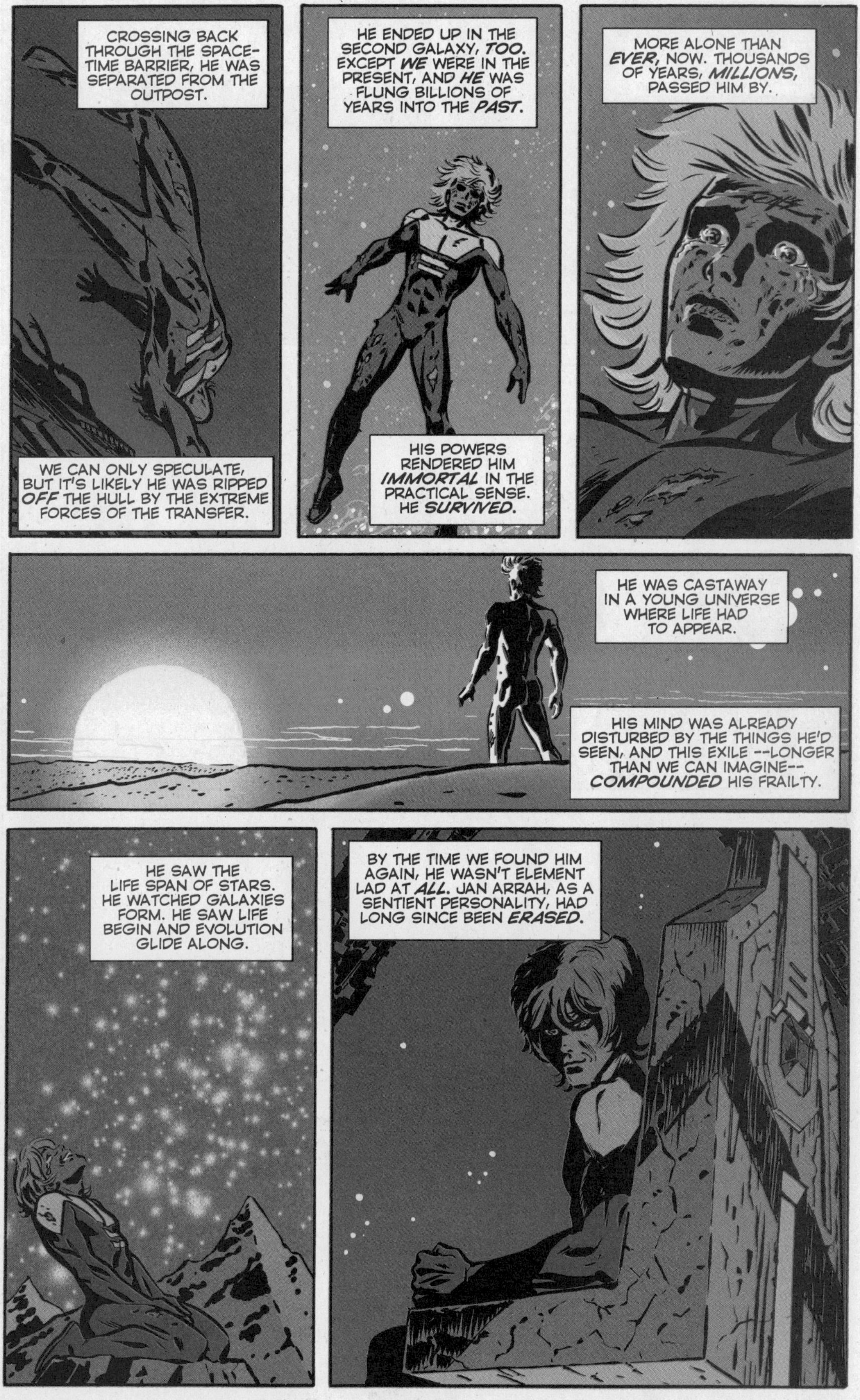
CROSSING BACK THROUGH THE SPACE-TIME BARRIER, HE WAS SEPARATED FROM THE OUTPOST.
WE CAN ONLY SPECULATE, BUT IT'S LIKELY HE WAS RIPPED OFF THE HULL BY THE EXTREME FORCES OF THE TRANSFER.
HE ENDED UP IN THE SECOND GALAXY, TOO. EXCEPT WE WERE IN THE PRESENT, AND HE WAS FLUNG BILLIONS OF YEARS INTO THE PAST.
HIS POWERS RENDERED HIM IMMORTAL IN THE PRACTICAL SENSE. HE SURVIVED.
MORE ALONE THAN EVER, NOW. THOUSANDS OF YEARS, MILLIONS, PASSED HIM BY.
HE WAS CASTAWAY IN A YOUNG UNIVERSE WHERE LIFE HAD TO APPEAR.
HIS MIND WAS ALREADY DISTURBED BY THE THINGS HE'D SEEN, AND THIS EXILE --LONGER THAN WE CAN IMAGINE-- COMPOUNDED HIS FRAILTY.
HE SAW THE LIFE SPAN OF STARS. HE WATCHED GALAXIES FORM. HE SAW LIFE BEGIN AND EVOLUTION GLIDE ALONG.
BY THE TIME WE FOUND HIM AGAIN, HE WASN'T ELEMENT LAD AT ALL. JAN ARRAH, AS A SENTIENT PERSONALITY, HAD LONG SINCE BEEN ERASED.

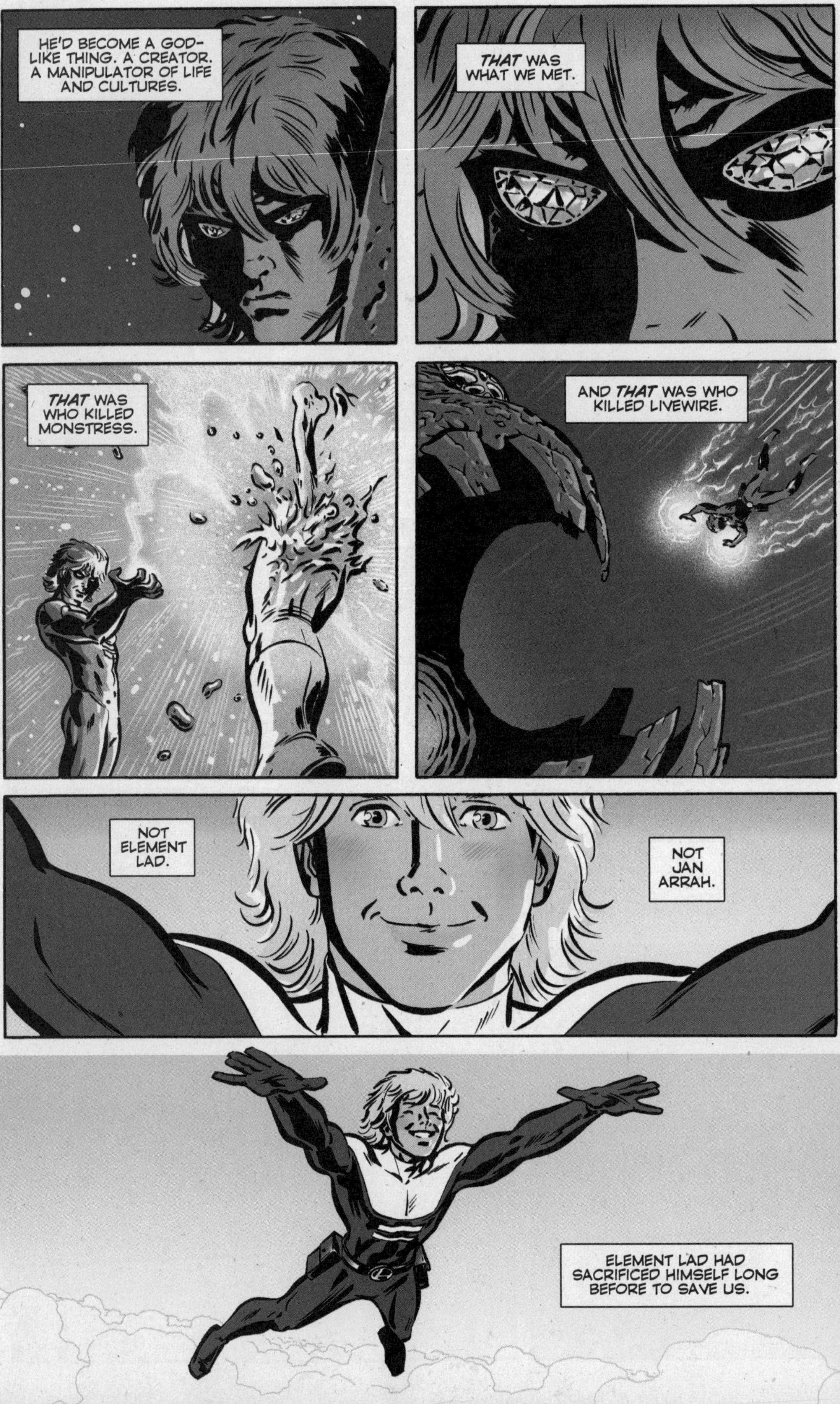
HE'D BECOME A GOD-LIKE THING. A CREATOR. A MANIPULATOR OF LIFE AND CULTURES.
THAT WAS WHAT WE MET.
THAT WAS WHO KILLED MONSTRESS.
AND THAT WAS WHO KILLED LIVEWIRE.
NOT ELEMENT LAD.
NOT JAN ARRAH.
ELEMENT LAD HAD SACRIFICED HIMSELF LONG BEFORE TO SAVE US.

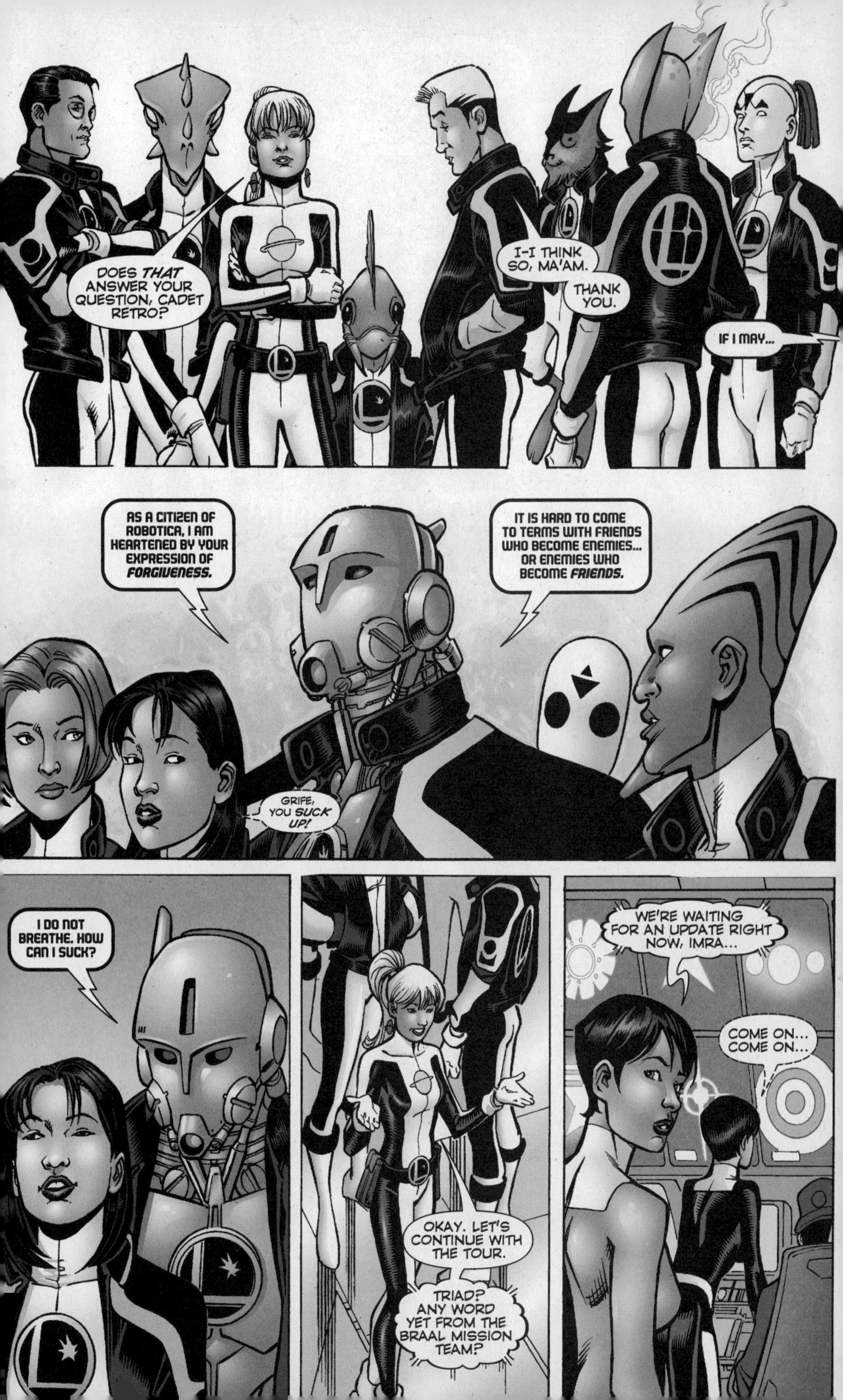
DOES THAT ANSWER YOUR QUESTION, CADET RETRO?
I-I THINK SO, MA'AM.
THANK YOU.
IF I MAY...
AS A CITIZEN OF ROBOTICA, I AM HEARTENED BY YOUR EXPRESSION OF FORGIVENESS.
IT IS HARD TO COME TO TERMS WITH FRIENDS WHO BECOME ENEMIES... OR ENEMIES WHO BECOME FRIENDS.
GRIFE, YOU SUCK UP!
I DO NOT BREATHE. HOW CAN I SUCK?
OKAY. LET'S CONTINUE WITH THE TOUR.
TRIAD? ANY WORD YET FROM THE BRAAL MISSION TEAM?
WE'RE WAITING FOR AN UPDATE RIGHT NOW, IMRA...
COME ON... COME ON...

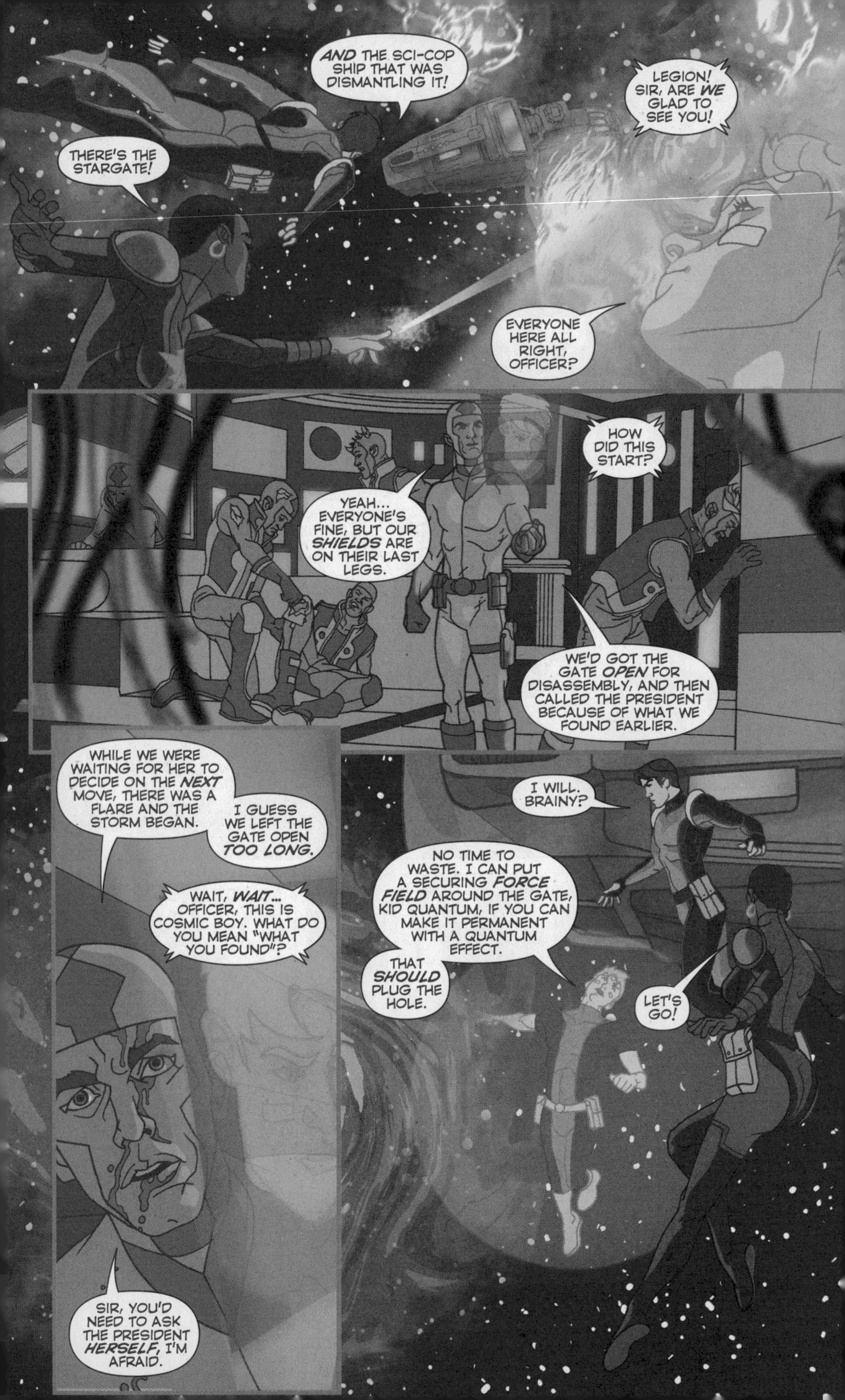
AND THE SCI-COP SHIP THAT WAS DISMANTLING IT!
LEGION! SIR, ARE WE GLAD TO SEE YOU!
THERE'S THE STARGATE!
EVERYONE HERE ALL RIGHT, OFFICER?
HOW DID THIS START?
YEAH... EVERYONE'S FINE, BUT OUR SHIELDS ARE ON THEIR LAST LEGS.
WE'D GOT THE GATE OPEN FOR DISASSEMBLY, AND THEN CALLED THE PRESIDENT BECAUSE OF WHAT WE FOUND EARLIER.
WHILE WE WERE WAITING FOR HER TO DECIDE ON THE NEXT MOVE, THERE WAS A FLARE AND THE STORM BEGAN.
I GUESS WE LEFT THE GATE OPEN TOO LONG.
WAIT, WAIT... OFFICER, THIS IS COSMIC BOY. WHAT DO YOU MEAN "WHAT YOU FOUND"?
SIR, YOU'D NEED TO ASK THE PRESIDENT HERSELF, I'M AFRAID.
I WILL. BRAINY?
NO TIME TO WASTE. I CAN PUT A SECURING FORCE FIELD AROUND THE GATE, KID QUANTUM, IF YOU CAN MAKE IT PERMANENT WITH A QUANTUM EFFECT.
THAT SHOULD PLUG THE HOLE.
LET'S GO!

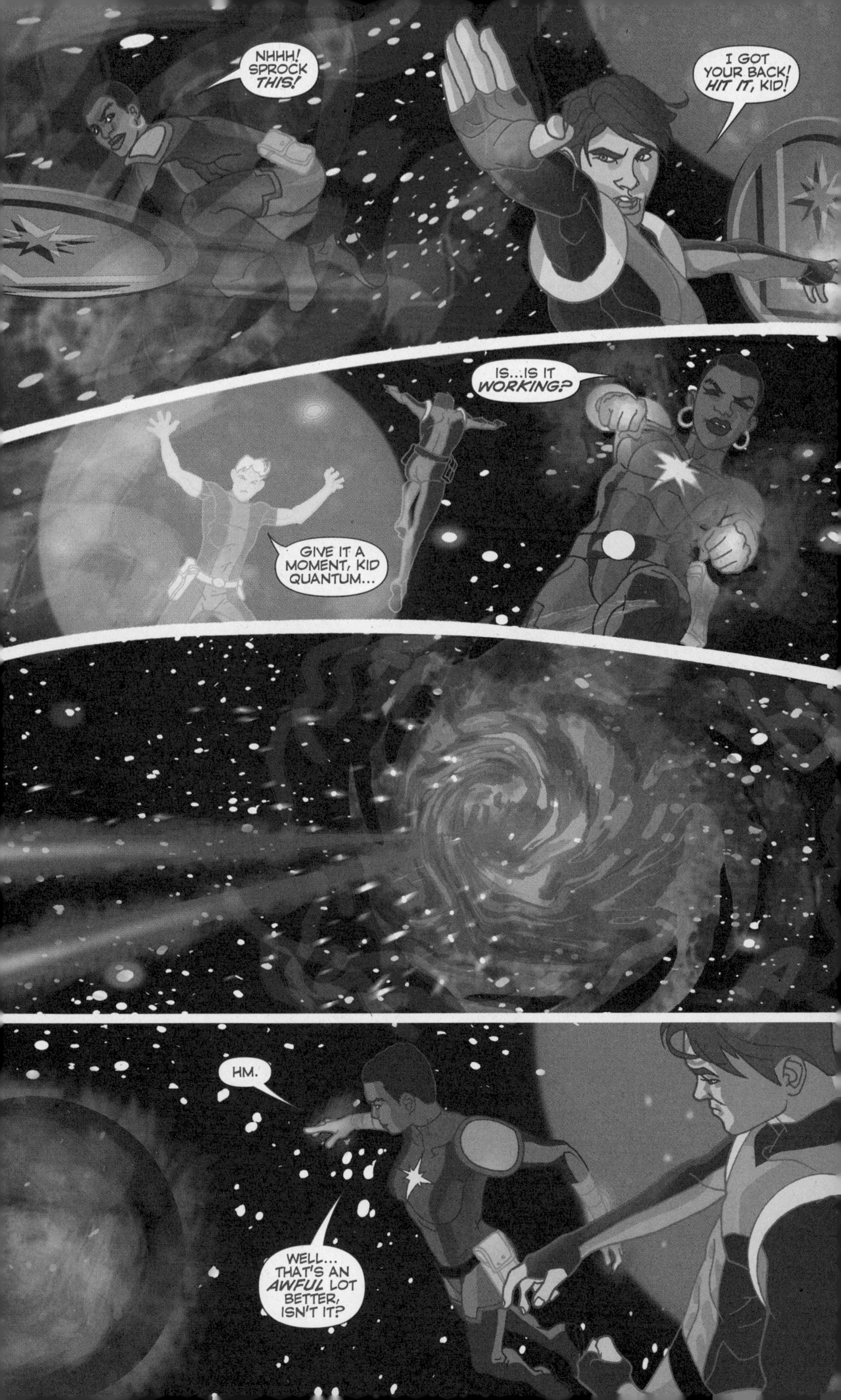
NHHH! SPROCK *THIS!*
I GOT YOUR BACK! *HIT IT,* KID!
IS...IS IT *WORKING?*
GIVE IT A MOMENT, KID QUANTUM...
HM.
WELL... THAT'S AN *AWFUL* LOT BETTER, ISN'T IT?

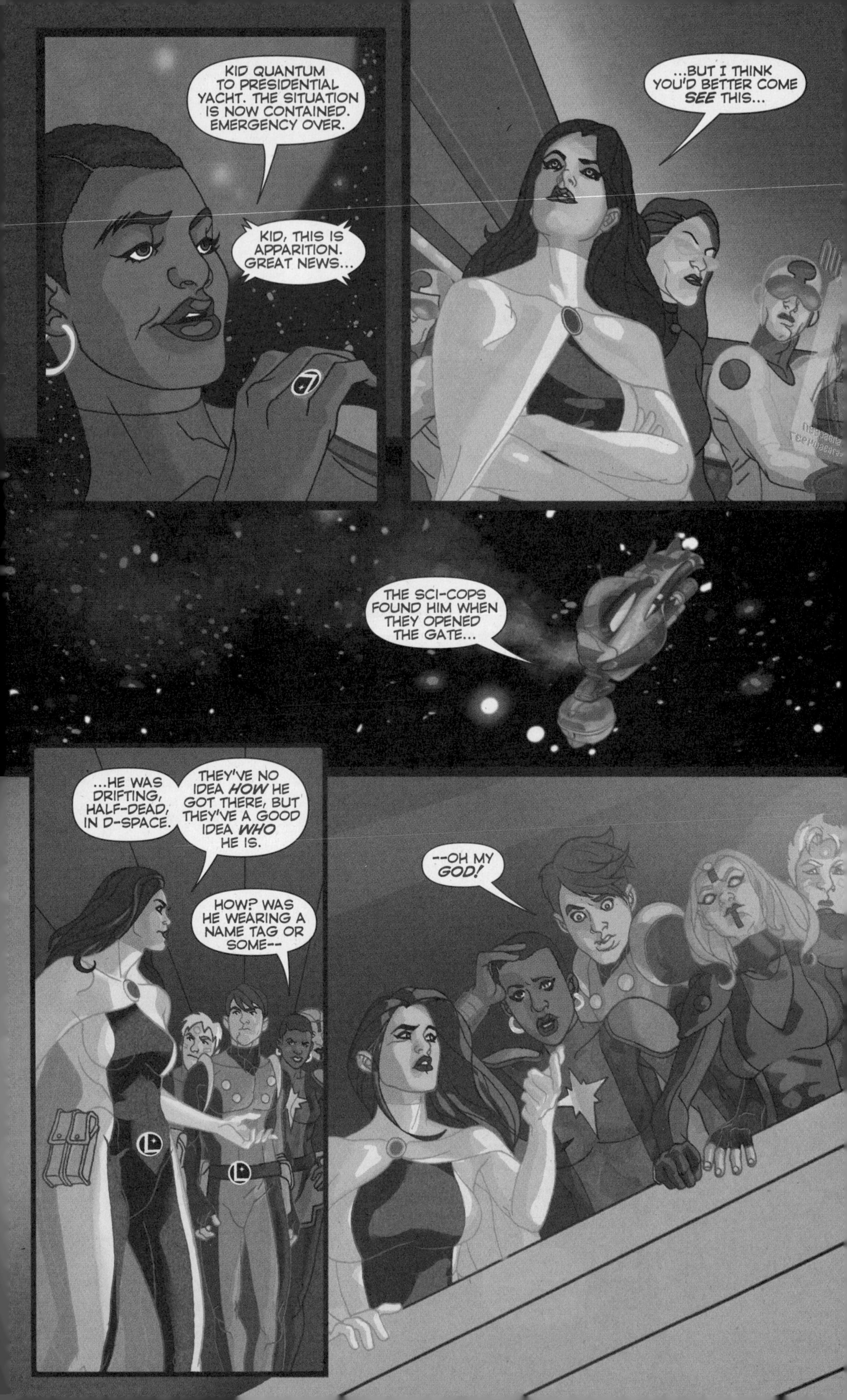
KID QUANTUM TO PRESIDENTIAL YACHT. THE SITUATION IS NOW CONTAINED. EMERGENCY OVER.
KID, THIS IS APPARITION. GREAT NEWS...
...BUT I THINK YOU'D BETTER COME SEE THIS...
THE SCI-COPS FOUND HIM WHEN THEY OPENED THE GATE...
...HE WAS DRIFTING, HALF-DEAD, IN D-SPACE.
THEY'VE NO IDEA HOW HE GOT THERE, BUT THEY'VE A GOOD IDEA WHO HE IS.
HOW? WAS HE WEARING A NAME TAG OR SOME--
--OH MY GOD!

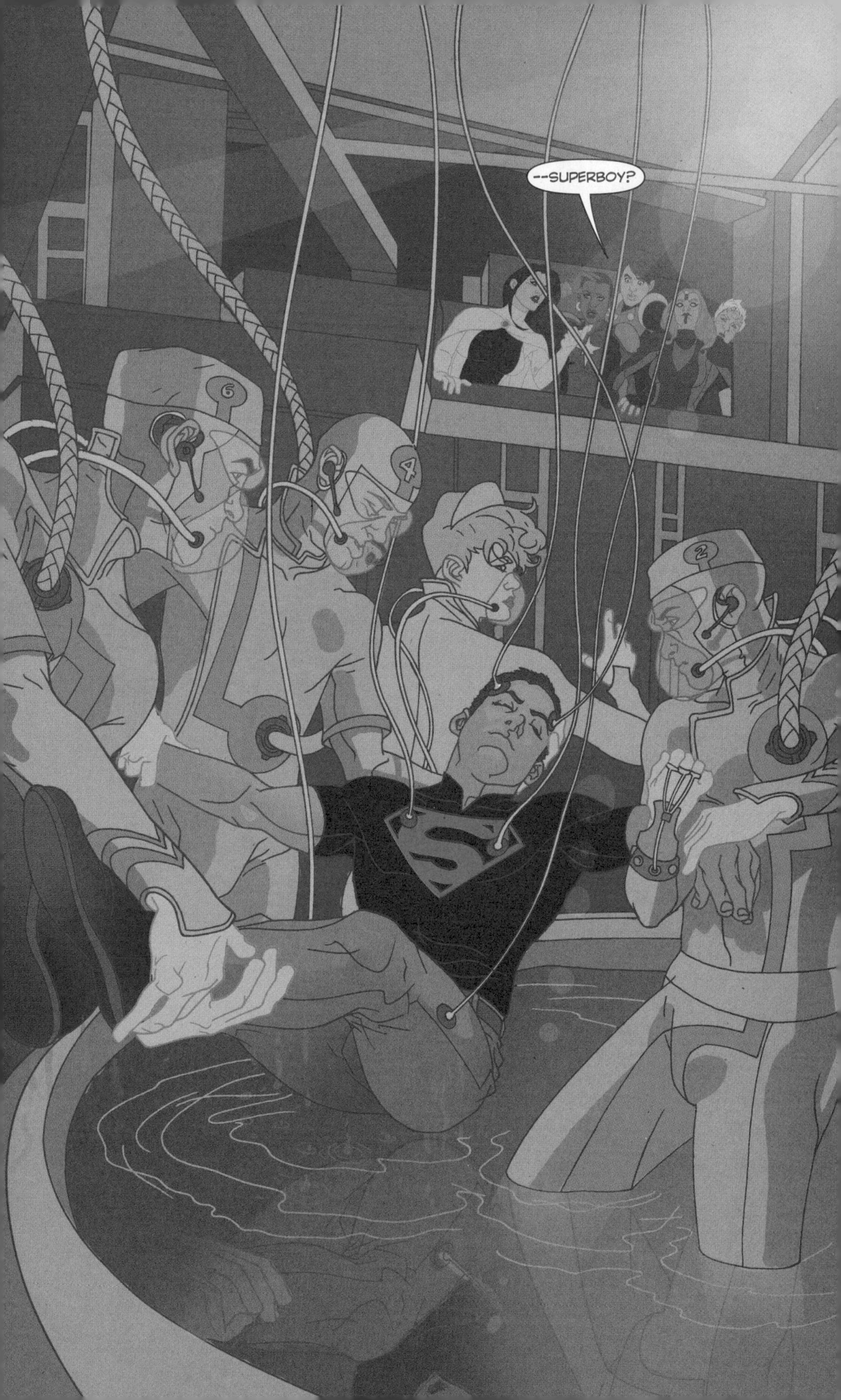
--SUPERBOY?

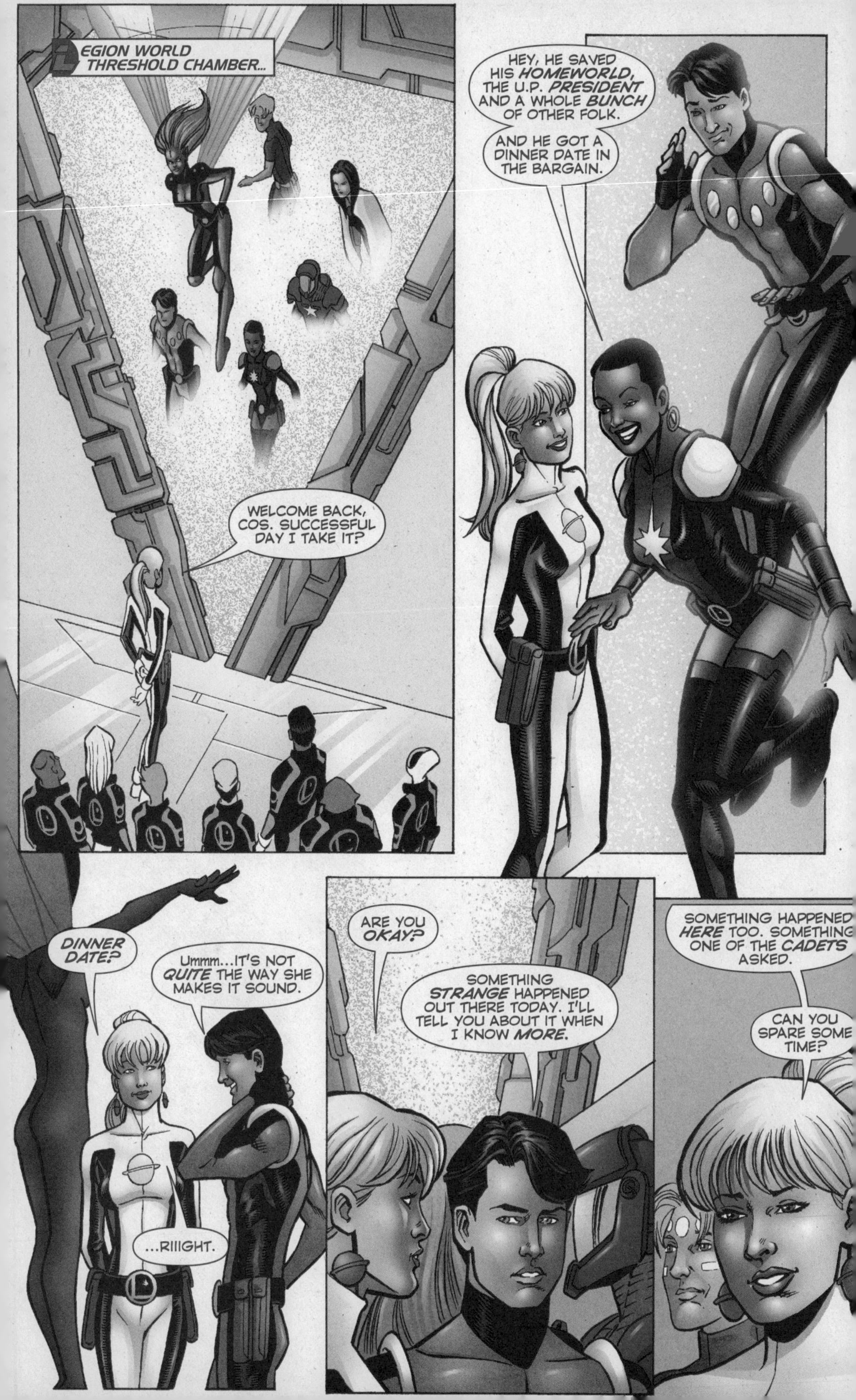
LEGION WORLD THRESHOLD CHAMBER...
WELCOME BACK, COS. SUCCESSFUL DAY I TAKE IT?
HEY, HE SAVED HIS HOMEWORLD, THE U.P. PRESIDENT AND A WHOLE BUNCH OF OTHER FOLK.
AND HE GOT A DINNER DATE IN THE BARGAIN.
DINNER DATE?
Ummm...IT'S NOT QUITE THE WAY SHE MAKES IT SOUND.
...RIIIGHT.
ARE YOU OKAY?
SOMETHING STRANGE HAPPENED OUT THERE TODAY. I'LL TELL YOU ABOUT IT WHEN I KNOW MORE.
SOMETHING HAPPENED HERE TOO. SOMETHING ONE OF THE CADETS ASKED.
CAN YOU SPARE SOME TIME?

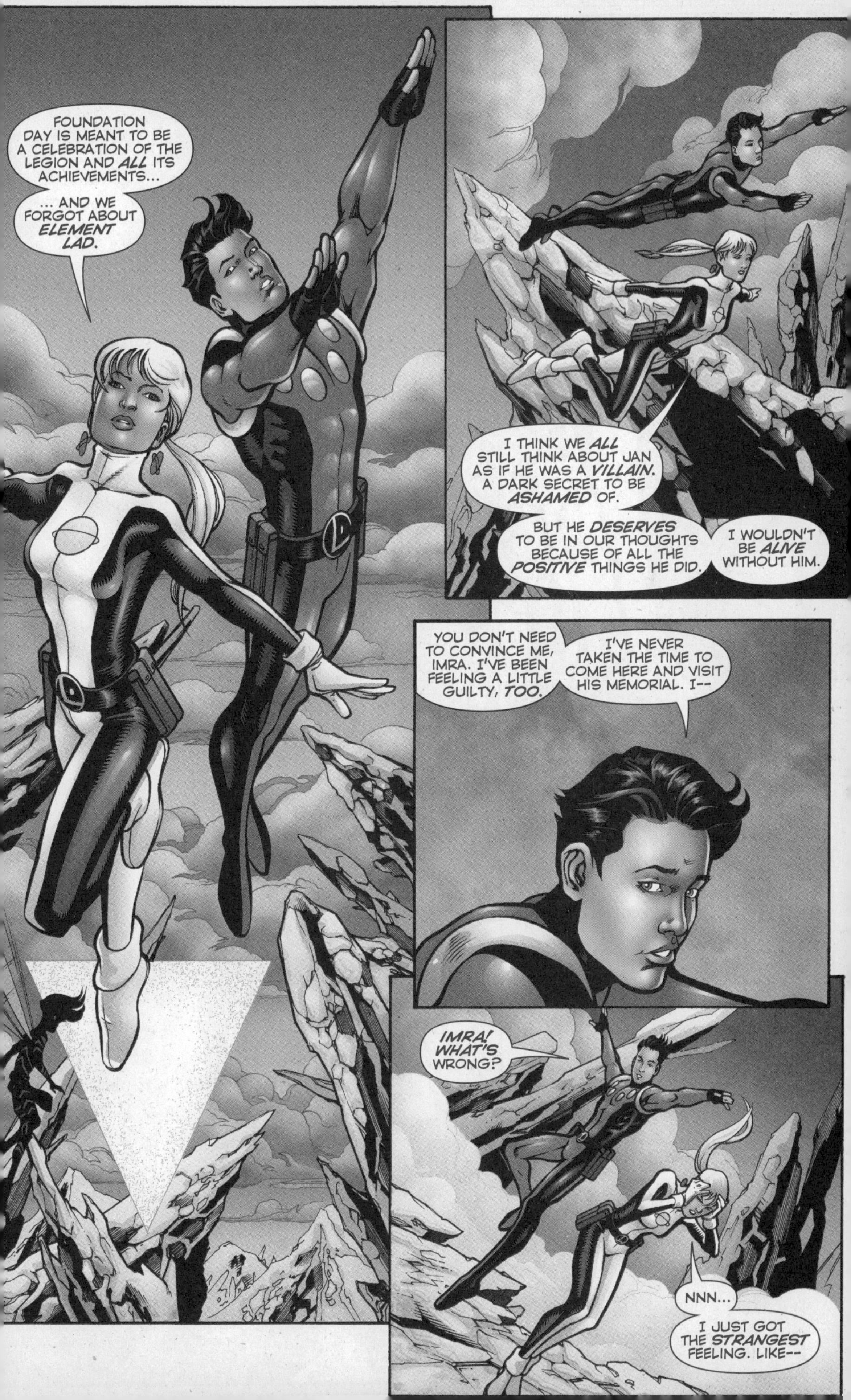
FOUNDATION DAY IS MEANT TO BE A CELEBRATION OF THE LEGION AND ALL ITS ACHIEVEMENTS...
... AND WE FORGOT ABOUT ELEMENT LAD.
I THINK WE ALL STILL THINK ABOUT JAN AS IF HE WAS A VILLAIN. A DARK SECRET TO BE ASHAMED OF.
BUT HE DESERVES TO BE IN OUR THOUGHTS BECAUSE OF ALL THE POSITIVE THINGS HE DID.
I WOULDN'T BE ALIVE WITHOUT HIM.
YOU DON'T NEED TO CONVINCE ME, IMRA. I'VE BEEN FEELING A LITTLE GUILTY, TOO.
I'VE NEVER TAKEN THE TIME TO COME HERE AND VISIT HIS MEMORIAL. I--
IMRA! WHAT'S WRONG?
NNN...
I JUST GOT THE STRANGEST FEELING. LIKE--

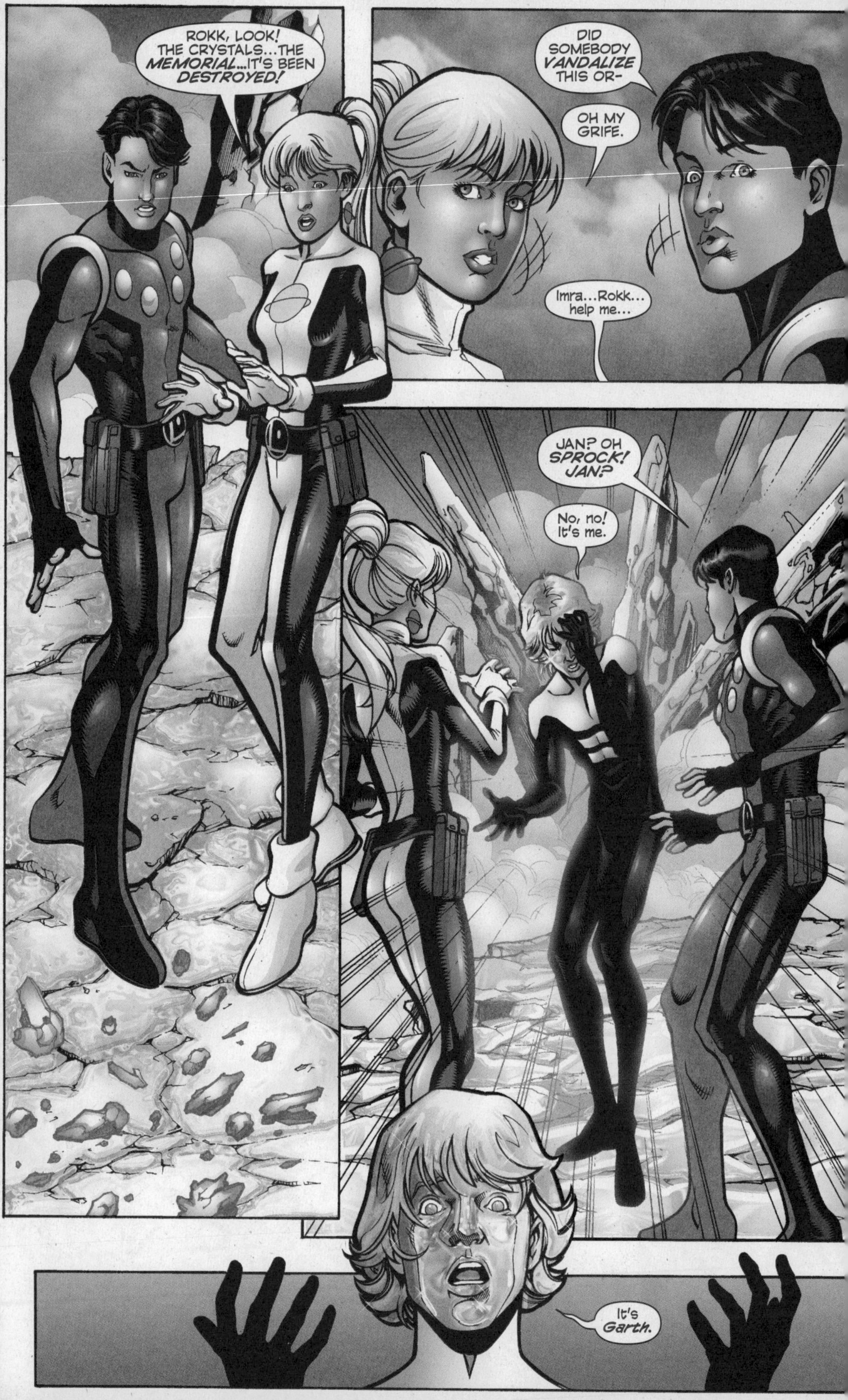
ROKK, LOOK! THE CRYSTALS...THE MEMORIAL...IT'S BEEN DESTROYED!
DID SOMEBODY VANDALIZE THIS OR-
OH MY GRIFE.
Imra...Rokk... help me...
JAN? OH SPROCK! JAN?
No, no! It's me.
It's Garth.

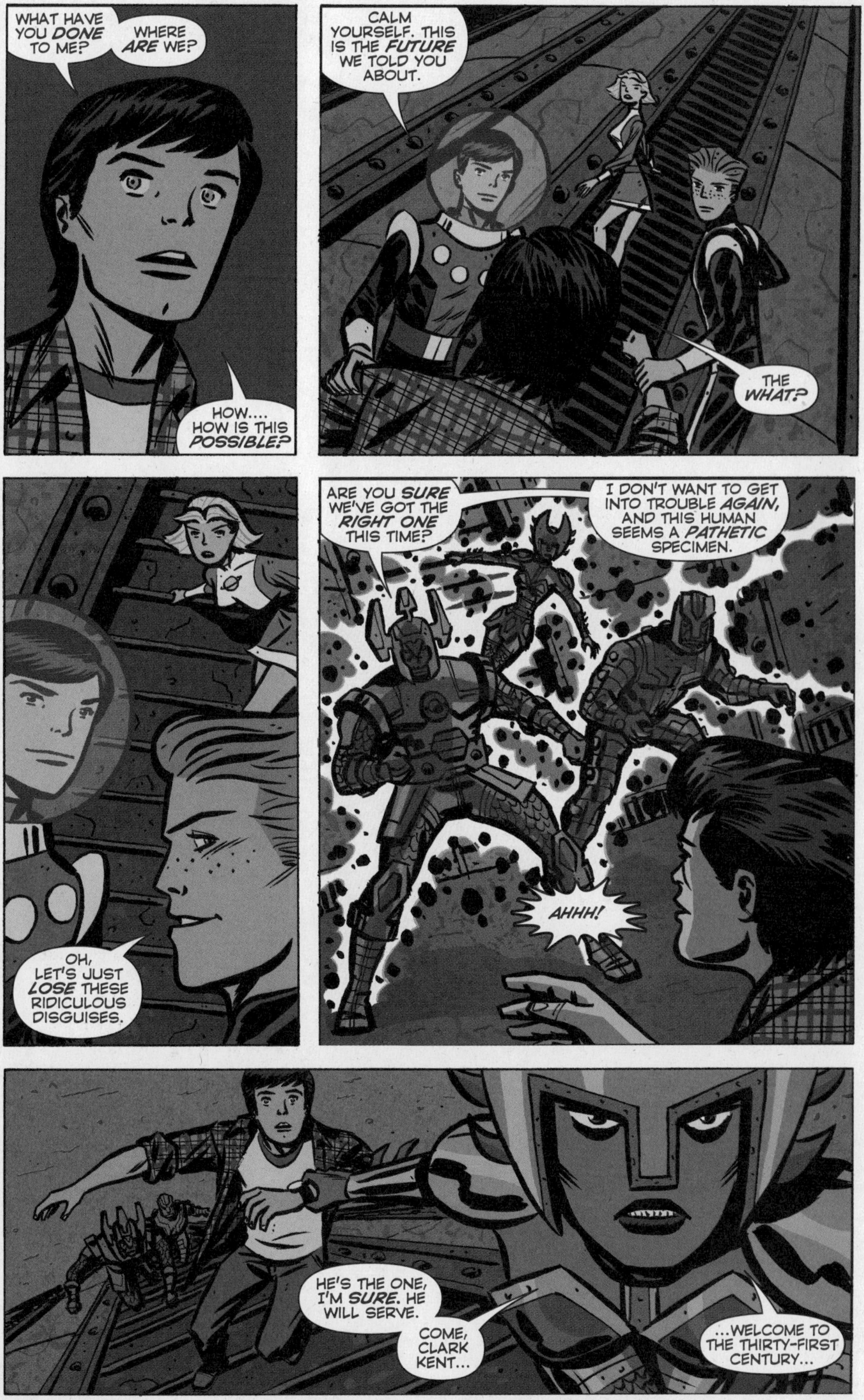
WHAT HAVE YOU DONE TO ME?
WHERE ARE WE?
HOW.... HOW IS THIS POSSIBLE?
CALM YOURSELF. THIS IS THE FUTURE WE TOLD YOU ABOUT.
THE WHAT?
OH, LET'S JUST LOSE THESE RIDICULOUS DISGUISES.
ARE YOU SURE WE'VE GOT THE RIGHT ONE THIS TIME?
I DON'T WANT TO GET INTO TROUBLE AGAIN, AND THIS HUMAN SEEMS A PATHETIC SPECIMEN.
AHHH!
HE'S THE ONE, I'M SURE. HE WILL SERVE.
COME, CLARK KENT...
...WELCOME TO THE THIRTY-FIRST CENTURY...

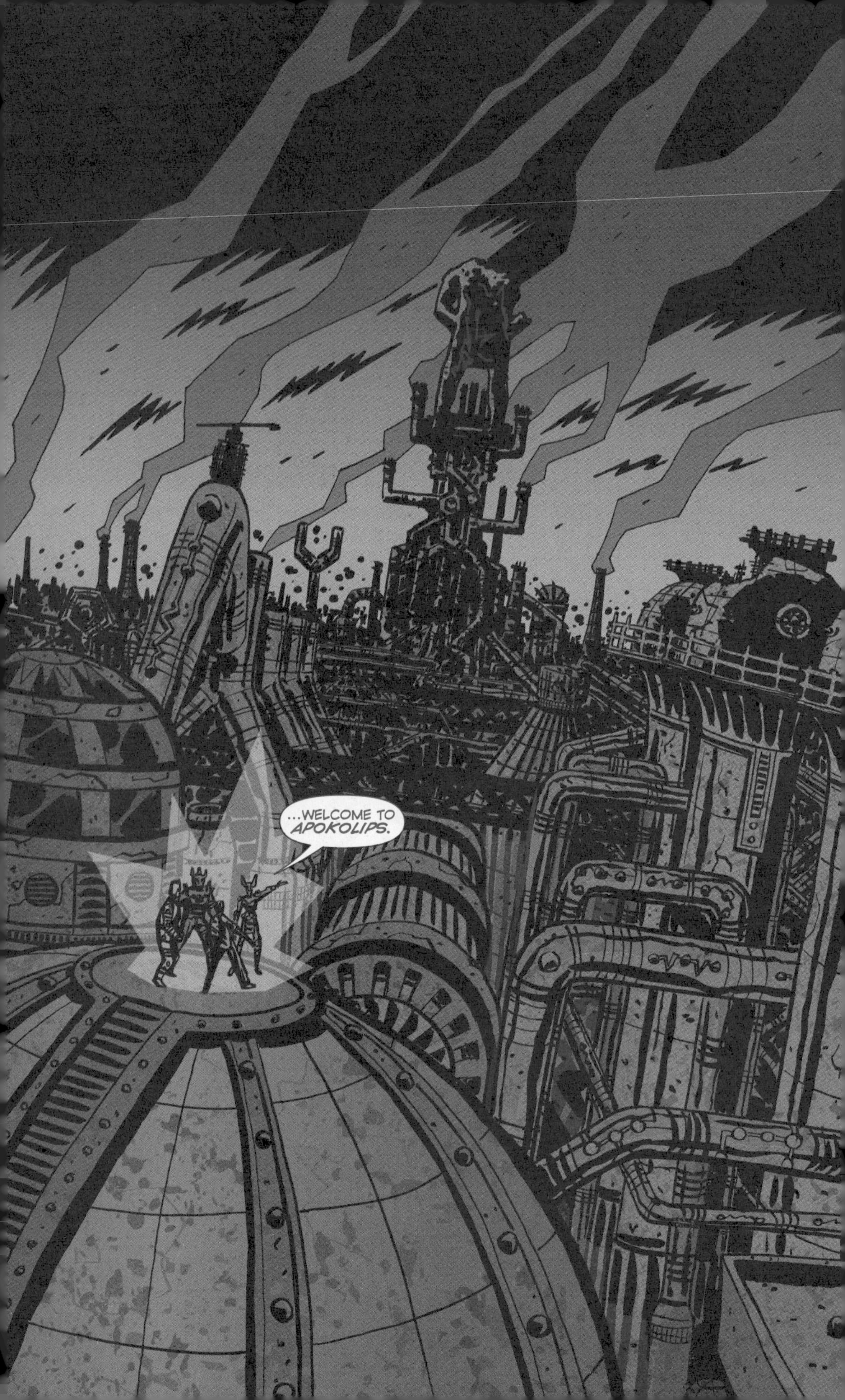
...WELCOME TO APOKOLIPS.

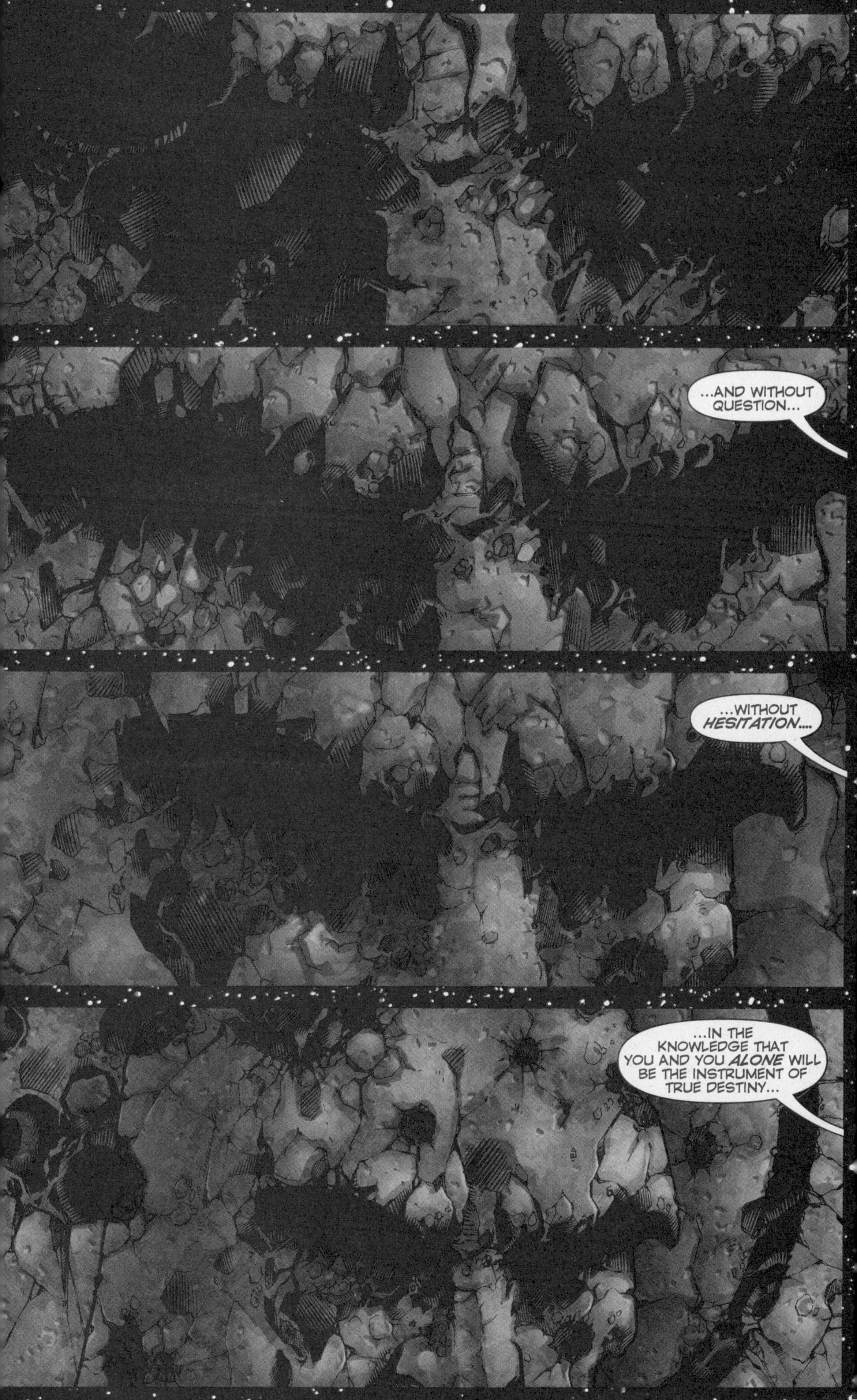
...AND WITHOUT QUESTION...
...WITHOUT *HESITATION*....
...IN THE KNOWLEDGE THAT YOU AND YOU *ALONE* WILL BE THE INSTRUMENT OF TRUE DESTINY...

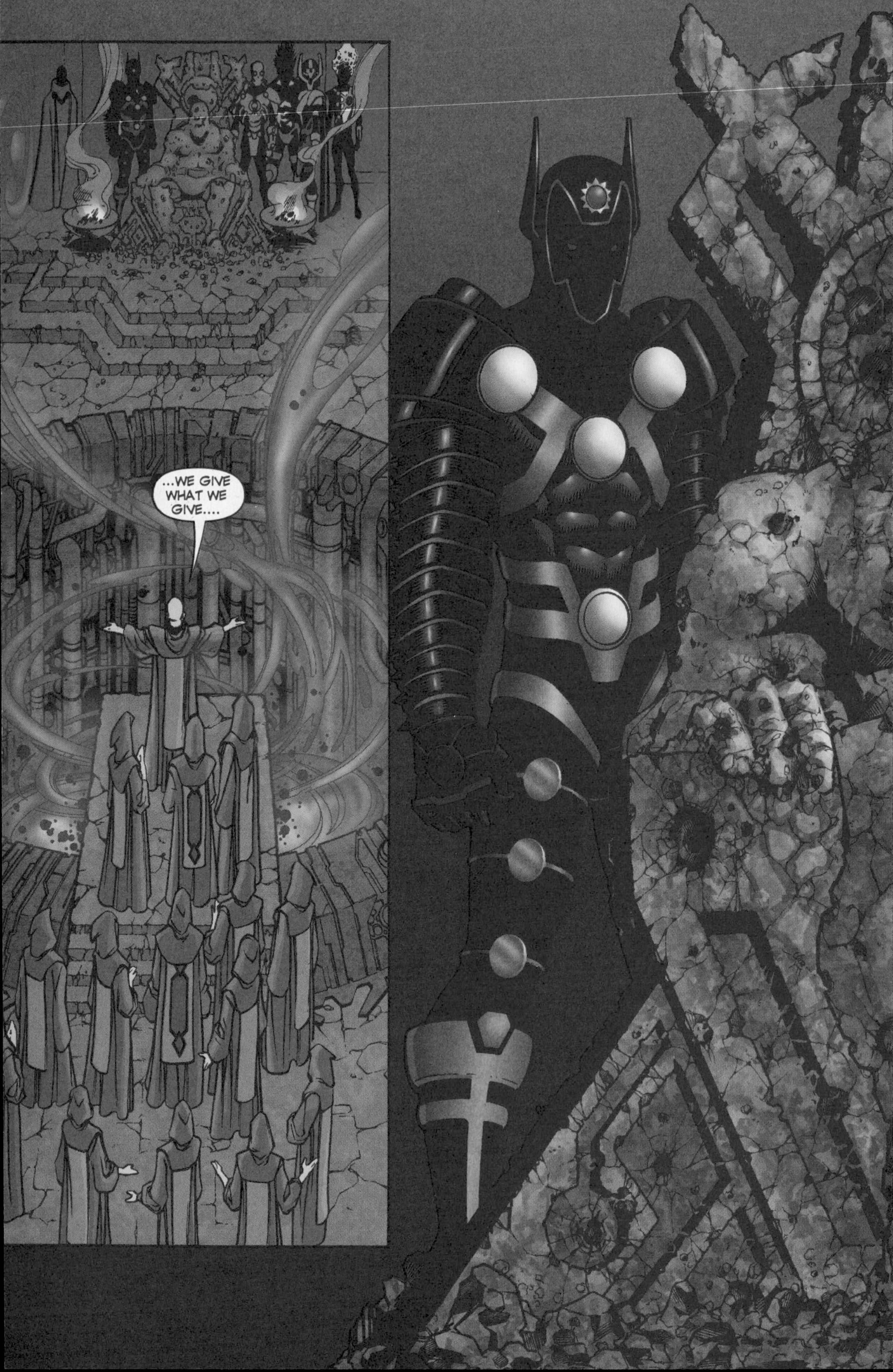
...WE GIVE WHAT WE GIVE....

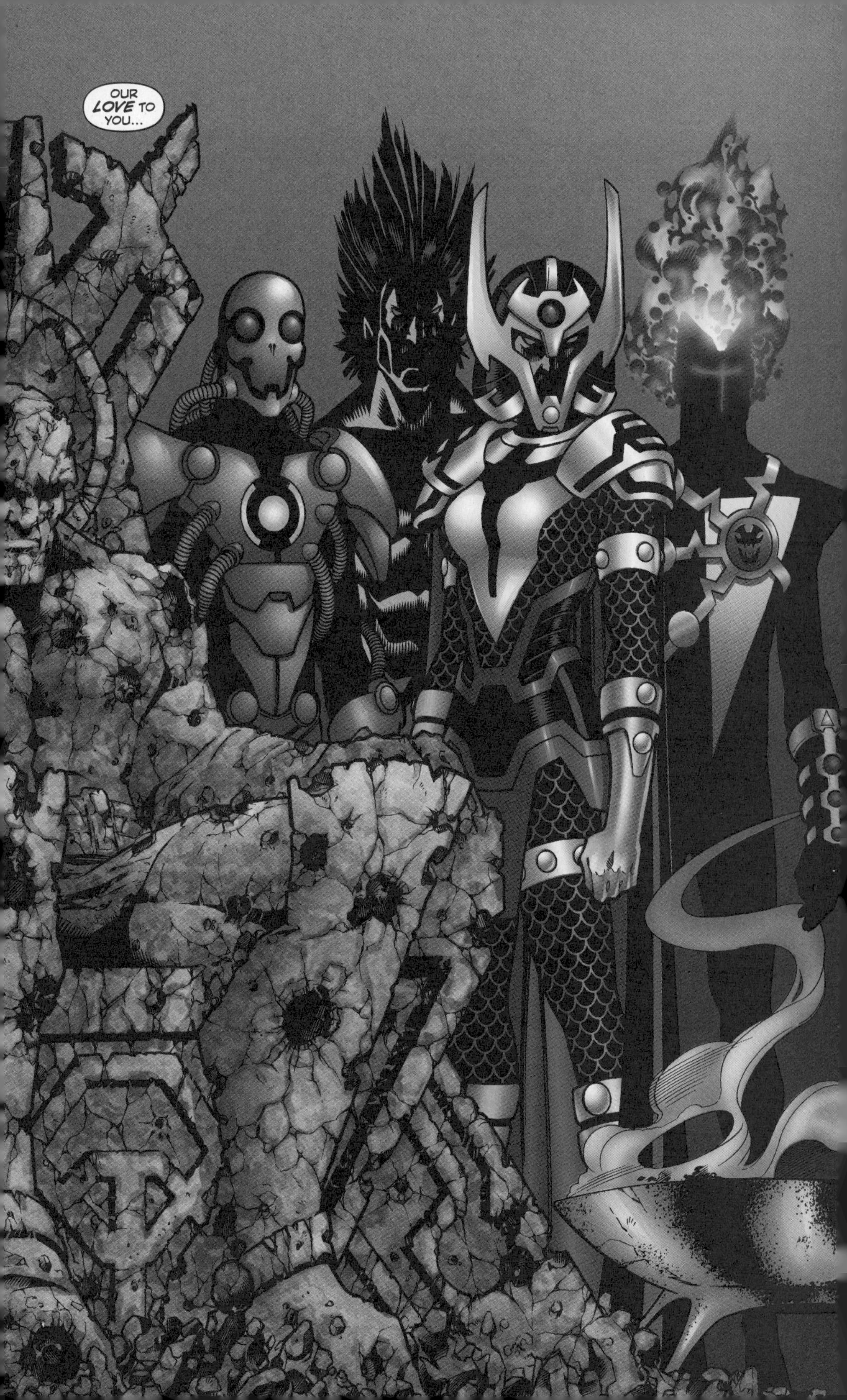
OUR LOVE TO YOU...

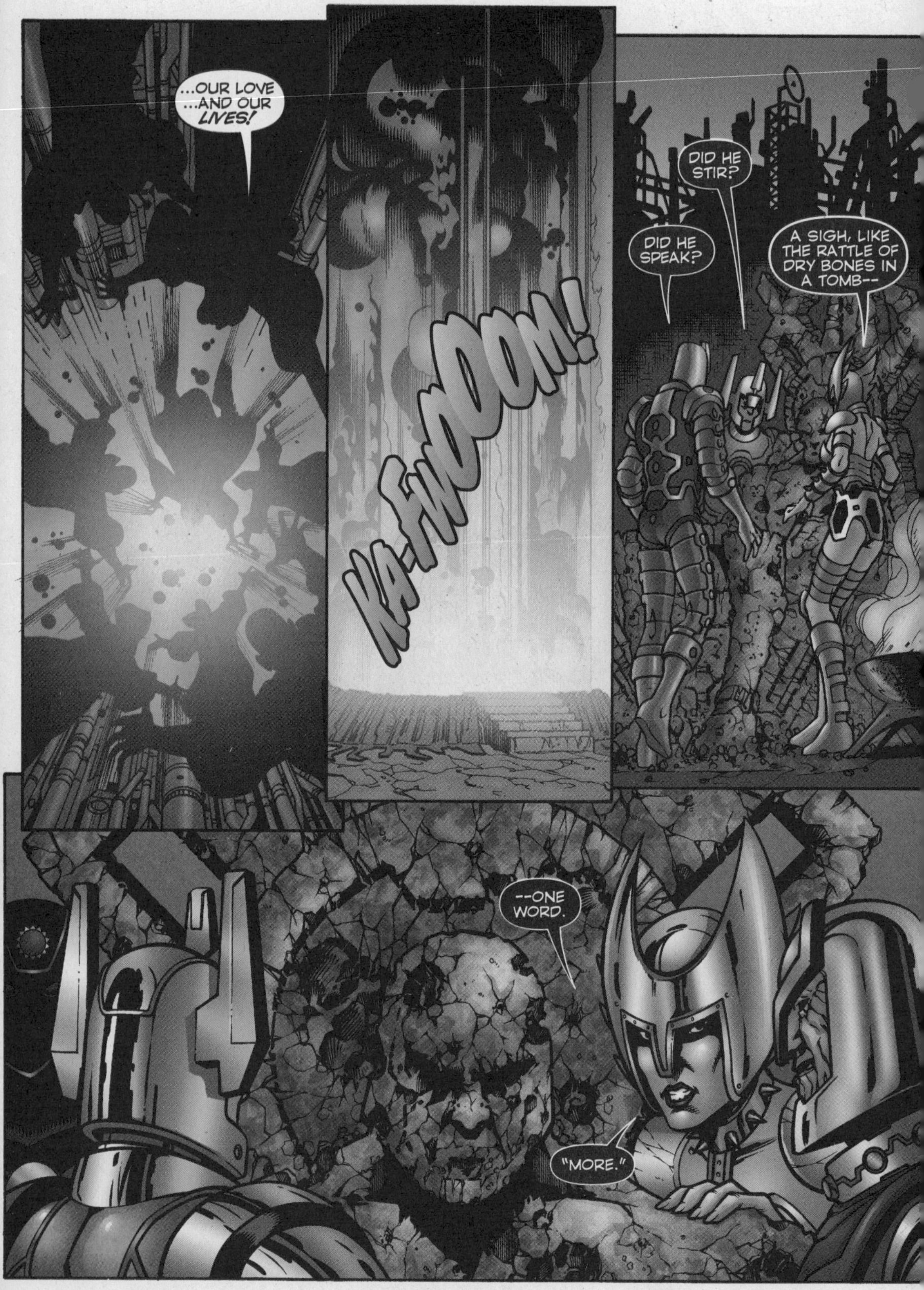
...OUR LOVE ...AND OUR LIVES!
KA-FWOOOM!
DID HE SPEAK?
DID HE STIR?
A SIGH, LIKE THE RATTLE OF DRY BONES IN A TOMB--
--ONE WORD.
"MORE."

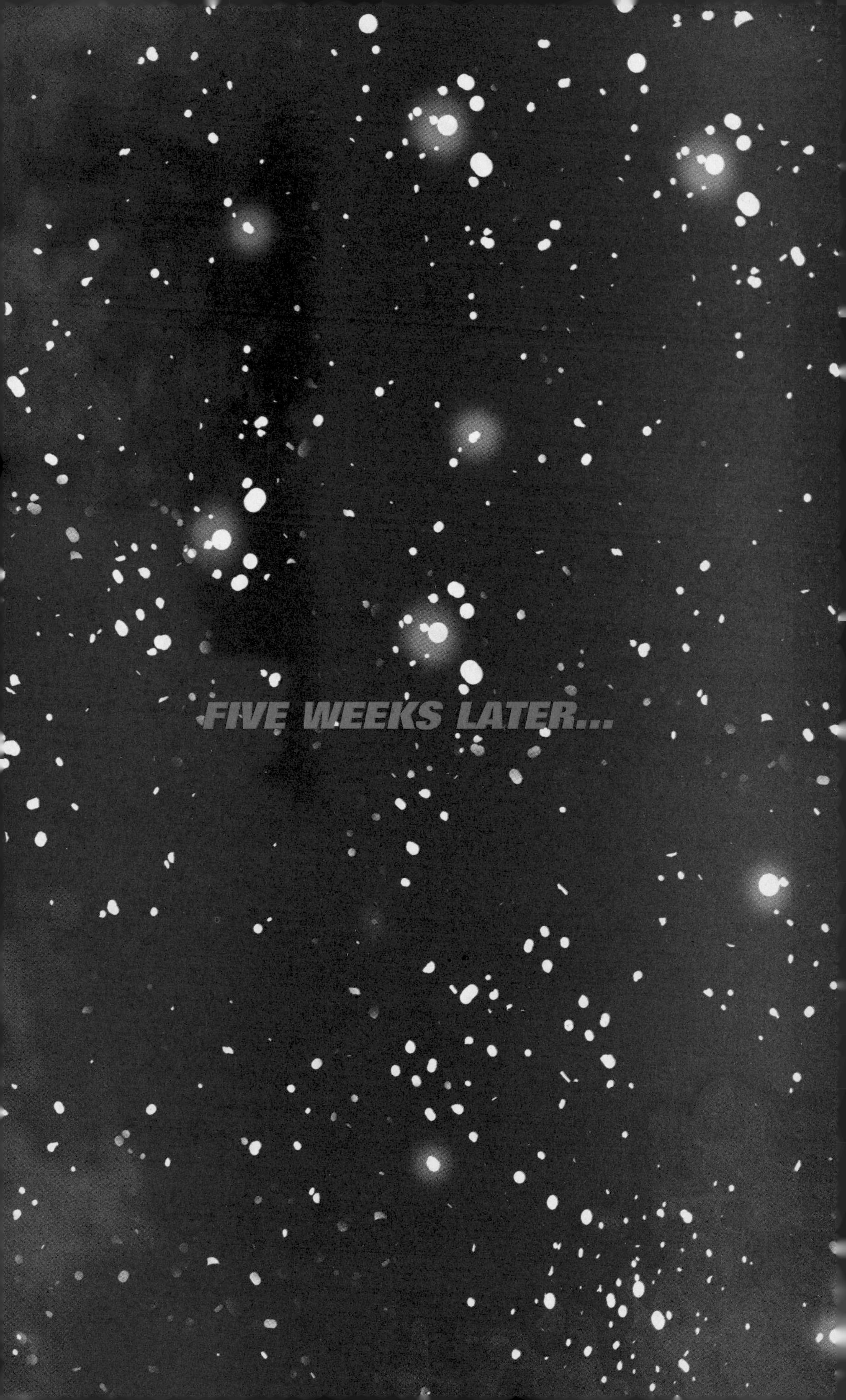
FIVE WEEKS LATER...

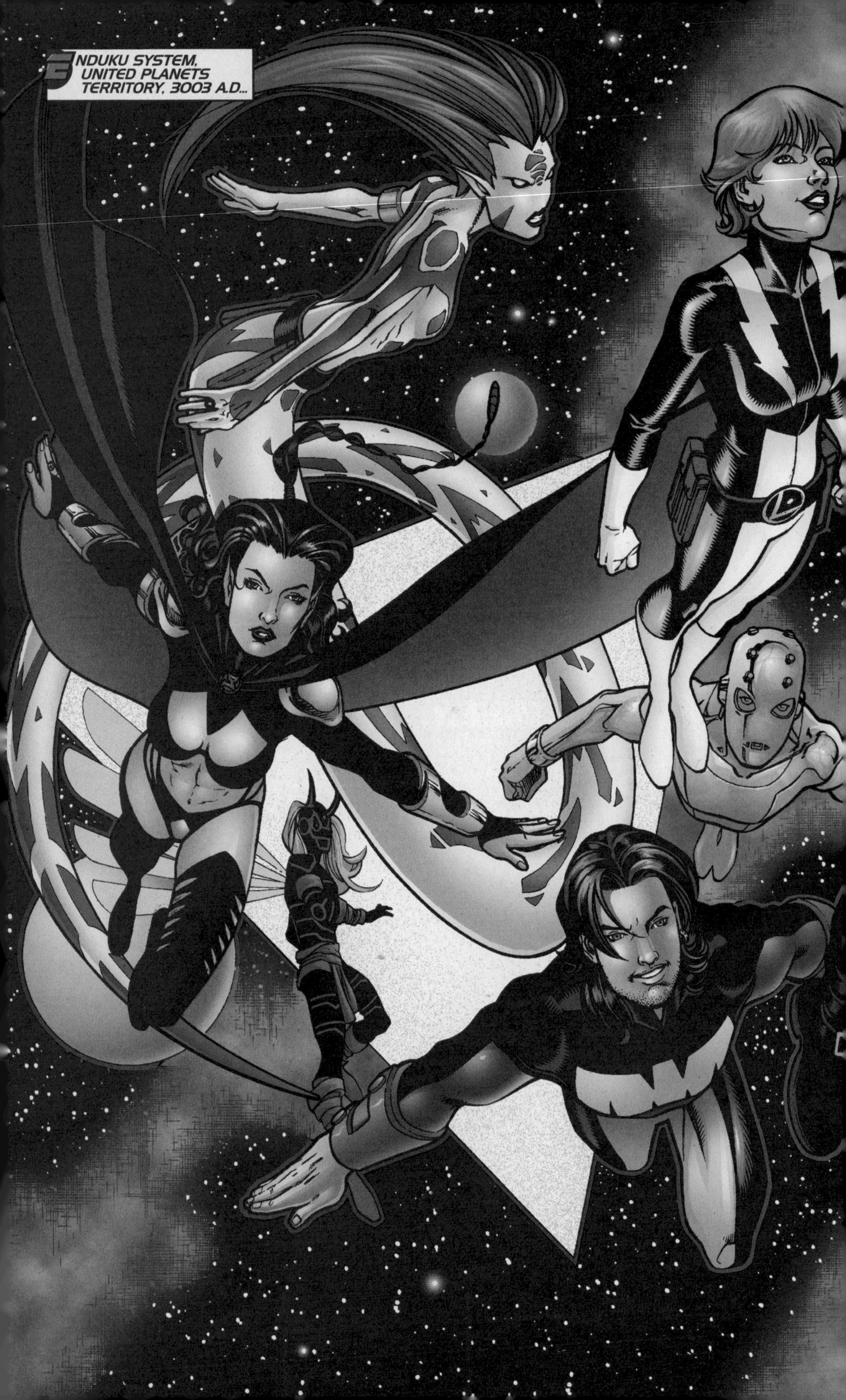
ENDUKU SYSTEM,
UNITED PLANETS
TERRITORY, 3003 A.D...

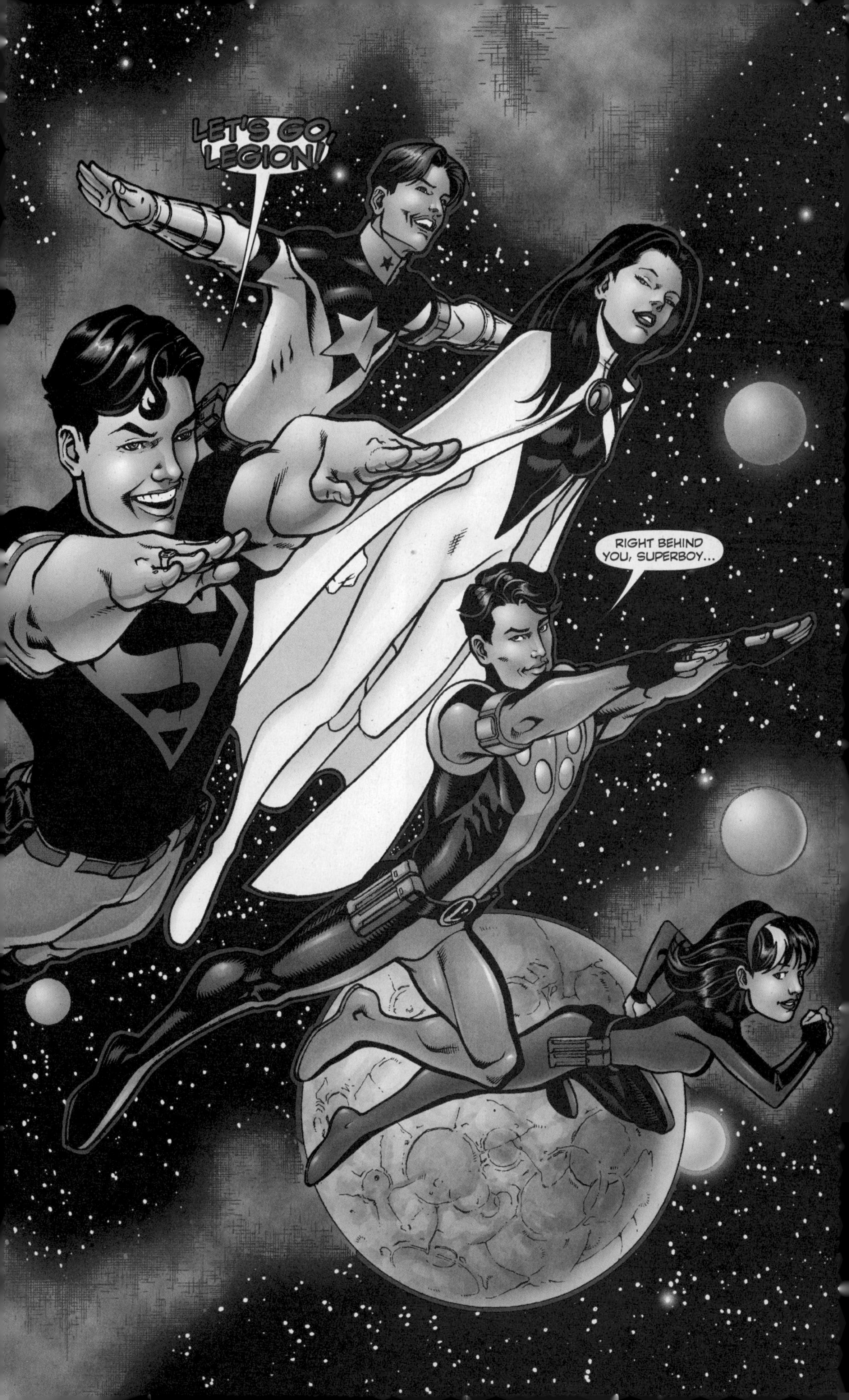
LET'S GO, LEGION!
RIGHT BEHIND YOU, SUPERBOY...

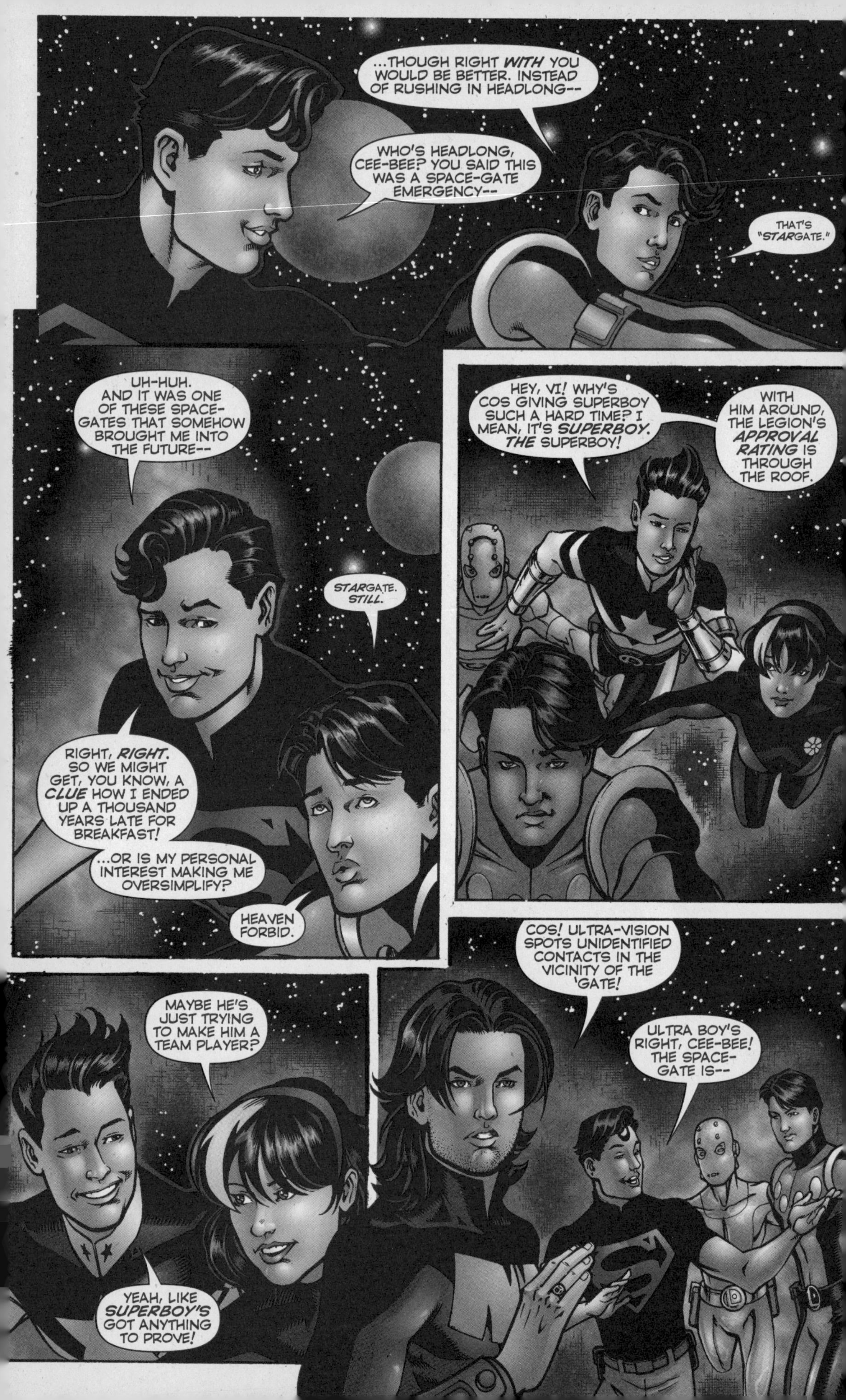
...THOUGH RIGHT WITH YOU WOULD BE BETTER. INSTEAD OF RUSHING IN HEADLONG--
WHO'S HEADLONG, CEE-BEE? YOU SAID THIS WAS A SPACE-GATE EMERGENCY--
THAT'S "STARGATE."
UH-HUH. AND IT WAS ONE OF THESE SPACE-GATES THAT SOMEHOW BROUGHT ME INTO THE FUTURE--
STARGATE. STILL.
RIGHT, RIGHT. SO WE MIGHT GET, YOU KNOW, A CLUE HOW I ENDED UP A THOUSAND YEARS LATE FOR BREAKFAST!
...OR IS MY PERSONAL INTEREST MAKING ME OVERSIMPLIFY?
HEAVEN FORBID.
HEY, VI! WHY'S COS GIVING SUPERBOY SUCH A HARD TIME? I MEAN, IT'S SUPERBOY. THE SUPERBOY!
WITH HIM AROUND, THE LEGION'S APPROVAL RATING IS THROUGH THE ROOF.
MAYBE HE'S JUST TRYING TO MAKE HIM A TEAM PLAYER?
YEAH, LIKE SUPERBOY'S GOT ANYTHING TO PROVE!
COS! ULTRA-VISION SPOTS UNIDENTIFIED CONTACTS IN THE VICINITY OF THE 'GATE!
ULTRA BOY'S RIGHT, CEE-BEE! THE SPACE-GATE IS--

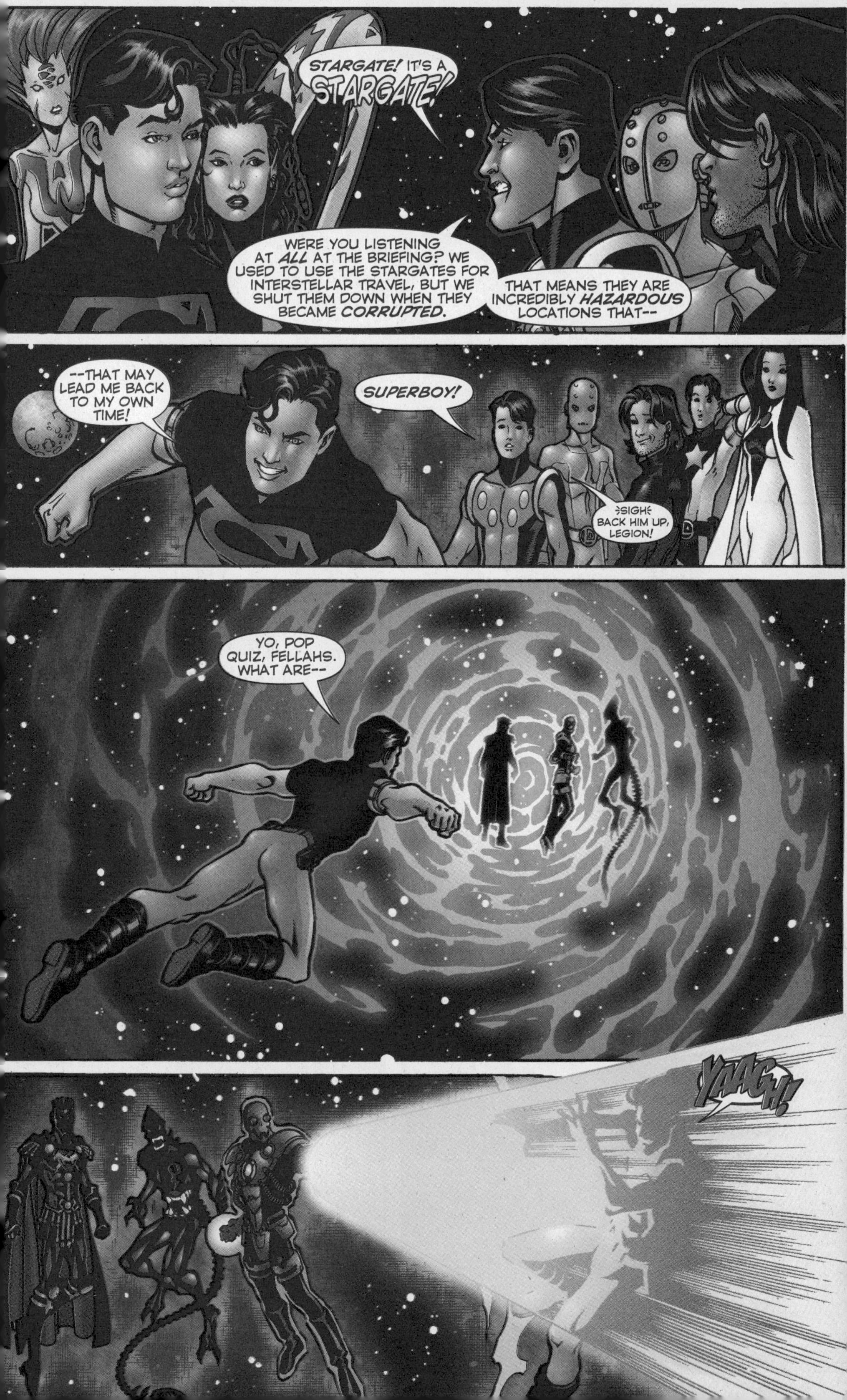
STARGATE! IT'S A STARGATE!
WERE YOU LISTENING AT ALL AT THE BRIEFING? WE USED TO USE THE STARGATES FOR INTERSTELLAR TRAVEL, BUT WE SHUT THEM DOWN WHEN THEY BECAME CORRUPTED.
THAT MEANS THEY ARE INCREDIBLY HAZARDOUS LOCATIONS THAT--
--THAT MAY LEAD ME BACK TO MY OWN TIME!
SUPERBOY!
SIGH BACK HIM UP, LEGION!
YO, POP QUIZ, FELLAHS. WHAT ARE--
YAAGH!

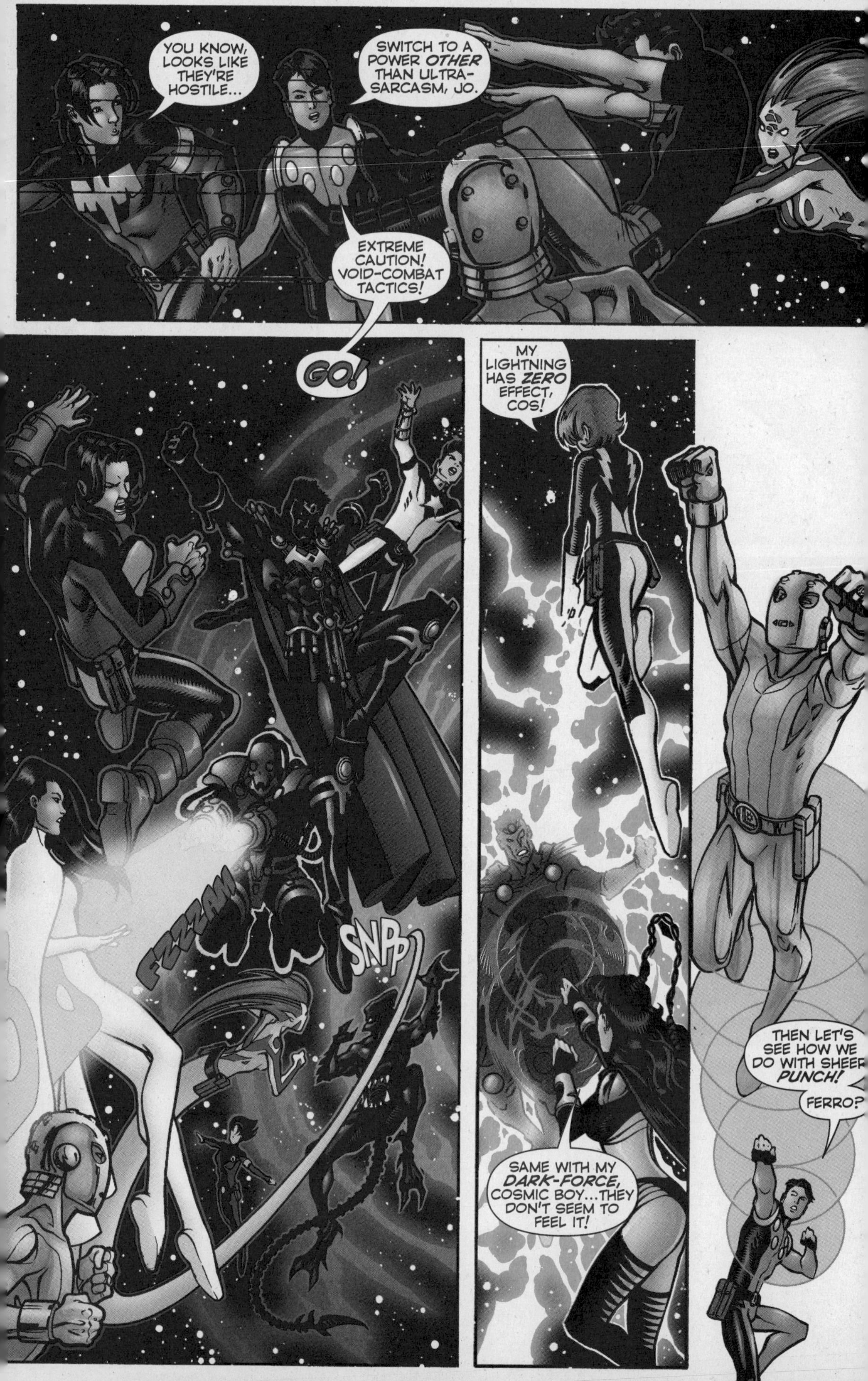
YOU KNOW, LOOKS LIKE THEY'RE HOSTILE...
SWITCH TO A POWER OTHER THAN ULTRA-SARCASM, JO.
EXTREME CAUTION! VOID-COMBAT TACTICS!
GO!
FZZZZAM
SNPP
MY LIGHTNING HAS ZERO EFFECT, COS!
SAME WITH MY DARK-FORCE, COSMIC BOY...THEY DON'T SEEM TO FEEL IT!
THEN LET'S SEE HOW WE DO WITH SHEER PUNCH!
FERRO?

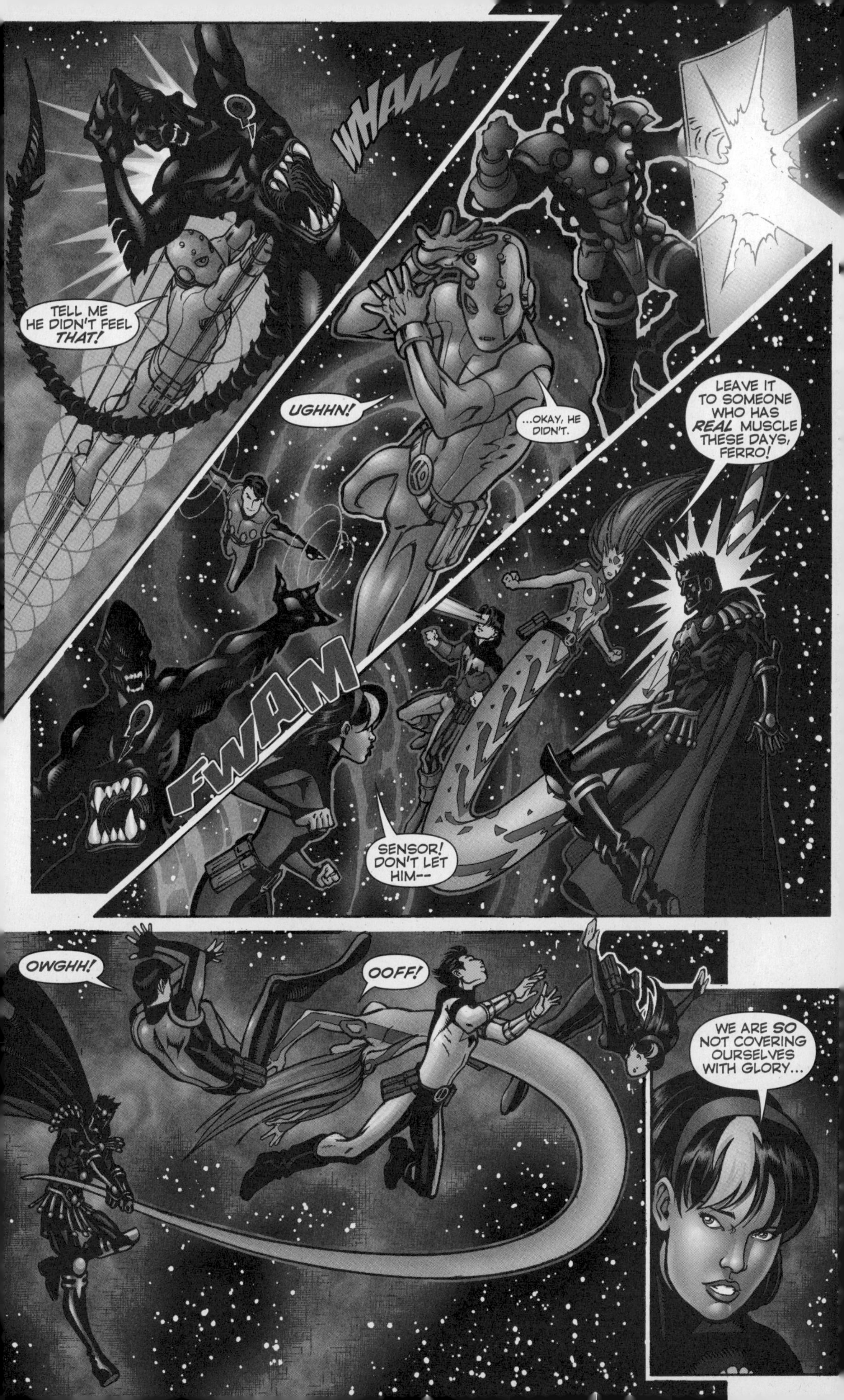
WHAM
TELL ME HE DIDN'T FEEL THAT!
UGHHN!
...OKAY, HE DIDN'T.
LEAVE IT TO SOMEONE WHO HAS REAL MUSCLE THESE DAYS, FERRO!
FWAM
SENSOR! DON'T LET HIM--
OWGHH!
OOFF!
WE ARE SO NOT COVERING OURSELVES WITH GLORY...

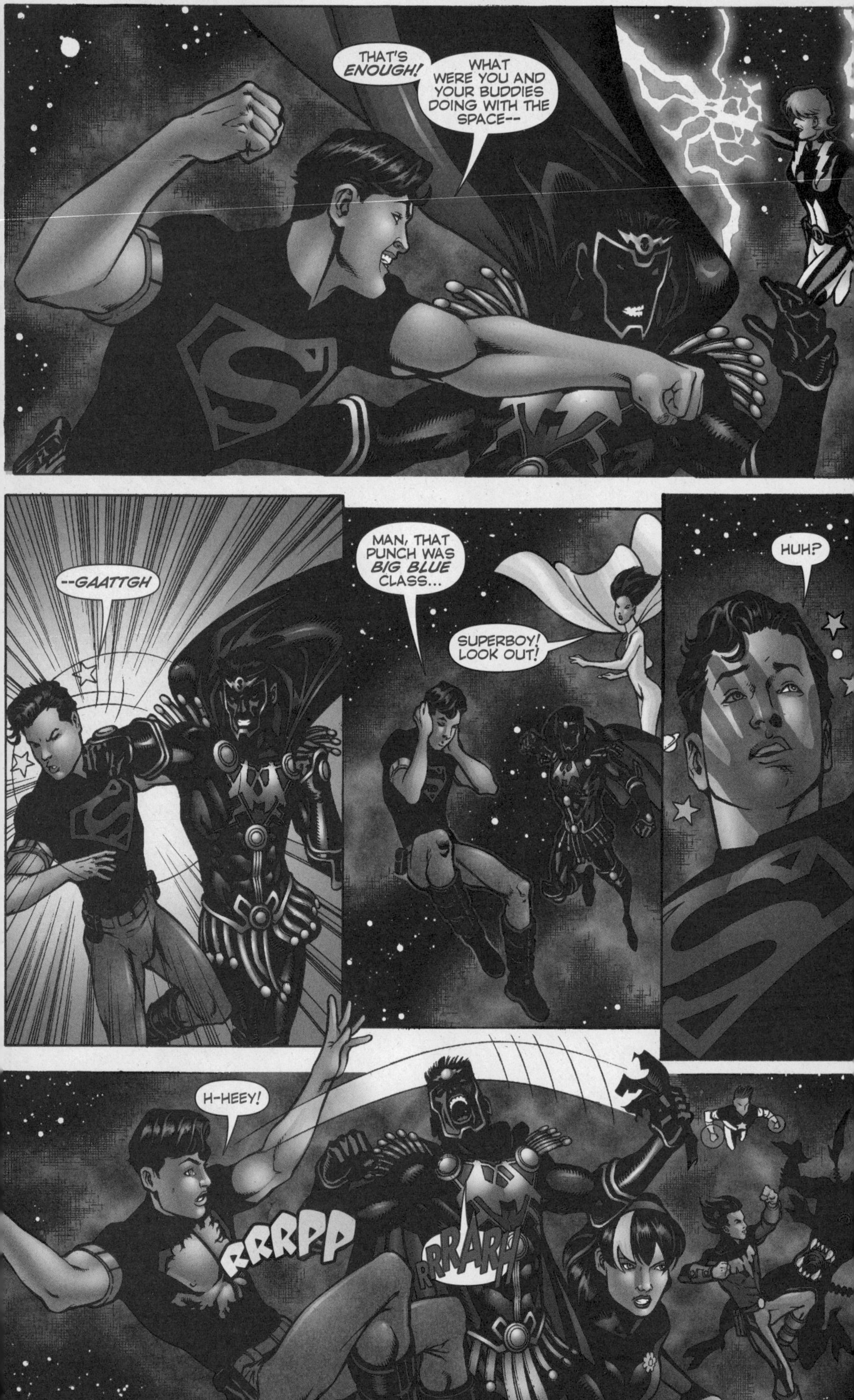
THAT'S ENOUGH!
WHAT WERE YOU AND YOUR BUDDIES DOING WITH THE SPACE--
--GAATTGH
MAN, THAT PUNCH WAS BIG BLUE CLASS...
SUPERBOY! LOOK OUT!
HUH?
H-HEEY!
RRRPP
RRRARH

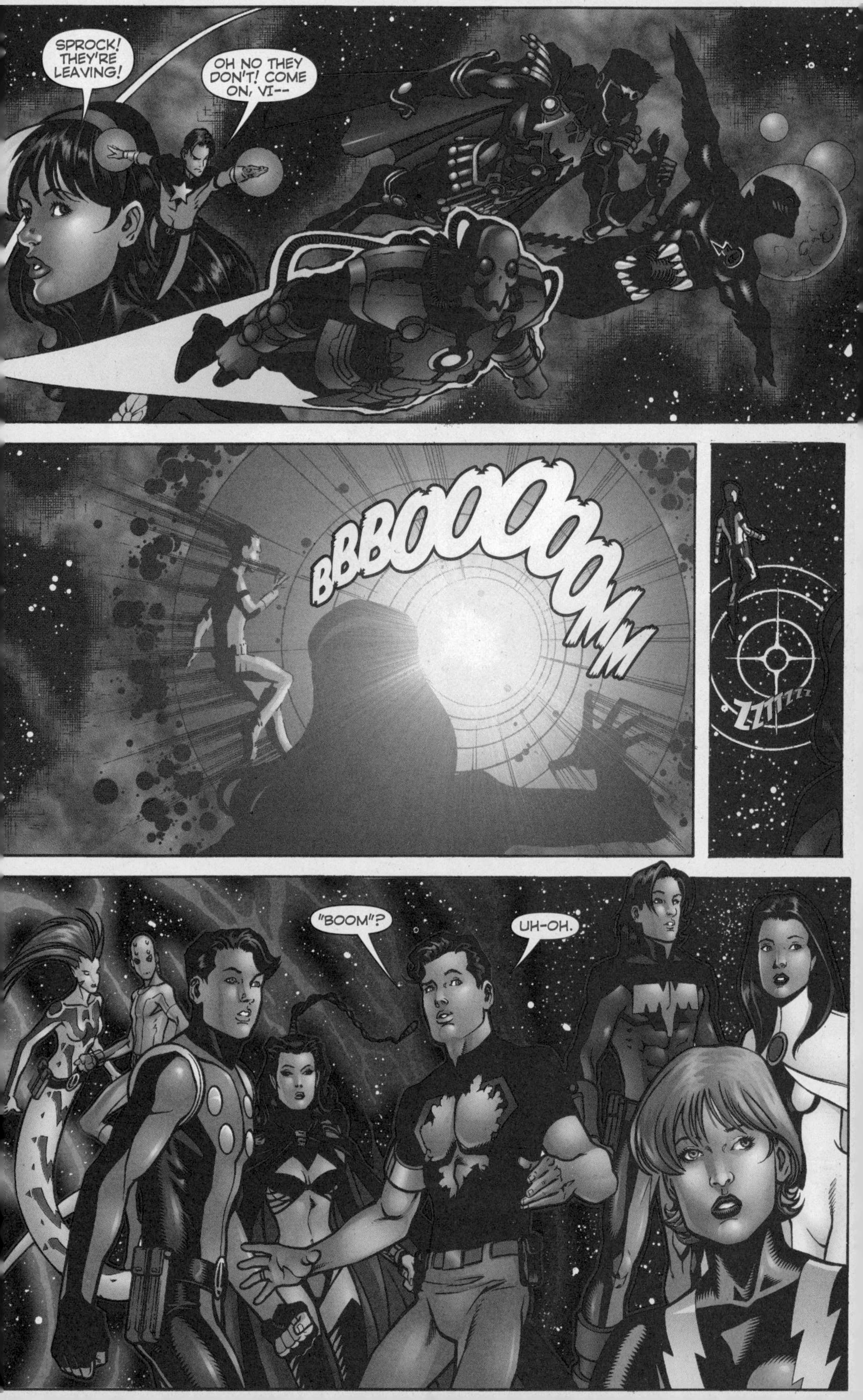
SPROCK! THEY'RE LEAVING!
OH NO THEY DON'T! COME ON, VI--
BBBOOOOOMM
ZZTTZZZ
"BOOM"?
UH-OH.

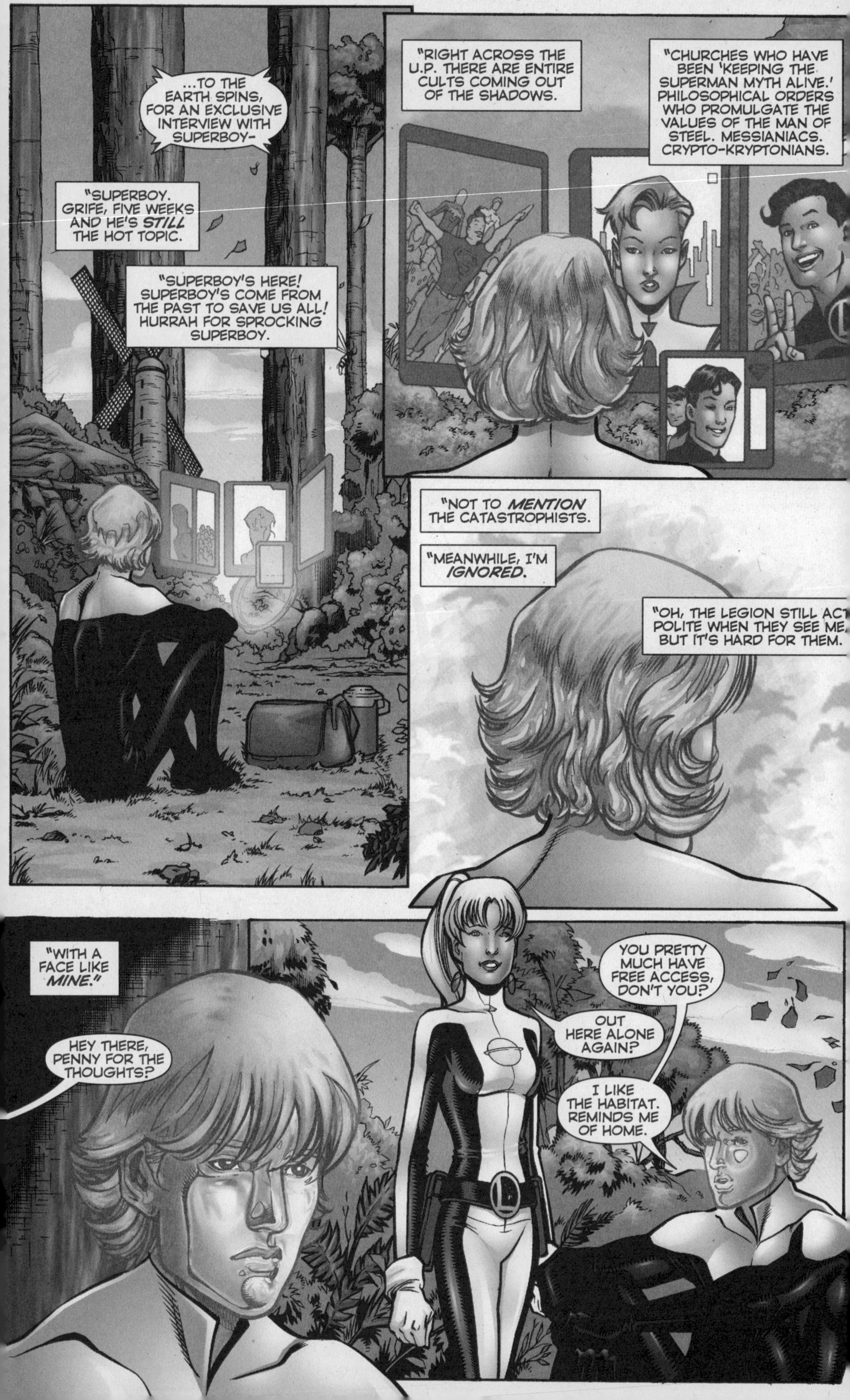
...TO THE EARTH SPINS, FOR AN EXCLUSIVE INTERVIEW WITH SUPERBOY-
"SUPERBOY. GRIFE, FIVE WEEKS AND HE'S STILL THE HOT TOPIC.
"SUPERBOY'S HERE! SUPERBOY'S COME FROM THE PAST TO SAVE US ALL! HURRAH FOR SPROCKING SUPERBOY.
"RIGHT ACROSS THE U.P. THERE ARE ENTIRE CULTS COMING OUT OF THE SHADOWS.
"CHURCHES WHO HAVE BEEN 'KEEPING THE SUPERMAN MYTH ALIVE.' PHILOSOPHICAL ORDERS WHO PROMULGATE THE VALUES OF THE MAN OF STEEL. MESSIANIACS. CRYPTO-KRYPTONIANS.
"NOT TO MENTION THE CATASTROPHISTS.
"MEANWHILE, I'M IGNORED.
"OH, THE LEGION STILL ACT POLITE WHEN THEY SEE ME, BUT IT'S HARD FOR THEM.
"WITH A FACE LIKE MINE."
HEY THERE, PENNY FOR THE THOUGHTS?
OUT HERE ALONE AGAIN?
I LIKE THE HABITAT. REMINDS ME OF HOME.
YOU PRETTY MUCH HAVE FREE ACCESS, DON'T YOU?

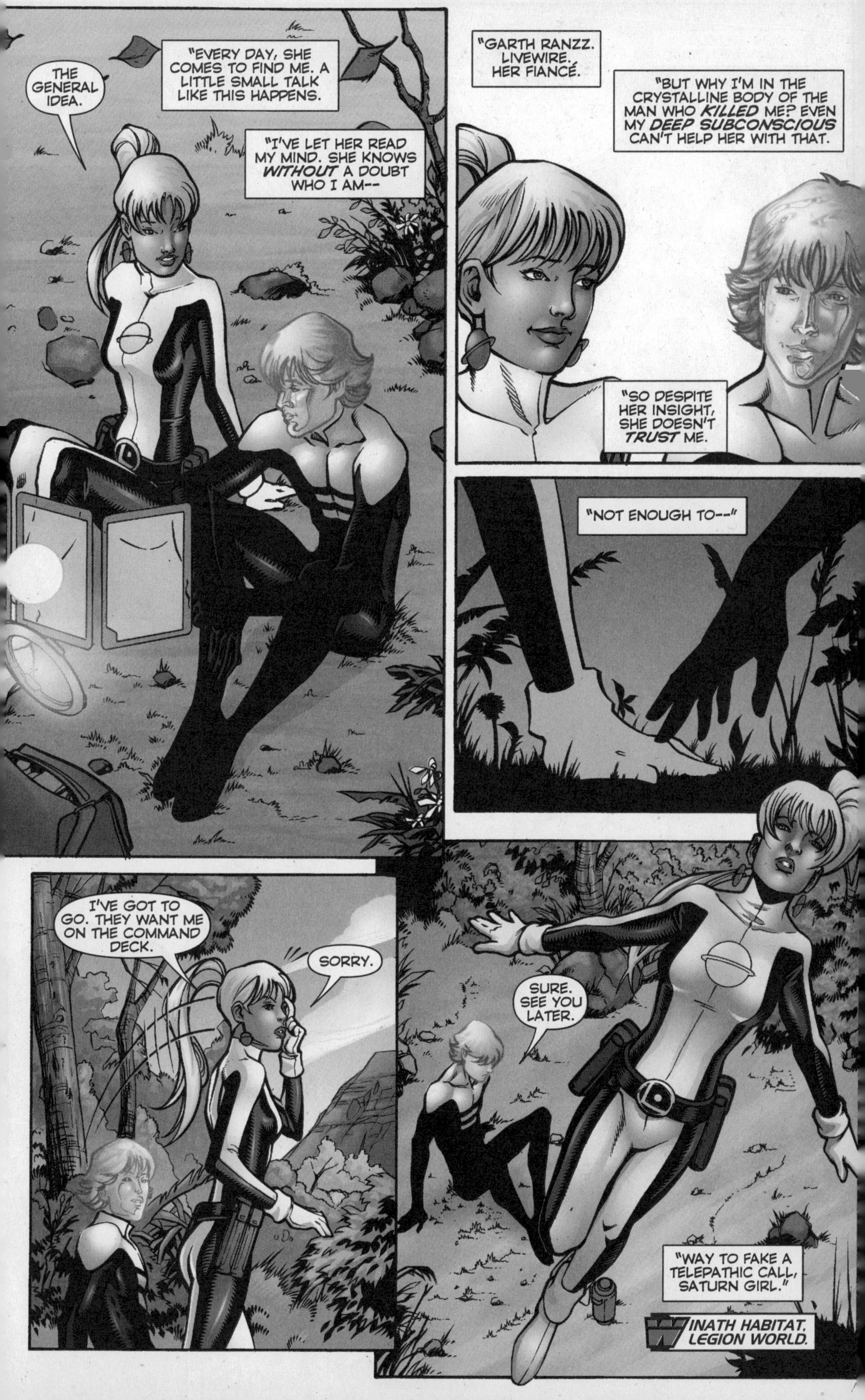
"EVERY DAY, SHE COMES TO FIND ME. A LITTLE SMALL TALK LIKE THIS HAPPENS.
THE GENERAL IDEA.
"I'VE LET HER READ MY MIND. SHE KNOWS *WITHOUT* A DOUBT WHO I AM--
"GARTH RANZZ. LIVEWIRE. HER FIANCÉ.
"BUT WHY I'M IN THE CRYSTALLINE BODY OF THE MAN WHO *KILLED* ME? EVEN MY *DEEP SUBCONSCIOUS* CAN'T HELP HER WITH THAT.
"SO DESPITE HER INSIGHT, SHE DOESN'T *TRUST* ME.
"NOT ENOUGH TO--"
I'VE GOT TO GO. THEY WANT ME ON THE COMMAND DECK.
SORRY.
SURE. SEE YOU LATER.
"WAY TO FAKE A TELEPATHIC CALL, SATURN GIRL."
WINATH HABITAT, LEGION WORLD.

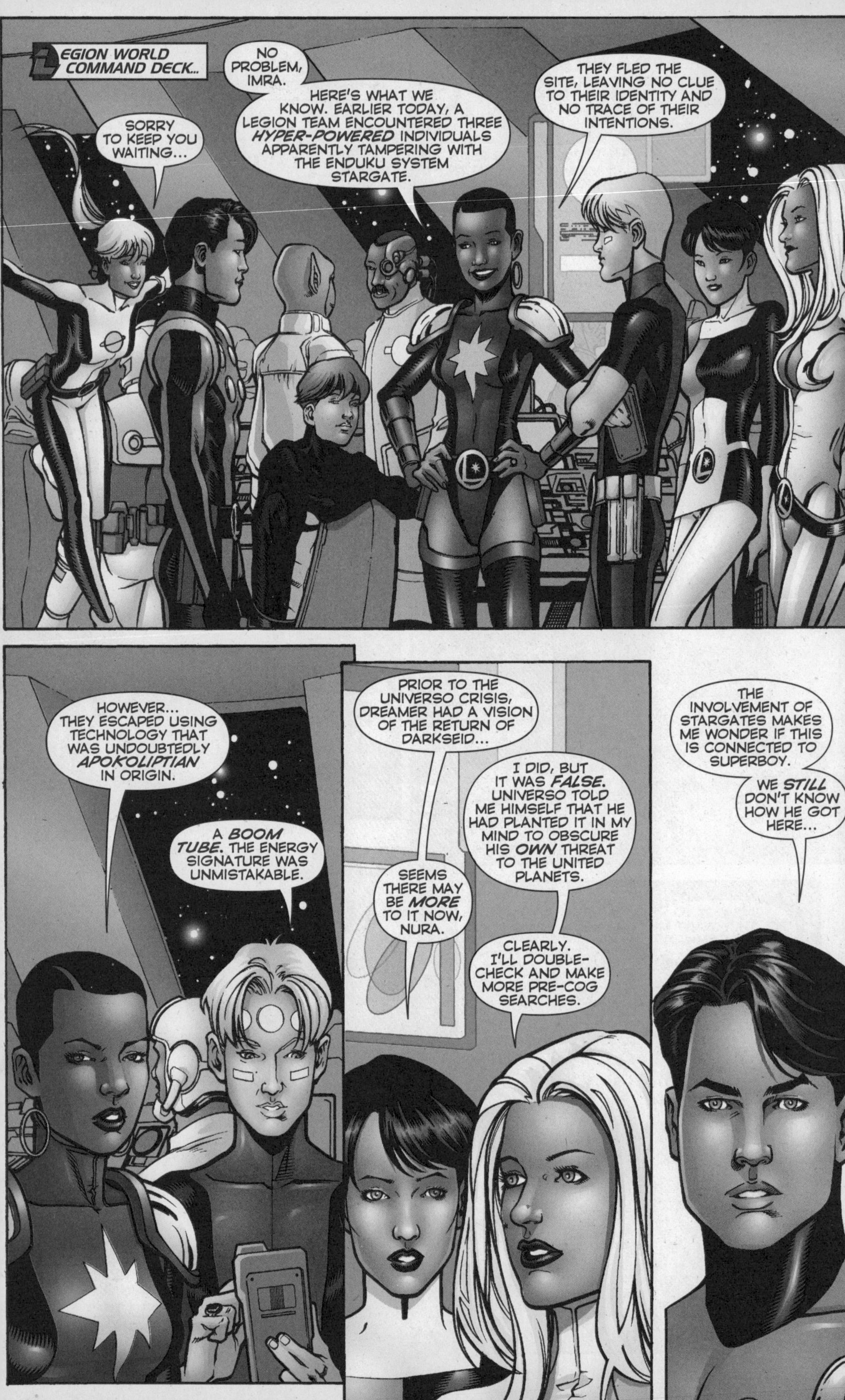
LEGION WORLD COMMAND DECK...
SORRY TO KEEP YOU WAITING...
NO PROBLEM, IMRA.
HERE'S WHAT WE KNOW. EARLIER TODAY, A LEGION TEAM ENCOUNTERED THREE *HYPER-POWERED* INDIVIDUALS APPARENTLY TAMPERING WITH THE ENDUKU SYSTEM STARGATE.
THEY FLED THE SITE, LEAVING NO CLUE TO THEIR IDENTITY AND NO TRACE OF THEIR INTENTIONS.
HOWEVER... THEY ESCAPED USING TECHNOLOGY THAT WAS UNDOUBTEDLY *APOKOLIPTIAN* IN ORIGIN.
A *BOOM TUBE*. THE ENERGY SIGNATURE WAS UNMISTAKABLE.
PRIOR TO THE UNIVERSO CRISIS, DREAMER HAD A VISION OF THE RETURN OF DARKSEID...
I DID, BUT IT WAS *FALSE*. UNIVERSO TOLD ME HIMSELF THAT HE HAD PLANTED IT IN MY MIND TO OBSCURE HIS *OWN* THREAT TO THE UNITED PLANETS.
SEEMS THERE MAY BE *MORE* TO IT NOW, NURA.
CLEARLY. I'LL DOUBLE-CHECK AND MAKE MORE PRE-COG SEARCHES.
THE INVOLVEMENT OF STARGATES MAKES ME WONDER IF THIS IS CONNECTED TO SUPERBOY.
WE *STILL* DON'T KNOW HOW HE GOT HERE...

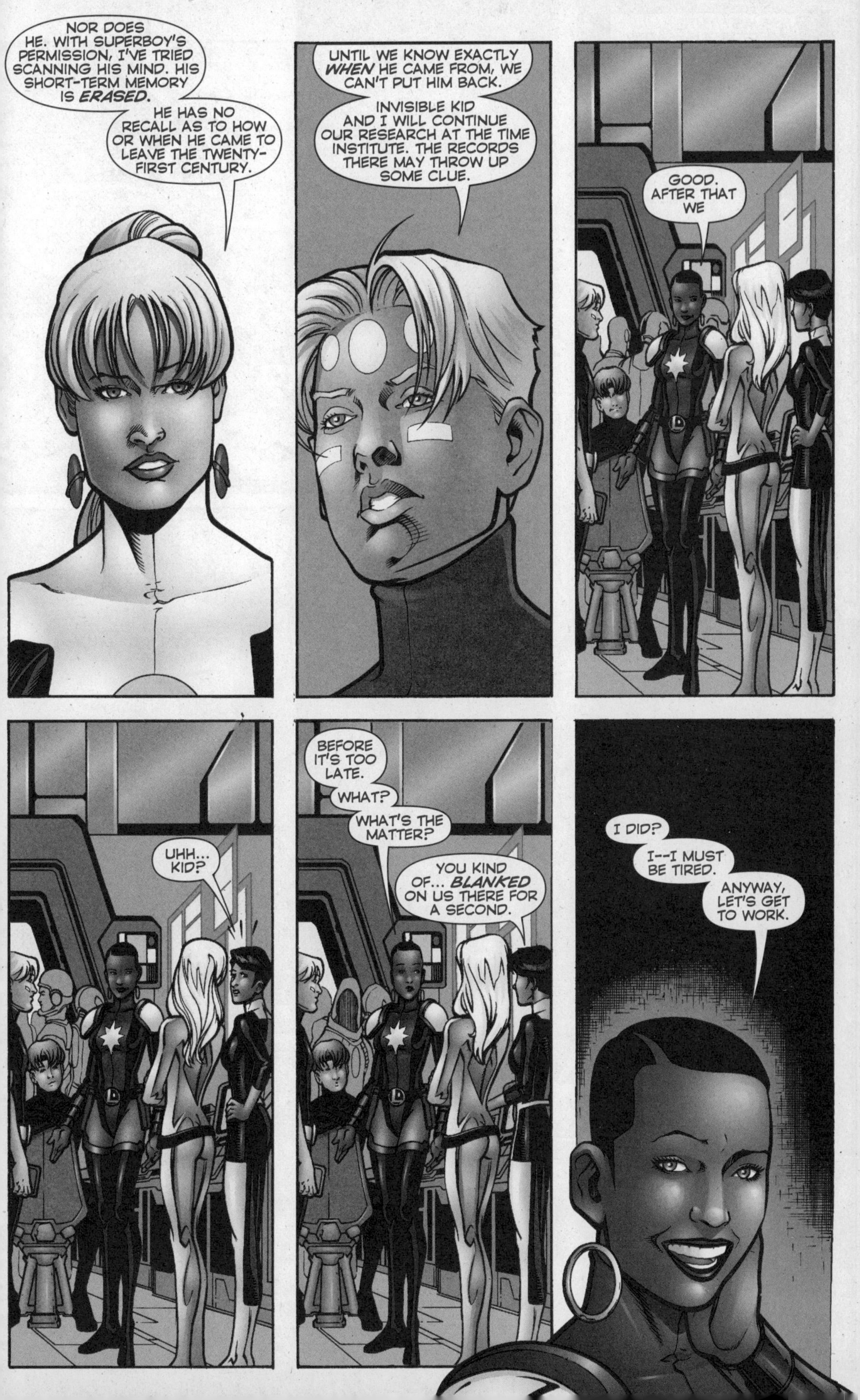
NOR DOES HE. WITH SUPERBOY'S PERMISSION, I'VE TRIED SCANNING HIS MIND. HIS SHORT-TERM MEMORY IS ERASED.
HE HAS NO RECALL AS TO HOW OR WHEN HE CAME TO LEAVE THE TWENTY-FIRST CENTURY.
UNTIL WE KNOW EXACTLY WHEN HE CAME FROM, WE CAN'T PUT HIM BACK.
INVISIBLE KID AND I WILL CONTINUE OUR RESEARCH AT THE TIME INSTITUTE. THE RECORDS THERE MAY THROW UP SOME CLUE.
GOOD. AFTER THAT WE
UHH... KID?
BEFORE IT'S TOO LATE.
WHAT?
WHAT'S THE MATTER?
YOU KIND OF... BLANKED ON US THERE FOR A SECOND.
I DID?
I--I MUST BE TIRED.
ANYWAY, LET'S GET TO WORK.

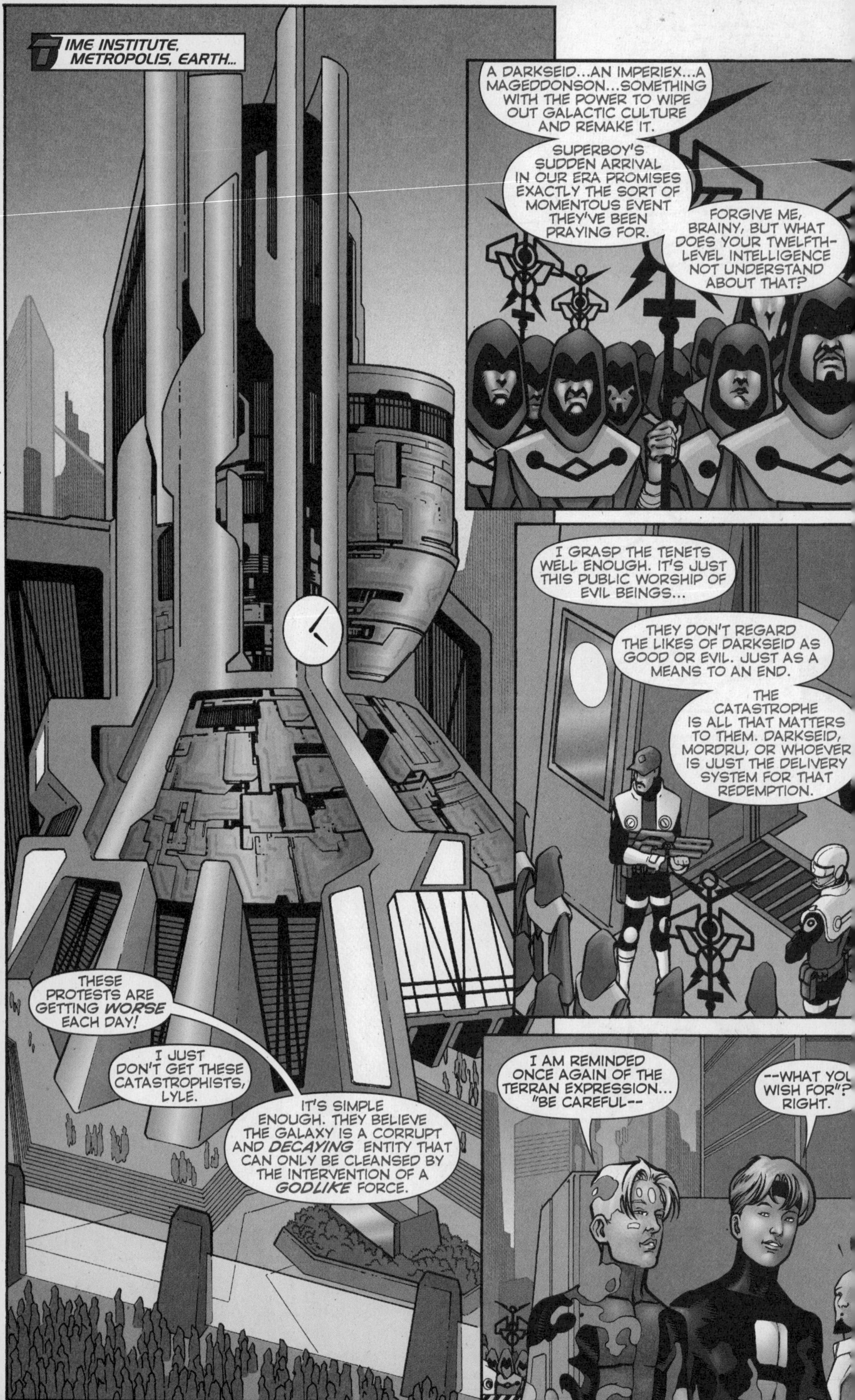
TIME INSTITUTE,
METROPOLIS, EARTH...
THESE PROTESTS ARE GETTING WORSE EACH DAY!
I JUST DON'T GET THESE CATASTROPHISTS, LYLE.
IT'S SIMPLE ENOUGH. THEY BELIEVE THE GALAXY IS A CORRUPT AND DECAYING ENTITY THAT CAN ONLY BE CLEANSED BY THE INTERVENTION OF A GODLIKE FORCE.
A DARKSEID...AN IMPERIEX...A MAGEDDONSON...SOMETHING WITH THE POWER TO WIPE OUT GALACTIC CULTURE AND REMAKE IT.
SUPERBOY'S SUDDEN ARRIVAL IN OUR ERA PROMISES EXACTLY THE SORT OF MOMENTOUS EVENT THEY'VE BEEN PRAYING FOR.
FORGIVE ME, BRAINY, BUT WHAT DOES YOUR TWELFTH-LEVEL INTELLIGENCE NOT UNDERSTAND ABOUT THAT?
I GRASP THE TENETS WELL ENOUGH. IT'S JUST THIS PUBLIC WORSHIP OF EVIL BEINGS...
THEY DON'T REGARD THE LIKES OF DARKSEID AS GOOD OR EVIL. JUST AS A MEANS TO AN END.
THE CATASTROPHE IS ALL THAT MATTERS TO THEM. DARKSEID, MORDRU, OR WHOEVER IS JUST THE DELIVERY SYSTEM FOR THAT REDEMPTION.
I AM REMINDED ONCE AGAIN OF THE TERRAN EXPRESSION... "BE CAREFUL--
--WHAT YOU WISH FOR"? RIGHT.

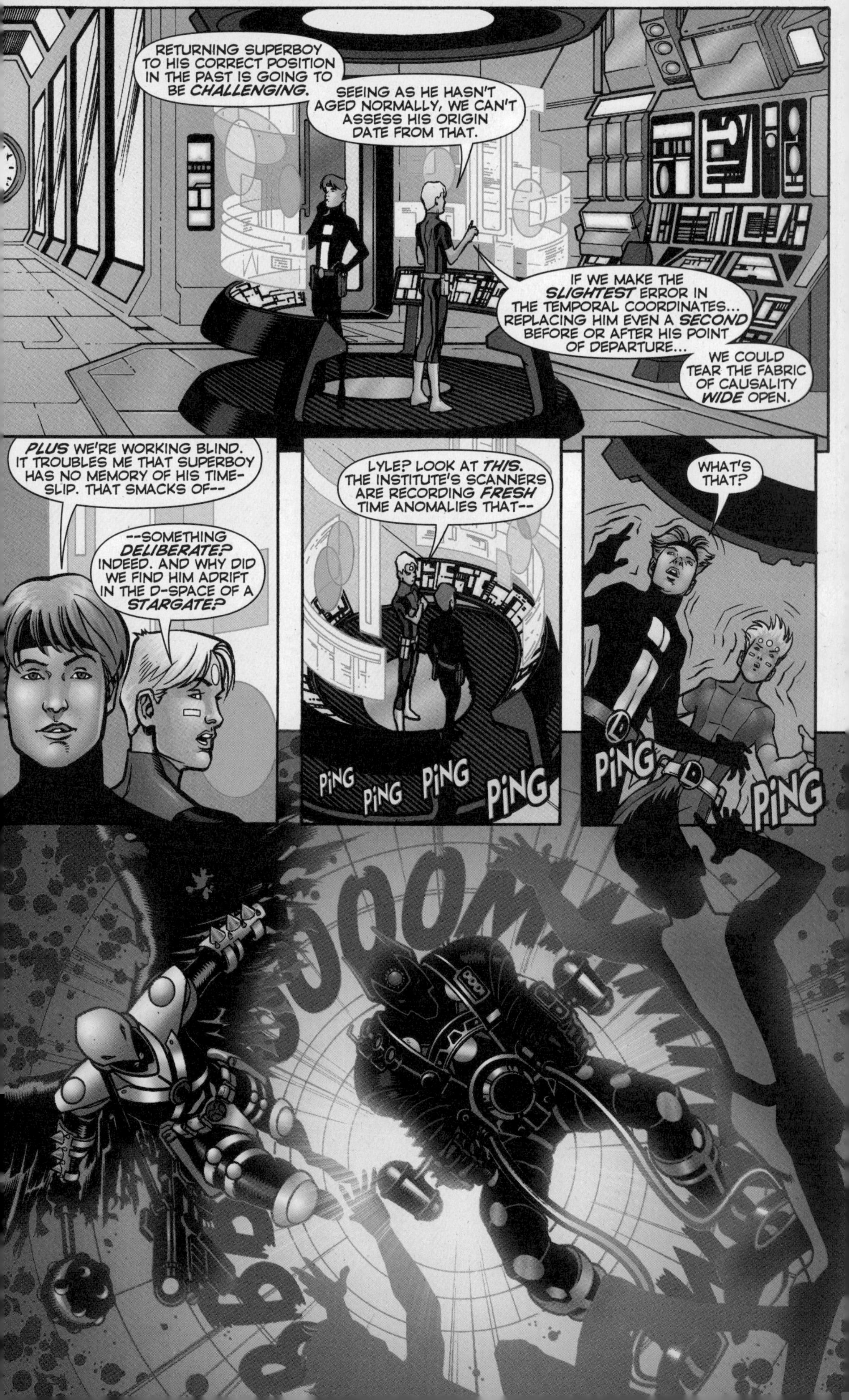
RETURNING SUPERBOY TO HIS CORRECT POSITION IN THE PAST IS GOING TO BE *CHALLENGING*.
SEEING AS HE HASN'T AGED NORMALLY, WE CAN'T ASSESS HIS ORIGIN DATE FROM THAT.
IF WE MAKE THE *SLIGHTEST* ERROR IN THE TEMPORAL COORDINATES... REPLACING HIM EVEN A *SECOND* BEFORE OR AFTER HIS POINT OF DEPARTURE...
WE COULD TEAR THE FABRIC OF CAUSALITY *WIDE* OPEN.
PLUS WE'RE WORKING BLIND. IT TROUBLES ME THAT SUPERBOY HAS NO MEMORY OF HIS TIME-SLIP. THAT SMACKS OF--
--SOMETHING *DELIBERATE?* INDEED. AND WHY DID WE FIND HIM ADRIFT IN THE D-SPACE OF A *STARGATE?*
LYLE? LOOK AT *THIS*. THE INSTITUTE'S SCANNERS ARE RECORDING *FRESH* TIME ANOMALIES THAT--
PING
PING
PING
PING
WHAT'S THAT?
PING
PING
BOOOM

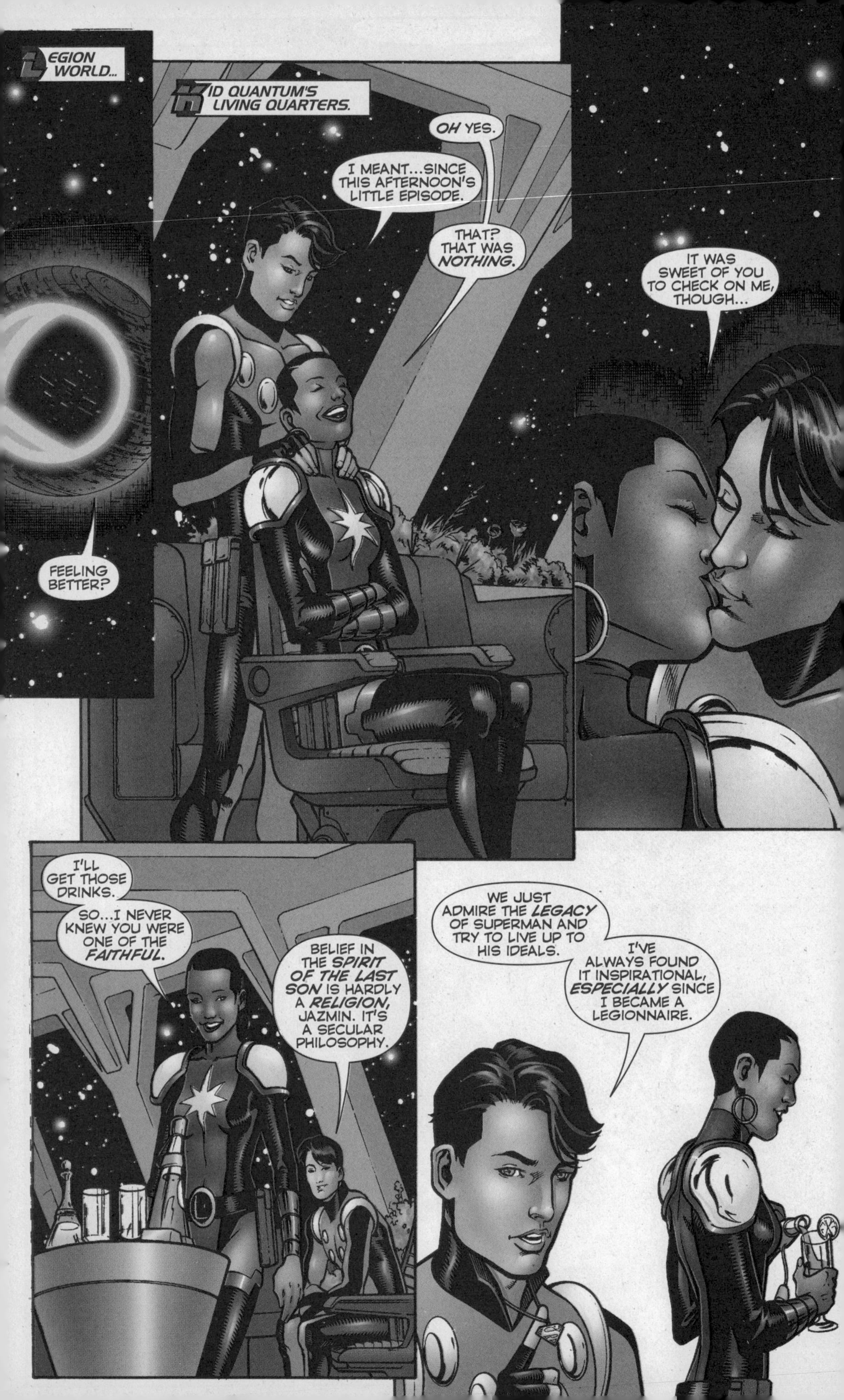
LEGION WORLD...
KID QUANTUM'S LIVING QUARTERS.
FEELING BETTER?
I MEANT...SINCE THIS AFTERNOON'S LITTLE EPISODE.
OH YES.
THAT? THAT WAS NOTHING.
IT WAS SWEET OF YOU TO CHECK ON ME, THOUGH...
I'LL GET THOSE DRINKS.
SO...I NEVER KNEW YOU WERE ONE OF THE FAITHFUL.
BELIEF IN THE SPIRIT OF THE LAST SON IS HARDLY A RELIGION, JAZMIN. IT'S A SECULAR PHILOSOPHY.
WE JUST ADMIRE THE LEGACY OF SUPERMAN AND TRY TO LIVE UP TO HIS IDEALS.
I'VE ALWAYS FOUND IT INSPIRATIONAL, ESPECIALLY SINCE I BECAME A LEGIONNAIRE.

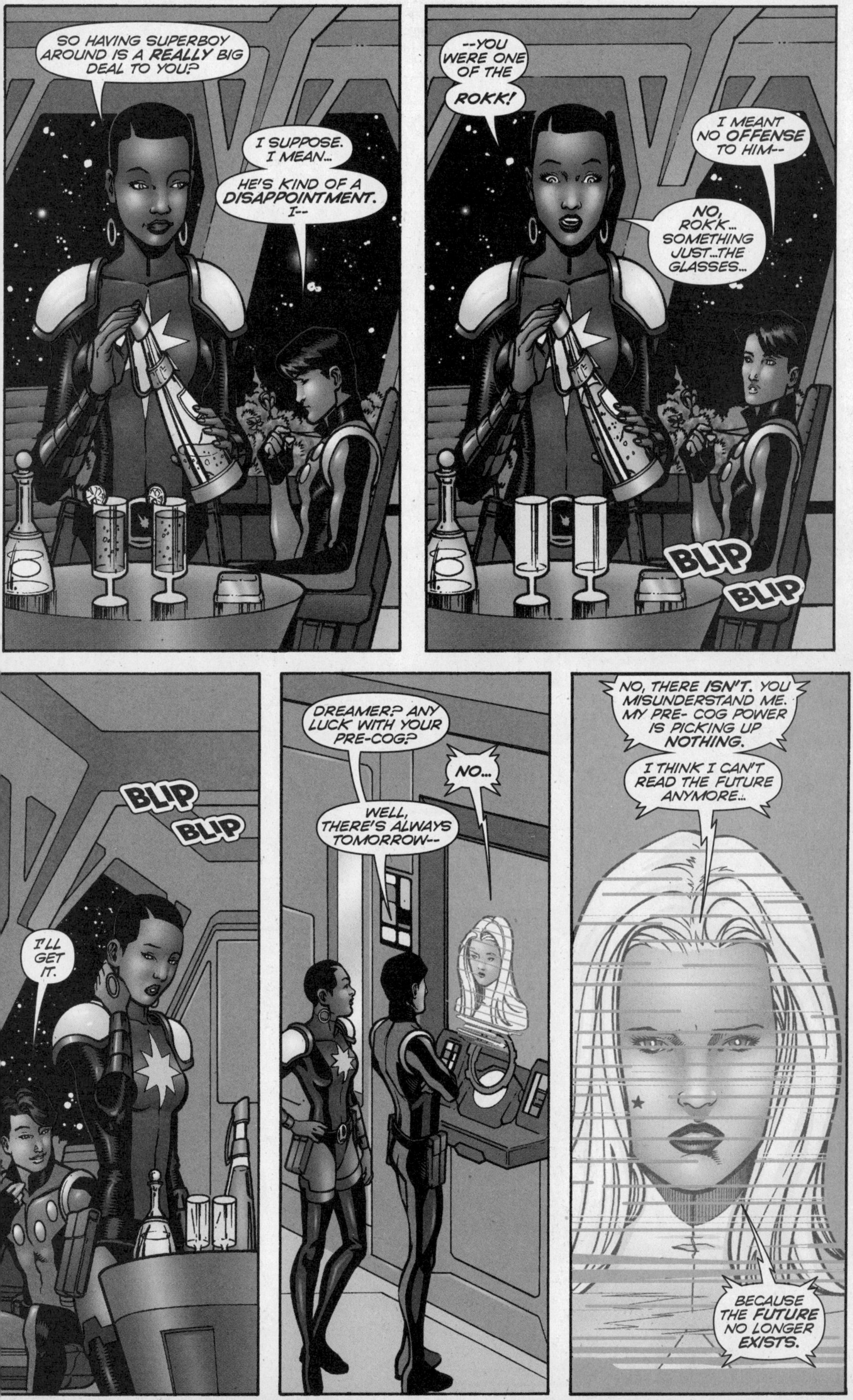
SO HAVING SUPERBOY AROUND IS A REALLY BIG DEAL TO YOU?
I SUPPOSE. I MEAN...
HE'S KIND OF A DISAPPOINTMENT. I--
--YOU WERE ONE OF THE
ROKK!
I MEANT NO OFFENSE TO HIM--
NO, ROKK... SOMETHING JUST...THE GLASSES...
BLIP
BLIP
BLIP
BLIP
I'LL GET IT.
DREAMER? ANY LUCK WITH YOUR PRE-COG?
NO...
WELL, THERE'S ALWAYS TOMORROW--
NO, THERE ISN'T. YOU MISUNDERSTAND ME. MY PRE- COG POWER IS PICKING UP NOTHING.
I THINK I CAN'T READ THE FUTURE ANYMORE...
BECAUSE THE FUTURE NO LONGER EXISTS.

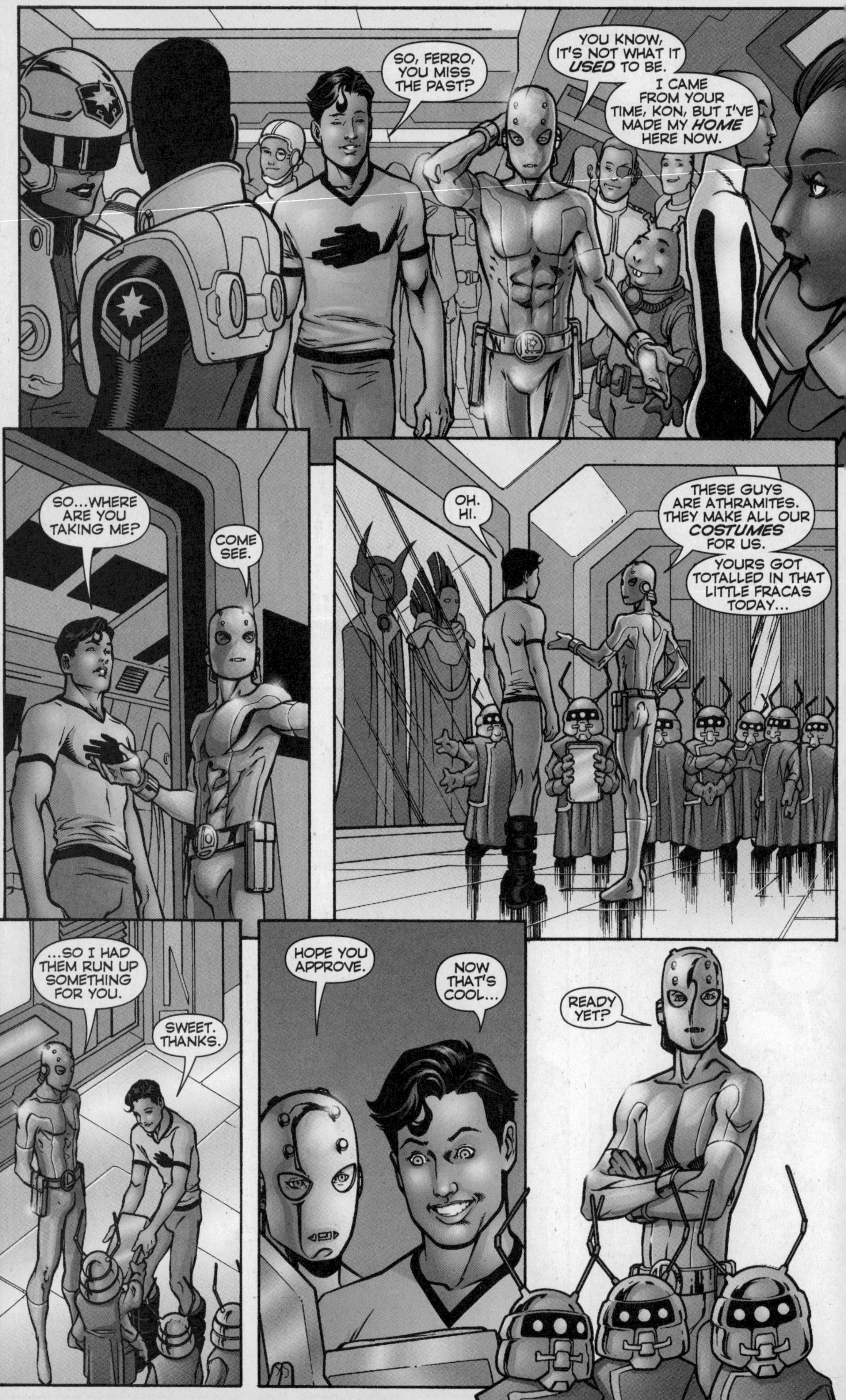
SO, FERRO, YOU MISS THE PAST?
YOU KNOW, IT'S NOT WHAT IT *USED* TO BE.
I CAME FROM YOUR TIME, KON, BUT I'VE MADE MY *HOME* HERE NOW.
SO...WHERE ARE YOU TAKING ME?
COME SEE.
OH. HI.
THESE GUYS ARE ATHRAMITES. THEY MAKE ALL OUR *COSTUMES* FOR US.
YOURS GOT TOTALLED IN THAT LITTLE FRACAS TODAY...
...SO I HAD THEM RUN UP SOMETHING FOR YOU.
SWEET. THANKS.
HOPE YOU APPROVE.
NOW THAT'S COOL...
READY YET?

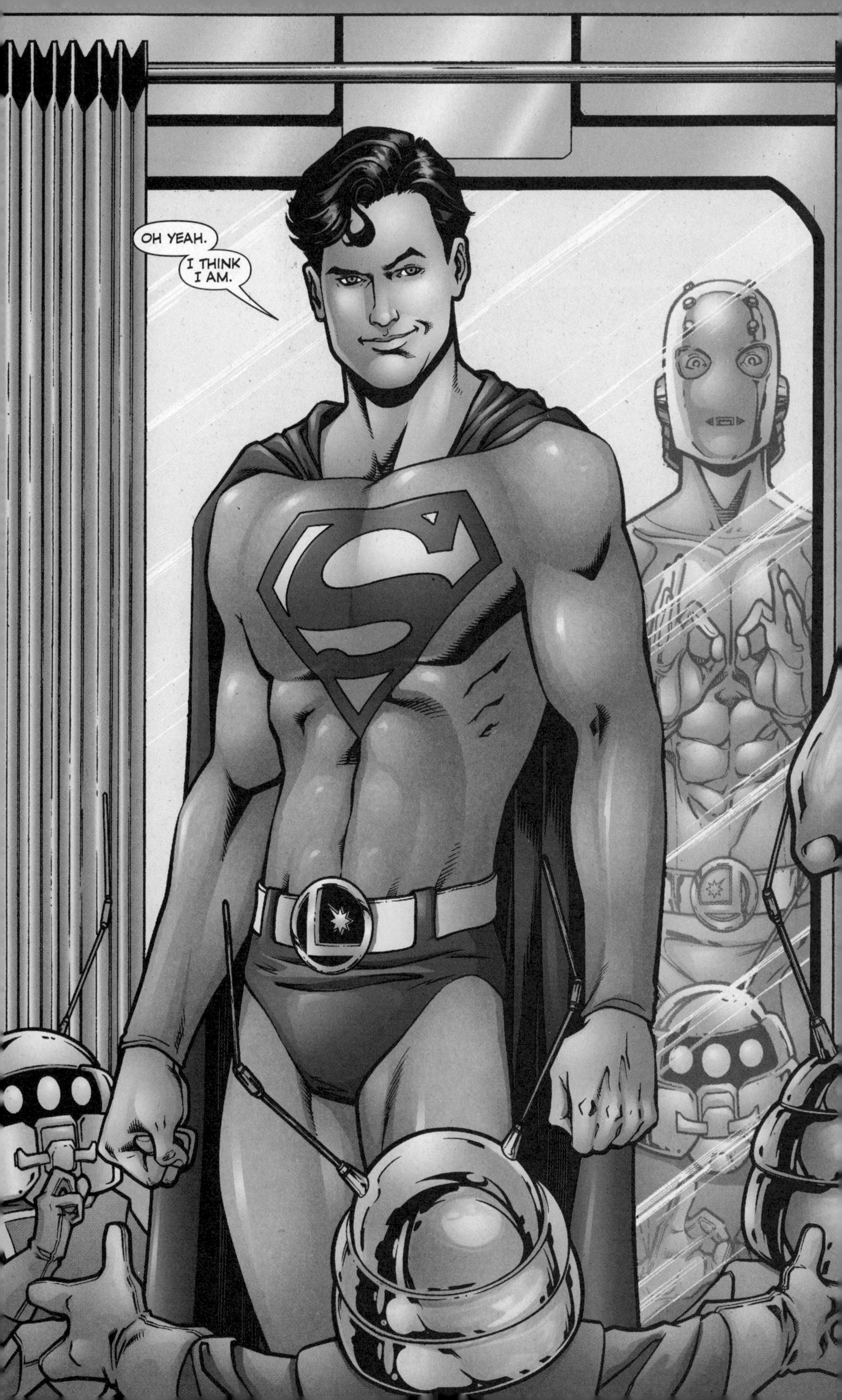
OH YEAH.
I THINK I AM.

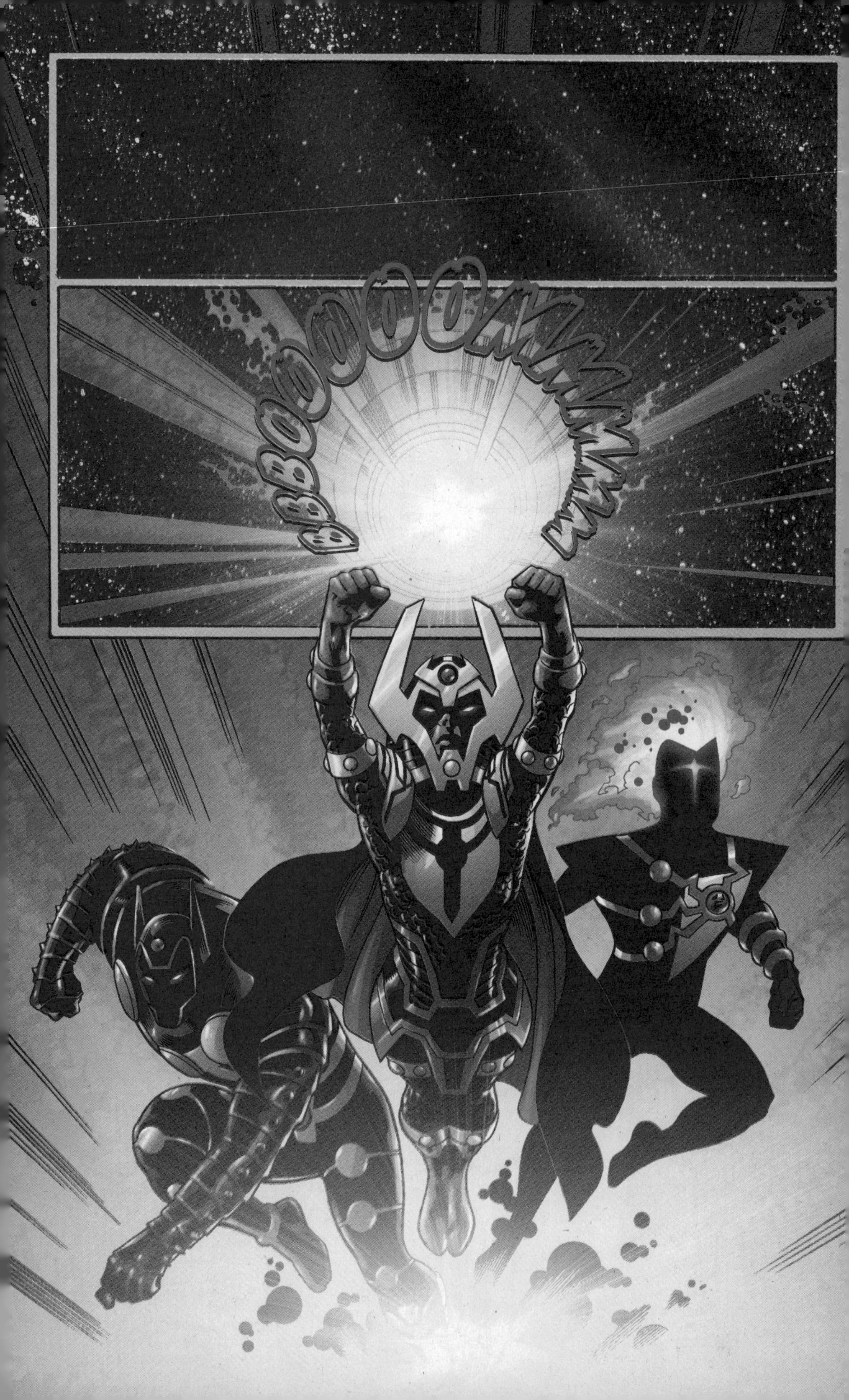
BBBOOOOOOMMMMMM

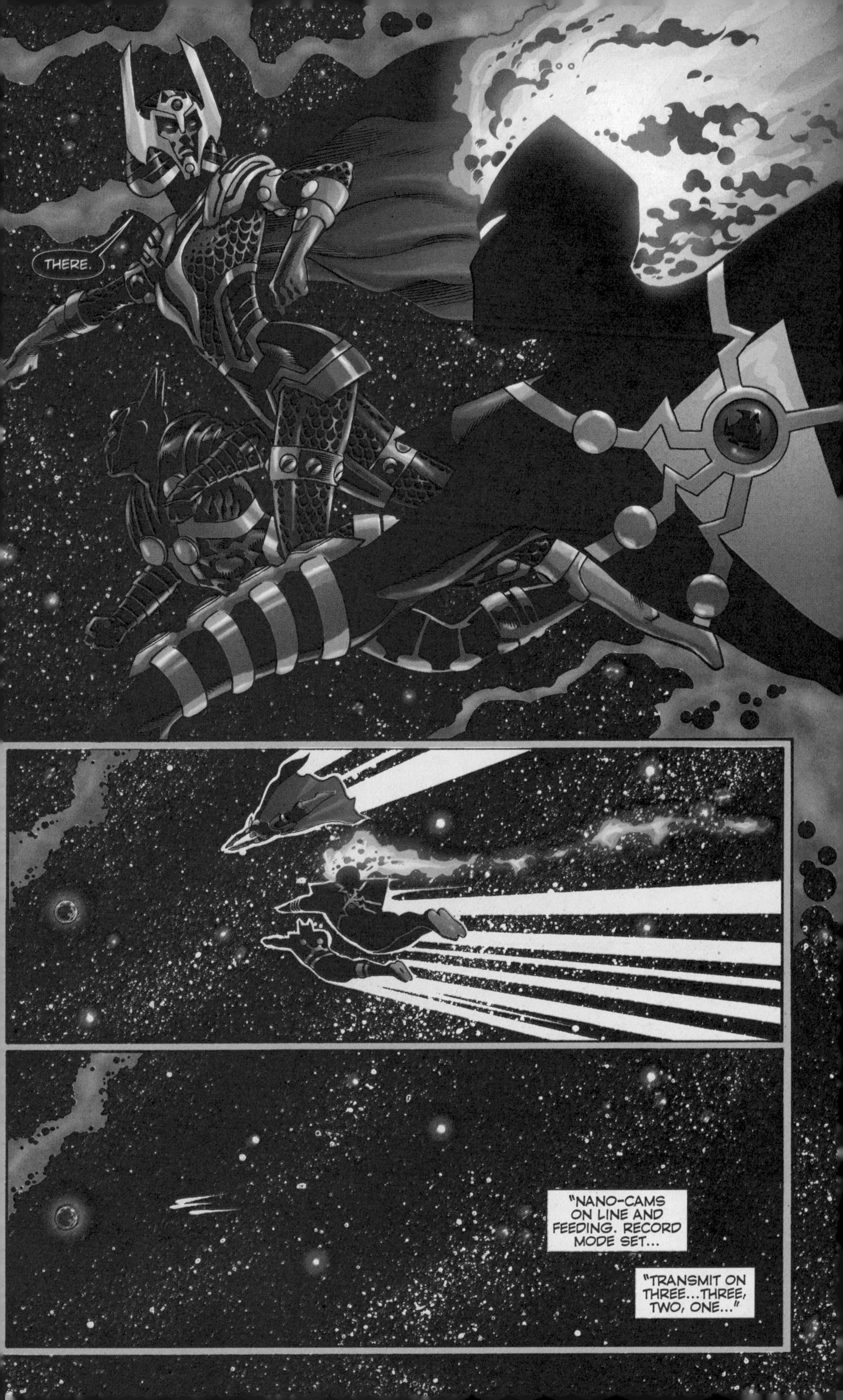
THERE.
"NANO-CAMS ON LINE AND FEEDING. RECORD MODE SET...
"TRANSMIT ON THREE...THREE, TWO, ONE..."

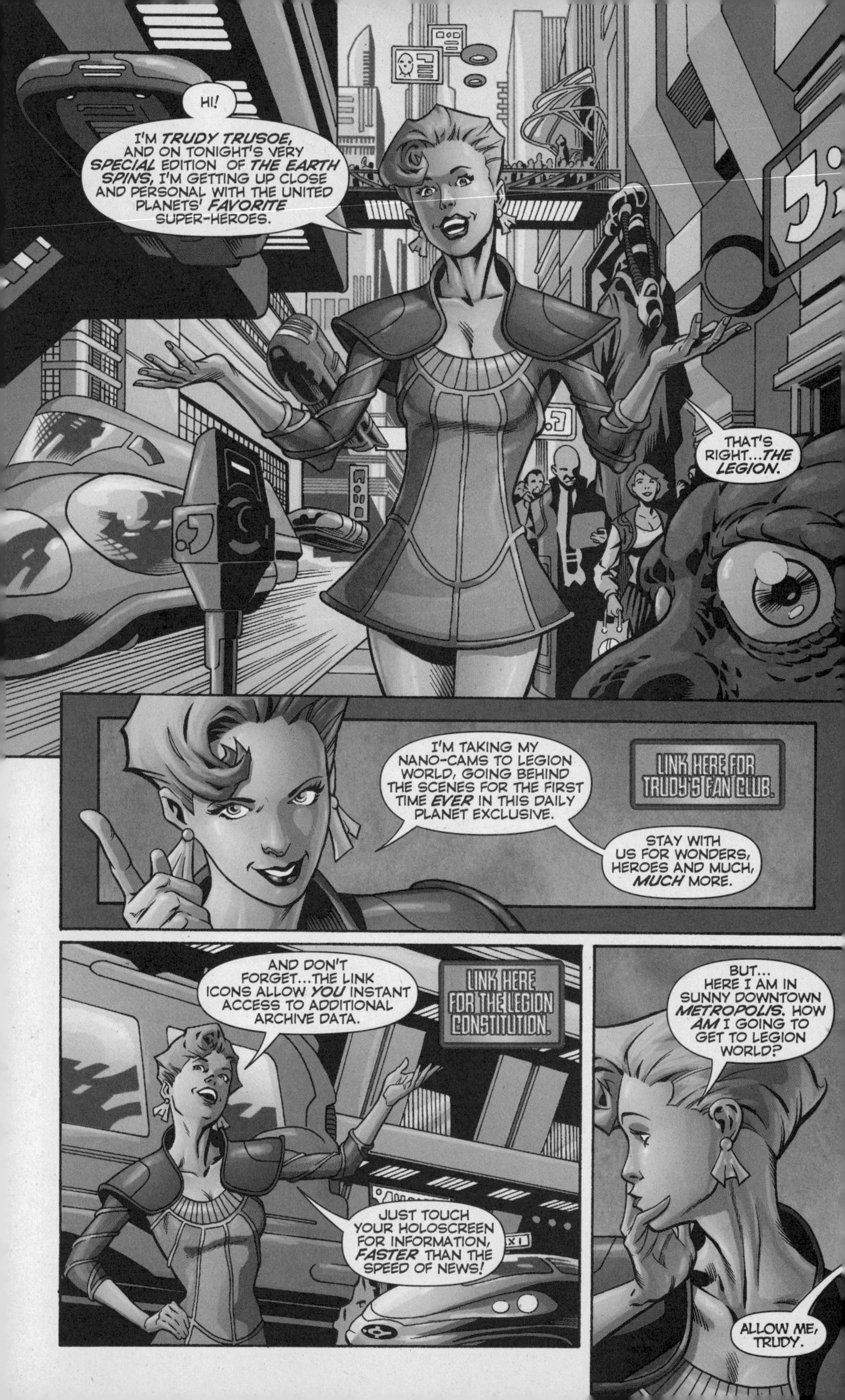
HI!
I'M TRUDY TRUSOE, AND ON TONIGHT'S VERY SPECIAL EDITION OF THE EARTH SPINS, I'M GETTING UP CLOSE AND PERSONAL WITH THE UNITED PLANETS' FAVORITE SUPER-HEROES.
THAT'S RIGHT...THE LEGION.
I'M TAKING MY NANO-CAMS TO LEGION WORLD, GOING BEHIND THE SCENES FOR THE FIRST TIME EVER IN THIS DAILY PLANET EXCLUSIVE.
LINK HERE FOR TRUDY'S FAN CLUB.
STAY WITH US FOR WONDERS, HEROES AND MUCH, MUCH MORE.
AND DON'T FORGET...THE LINK ICONS ALLOW YOU INSTANT ACCESS TO ADDITIONAL ARCHIVE DATA.
LINK HERE FOR THE LEGION CONSTITUTION.
JUST TOUCH YOUR HOLOSCREEN FOR INFORMATION, FASTER THAN THE SPEED OF NEWS!
BUT... HERE I AM IN SUNNY DOWNTOWN METROPOLIS. HOW AM I GOING TO GET TO LEGION WORLD?
ALLOW ME, TRUDY.

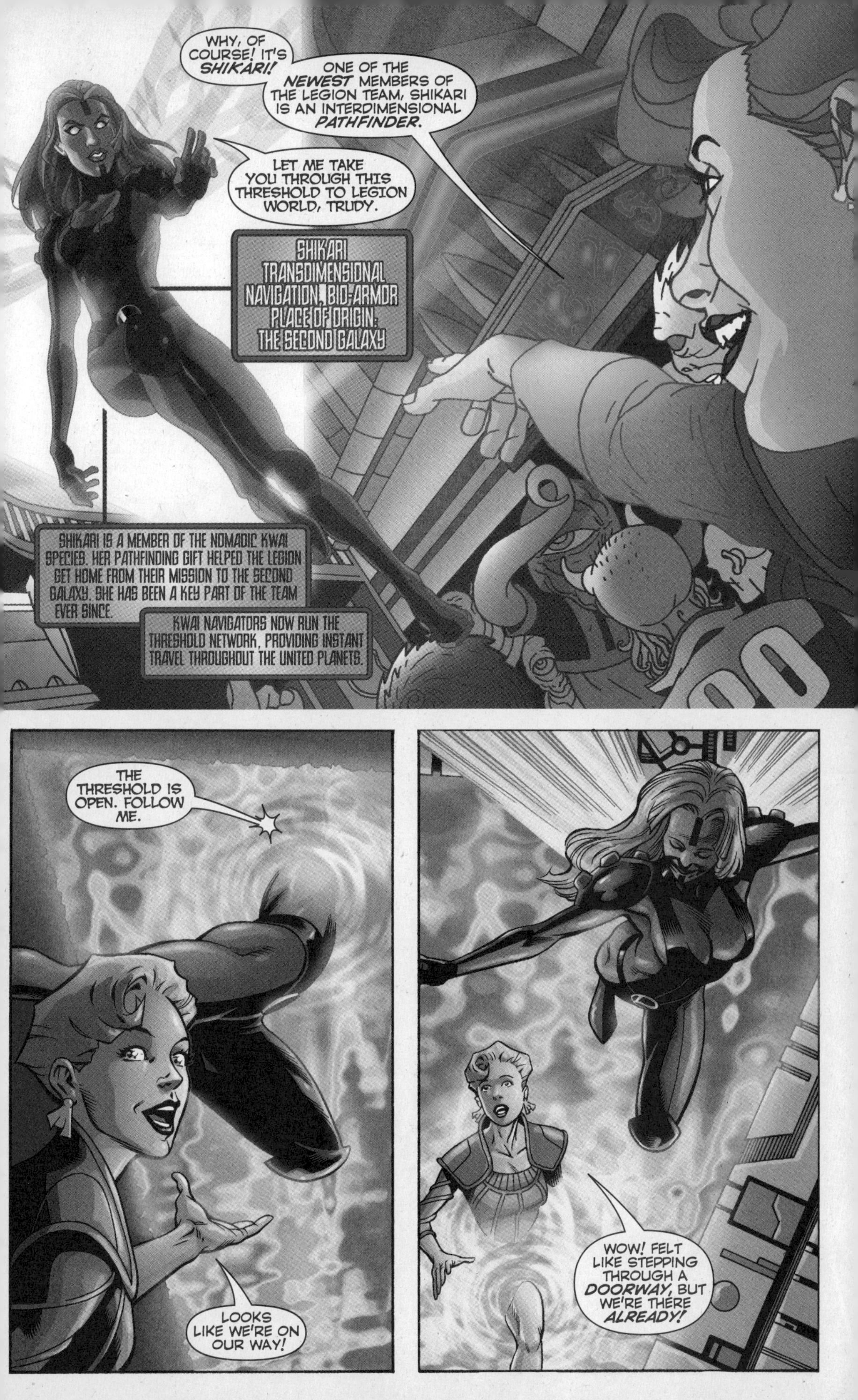
WHY, OF COURSE! IT'S SHIKARI!
ONE OF THE NEWEST MEMBERS OF THE LEGION TEAM, SHIKARI IS AN INTERDIMENSIONAL PATHFINDER.
LET ME TAKE YOU THROUGH THIS THRESHOLD TO LEGION WORLD, TRUDY.
SHIKARI
TRANSDIMENSIONAL NAVIGATION, BIO-ARMOR
PLACE OF ORIGIN: THE SECOND GALAXY
SHIKARI IS A MEMBER OF THE NOMADIC KWAI SPECIES. HER PATHFINDING GIFT HELPED THE LEGION GET HOME FROM THEIR MISSION TO THE SECOND GALAXY. SHE HAS BEEN A KEY PART OF THE TEAM EVER SINCE.
KWAI NAVIGATORS NOW RUN THE THRESHOLD NETWORK, PROVIDING INSTANT TRAVEL THROUGHOUT THE UNITED PLANETS.
THE THRESHOLD IS OPEN. FOLLOW ME.
LOOKS LIKE WE'RE ON OUR WAY!
WOW! FELT LIKE STEPPING THROUGH A DOORWAY, BUT WE'RE THERE ALREADY!

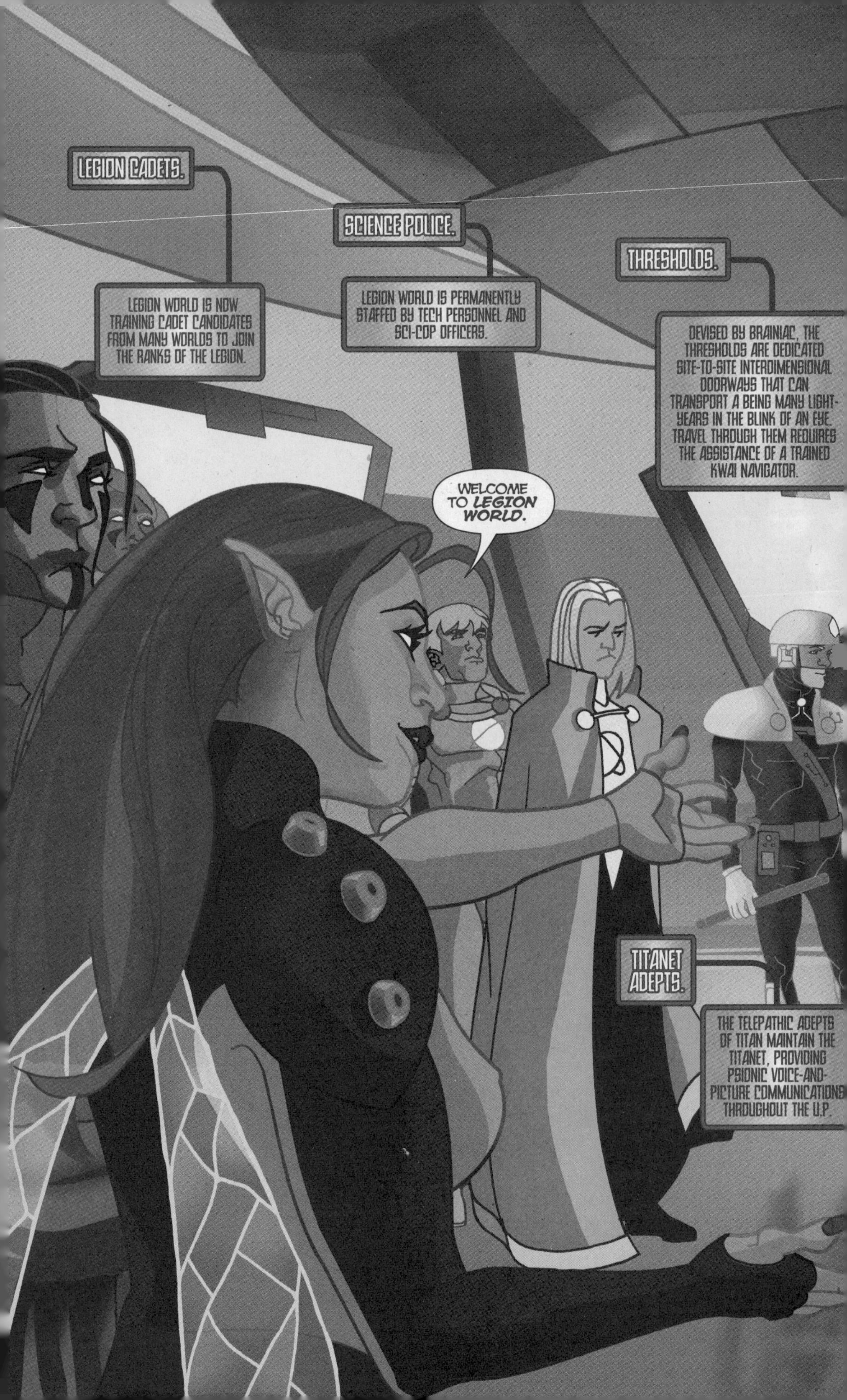
LEGION CADETS.
LEGION WORLD IS NOW TRAINING CADET CANDIDATES FROM MANY WORLDS TO JOIN THE RANKS OF THE LEGION.
SCIENCE POLICE.
LEGION WORLD IS PERMANENTLY STAFFED BY TECH PERSONNEL AND SCI-COP OFFICERS.
THRESHOLDS.
DEVISED BY BRAINIAC, THE THRESHOLDS ARE DEDICATED SITE-TO-SITE INTERDIMENSIONAL DOORWAYS THAT CAN TRANSPORT A BEING MANY LIGHT-YEARS IN THE BLINK OF AN EYE. TRAVEL THROUGH THEM REQUIRES THE ASSISTANCE OF A TRAINED KWAI NAVIGATOR.
WELCOME TO *LEGION WORLD*.
TITANET ADEPTS.
THE TELEPATHIC ADEPTS OF TITAN MAINTAIN THE TITANET, PROVIDING PSIONIC VOICE-AND-PICTURE COMMUNICATIONS THROUGHOUT THE U.P.

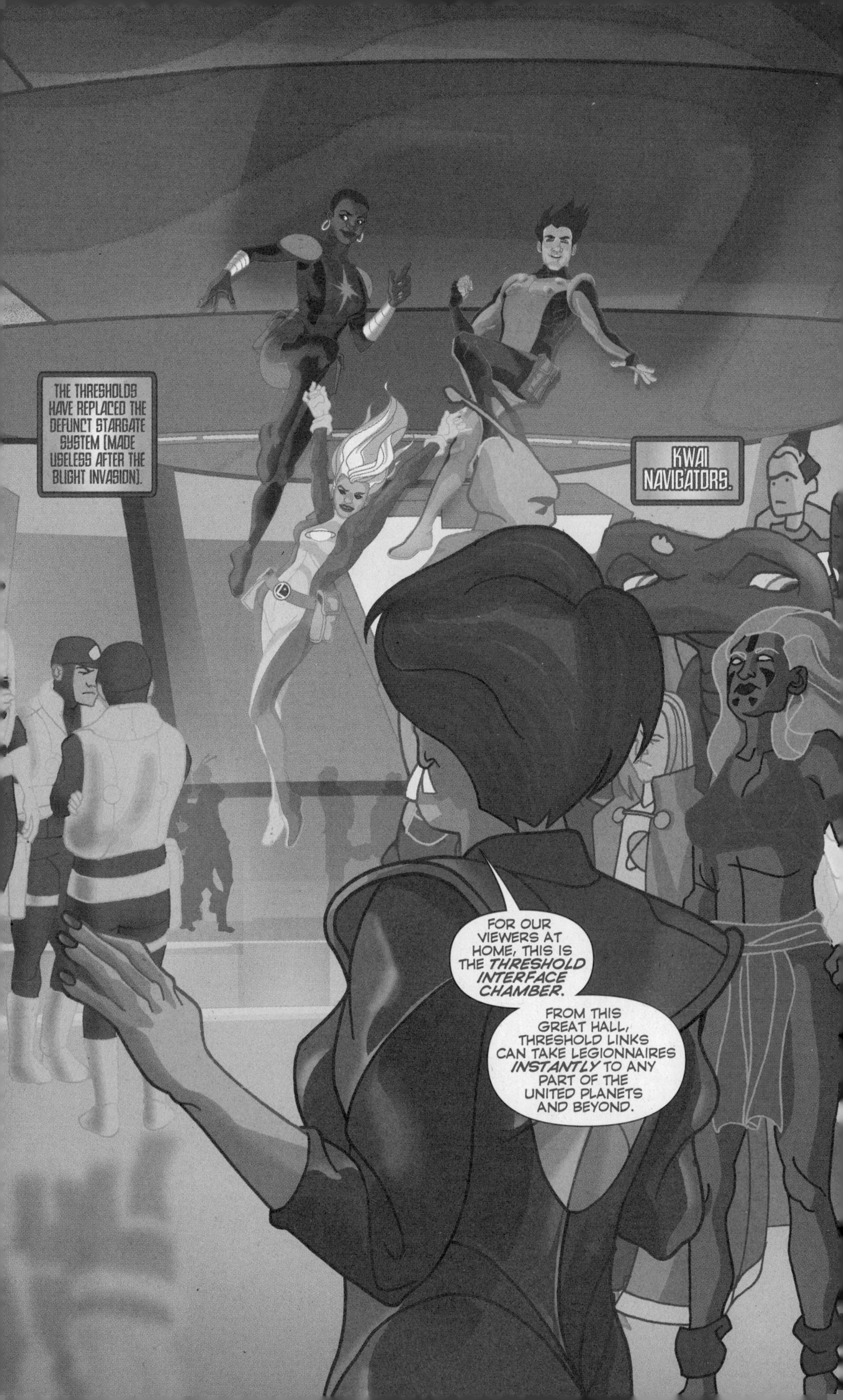

THE THRESHOLDS HAVE REPLACED THE DEFUNCT STARGATE SYSTEM (MADE USELESS AFTER THE BLIGHT INVASION).
KWAI NAVIGATORS.
FOR OUR VIEWERS AT HOME, THIS IS THE *THRESHOLD INTERFACE CHAMBER*.
FROM THIS GREAT HALL, THRESHOLD LINKS CAN TAKE LEGIONNAIRES *INSTANTLY* TO ANY PART OF THE UNITED PLANETS AND BEYOND.

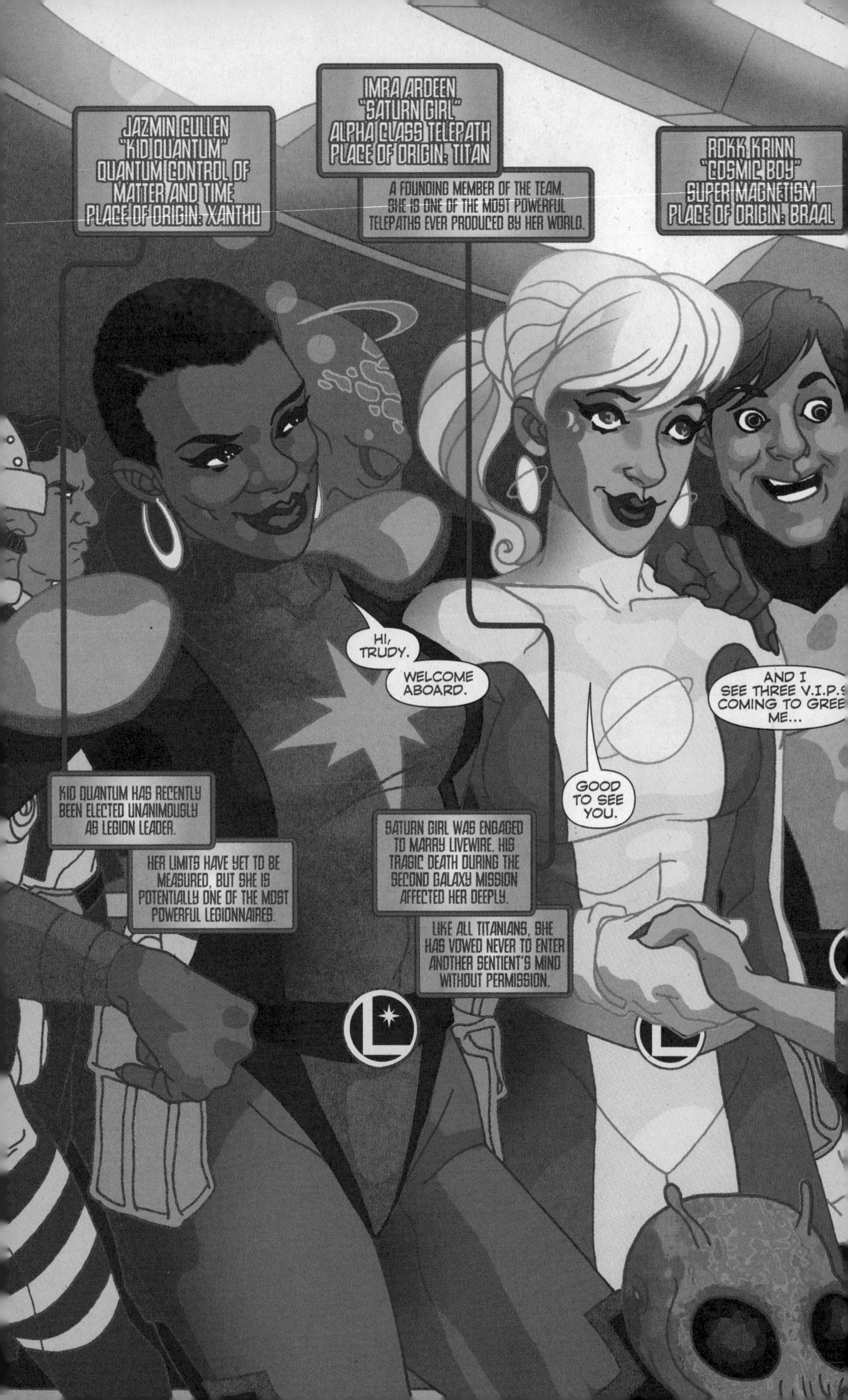
JAZMIN CULLEN
"KID QUANTUM"
QUANTUM CONTROL OF
MATTER AND TIME
PLACE OF ORIGIN: XANTHU
IMRA ARDEEN
"SATURN GIRL"
ALPHA CLASS TELEPATH
PLACE OF ORIGIN: TITAN
A FOUNDING MEMBER OF THE TEAM. SHE IS ONE OF THE MOST POWERFUL TELEPATHS EVER PRODUCED BY HER WORLD.
ROKK KRINN
"COSMIC BOY"
SUPER MAGNETISM
PLACE OF ORIGIN: BRAAL
HI, TRUDY.
WELCOME ABOARD.
KID QUANTUM HAS RECENTLY BEEN ELECTED UNANIMOUSLY AS LEGION LEADER.
HER LIMITS HAVE YET TO BE MEASURED, BUT SHE IS POTENTIALLY ONE OF THE MOST POWERFUL LEGIONNAIRES.
GOOD TO SEE YOU.
SATURN GIRL WAS ENGAGED TO MARRY LIVEWIRE. HIS TRAGIC DEATH DURING THE SECOND GALAXY MISSION AFFECTED HER DEEPLY.
LIKE ALL TITANIANS, SHE HAS VOWED NEVER TO ENTER ANOTHER SENTIENT'S MIND WITHOUT PERMISSION.
AND I SEE THREE V.I.P.S COMING TO GREE ME...

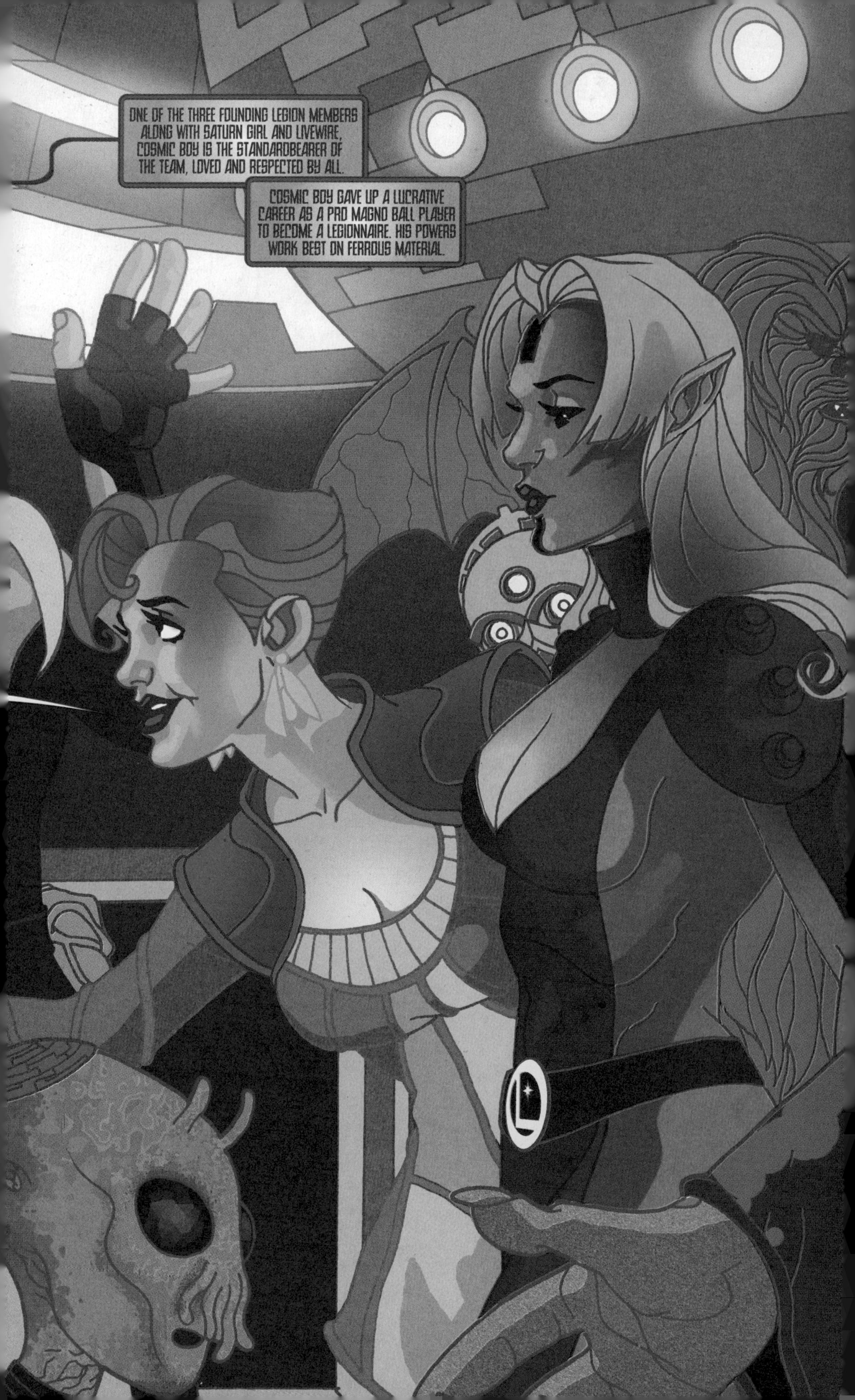
ONE OF THE THREE FOUNDING LEGION MEMBERS ALONG WITH SATURN GIRL AND LIVEWIRE, COSMIC BOY IS THE STANDARDBEARER OF THE TEAM, LOVED AND RESPECTED BY ALL.
COSMIC BOY GAVE UP A LUCRATIVE CAREER AS A PRO MAGNO BALL PLAYER TO BECOME A LEGIONNAIRE. HIS POWERS WORK BEST ON FERROUS MATERIAL.

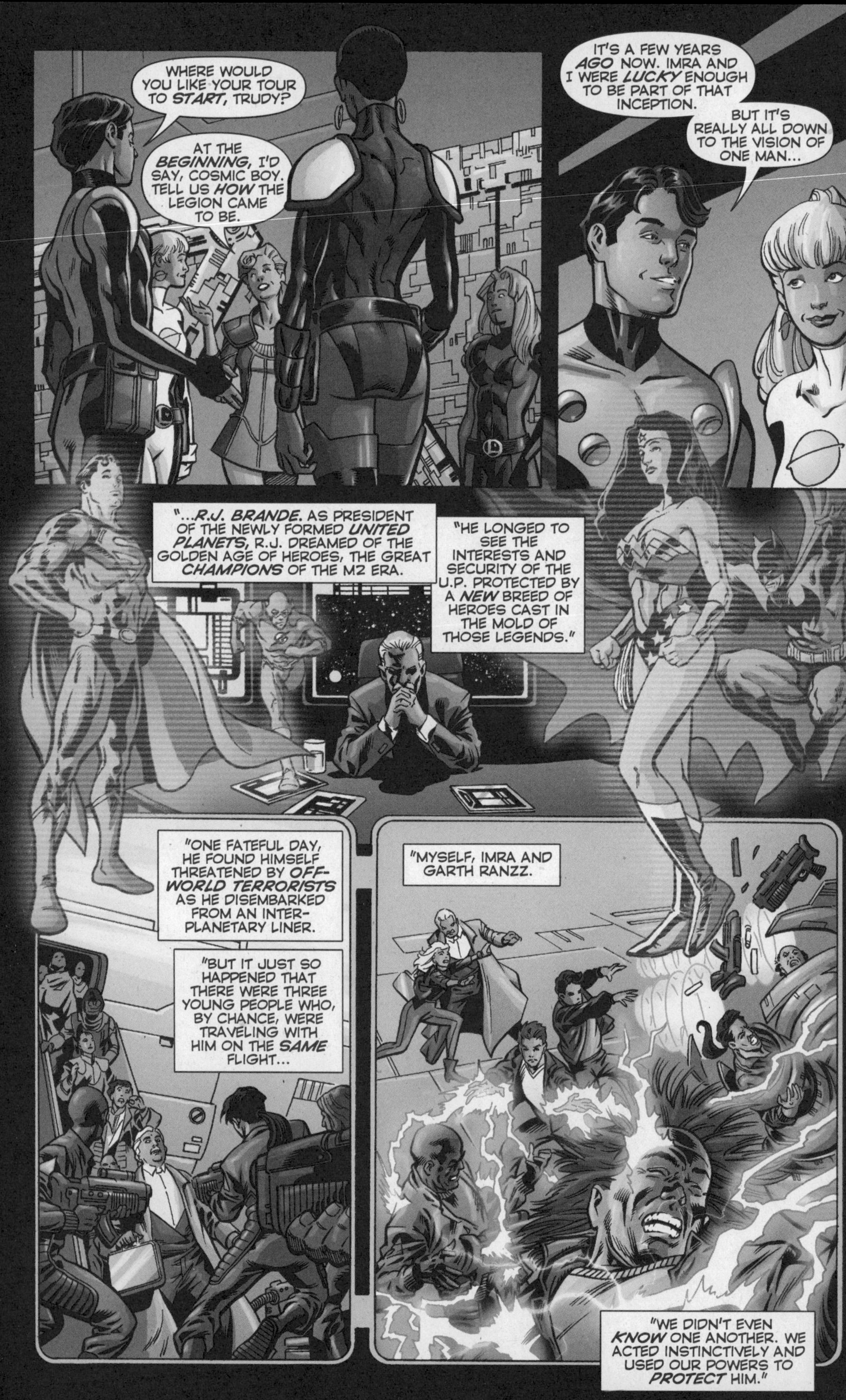

WHERE WOULD YOU LIKE YOUR TOUR TO START, TRUDY?
AT THE BEGINNING, I'D SAY, COSMIC BOY. TELL US HOW THE LEGION CAME TO BE.
IT'S A FEW YEARS AGO NOW. IMRA AND I WERE LUCKY ENOUGH TO BE PART OF THAT INCEPTION.
BUT IT'S REALLY ALL DOWN TO THE VISION OF ONE MAN...
"...R.J. BRANDE. AS PRESIDENT OF THE NEWLY FORMED UNITED PLANETS, R.J. DREAMED OF THE GOLDEN AGE OF HEROES, THE GREAT CHAMPIONS OF THE M2 ERA.
"HE LONGED TO SEE THE INTERESTS AND SECURITY OF THE U.P. PROTECTED BY A NEW BREED OF HEROES CAST IN THE MOLD OF THOSE LEGENDS."
"ONE FATEFUL DAY, HE FOUND HIMSELF THREATENED BY OFF-WORLD TERRORISTS AS HE DISEMBARKED FROM AN INTER-PLANETARY LINER.
"BUT IT JUST SO HAPPENED THAT THERE WERE THREE YOUNG PEOPLE WHO, BY CHANCE, WERE TRAVELING WITH HIM ON THE SAME FLIGHT...
"MYSELF, IMRA AND GARTH RANZZ.
"WE DIDN'T EVEN KNOW ONE ANOTHER. WE ACTED INSTINCTIVELY AND USED OUR POWERS TO PROTECT HIM."

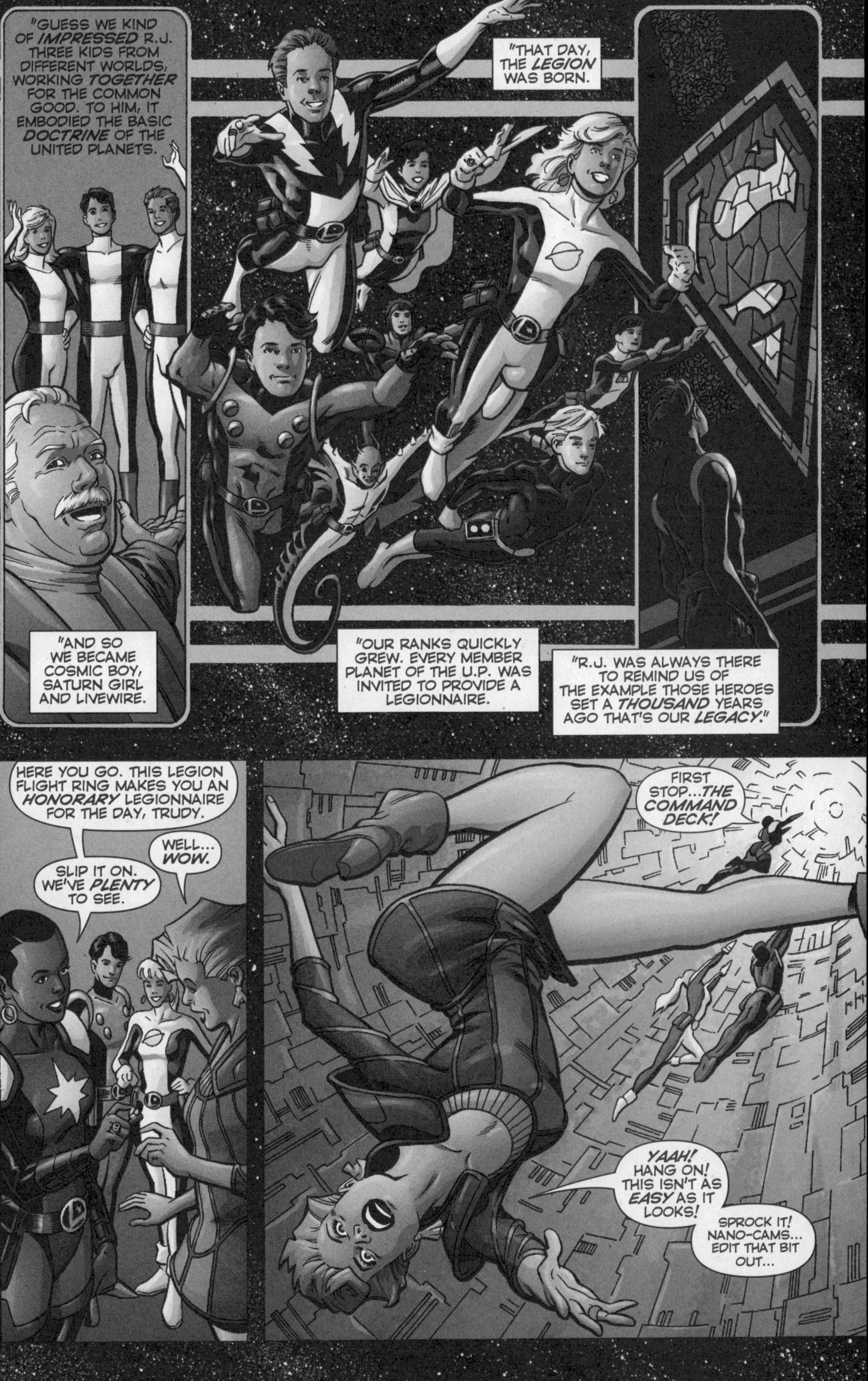
"GUESS WE KIND OF *IMPRESSED* R.J. THREE KIDS FROM DIFFERENT WORLDS, WORKING *TOGETHER* FOR THE COMMON GOOD. TO HIM, IT EMBODIED THE BASIC *DOCTRINE* OF THE UNITED PLANETS.
"AND SO WE BECAME COSMIC BOY, SATURN GIRL AND LIVEWIRE.
"THAT DAY, THE *LEGION* WAS BORN.
"OUR RANKS QUICKLY GREW. EVERY MEMBER PLANET OF THE U.P. WAS INVITED TO PROVIDE A LEGIONNAIRE.
"R.J. WAS ALWAYS THERE TO REMIND US OF THE EXAMPLE THOSE HEROES SET A *THOUSAND* YEARS AGO THAT'S OUR *LEGACY.*"
HERE YOU GO. THIS LEGION FLIGHT RING MAKES YOU AN *HONORARY* LEGIONNAIRE FOR THE DAY, TRUDY.
SLIP IT ON. WE'VE *PLENTY* TO SEE.
WELL... *WOW.*
FIRST STOP...*THE COMMAND DECK!*
YAAH! HANG ON! THIS ISN'T AS *EASY* AS IT LOOKS!
SPROCK IT! NANO-CAMS... EDIT THAT BIT OUT...

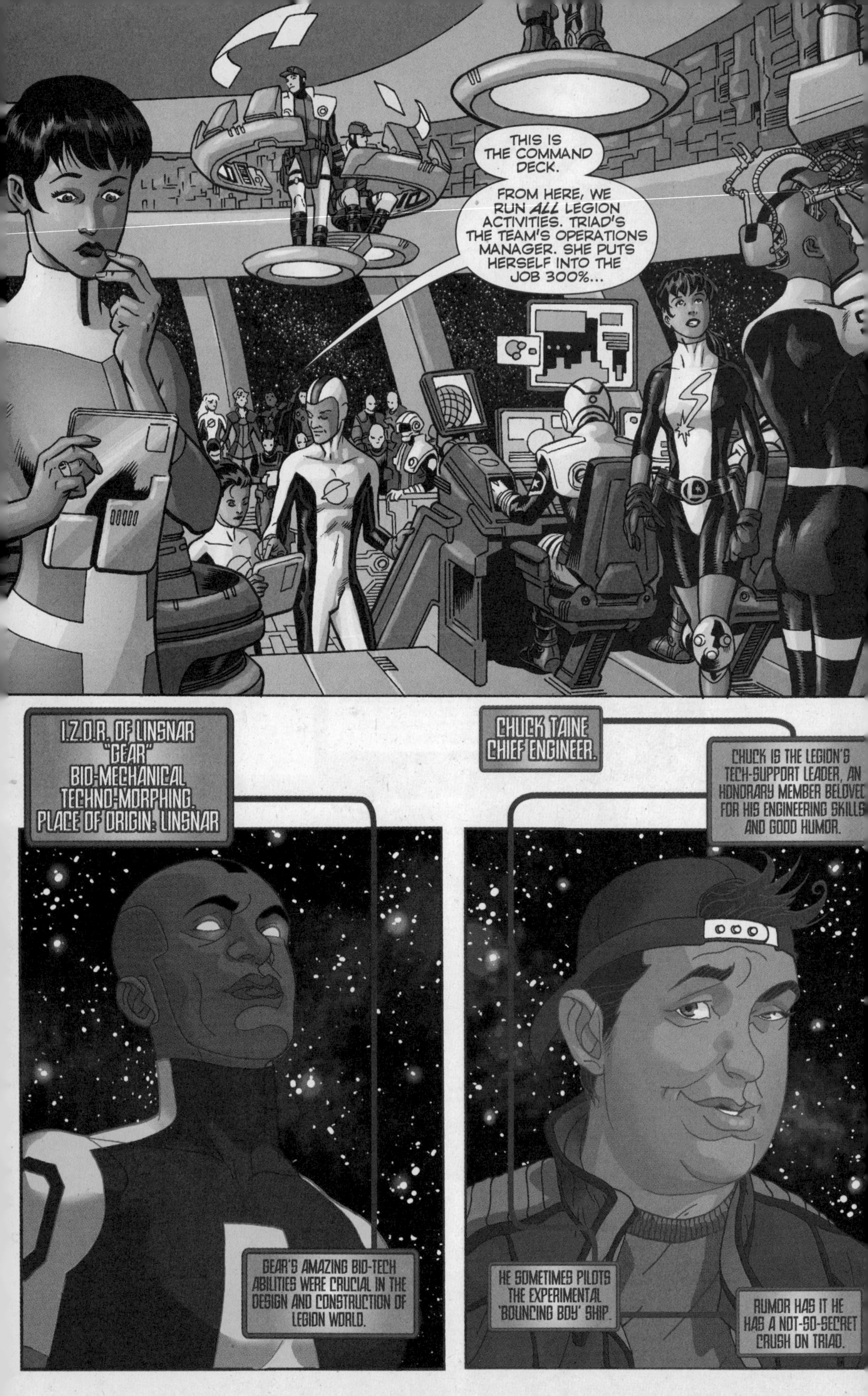
THIS IS THE COMMAND DECK.
FROM HERE, WE RUN ALL LEGION ACTIVITIES. TRIAD'S THE TEAM'S OPERATIONS MANAGER. SHE PUTS HERSELF INTO THE JOB 300%...
I.Z.O.R. OF LINSNAR "GEAR" BIO-MECHANICAL TECHNO-MORPHING. PLACE OF ORIGIN: LINSNAR
GEAR'S AMAZING BIO-TECH ABILITIES WERE CRUCIAL IN THE DESIGN AND CONSTRUCTION OF LEGION WORLD.
CHUCK TAINE CHIEF ENGINEER.
CHUCK IS THE LEGION'S TECH-SUPPORT LEADER, AN HONORARY MEMBER BELOVED FOR HIS ENGINEERING SKILLS AND GOOD HUMOR.
HE SOMETIMES PILOTS THE EXPERIMENTAL 'BOUNCING BOY' SHIP.
RUMOR HAS IT HE HAS A NOT-SO-SECRET CRUSH ON TRIAD.

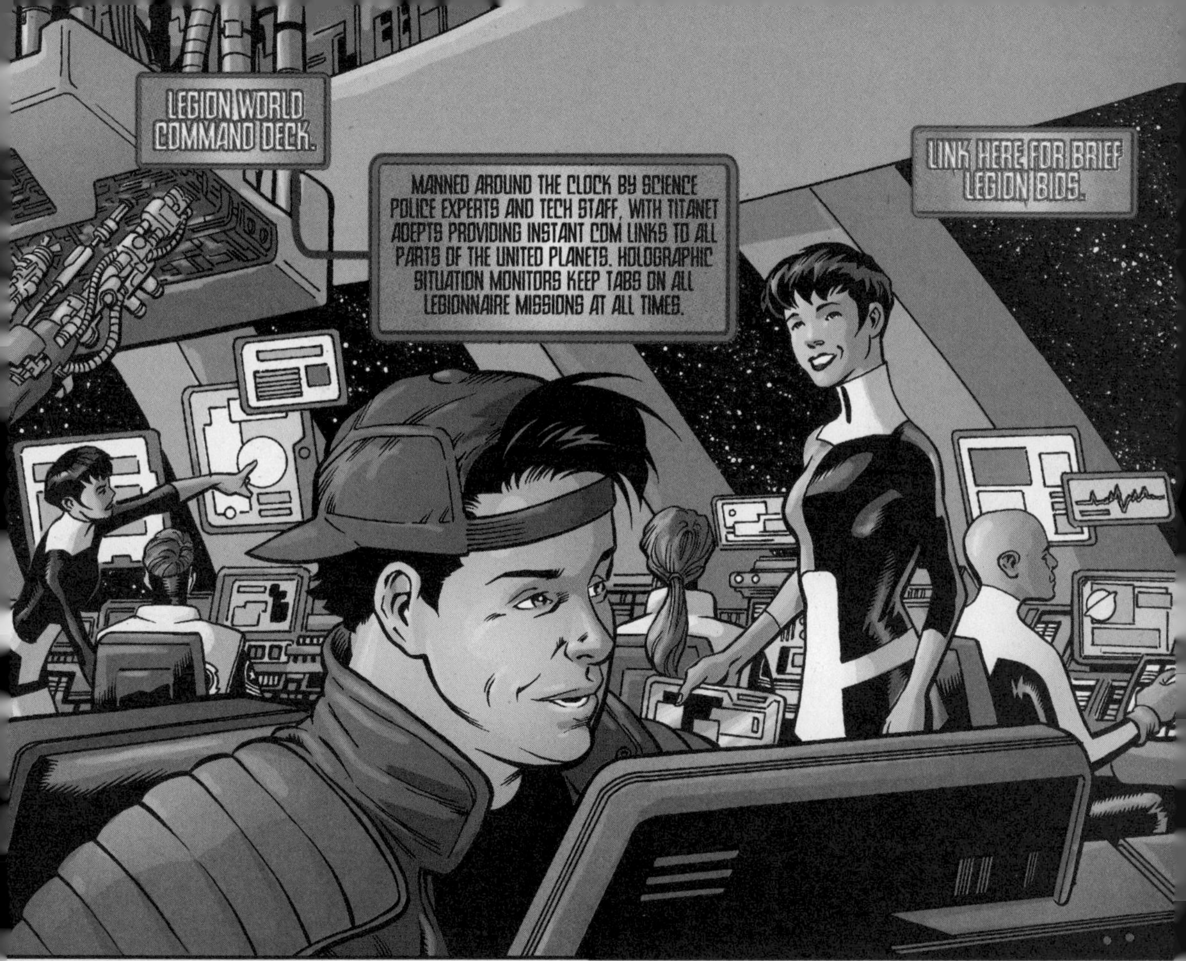
LEGION WORLD COMMAND DECK.
MANNED AROUND THE CLOCK BY SCIENCE POLICE EXPERTS AND TECH STAFF, WITH TITANET ADEPTS PROVIDING INSTANT COM LINKS TO ALL PARTS OF THE UNITED PLANETS. HOLOGRAPHIC SITUATION MONITORS KEEP TABS ON ALL LEGIONNAIRE MISSIONS AT ALL TIMES.
LINK HERE FOR BRIEF LEGION BIOS.

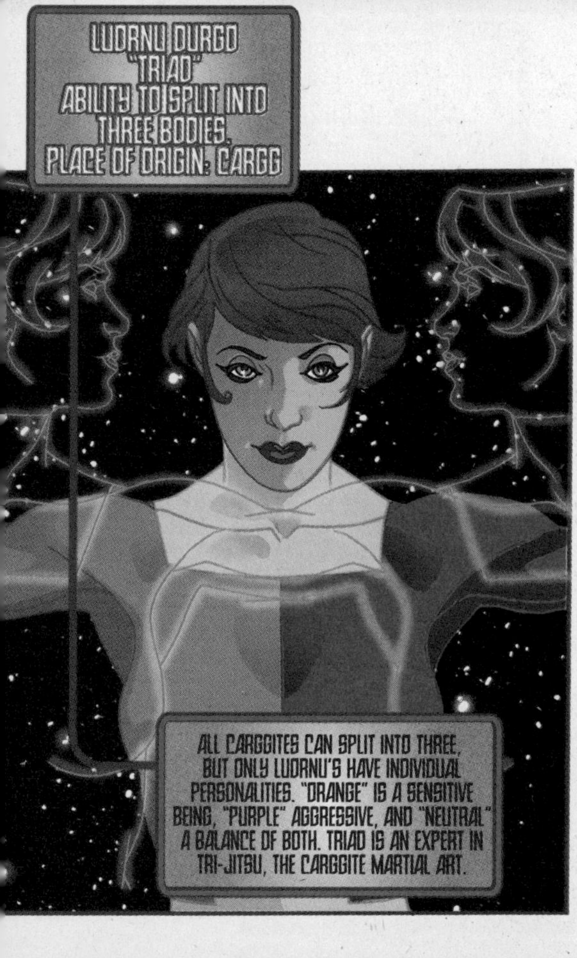
LUORNU DURGO "TRIAD" ABILITY TO SPLIT INTO THREE BODIES. PLACE OF ORIGIN: CARGG
ALL CARGGITES CAN SPLIT INTO THREE, BUT ONLY LUORNU'S HAVE INDIVIDUAL PERSONALITIES. "ORANGE" IS A SENSITIVE BEING, "PURPLE" AGGRESSIVE, AND "NEUTRAL" A BALANCE OF BOTH. TRIAD IS AN EXPERT IN TRI-JITSU, THE CARGGITE MARTIAL ART.

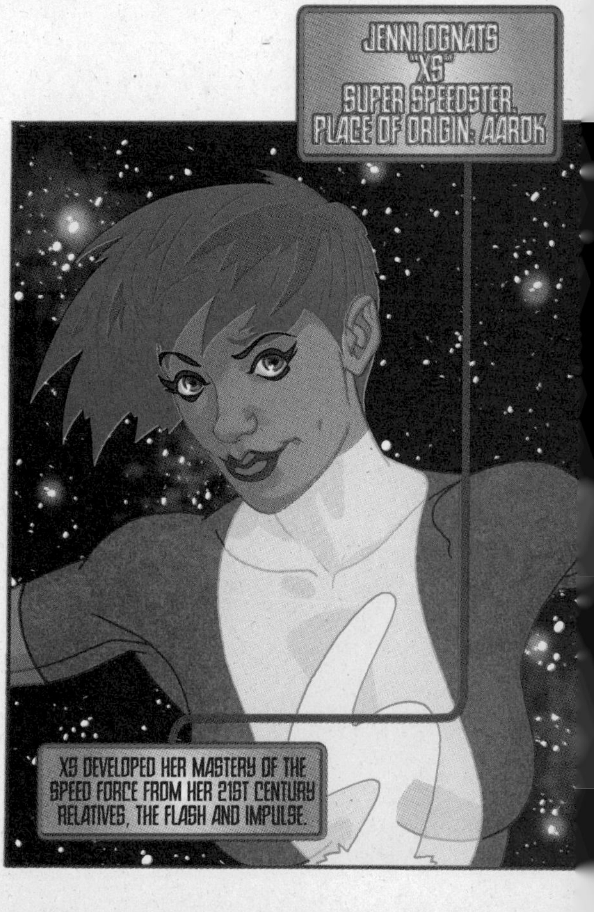
JENNI OGNATS "XS" SUPER SPEEDSTER. PLACE OF ORIGIN: AAROK
XS DEVELOPED HER MASTERY OF THE SPEED FORCE FROM HER 21ST CENTURY RELATIVES, THE FLASH AND IMPULSE.

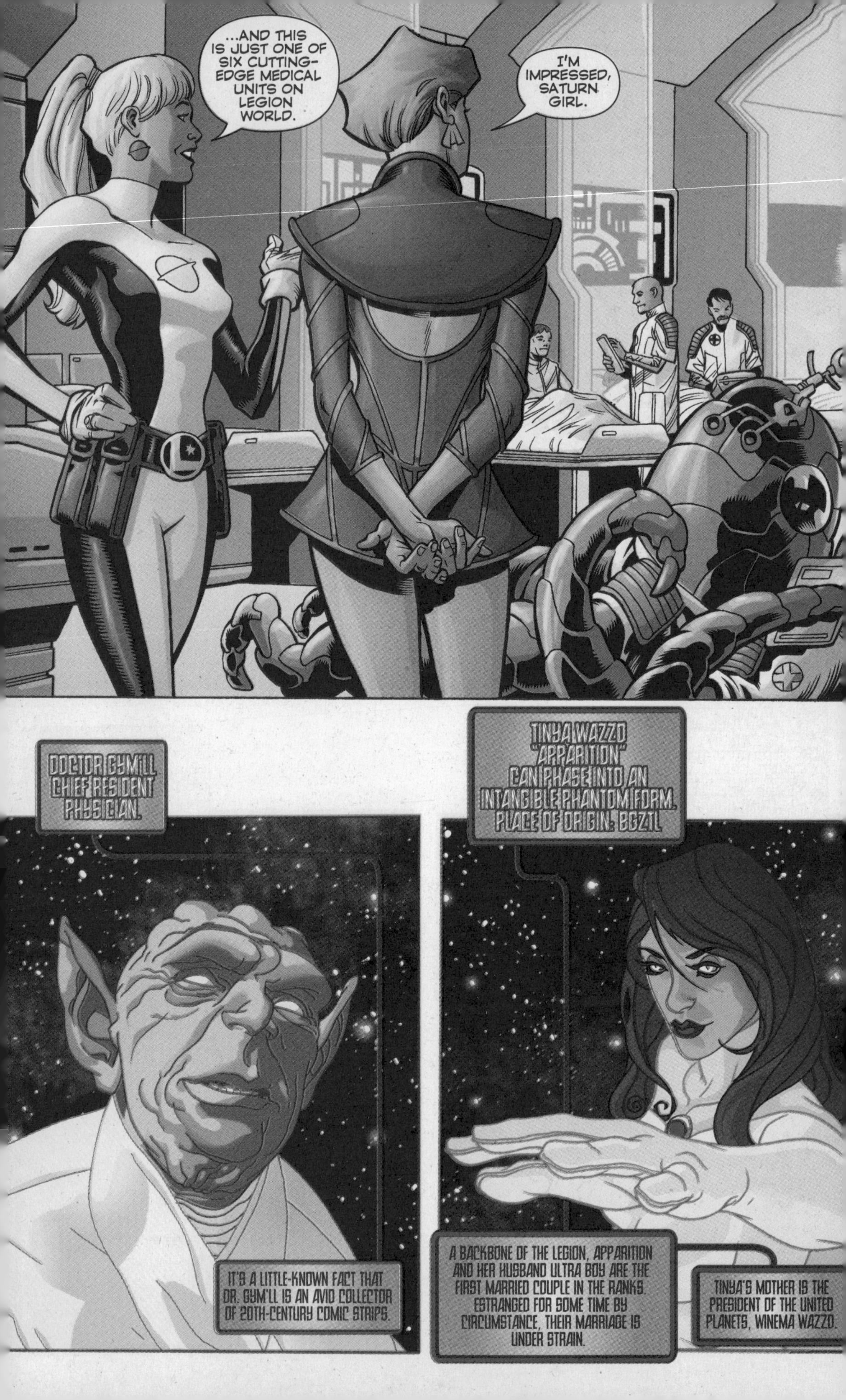
...AND THIS IS JUST ONE OF SIX CUTTING-EDGE MEDICAL UNITS ON LEGION WORLD.
I'M IMPRESSED, SATURN GIRL.
DOCTOR GYM'LL CHIEF RESIDENT PHYSICIAN.
IT'S A LITTLE-KNOWN FACT THAT DR. GYM'LL IS AN AVID COLLECTOR OF 20TH-CENTURY COMIC STRIPS.
TINYA WAZZO "APPARITION" CAN PHASE INTO AN INTANGIBLE PHANTOM FORM. PLACE OF ORIGIN: BGZTL
A BACKBONE OF THE LEGION, APPARITION AND HER HUSBAND ULTRA BOY ARE THE FIRST MARRIED COUPLE IN THE RANKS. ESTRANGED FOR SOME TIME BY CIRCUMSTANCE, THEIR MARRIAGE IS UNDER STRAIN.
TINYA'S MOTHER IS THE PRESIDENT OF THE UNITED PLANETS, WINEMA WAZZO.

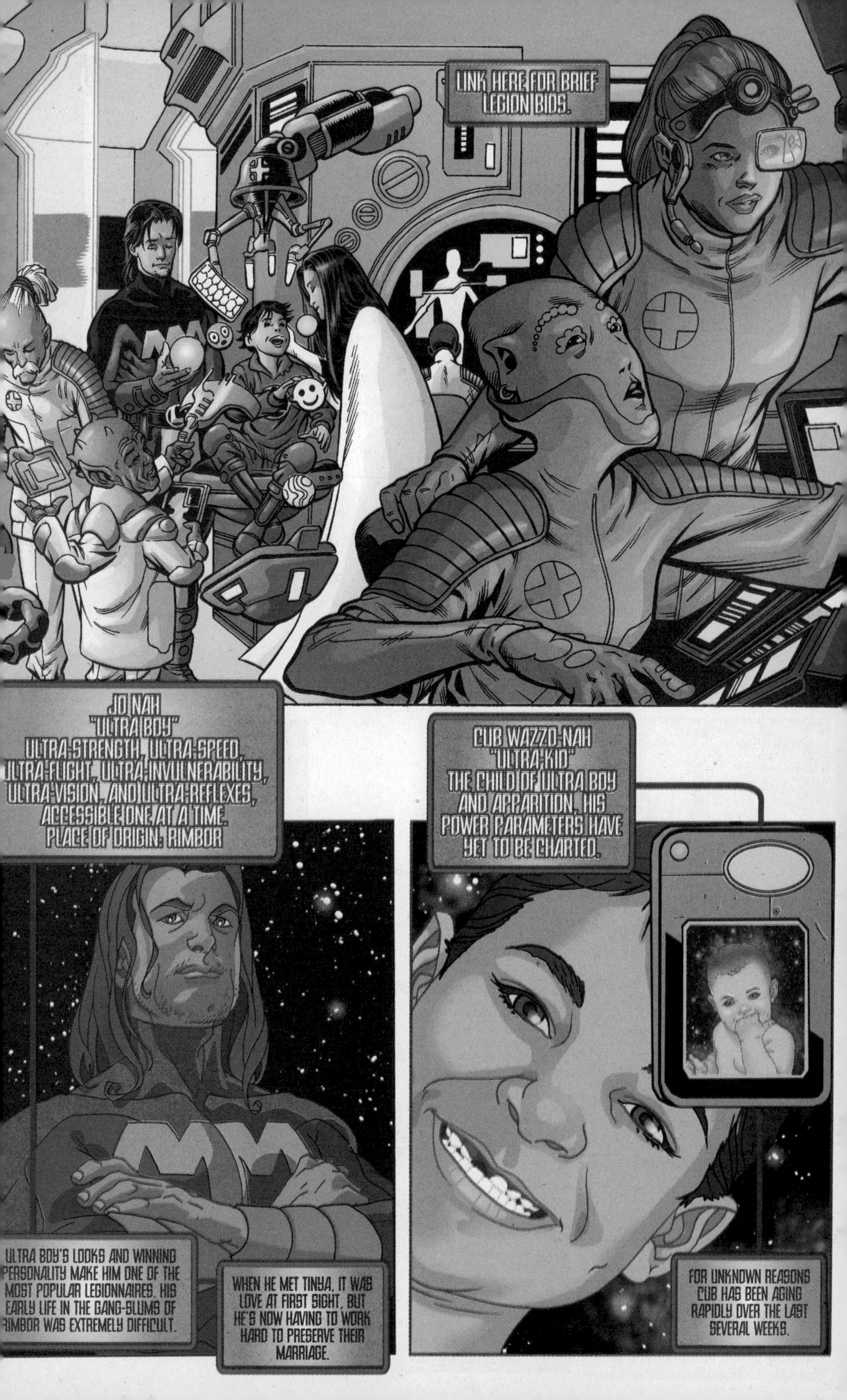
LINK HERE FOR BRIEF LEGION BIOS.
JO NAH "ULTRA BOY" ULTRA-STRENGTH, ULTRA-SPEED, ULTRA-FLIGHT, ULTRA-INVULNERABILITY, ULTRA-VISION, AND ULTRA-REFLEXES, ACCESSIBLE ONE AT A TIME. PLACE OF ORIGIN: RIMBOR
CUB WAZZO-NAH "ULTRA-KID" THE CHILD OF ULTRA BOY AND APPARITION, HIS POWER PARAMETERS HAVE YET TO BE CHARTED.
ULTRA BOY'S LOOKS AND WINNING PERSONALITY MAKE HIM ONE OF THE MOST POPULAR LEGIONNAIRES. HIS EARLY LIFE IN THE GANG-SLUMS OF RIMBOR WAS EXTREMELY DIFFICULT.
WHEN HE MET TINYA, IT WAS LOVE AT FIRST SIGHT, BUT HE'S NOW HAVING TO WORK HARD TO PRESERVE THEIR MARRIAGE.
FOR UNKNOWN REASONS CUB HAS BEEN AGING RAPIDLY OVER THE LAST SEVERAL WEEKS.

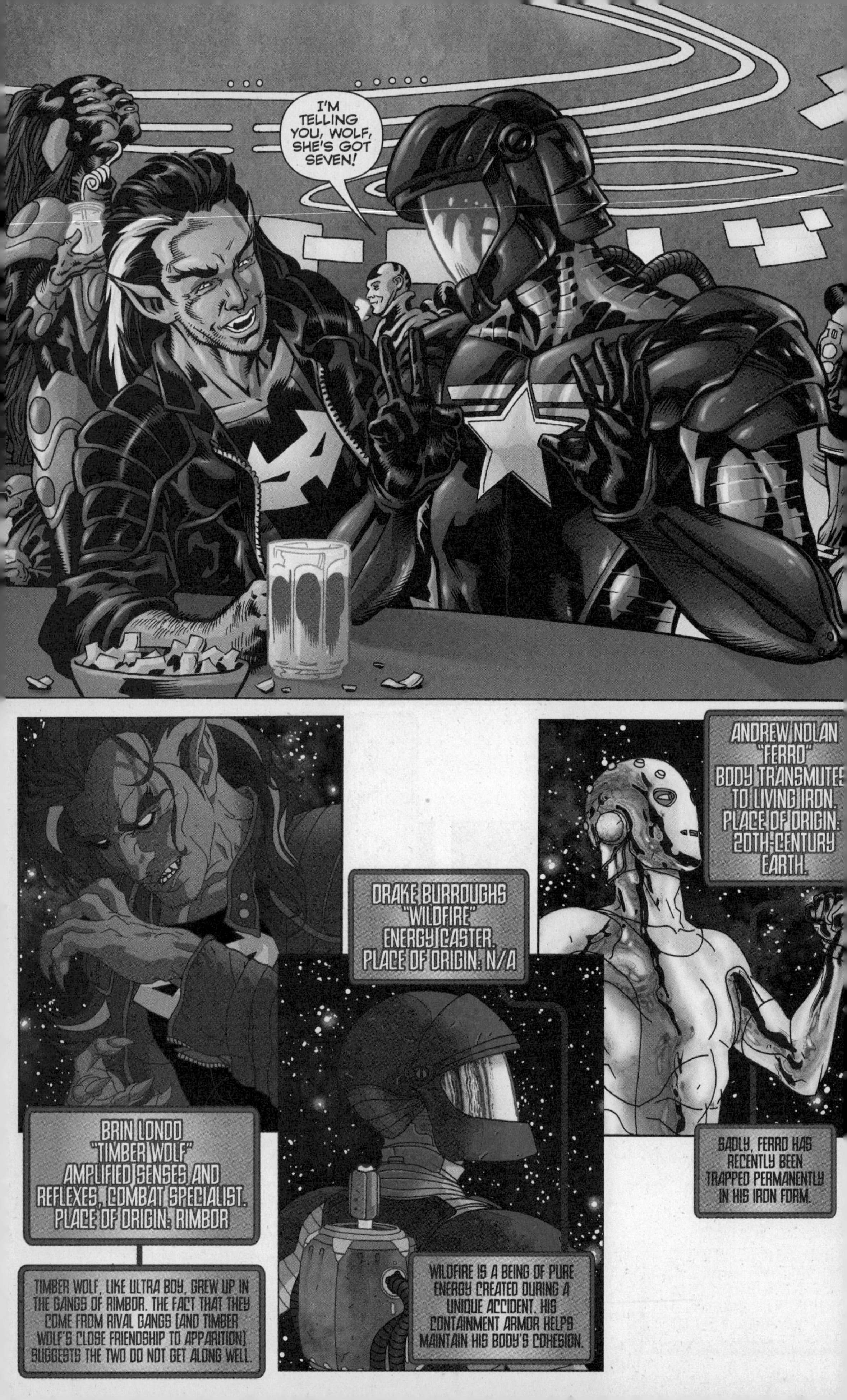

I'M TELLING YOU, WOLF, SHE'S GOT SEVEN!
BRIN LONDO "TIMBER WOLF" AMPLIFIED SENSES AND REFLEXES, COMBAT SPECIALIST. PLACE OF ORIGIN: RIMBOR
TIMBER WOLF, LIKE ULTRA BOY, GREW UP IN THE GANGS OF RIMBOR. THE FACT THAT THEY COME FROM RIVAL GANGS (AND TIMBER WOLF'S CLOSE FRIENDSHIP TO APPARITION) SUGGESTS THE TWO DO NOT GET ALONG WELL.
DRAKE BURROUGHS "WILDFIRE" ENERGY CASTER. PLACE OF ORIGIN: N/A
WILDFIRE IS A BEING OF PURE ENERGY CREATED DURING A UNIQUE ACCIDENT. HIS CONTAINMENT ARMOR HELPS MAINTAIN HIS BODY'S COHESION.
ANDREW NOLAN "FERRO" BODY TRANSMUTES TO LIVING IRON. PLACE OF ORIGIN: 20TH-CENTURY EARTH.
SADLY, FERRO HAS RECENTLY BEEN TRAPPED PERMANENTLY IN HIS IRON FORM.

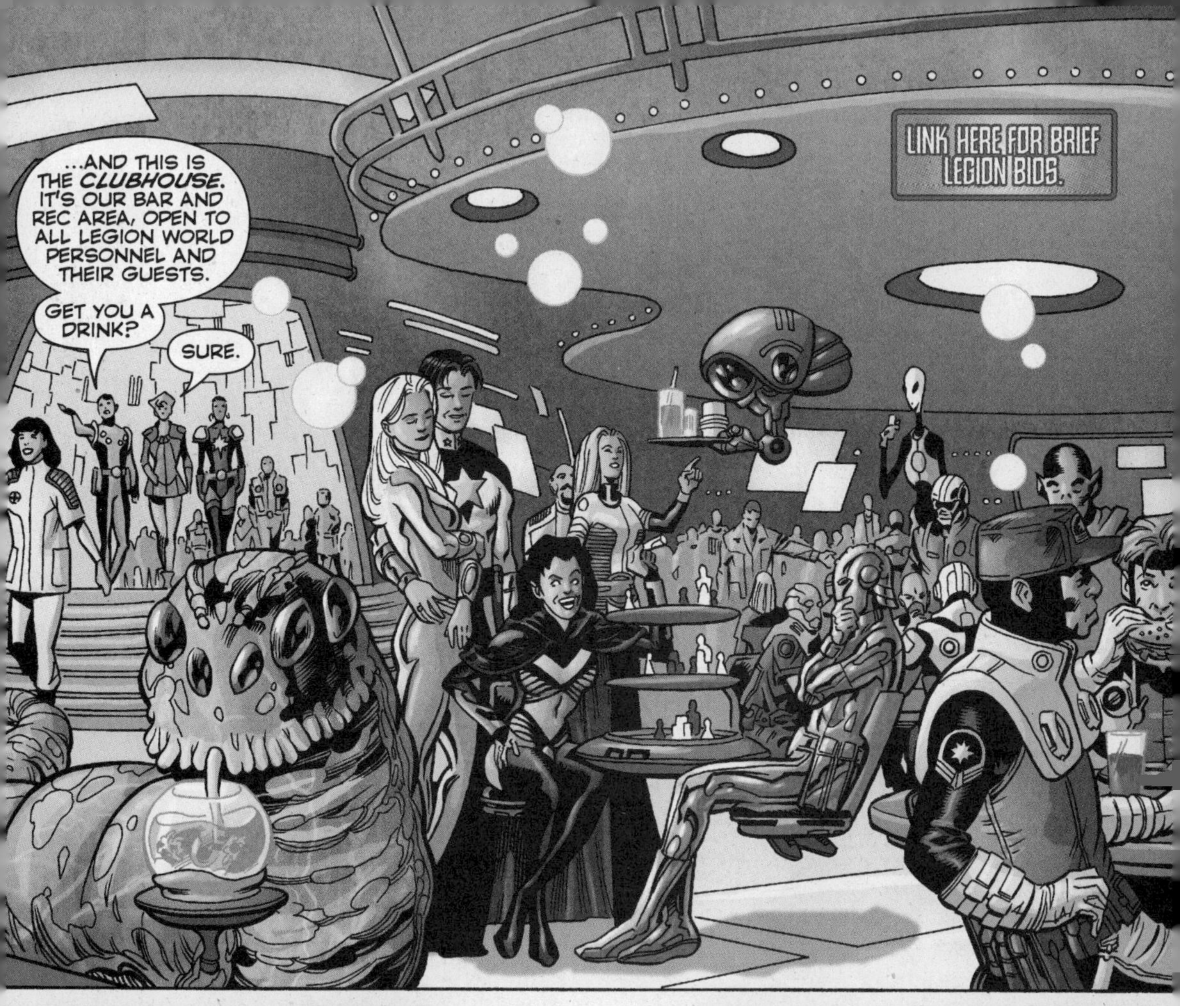

LINK HERE FOR BRIEF LEGION BIOS.
...AND THIS IS THE CLUBHOUSE. IT'S OUR BAR AND REC AREA, OPEN TO ALL LEGION WORLD PERSONNEL AND THEIR GUESTS.
GET YOU A DRINK?
SURE.

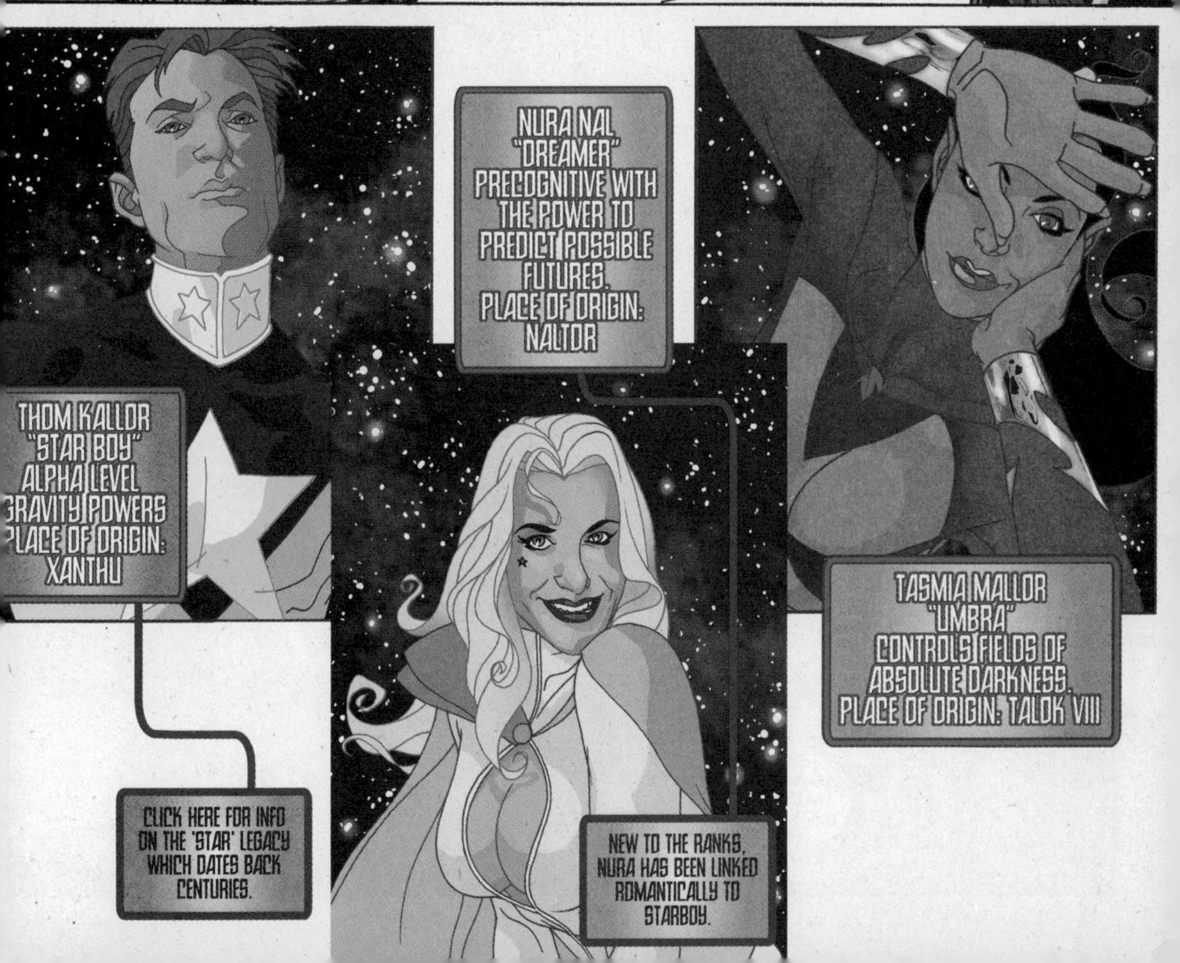

THOM KALLOR "STAR BOY" ALPHA LEVEL GRAVITY POWERS PLACE OF ORIGIN: XANTHU
CLICK HERE FOR INFO ON THE 'STAR' LEGACY WHICH DATES BACK CENTURIES.
NURA NAL "DREAMER" PRECOGNITIVE WITH THE POWER TO PREDICT POSSIBLE FUTURES. PLACE OF ORIGIN: NALTOR
NEW TO THE RANKS, NURA HAS BEEN LINKED ROMANTICALLY TO STARBOY.
TASMIA MALLOR "UMBRA" CONTROLS FIELDS OF ABSOLUTE DARKNESS. PLACE OF ORIGIN: TALOK VIII

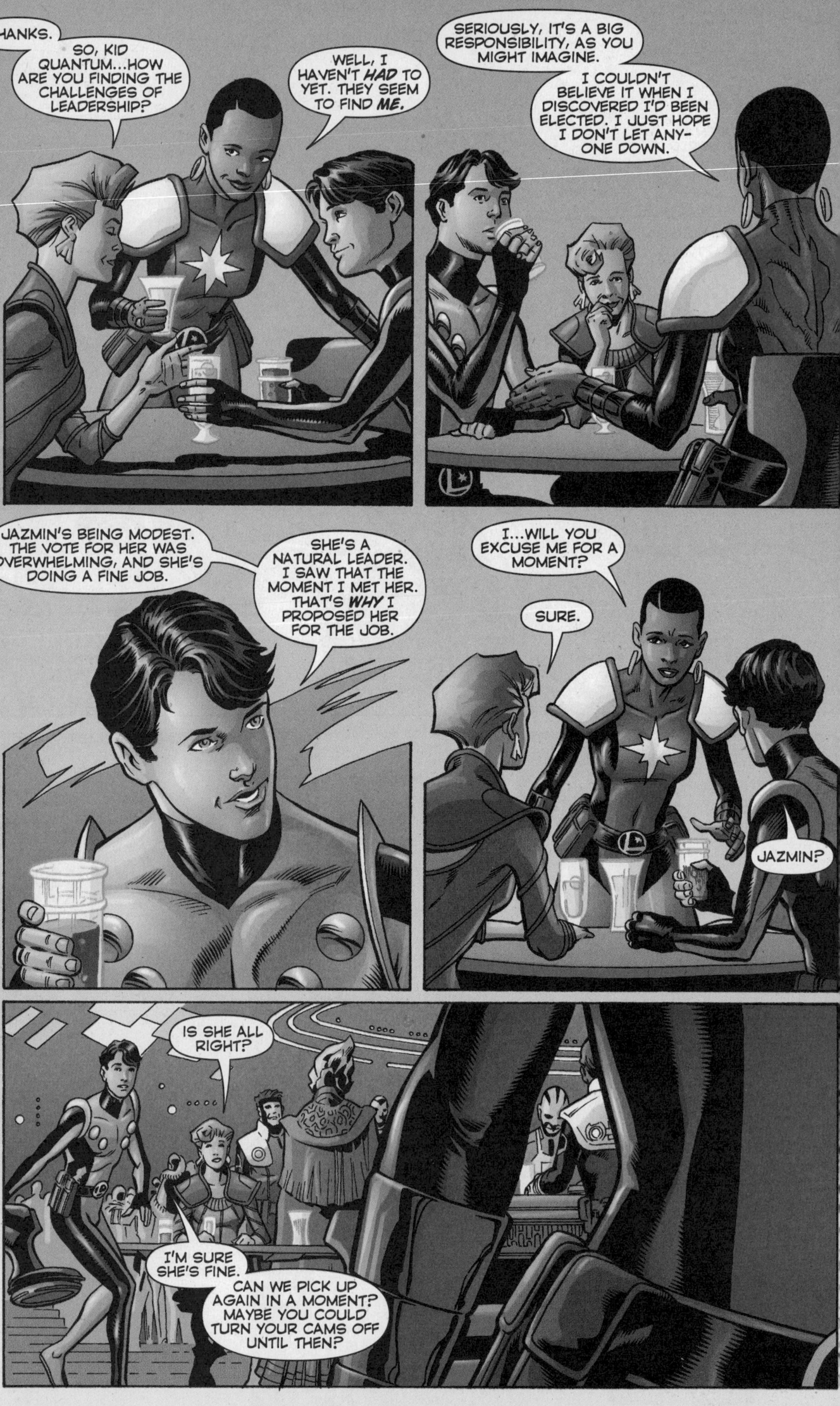
THANKS.
SO, KID QUANTUM...HOW ARE YOU FINDING THE CHALLENGES OF LEADERSHIP?
WELL, I HAVEN'T HAD TO YET. THEY SEEM TO FIND ME.
SERIOUSLY, IT'S A BIG RESPONSIBILITY, AS YOU MIGHT IMAGINE.
I COULDN'T BELIEVE IT WHEN I DISCOVERED I'D BEEN ELECTED. I JUST HOPE I DON'T LET ANYONE DOWN.
JAZMIN'S BEING MODEST. THE VOTE FOR HER WAS OVERWHELMING, AND SHE'S DOING A FINE JOB.
SHE'S A NATURAL LEADER. I SAW THAT THE MOMENT I MET HER. THAT'S WHY I PROPOSED HER FOR THE JOB.
I...WILL YOU EXCUSE ME FOR A MOMENT?
SURE.
JAZMIN?
IS SHE ALL RIGHT?
I'M SURE SHE'S FINE.
CAN WE PICK UP AGAIN IN A MOMENT? MAYBE YOU COULD TURN YOUR CAMS OFF UNTIL THEN?

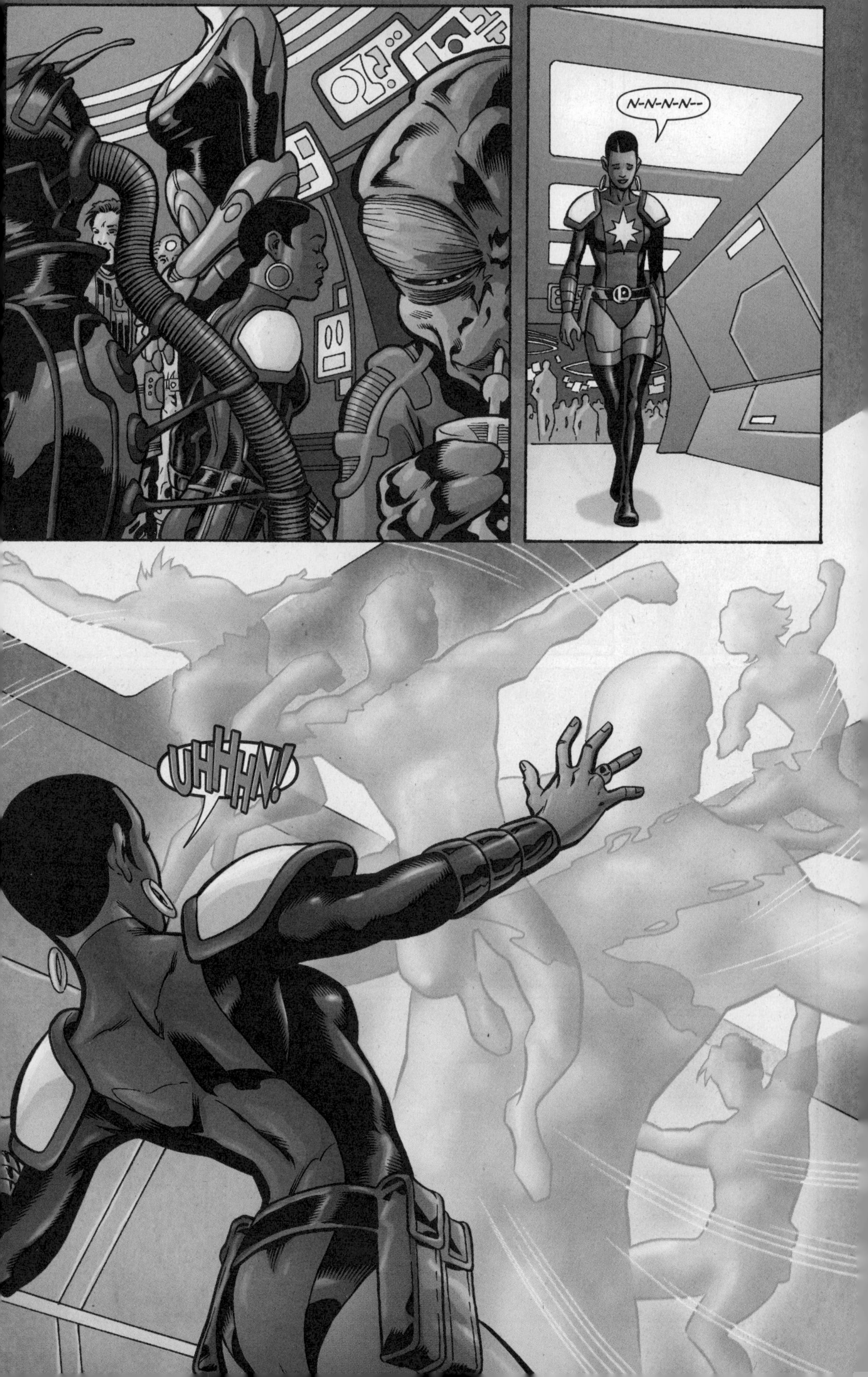
N-N-N-N-N--
UHHHN!

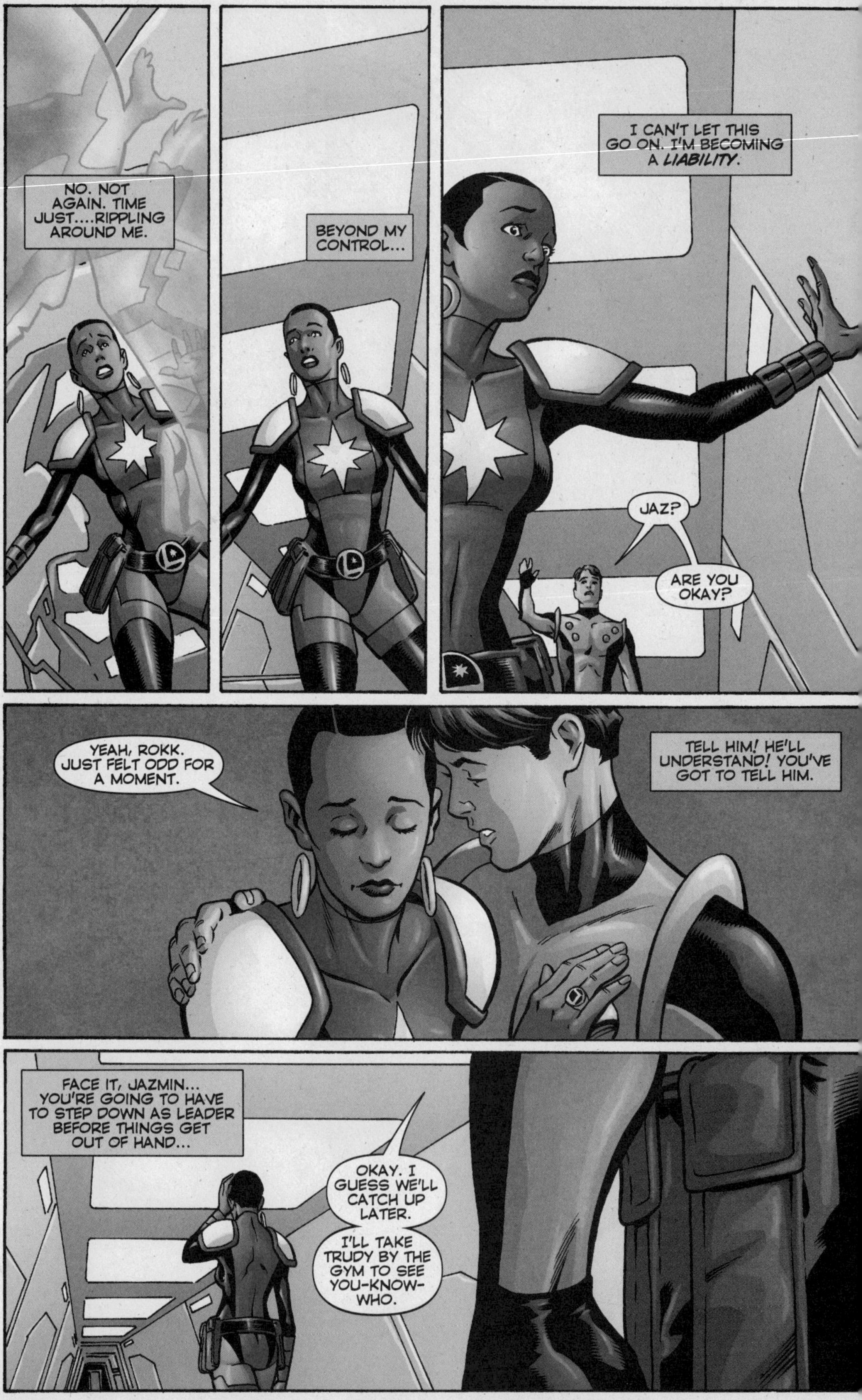
NO. NOT AGAIN. TIME JUST....RIPPLING AROUND ME.
BEYOND MY CONTROL...
I CAN'T LET THIS GO ON. I'M BECOMING A LIABILITY.
JAZ?
ARE YOU OKAY?
YEAH, ROKK. JUST FELT ODD FOR A MOMENT.
TELL HIM! HE'LL UNDERSTAND! YOU'VE GOT TO TELL HIM.
FACE IT, JAZMIN... YOU'RE GOING TO HAVE TO STEP DOWN AS LEADER BEFORE THINGS GET OUT OF HAND...
OKAY. I GUESS WE'LL CATCH UP LATER.
I'LL TAKE TRUDY BY THE GYM TO SEE YOU-KNOW-WHO.

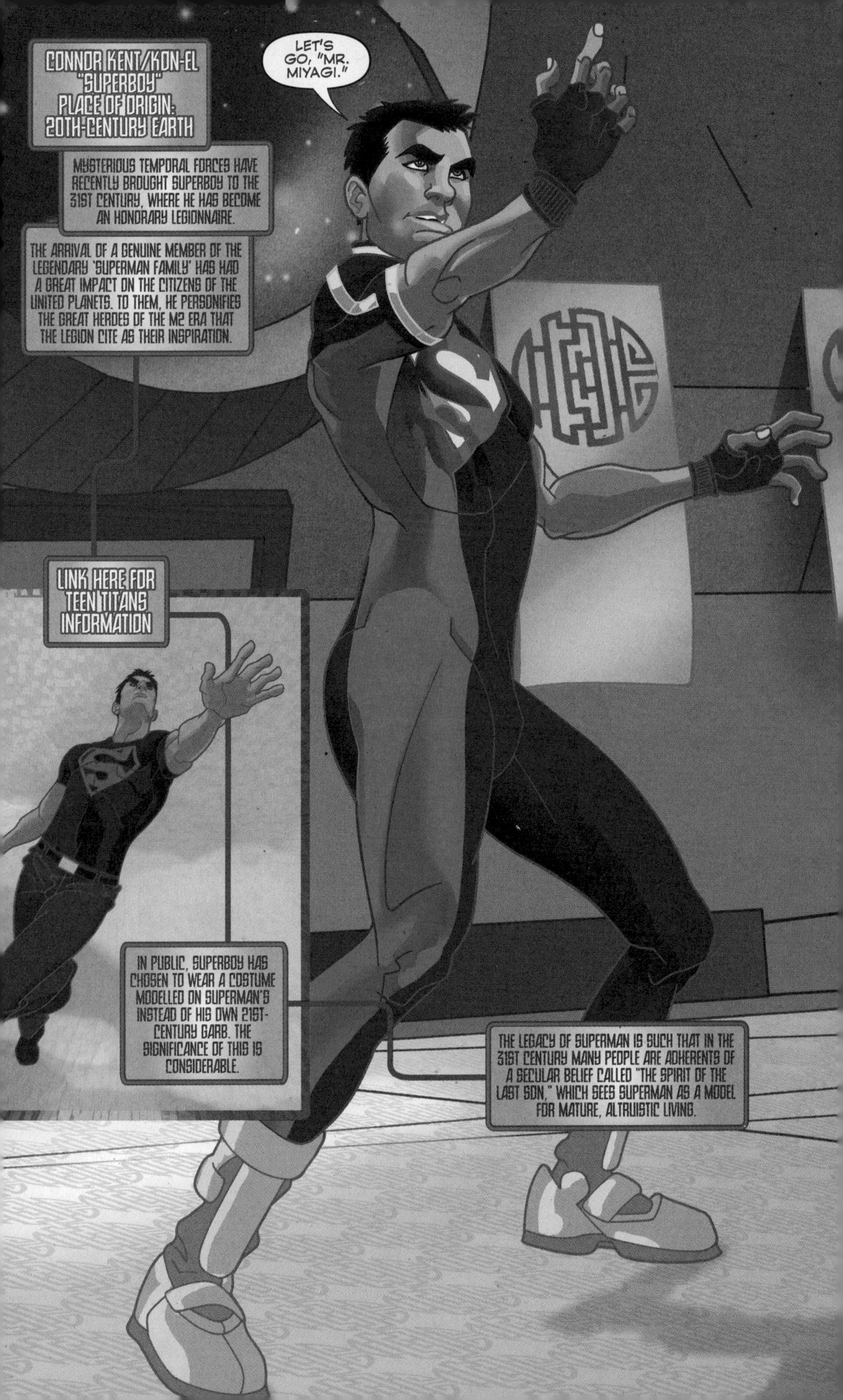
CONNOR KENT/KON-EL "SUPERBOY" PLACE OF ORIGIN: 20TH-CENTURY EARTH
LET'S GO, "MR. MIYAGI."
MYSTERIOUS TEMPORAL FORCES HAVE RECENTLY BROUGHT SUPERBOY TO THE 31ST CENTURY, WHERE HE HAS BECOME AN HONORARY LEGIONNAIRE.
THE ARRIVAL OF A GENUINE MEMBER OF THE LEGENDARY 'SUPERMAN FAMILY' HAS HAD A GREAT IMPACT ON THE CITIZENS OF THE UNITED PLANETS. TO THEM, HE PERSONIFIES THE GREAT HEROES OF THE M2 ERA THAT THE LEGION CITE AS THEIR INSPIRATION.
LINK HERE FOR TEEN TITANS INFORMATION
IN PUBLIC, SUPERBOY HAS CHOSEN TO WEAR A COSTUME MODELLED ON SUPERMAN'S INSTEAD OF HIS OWN 21ST-CENTURY GARB. THE SIGNIFICANCE OF THIS IS CONSIDERABLE.
THE LEGACY OF SUPERMAN IS SUCH THAT IN THE 31ST CENTURY MANY PEOPLE ARE ADHERENTS OF A SECULAR BELIEF CALLED "THE SPIRIT OF THE LAST SON," WHICH SEES SUPERMAN AS A MODEL FOR MATURE, ALTRUISTIC LIVING.

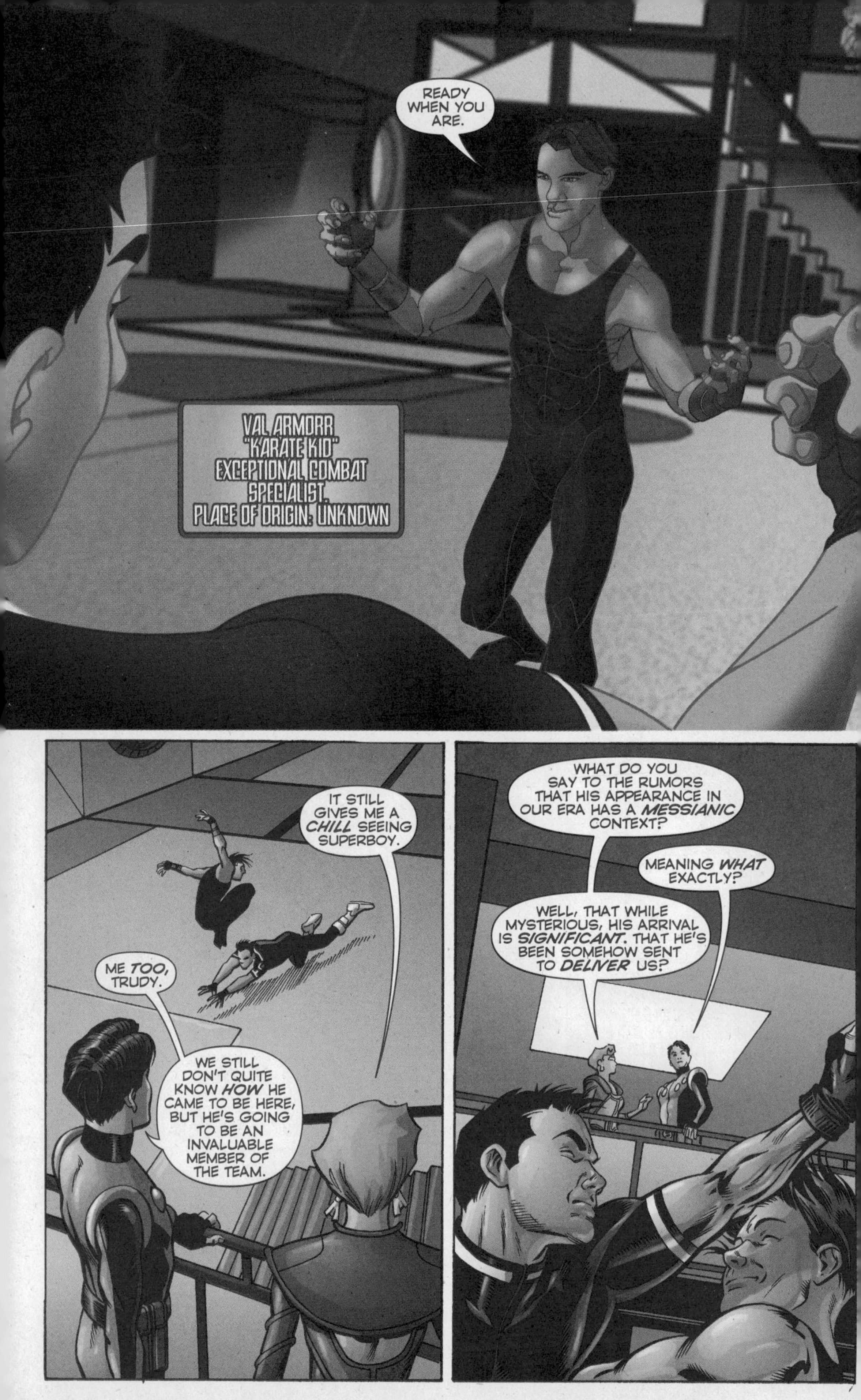
READY WHEN YOU ARE.
VAL ARMORR "KARATE KID" EXCEPTIONAL COMBAT SPECIALIST. PLACE OF ORIGIN: UNKNOWN
IT STILL GIVES ME A CHILL SEEING SUPERBOY.
ME TOO, TRUDY.
WE STILL DON'T QUITE KNOW HOW HE CAME TO BE HERE, BUT HE'S GOING TO BE AN INVALUABLE MEMBER OF THE TEAM.
WHAT DO YOU SAY TO THE RUMORS THAT HIS APPEARANCE IN OUR ERA HAS A MESSIANIC CONTEXT?
MEANING WHAT EXACTLY?
WELL, THAT WHILE MYSTERIOUS, HIS ARRIVAL IS SIGNIFICANT. THAT HE'S BEEN SOMEHOW SENT TO DELIVER US?

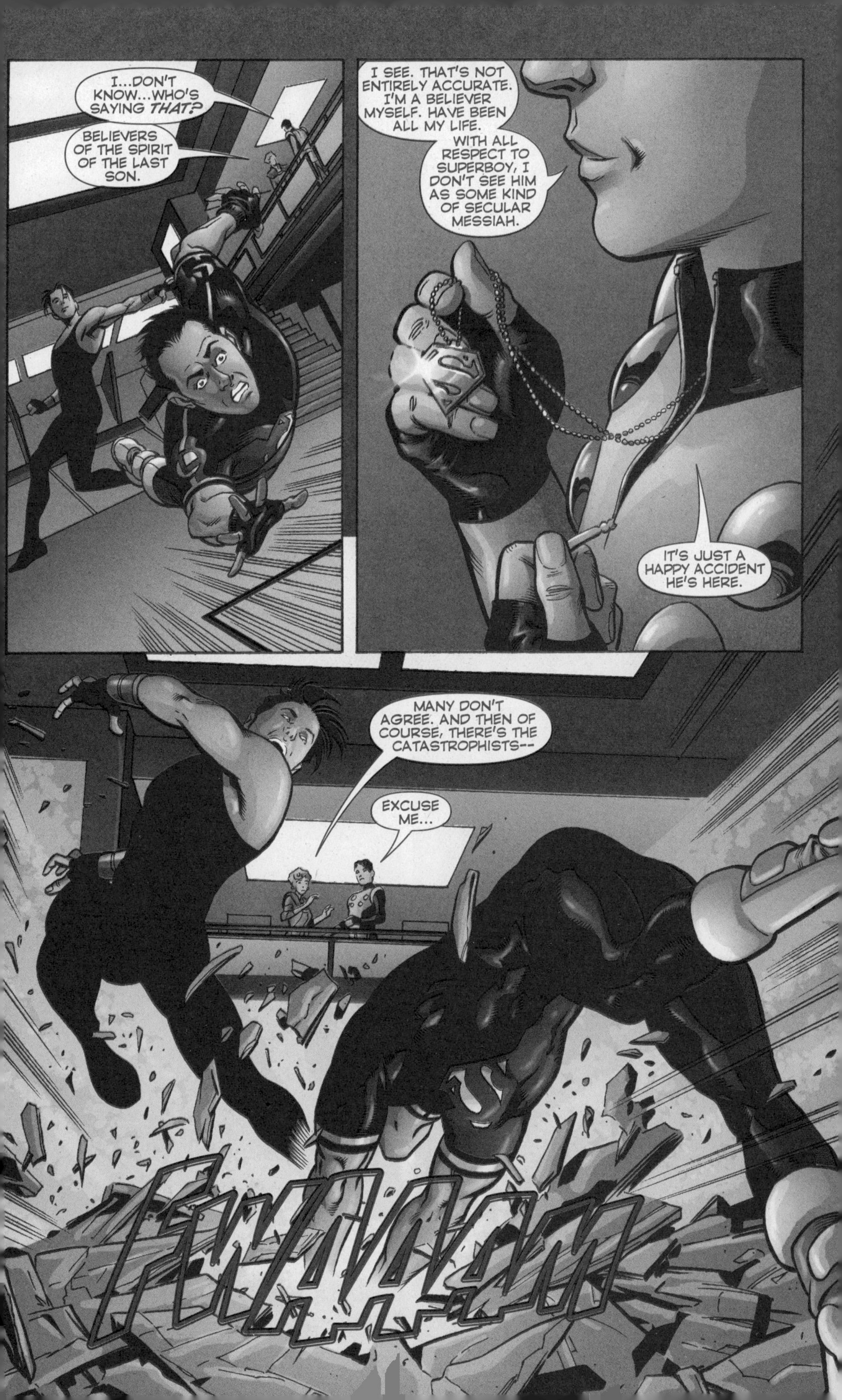

I...DON'T KNOW...WHO'S SAYING *THAT?*
BELIEVERS OF THE SPIRIT OF THE LAST SON.
I SEE. THAT'S NOT ENTIRELY ACCURATE. I'M A BELIEVER MYSELF. HAVE BEEN ALL MY LIFE.
WITH ALL RESPECT TO SUPERBOY, I DON'T SEE HIM AS SOME KIND OF SECULAR MESSIAH.
IT'S JUST A HAPPY ACCIDENT HE'S HERE.
MANY DON'T AGREE. AND THEN OF COURSE, THERE'S THE CATASTROPHISTS--
EXCUSE ME...

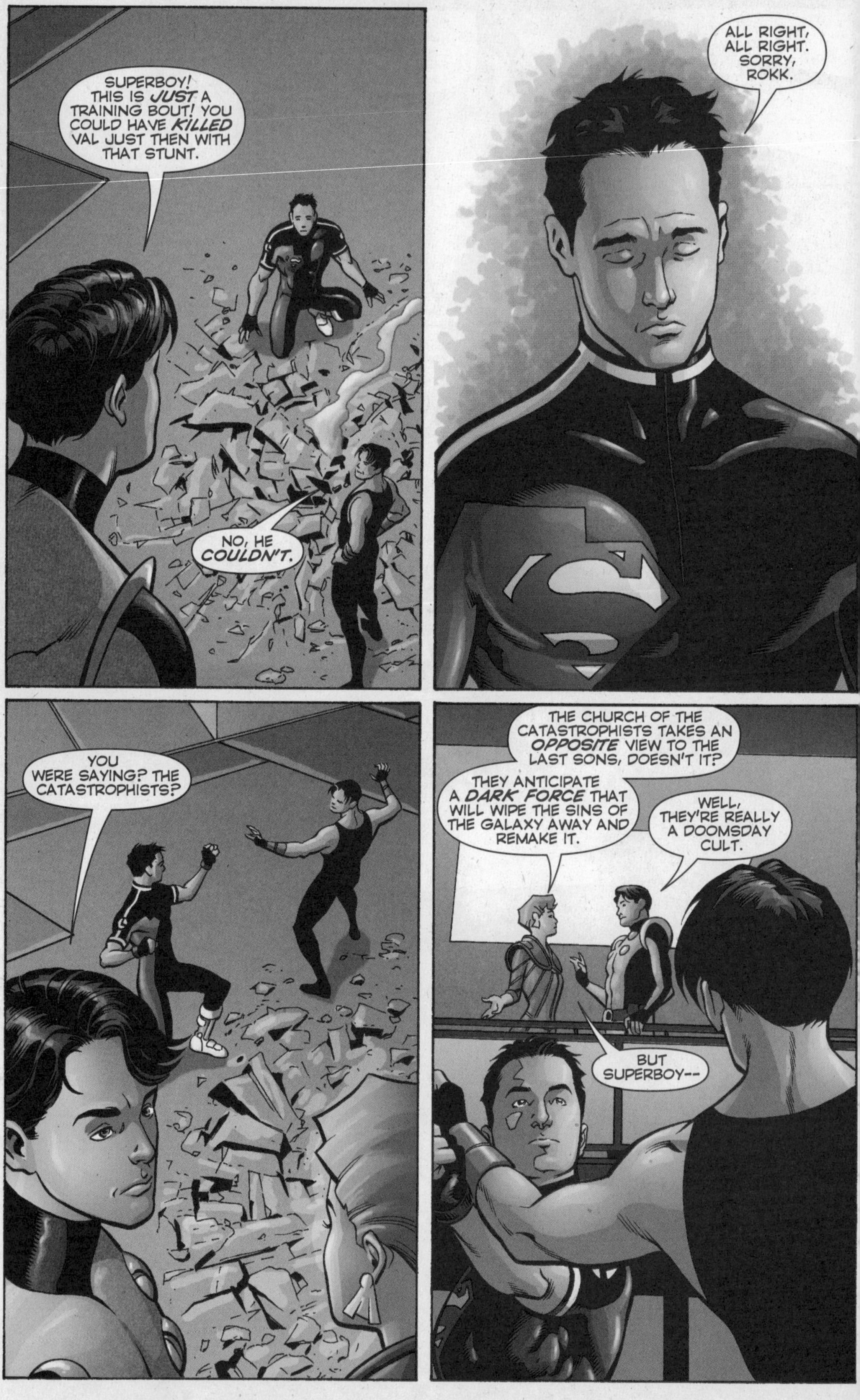
SUPERBOY! THIS IS JUST A TRAINING BOUT! YOU COULD HAVE KILLED VAL JUST THEN WITH THAT STUNT.
NO, HE COULDN'T.
ALL RIGHT, ALL RIGHT. SORRY, ROKK.
YOU WERE SAYING? THE CATASTROPHISTS?
THE CHURCH OF THE CATASTROPHISTS TAKES AN OPPOSITE VIEW TO THE LAST SONS, DOESN'T IT?
THEY ANTICIPATE A DARK FORCE THAT WILL WIPE THE SINS OF THE GALAXY AWAY AND REMAKE IT.
WELL, THEY'RE REALLY A DOOMSDAY CULT.
BUT SUPERBOY--

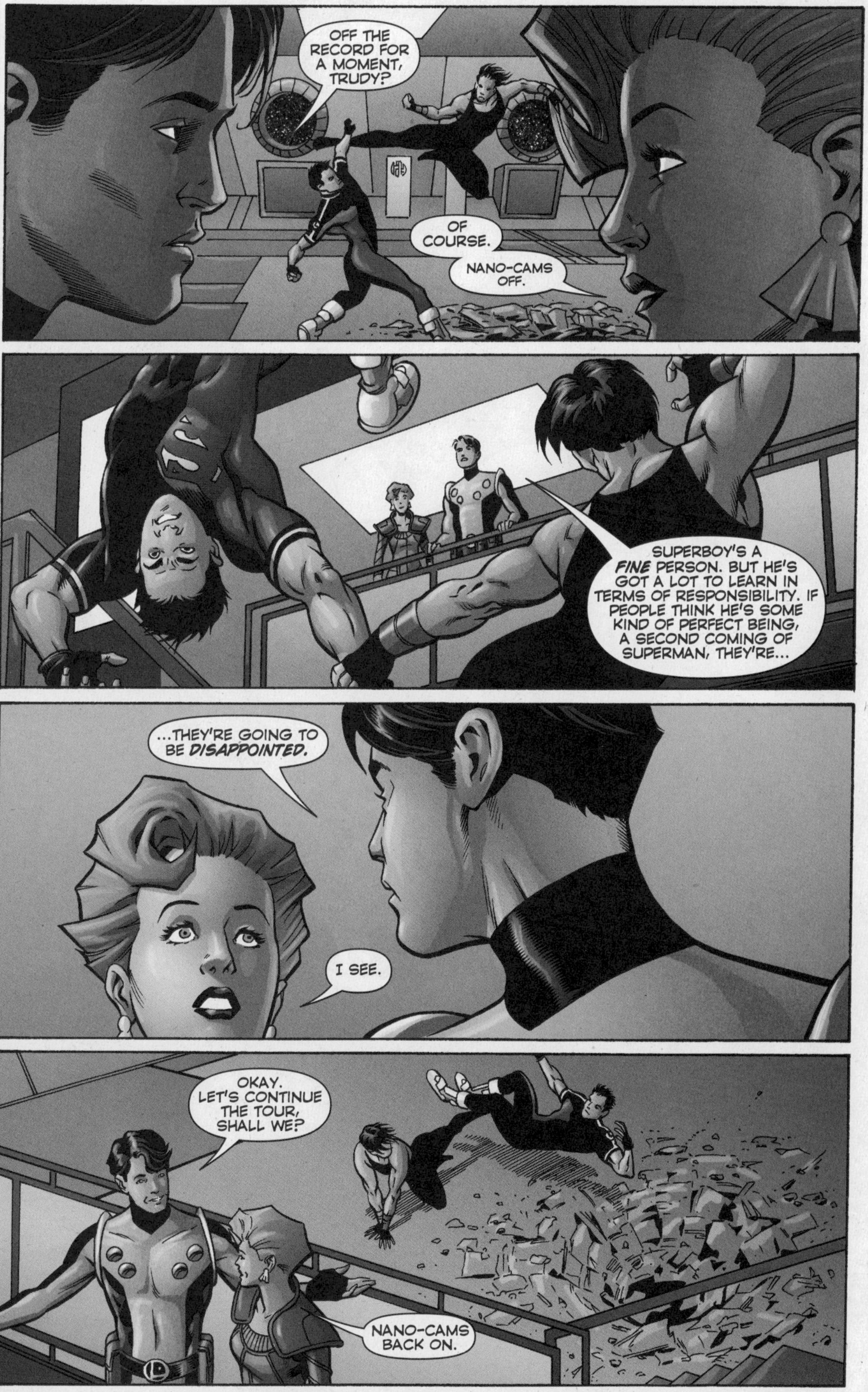
OFF THE RECORD FOR A MOMENT, TRUDY?
OF COURSE.
NANO-CAMS OFF.
SUPERBOY'S A *FINE* PERSON. BUT HE'S GOT A LOT TO LEARN IN TERMS OF RESPONSIBILITY. IF PEOPLE THINK HE'S SOME KIND OF PERFECT BEING, A SECOND COMING OF SUPERMAN, THEY'RE...
...THEY'RE GOING TO BE *DISAPPOINTED.*
I SEE.
OKAY. LET'S CONTINUE THE TOUR, SHALL WE?
NANO-CAMS BACK ON.

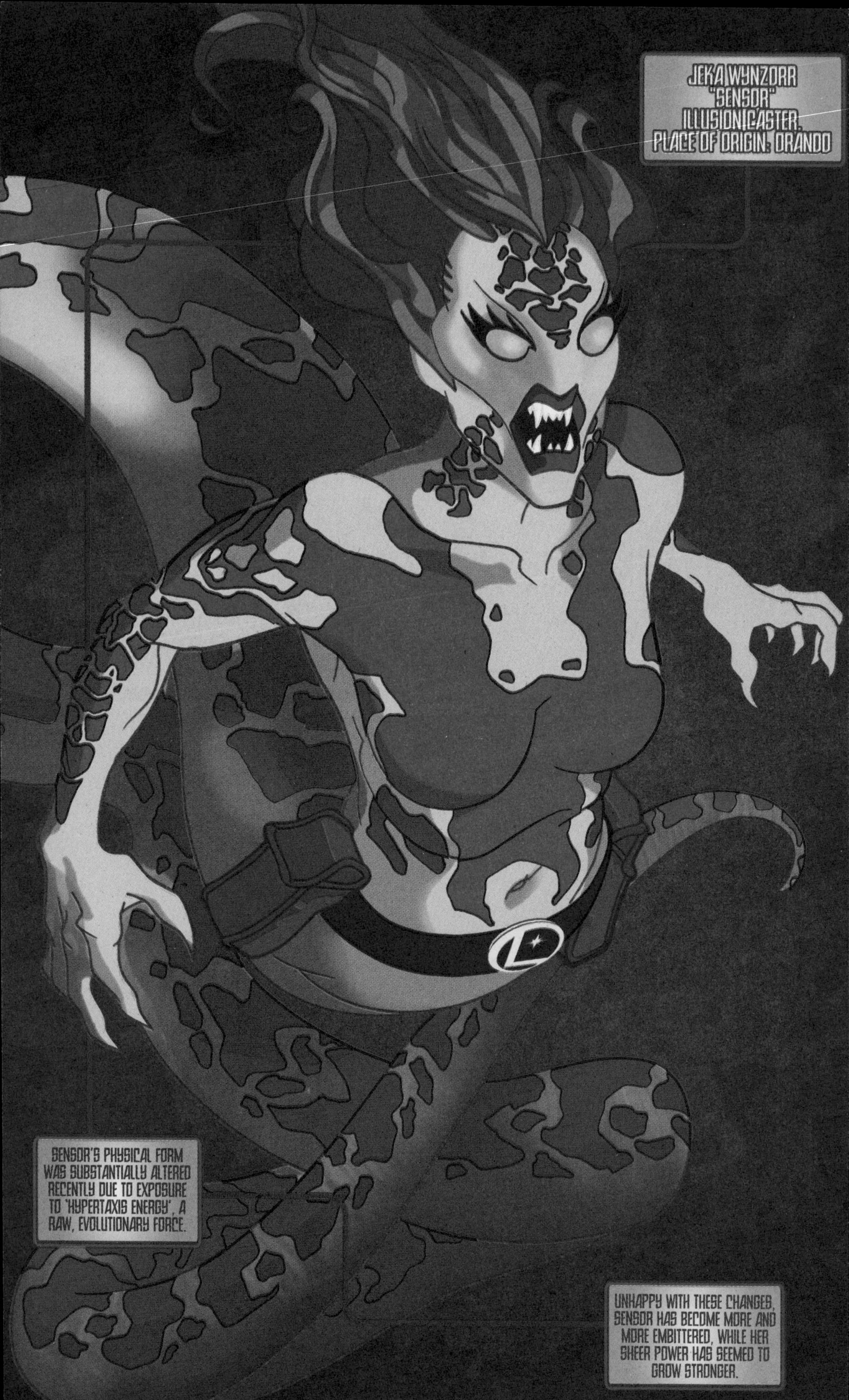
JEKA WYNZORR
"SENSOR"
ILLUSIONCASTER.
PLACE OF ORIGIN: ORANDO
SENSOR'S PHYSICAL FORM WAS SUBSTANTIALLY ALTERED RECENTLY DUE TO EXPOSURE TO "HYPERTAXIS ENERGY", A RAW, EVOLUTIONARY FORCE.
UNHAPPY WITH THESE CHANGES, SENSOR HAS BECOME MORE AND MORE EMBITTERED, WHILE HER SHEER POWER HAS SEEMED TO GROW STRONGER.

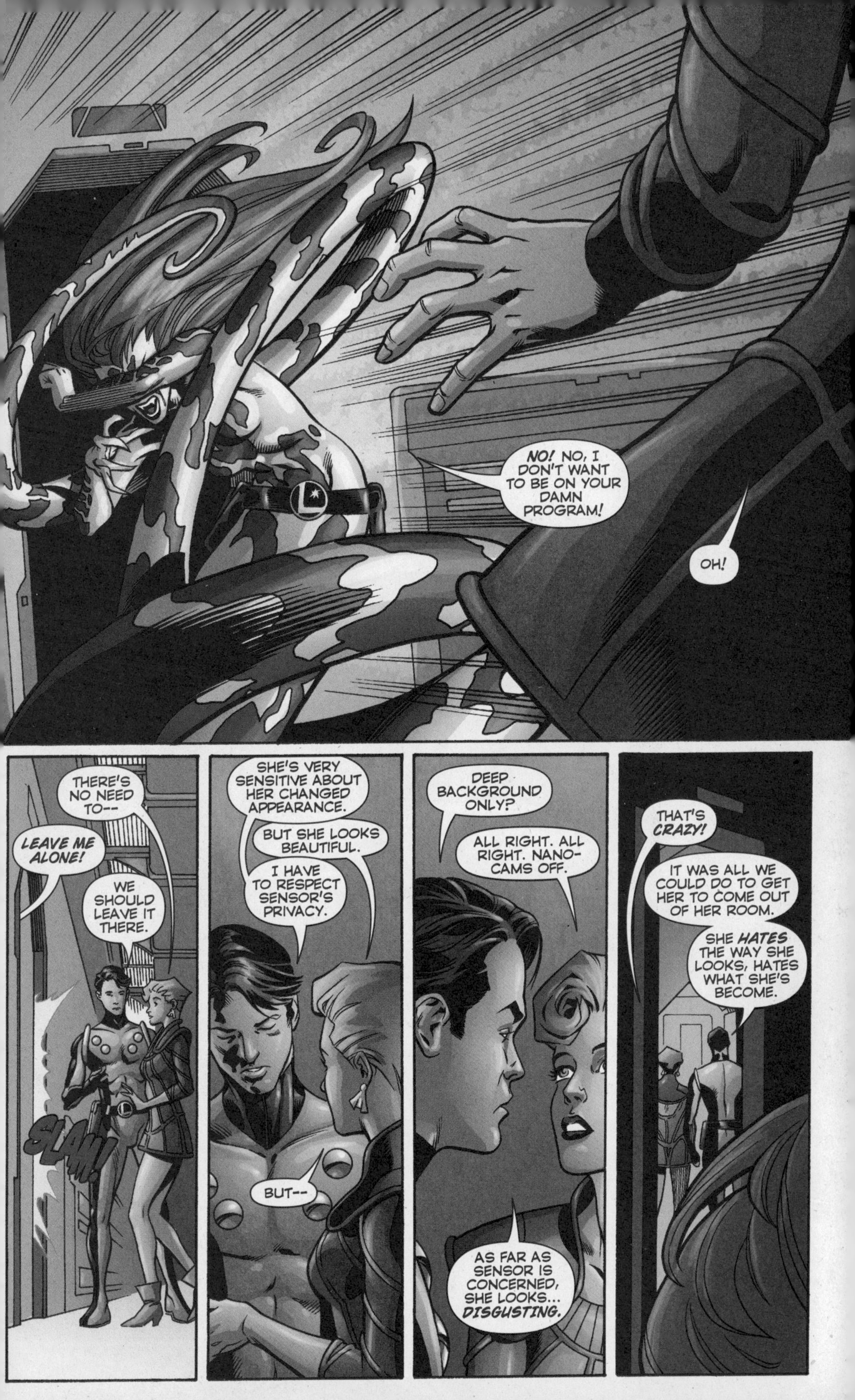
NO! NO, I DON'T WANT TO BE ON YOUR DAMN PROGRAM!
OH!
THERE'S NO NEED TO--
LEAVE ME ALONE!
WE SHOULD LEAVE IT THERE.
SLAM!
SHE'S VERY SENSITIVE ABOUT HER CHANGED APPEARANCE.
BUT SHE LOOKS BEAUTIFUL.
I HAVE TO RESPECT SENSOR'S PRIVACY.
BUT--
DEEP BACKGROUND ONLY?
ALL RIGHT. ALL RIGHT. NANO-CAMS OFF.
AS FAR AS SENSOR IS CONCERNED, SHE LOOKS... DISGUSTING.
THAT'S CRAZY!
IT WAS ALL WE COULD DO TO GET HER TO COME OUT OF HER ROOM.
SHE HATES THE WAY SHE LOOKS, HATES WHAT SHE'S BECOME.

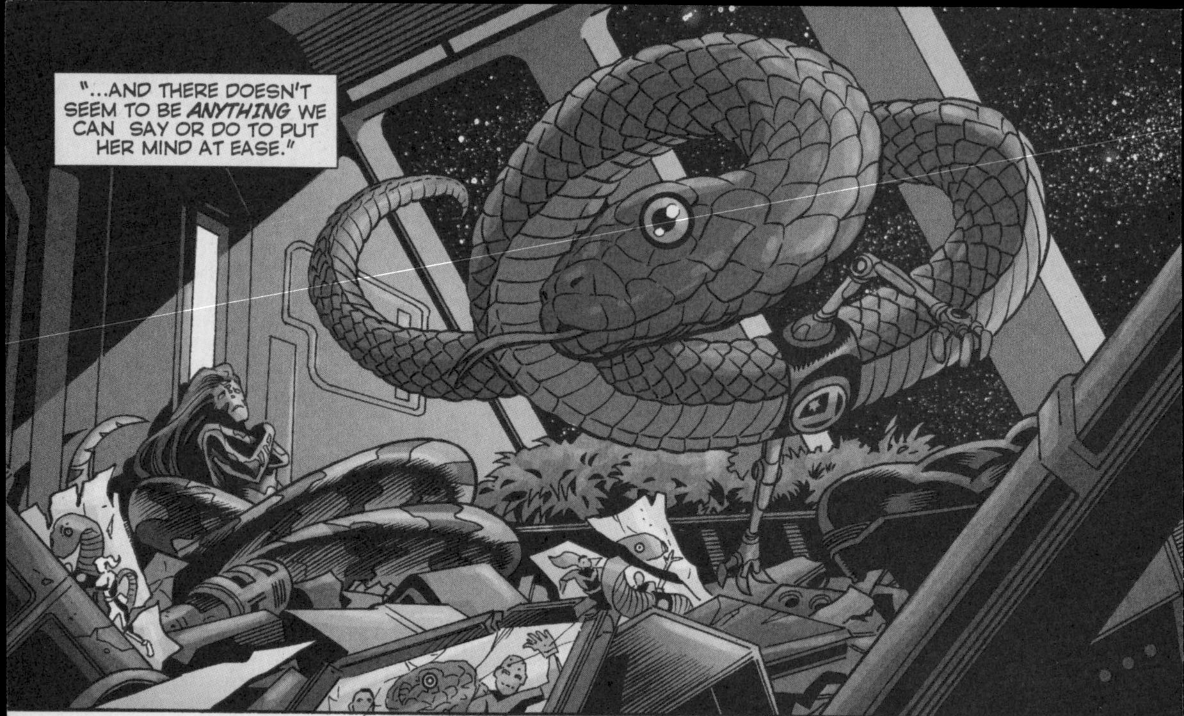
"...AND THERE DOESN'T SEEM TO BE ANYTHING WE CAN SAY OR DO TO PUT HER MIND AT EASE."

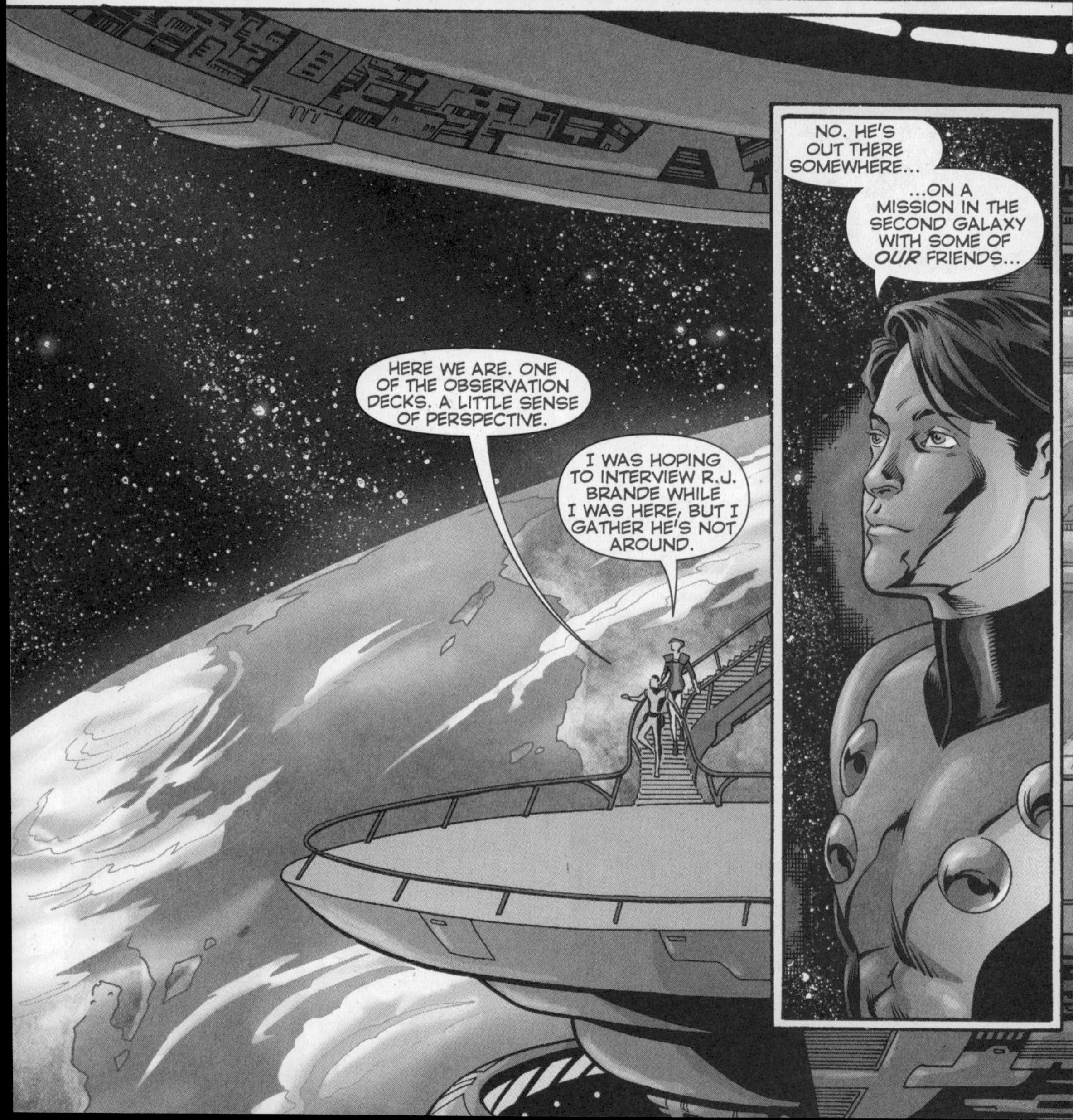
HERE WE ARE. ONE OF THE OBSERVATION DECKS. A LITTLE SENSE OF PERSPECTIVE.
I WAS HOPING TO INTERVIEW R.J. BRANDE WHILE I WAS HERE, BUT I GATHER HE'S NOT AROUND.
NO. HE'S OUT THERE SOMEWHERE...
...ON A MISSION IN THE SECOND GALAXY WITH SOME OF OUR FRIENDS...

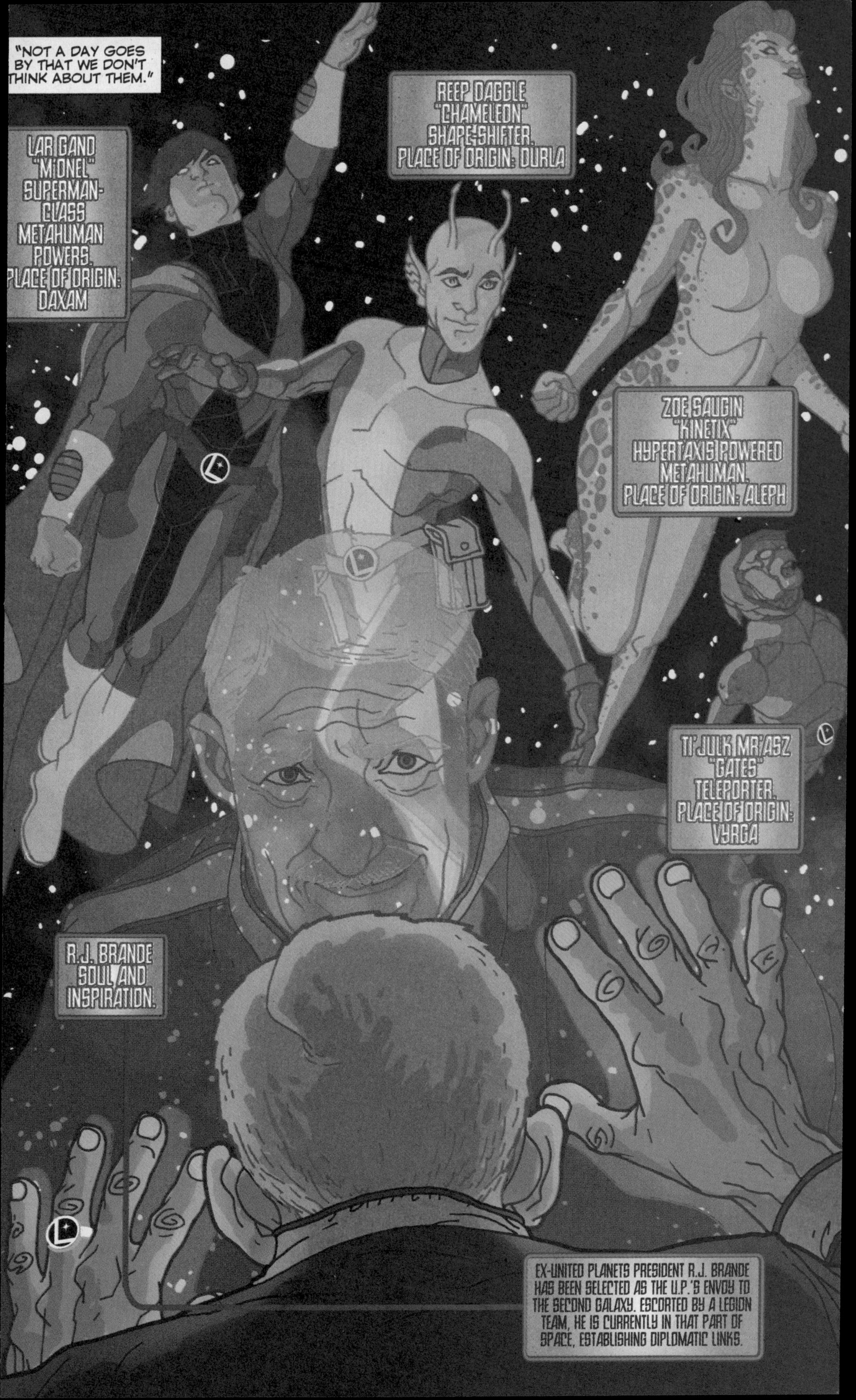
"NOT A DAY GOES BY THAT WE DON'T THINK ABOUT THEM."
LAR GAND "M'ONEL" SUPERMAN-CLASS METAHUMAN POWERS. PLACE OF ORIGIN: DAXAM
REEP DAGGLE "CHAMELEON" SHAPE-SHIFTER. PLACE OF ORIGIN: DURLA
ZOE SAUGIN "KINETIX" HYPERTAXIS POWERED METAHUMAN. PLACE OF ORIGIN: ALEPH
TI'JULK MR'ASZ "GATES" TELEPORTER. PLACE OF ORIGIN: VYRGA
R.J. BRANDE SOUL AND INSPIRATION.
EX-UNITED PLANETS PRESIDENT R.J. BRANDE HAS BEEN SELECTED AS THE U.P.'S ENVOY TO THE SECOND GALAXY. ESCORTED BY A LEGION TEAM, HE IS CURRENTLY IN THAT PART OF SPACE, ESTABLISHING DIPLOMATIC LINKS.

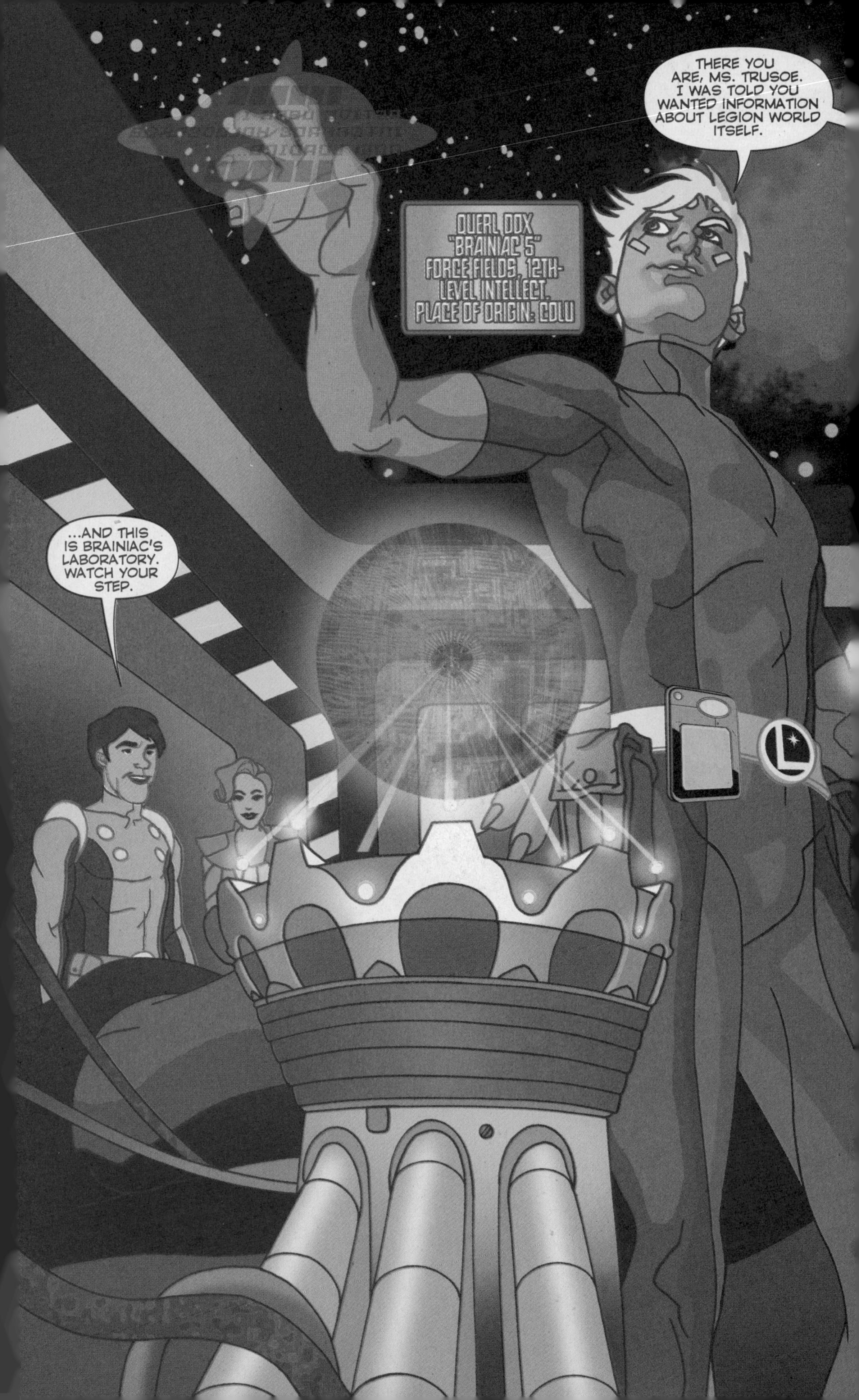
THERE YOU ARE, MS. TRUSOE. I WAS TOLD YOU WANTED INFORMATION ABOUT LEGION WORLD ITSELF.
QUERL DOX "BRAINIAC 5" FORCE FIELDS, 12TH-LEVEL INTELLECT. PLACE OF ORIGIN: COLU
...AND THIS IS BRAINIAC'S LABORATORY. WATCH YOUR STEP.

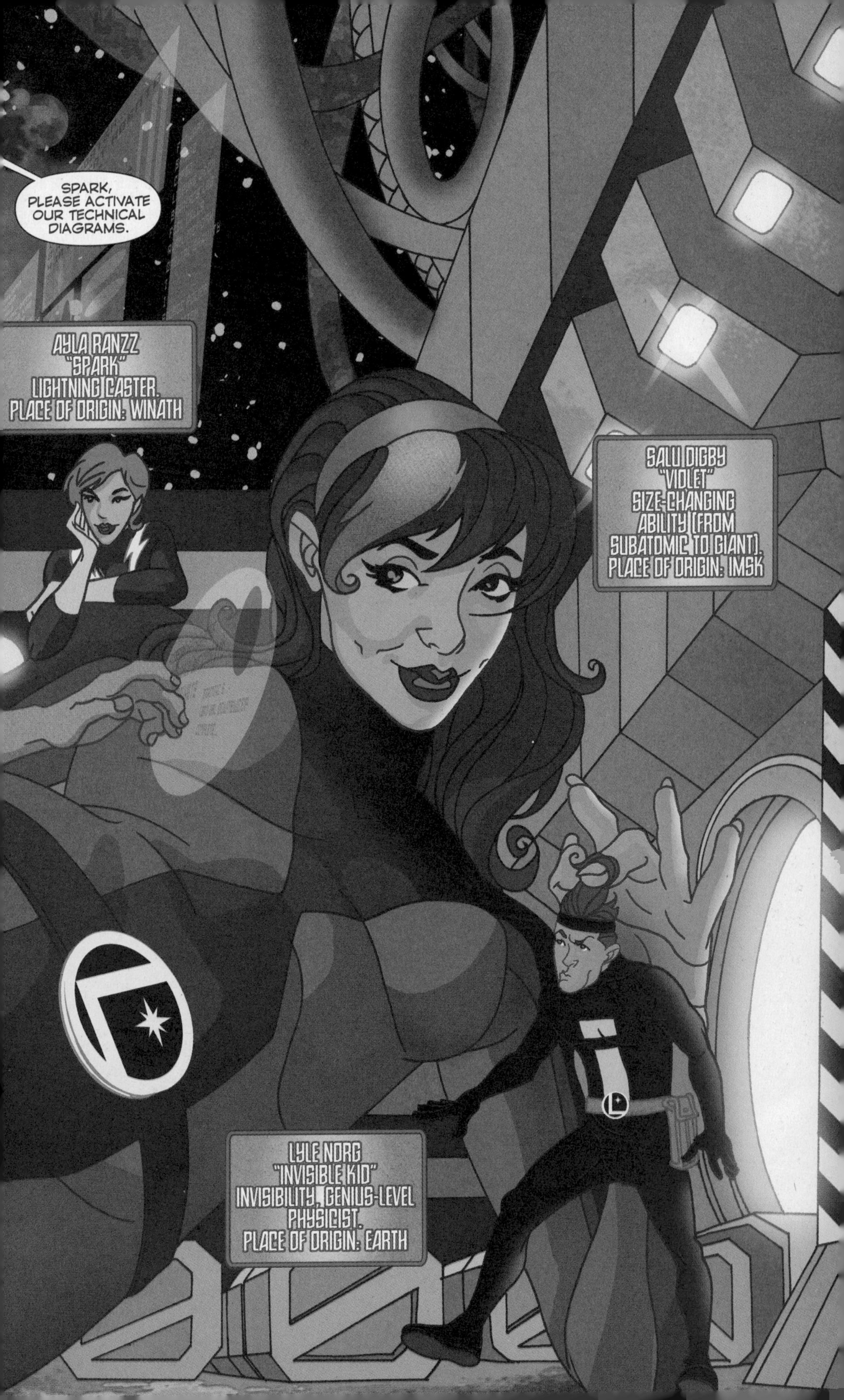
SPARK, PLEASE ACTIVATE OUR TECHNICAL DIAGRAMS.
AYLA RANZZ "SPARK" LIGHTNING CASTER. PLACE OF ORIGIN: WINATH
SALU DIGBY "VIOLET" SIZE-CHANGING ABILITY (FROM SUBATOMIC TO GIANT). PLACE OF ORIGIN: IMSK
LYLE NORG "INVISIBLE KID" INVISIBILITY, GENIUS-LEVEL PHYSICIST. PLACE OF ORIGIN: EARTH

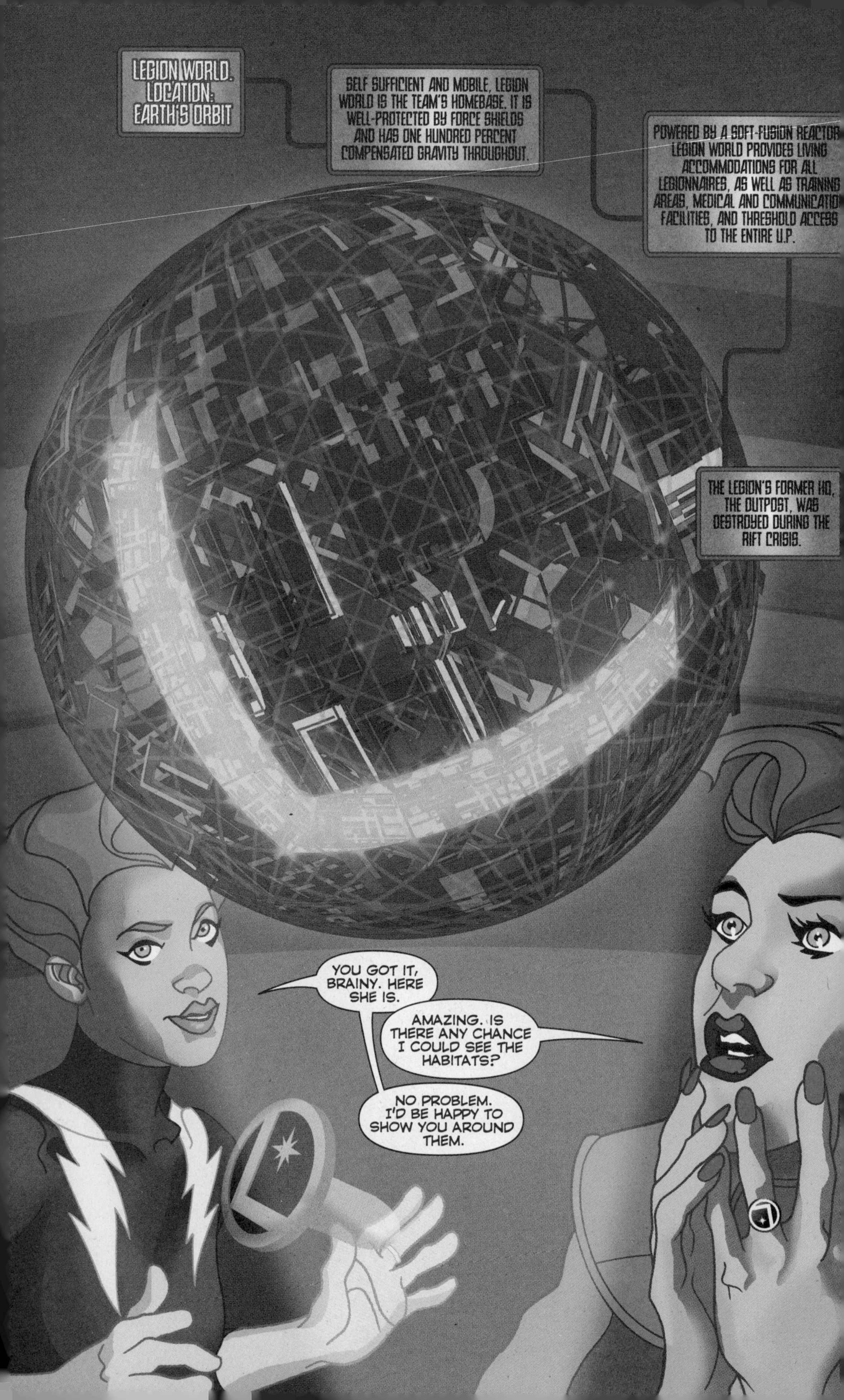
LEGION WORLD. LOCATION: EARTH'S ORBIT
SELF SUFFICIENT AND MOBILE, LEGION WORLD IS THE TEAM'S HOMEBASE. IT IS WELL-PROTECTED BY FORCE SHIELDS AND HAS ONE HUNDRED PERCENT COMPENSATED GRAVITY THROUGHOUT.
POWERED BY A SOFT-FUSION REACTOR LEGION WORLD PROVIDES LIVING ACCOMMODATIONS FOR ALL LEGIONNAIRES, AS WELL AS TRAINING AREAS, MEDICAL AND COMMUNICATIO FACILITIES, AND THRESHOLD ACCESS TO THE ENTIRE U.P.
THE LEGION'S FORMER HQ, THE OUTPOST, WAS DESTROYED DURING THE RIFT CRISIS.
YOU GOT IT, BRAINY. HERE SHE IS.
AMAZING. IS THERE ANY CHANCE I COULD SEE THE HABITATS?
NO PROBLEM. I'D BE HAPPY TO SHOW YOU AROUND THEM.

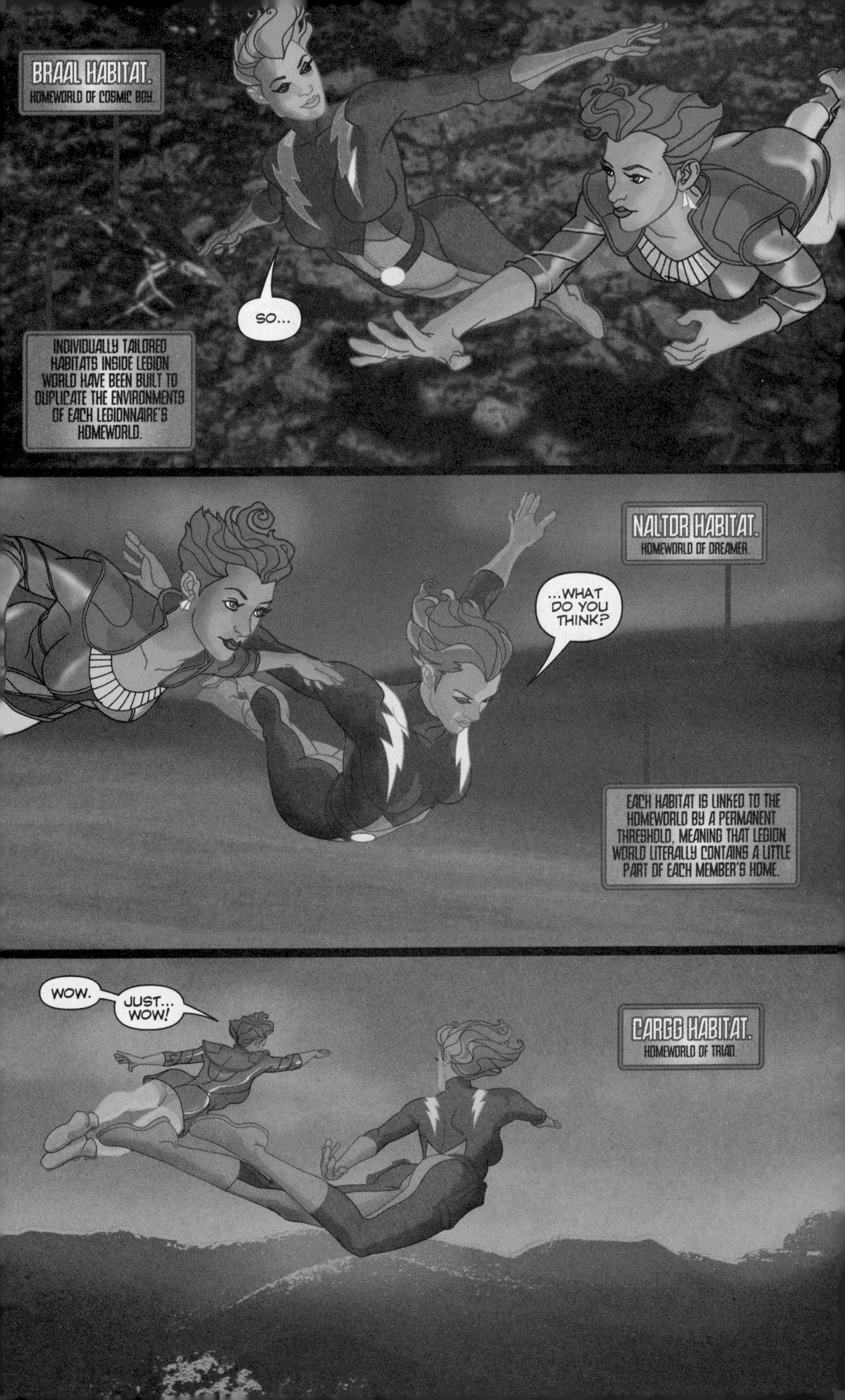
BRAAL HABITAT.
HOMEWORLD OF COSMIC BOY.
SO...
INDIVIDUALLY TAILORED HABITATS INSIDE LEGION WORLD HAVE BEEN BUILT TO DUPLICATE THE ENVIRONMENTS OF EACH LEGIONNAIRE'S HOMEWORLD.
NALTOR HABITAT.
HOMEWORLD OF DREAMER.
...WHAT DO YOU THINK?
EACH HABITAT IS LINKED TO THE HOMEWORLD BY A PERMANENT THRESHOLD, MEANING THAT LEGION WORLD LITERALLY CONTAINS A LITTLE PART OF EACH MEMBER'S HOME.
WOW.
JUST... WOW!
CARGG HABITAT.
HOMEWORLD OF TRIAD.

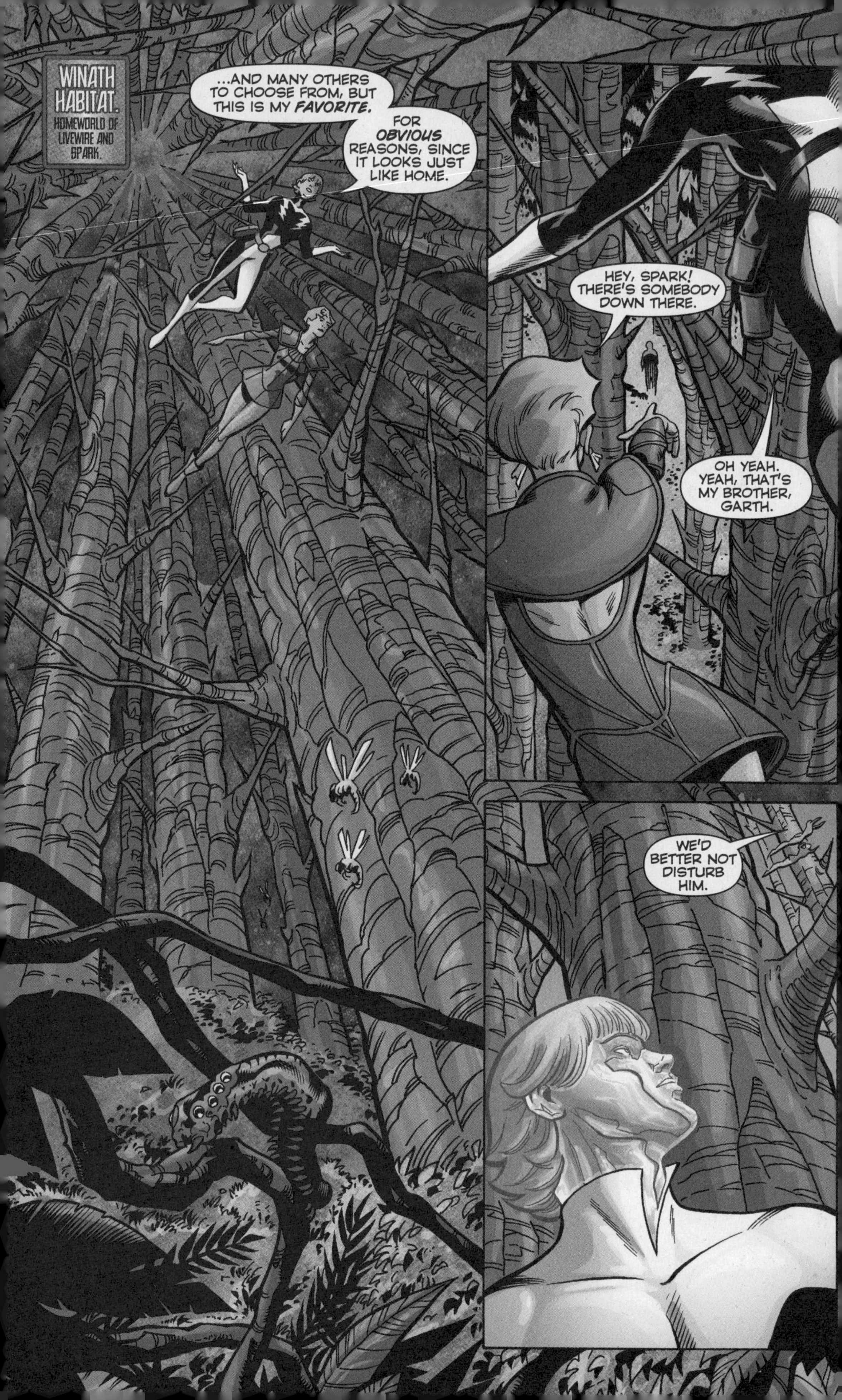
WINATH HABITAT.
HOMEWORLD OF LIVEWIRE AND SPARK.
...AND MANY OTHERS TO CHOOSE FROM, BUT THIS IS MY *FAVORITE.*
FOR *OBVIOUS* REASONS, SINCE IT LOOKS JUST LIKE HOME.
HEY, SPARK! THERE'S SOMEBODY DOWN THERE.
OH YEAH. YEAH, THAT'S MY BROTHER, GARTH.
WE'D BETTER NOT DISTURB HIM.

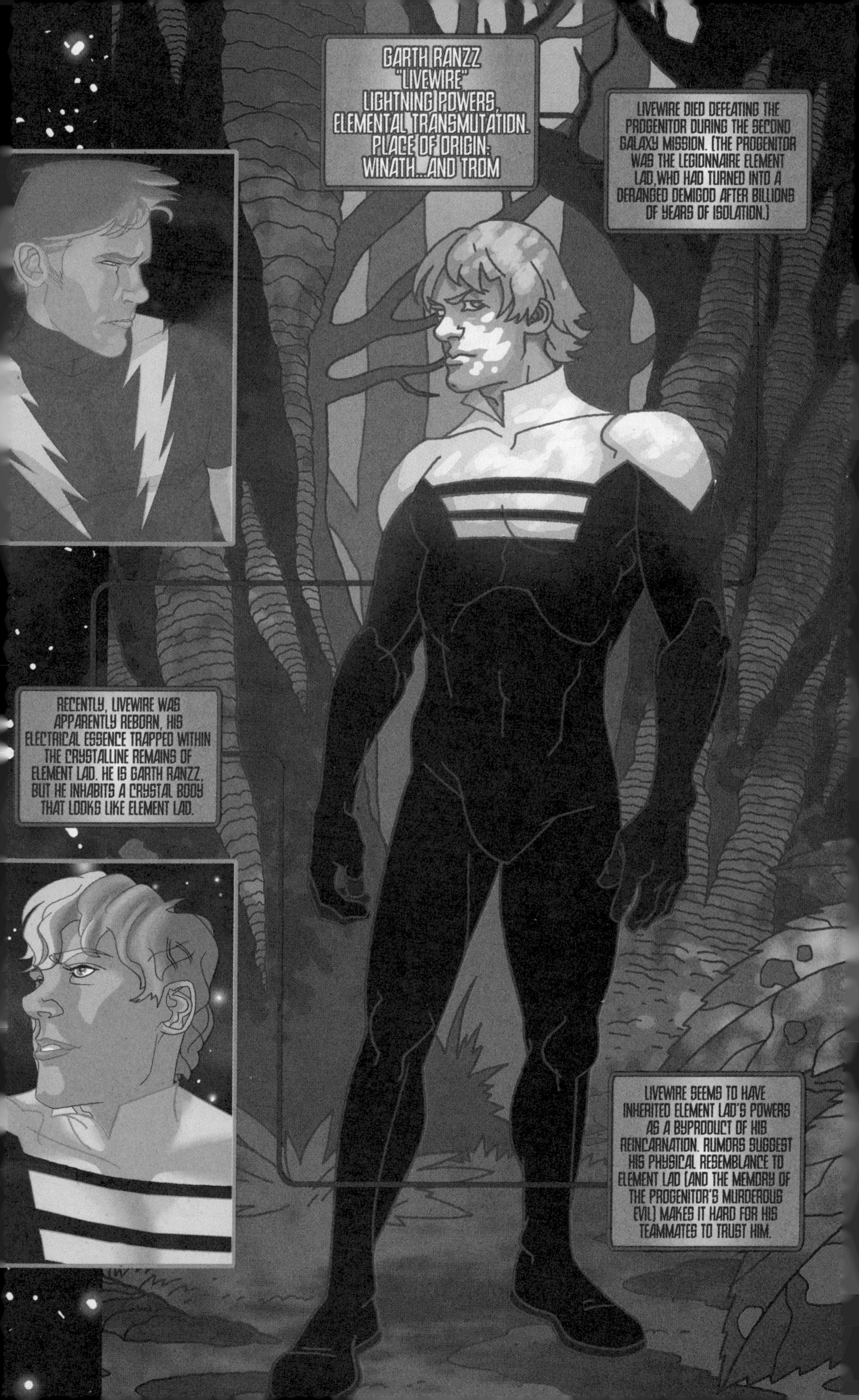
GARTH RANZZ "LIVEWIRE" LIGHTNING POWERS, ELEMENTAL TRANSMUTATION. PLACE OF ORIGIN: WINATH...AND TROM
LIVEWIRE DIED DEFEATING THE PROGENITOR DURING THE SECOND GALAXY MISSION. (THE PROGENITOR WAS THE LEGIONNAIRE ELEMENT LAD, WHO HAD TURNED INTO A DERANGED DEMIGOD AFTER BILLIONS OF YEARS OF ISOLATION.)
RECENTLY, LIVEWIRE WAS APPARENTLY REBORN, HIS ELECTRICAL ESSENCE TRAPPED WITHIN THE CRYSTALLINE REMAINS OF ELEMENT LAD. HE IS GARTH RANZZ, BUT HE INHABITS A CRYSTAL BODY THAT LOOKS LIKE ELEMENT LAD.
LIVEWIRE SEEMS TO HAVE INHERITED ELEMENT LAD'S POWERS AS A BYPRODUCT OF HIS REINCARNATION. RUMORS SUGGEST HIS PHYSICAL RESEMBLANCE TO ELEMENT LAD (AND THE MEMORY OF THE PROGENITOR'S MURDEROUS EVIL) MAKES IT HARD FOR HIS TEAMMATES TO TRUST HIM.

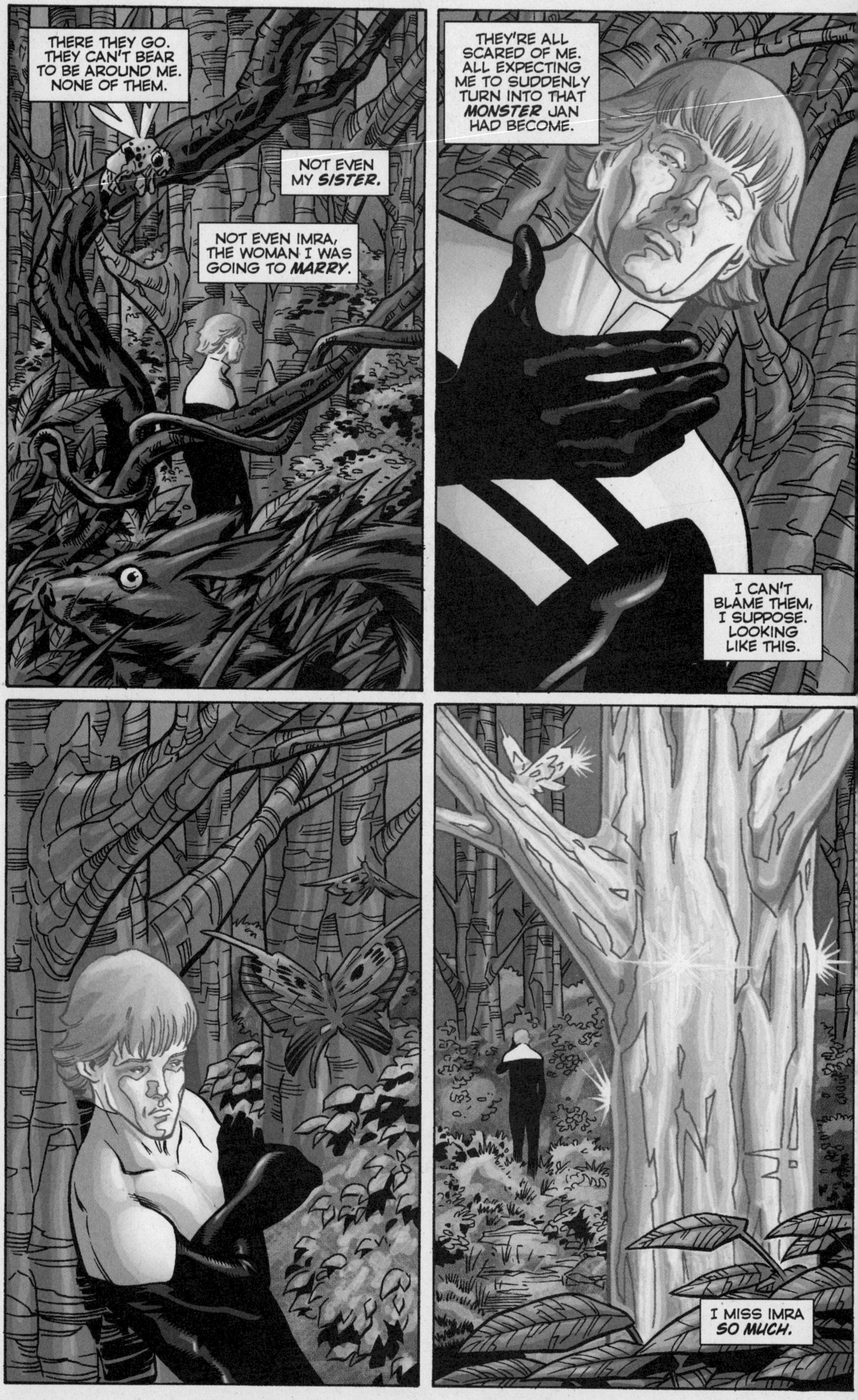
THERE THEY GO. THEY CAN'T BEAR TO BE AROUND ME. NONE OF THEM.
NOT EVEN MY *SISTER.*
NOT EVEN IMRA, THE WOMAN I WAS GOING TO *MARRY.*
THEY'RE ALL SCARED OF ME. ALL EXPECTING ME TO SUDDENLY TURN INTO THAT *MONSTER* JAN HAD BECOME.
I CAN'T BLAME THEM, I SUPPOSE. LOOKING LIKE THIS.
I MISS IMRA *SO MUCH.*

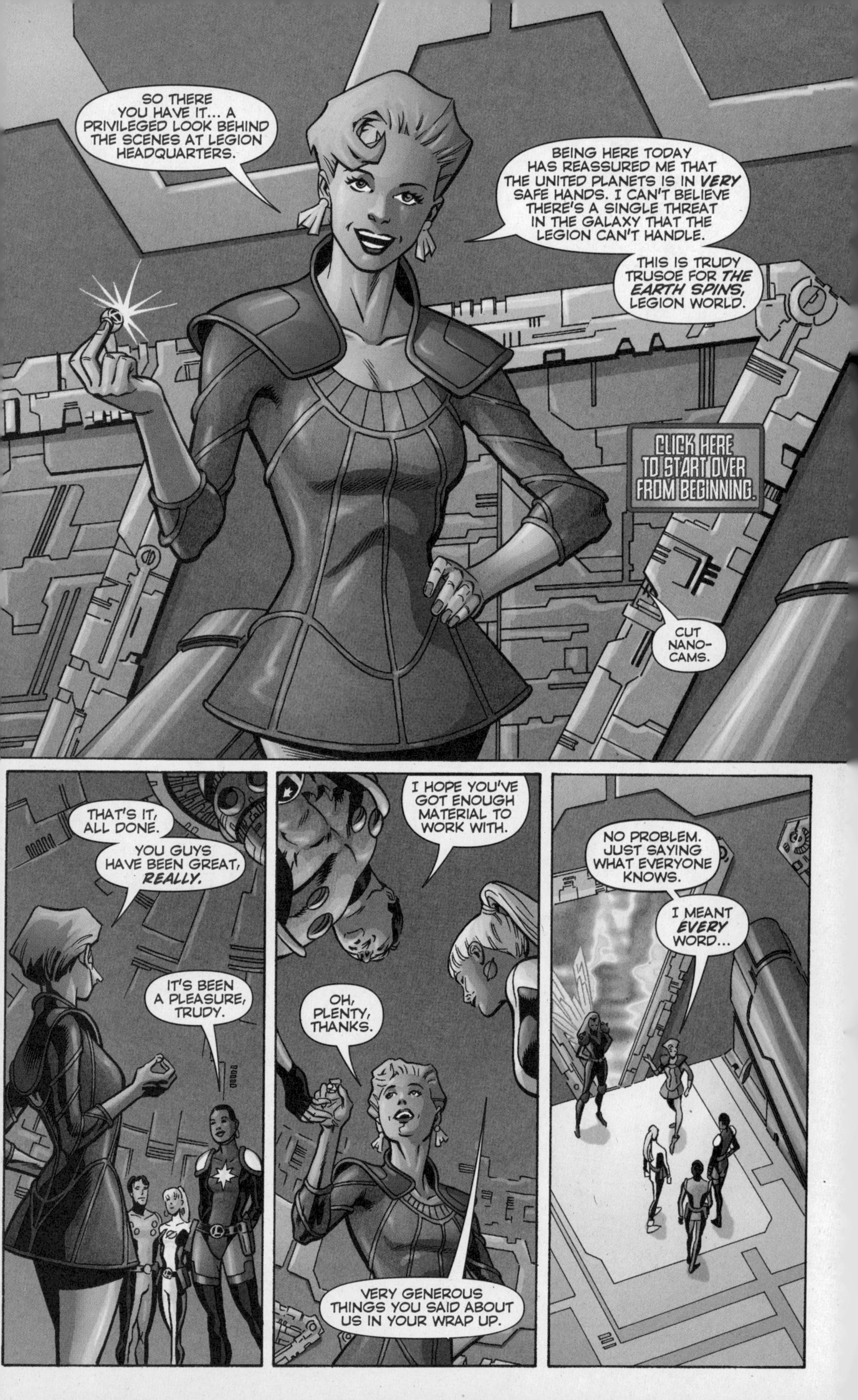

SO THERE YOU HAVE IT... A PRIVILEGED LOOK BEHIND THE SCENES AT LEGION HEADQUARTERS.
BEING HERE TODAY HAS REASSURED ME THAT THE UNITED PLANETS IS IN *VERY* SAFE HANDS. I CAN'T BELIEVE THERE'S A SINGLE THREAT IN THE GALAXY THAT THE LEGION CAN'T HANDLE.
THIS IS TRUDY TRUSOE FOR *THE EARTH SPINS,* LEGION WORLD.
CLICK HERE TO START OVER FROM BEGINNING.
CUT NANO-CAMS.
THAT'S IT, ALL DONE.
YOU GUYS HAVE BEEN GREAT, *REALLY.*
IT'S BEEN A PLEASURE, TRUDY.
I HOPE YOU'VE GOT ENOUGH MATERIAL TO WORK WITH.
OH, PLENTY, THANKS.
VERY GENEROUS THINGS YOU SAID ABOUT US IN YOUR WRAP UP.
NO PROBLEM. JUST SAYING WHAT EVERYONE KNOWS.
I MEANT *EVERY* WORD...

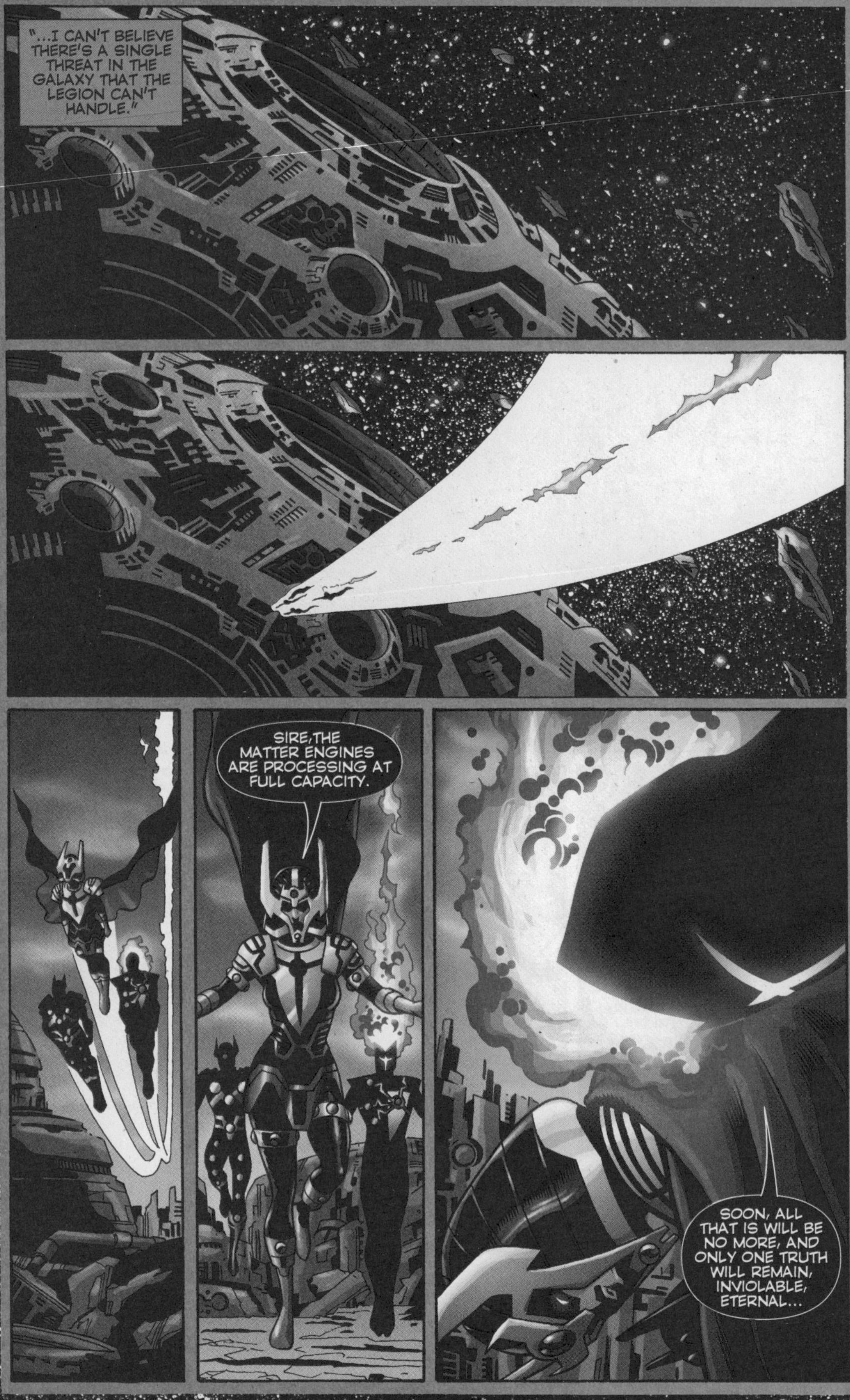
"...I CAN'T BELIEVE THERE'S A SINGLE THREAT IN THE GALAXY THAT THE LEGION CAN'T HANDLE."
SIRE, THE MATTER ENGINES ARE PROCESSING AT FULL CAPACITY.
SOON, ALL THAT IS WILL BE NO MORE, AND ONLY ONE TRUTH WILL REMAIN, INVIOLABLE, ETERNAL...

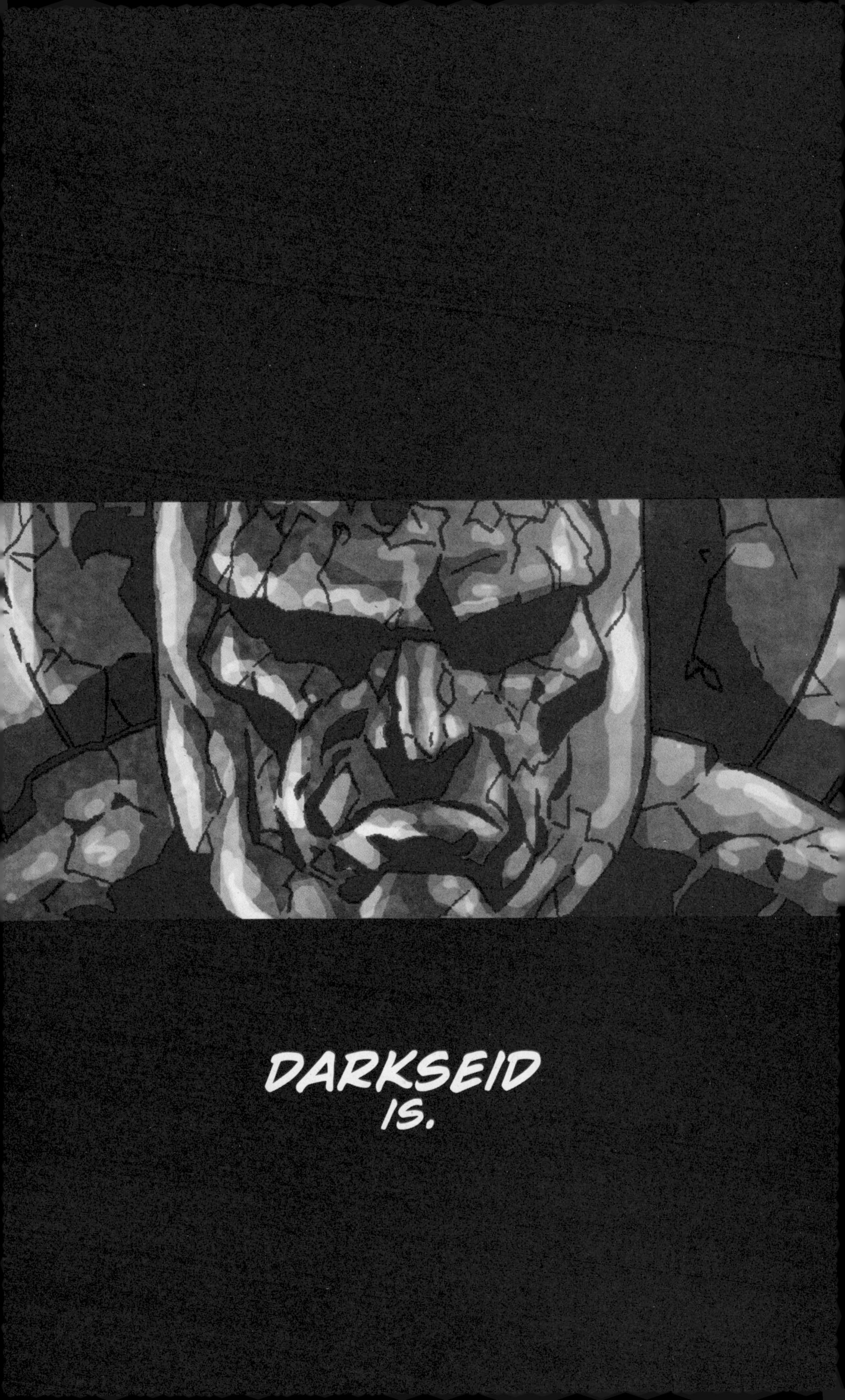
DARKSEID
IS.

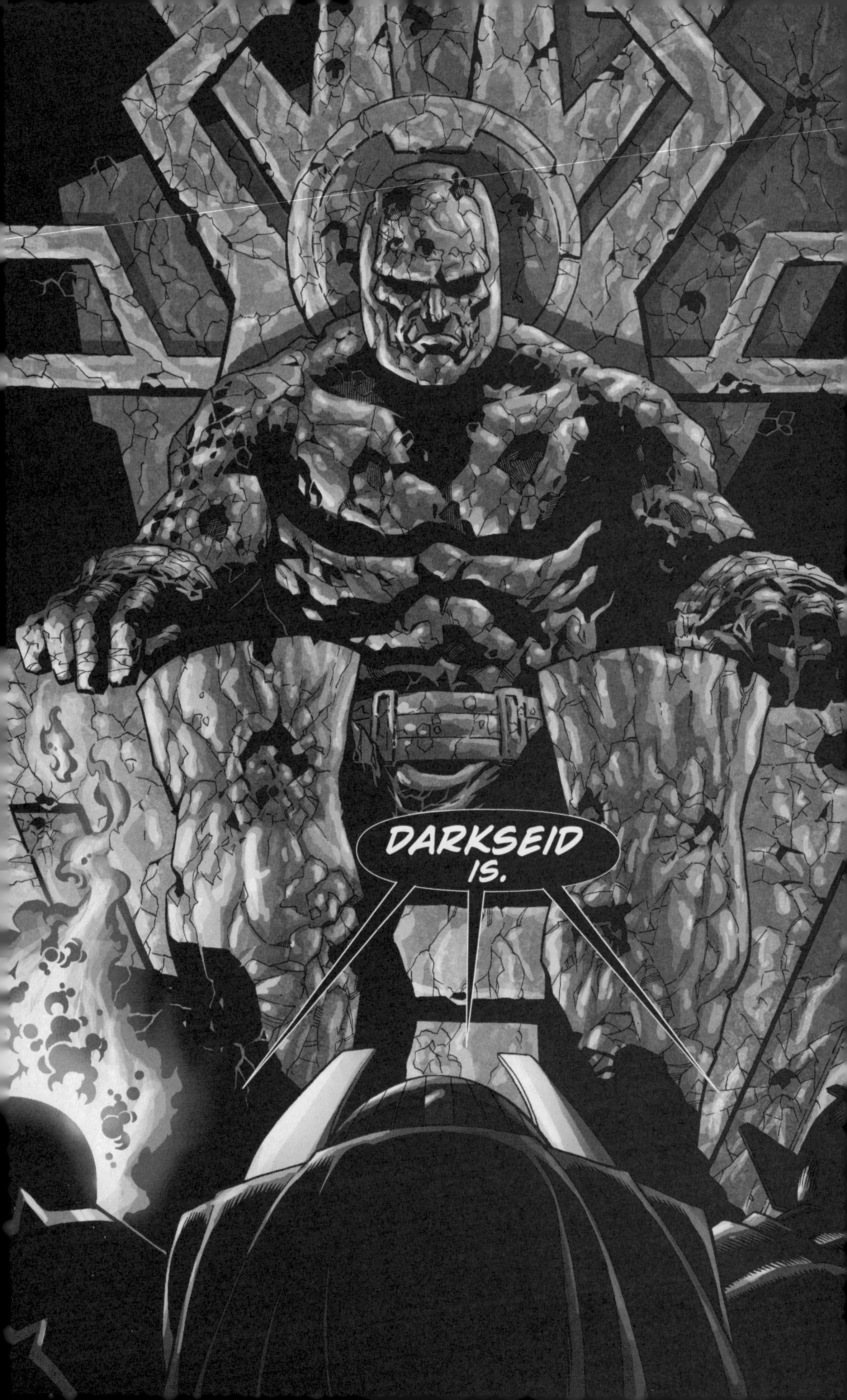
DARKSEID IS.

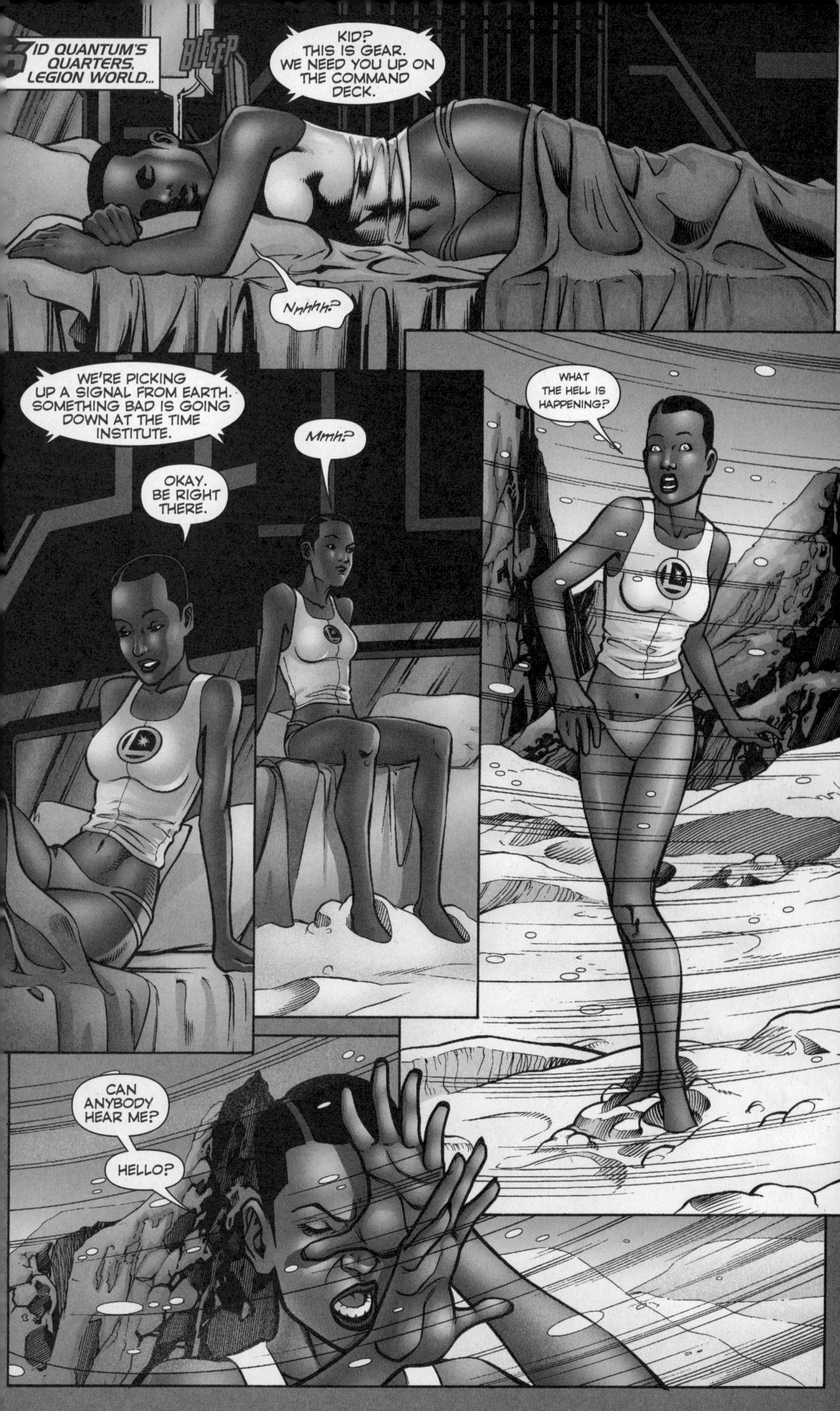

XS
ID QUANTUM'S QUARTERS, LEGION WORLD...
BLEEEP
KID? THIS IS GEAR. WE NEED YOU UP ON THE COMMAND DECK.
Nnhhh?
WE'RE PICKING UP A SIGNAL FROM EARTH. SOMETHING BAD IS GOING DOWN AT THE TIME INSTITUTE.
OKAY. BE RIGHT THERE.
Mmh?
WHAT THE HELL IS HAPPENING?
CAN ANYBODY HEAR ME?
HELLO?

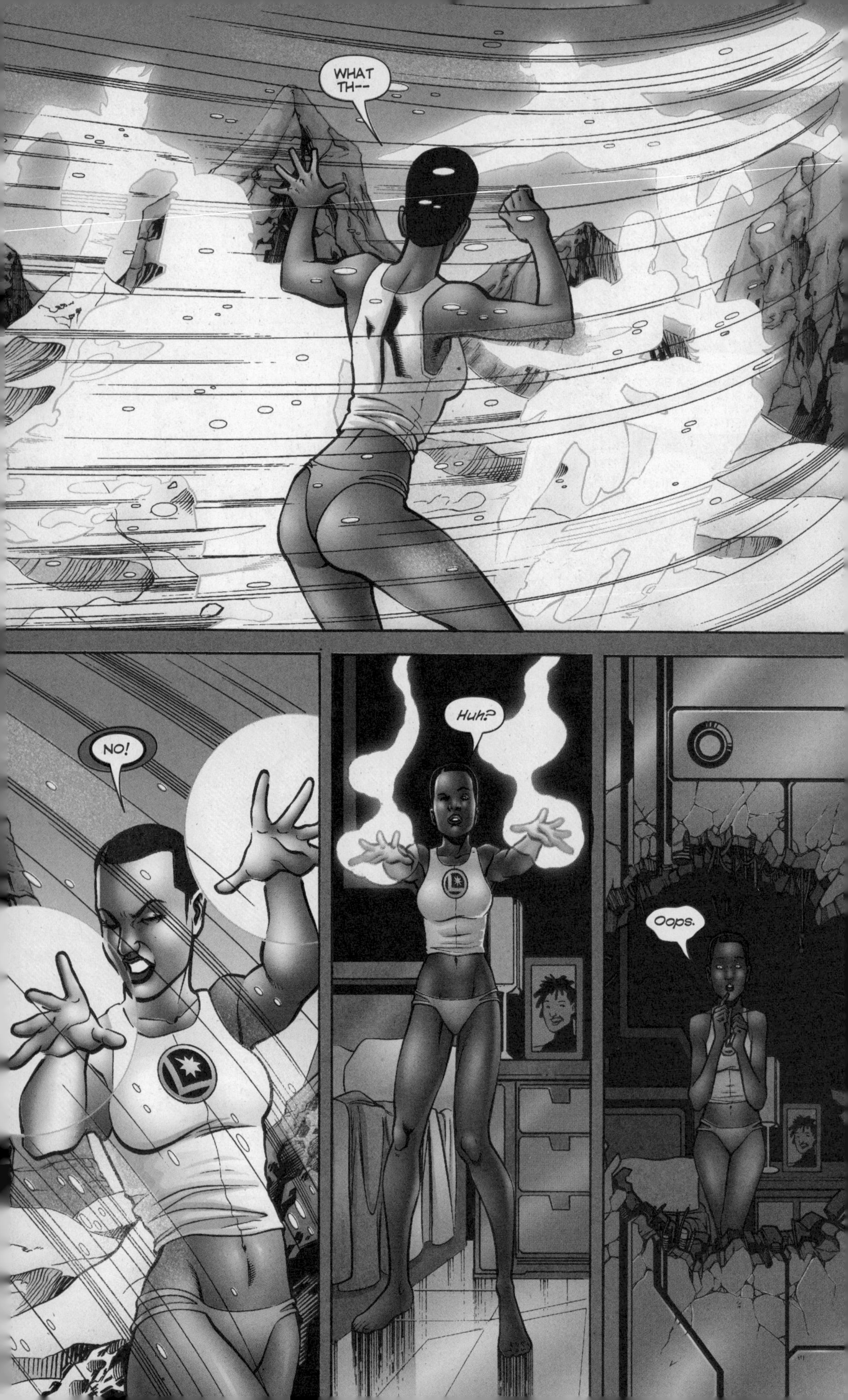
WHAT TH--
NO!
Huh?
Oops.

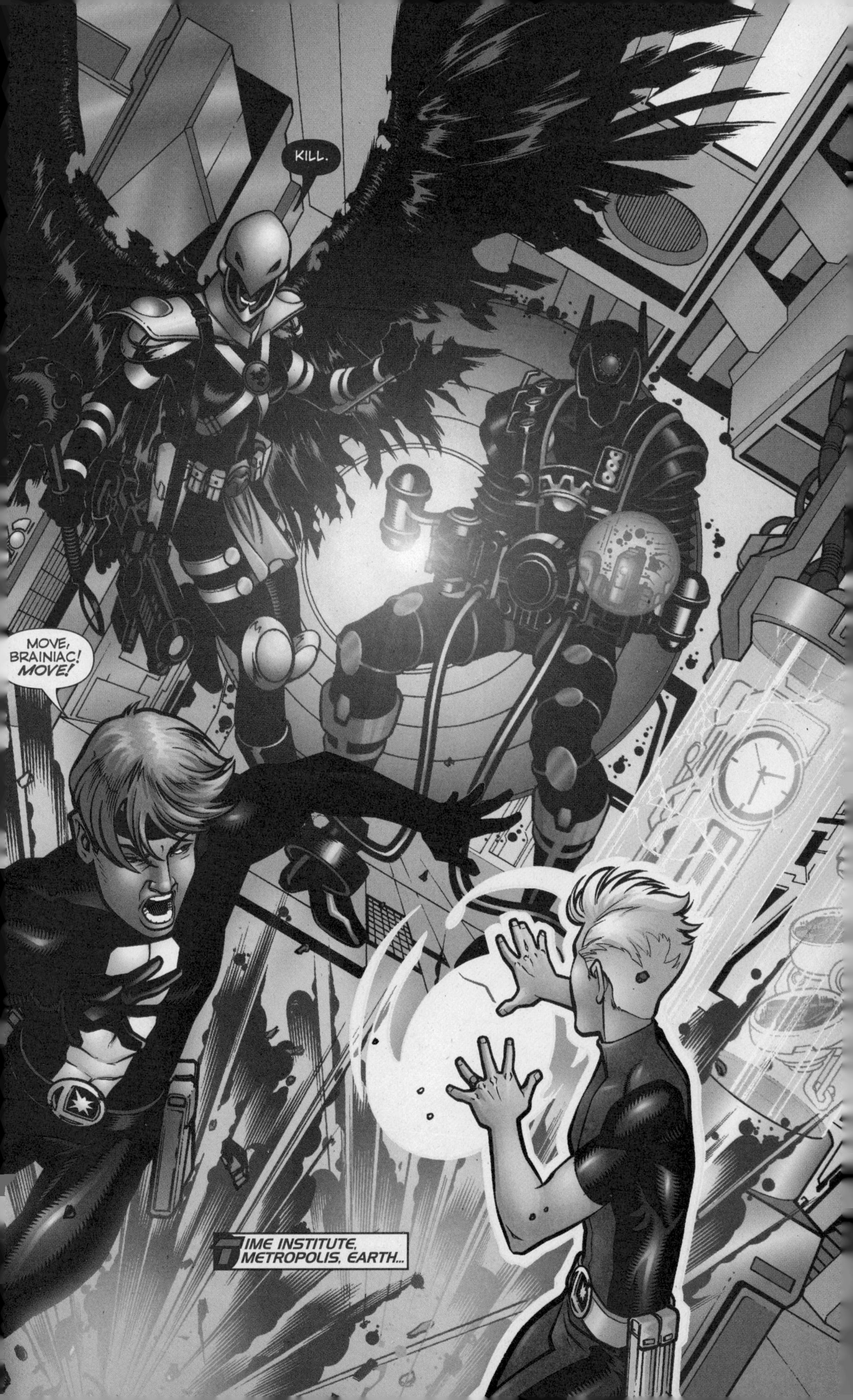
KILL.
MOVE, BRAINIAC! MOVE!
TIME INSTITUTE, METROPOLIS, EARTH...

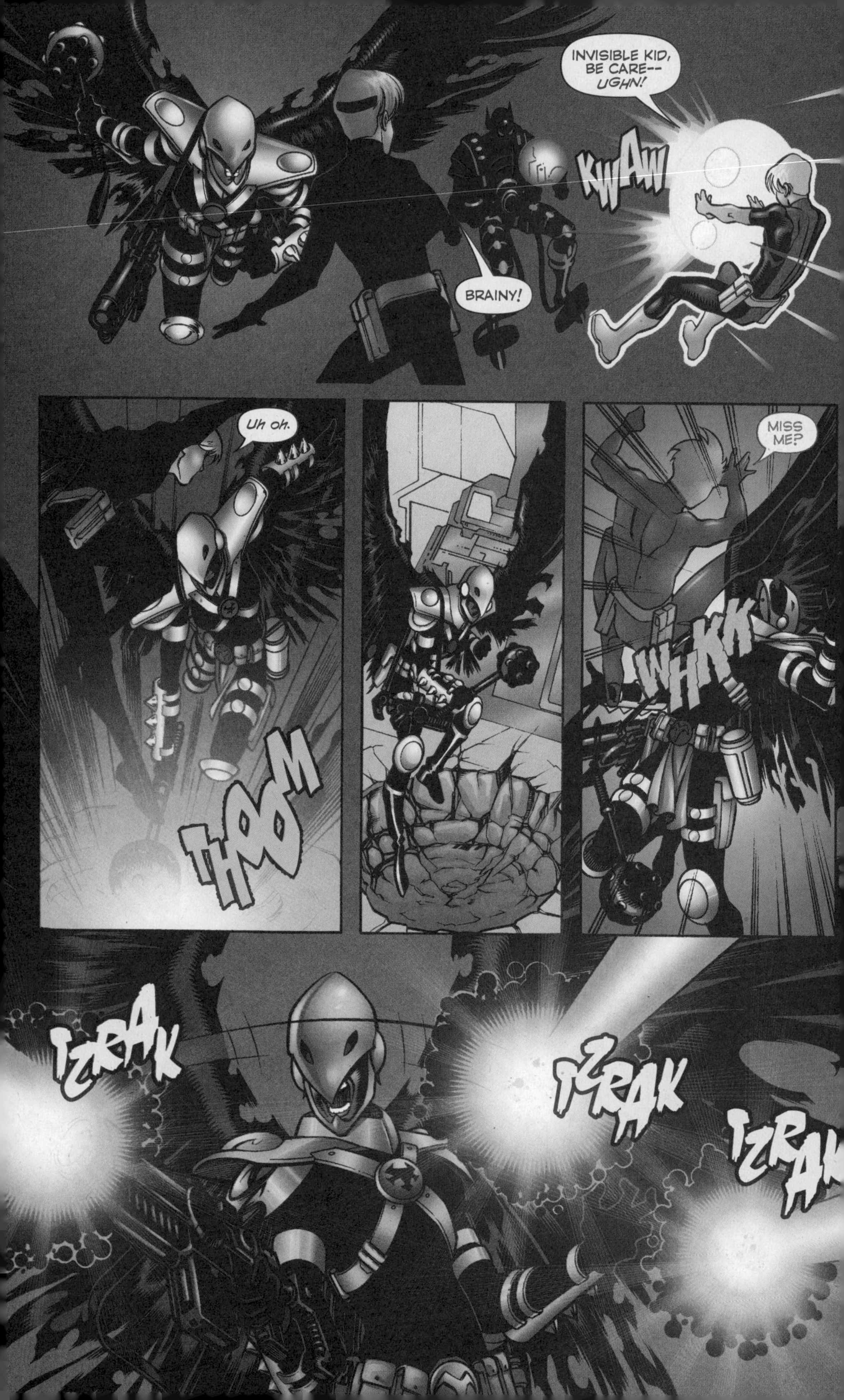
INVISIBLE KID, BE CARE-- UGHN!
KWAW
BRAINY!
Uh oh.
THOOM
MISS ME?
WHKK
TZRAK
TZRAK
TZRAK

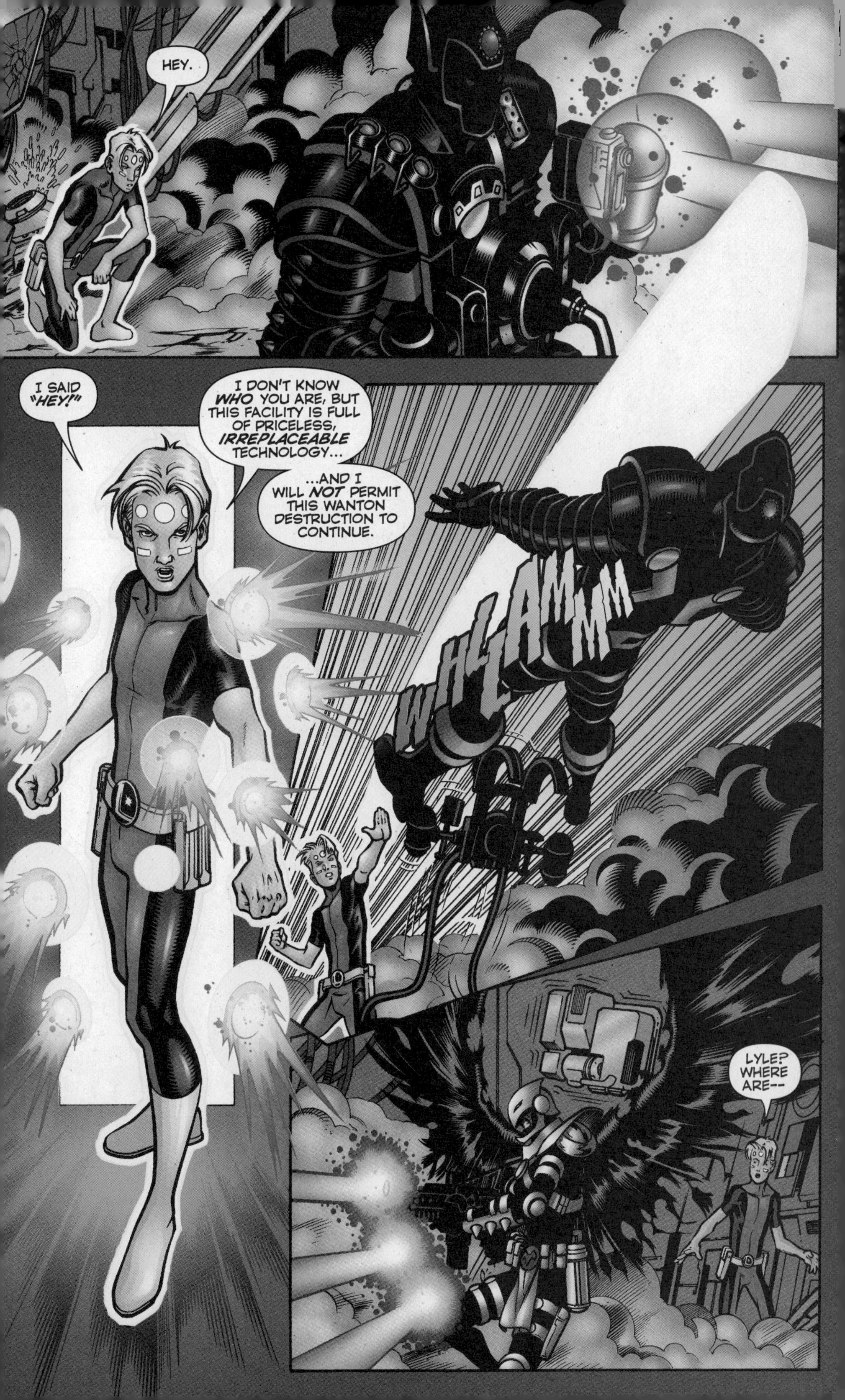
HEY.
I SAID "HEY!"
I DON'T KNOW WHO YOU ARE, BUT THIS FACILITY IS FULL OF PRICELESS, IRREPLACEABLE TECHNOLOGY...
...AND I WILL NOT PERMIT THIS WANTON DESTRUCTION TO CONTINUE.
WHLLAMMM
LYLE? WHERE ARE--

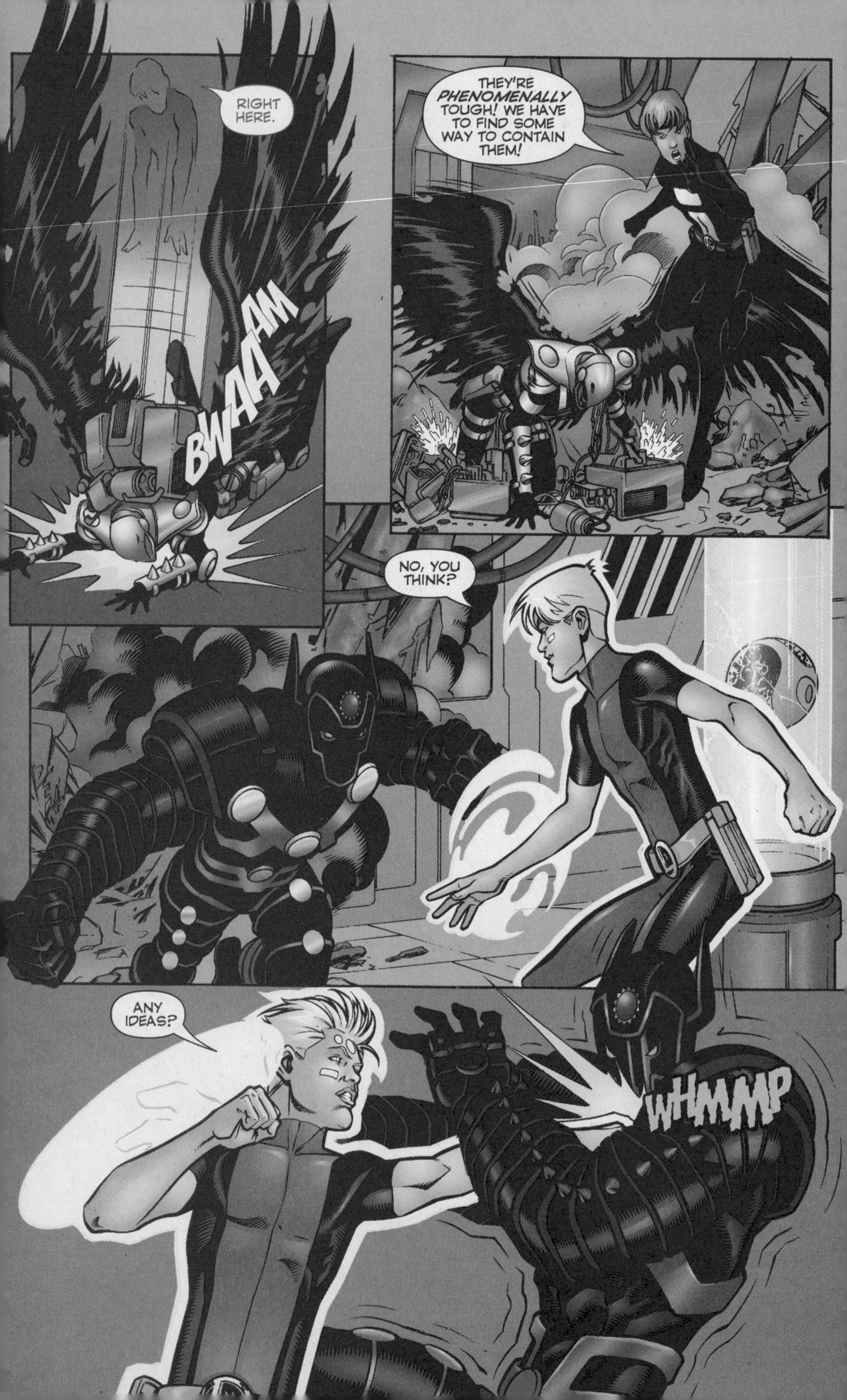
RIGHT HERE.
BWAAAM
THEY'RE PHENOMENALLY TOUGH! WE HAVE TO FIND SOME WAY TO CONTAIN THEM!
NO, YOU THINK?
ANY IDEAS?
WHMMP

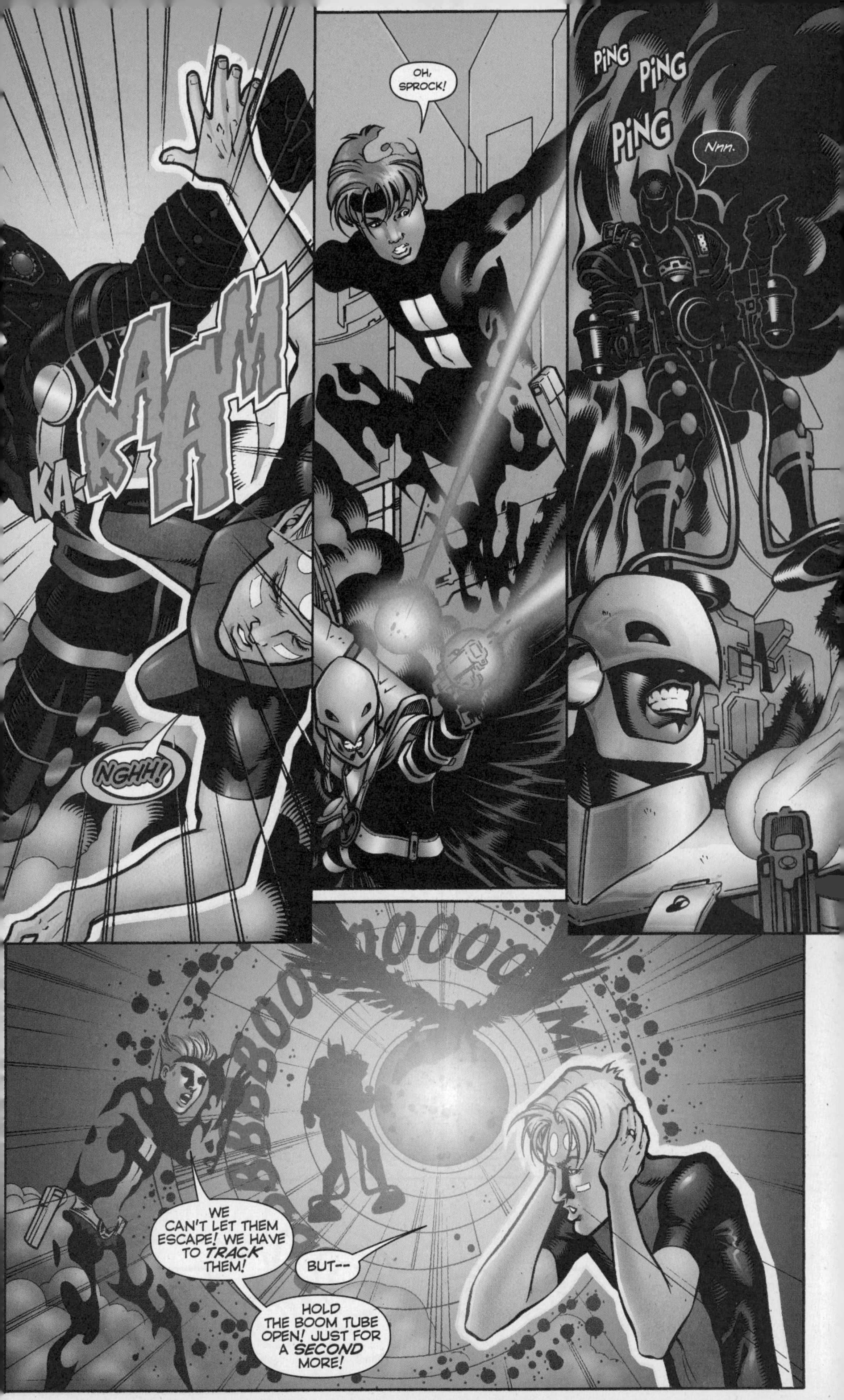

OH, SPROCK!
PING
PING
PING
Nnn.
KA-BLAM
NGHH!
BBBBOOOOOOOOOM
WE CAN'T LET THEM ESCAPE! WE HAVE TO TRACK THEM!
BUT--
HOLD THE BOOM TUBE OPEN! JUST FOR A SECOND MORE!

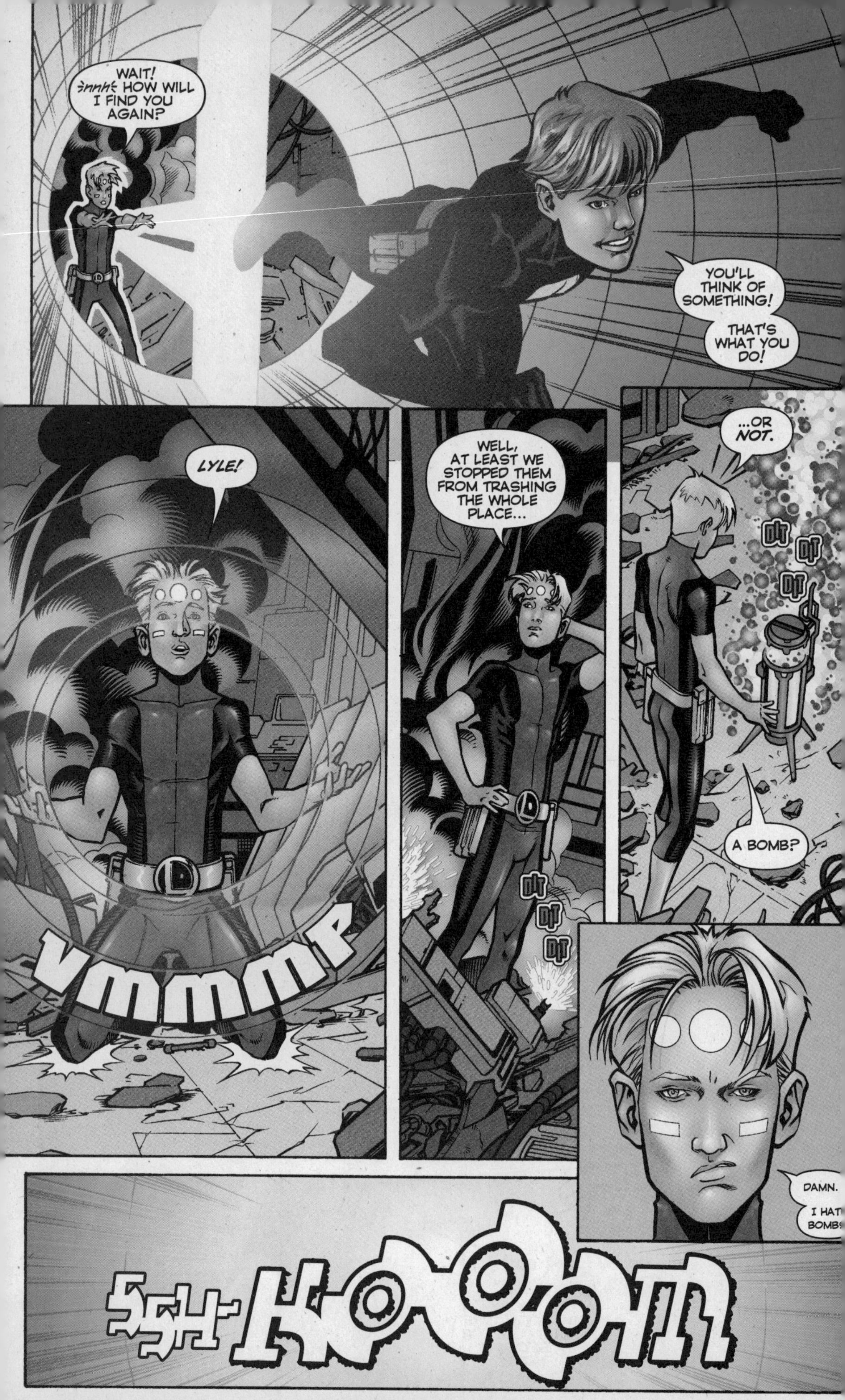

WAIT! nnh HOW WILL I FIND YOU AGAIN?
YOU'LL THINK OF SOMETHING!
THAT'S WHAT YOU DO!
LYLE!
VMMMP
WELL, AT LEAST WE STOPPED THEM FROM TRASHING THE WHOLE PLACE...
DIT DIT DIT
...OR NOT.
DIT DIT DIT
A BOMB?
DAMN.
I HAT BOMBS
SSH- HOOOM

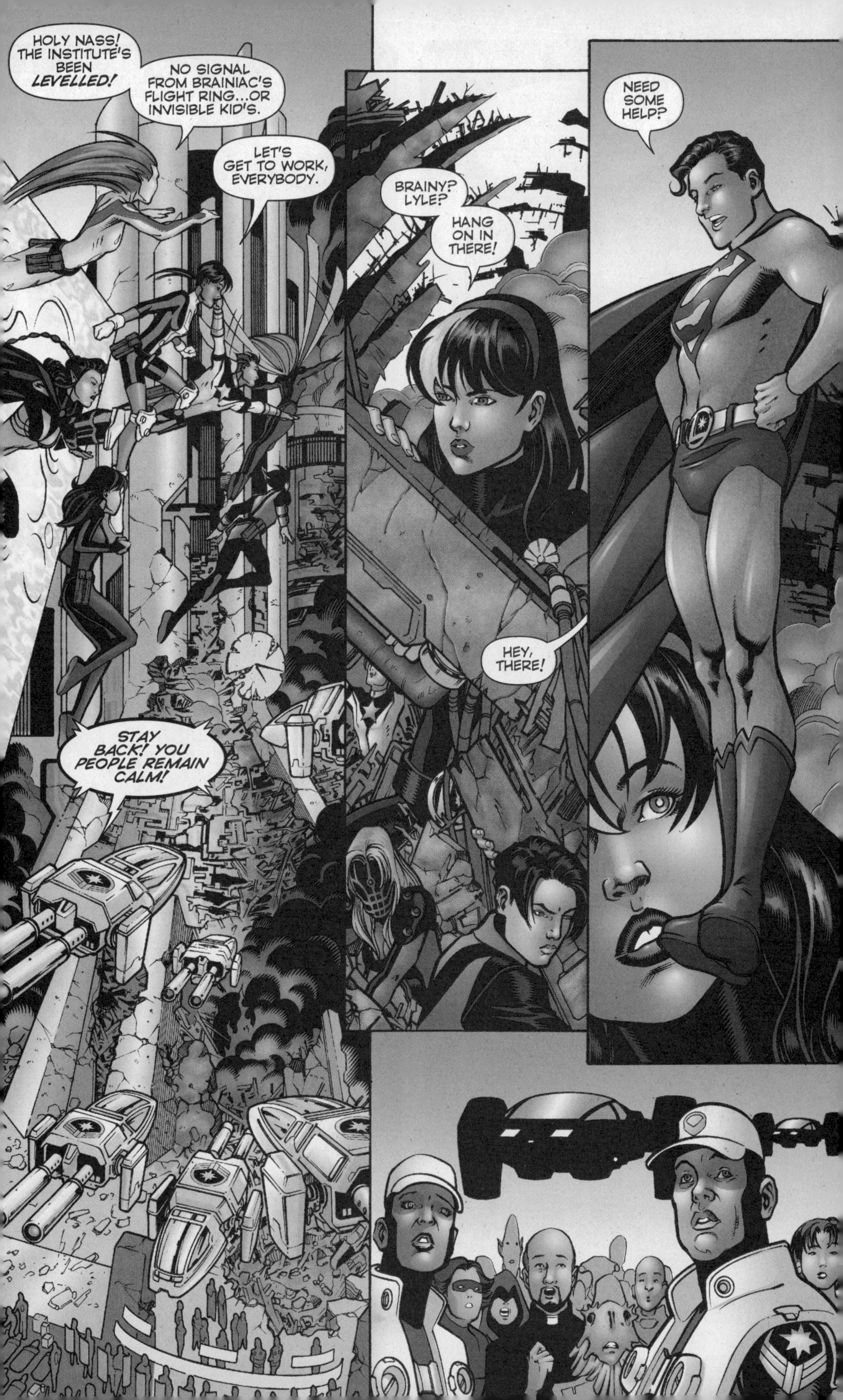
HOLY NASS! THE INSTITUTE'S BEEN LEVELLED!
NO SIGNAL FROM BRAINIAC'S FLIGHT RING...OR INVISIBLE KID'S.
LET'S GET TO WORK, EVERYBODY.
STAY BACK! YOU PEOPLE REMAIN CALM!
BRAINY? LYLE?
HANG ON IN THERE!
HEY, THERE!
NEED SOME HELP?

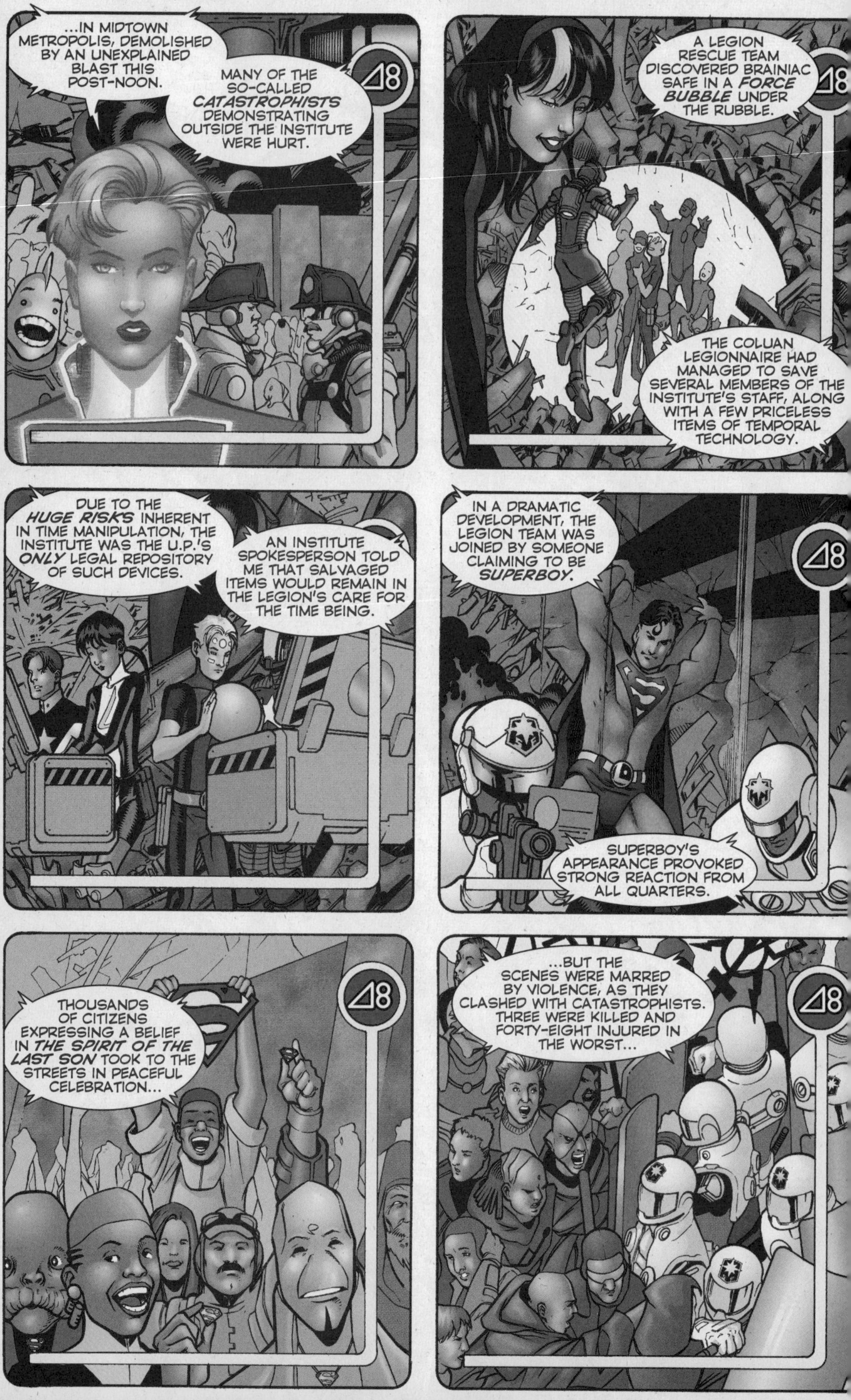
...IN MIDTOWN METROPOLIS, DEMOLISHED BY AN UNEXPLAINED BLAST THIS POST-NOON.
MANY OF THE SO-CALLED CATASTROPHISTS DEMONSTRATING OUTSIDE THE INSTITUTE WERE HURT.
Δ8
A LEGION RESCUE TEAM DISCOVERED BRAINIAC SAFE IN A FORCE BUBBLE UNDER THE RUBBLE.
THE COLUAN LEGIONNAIRE HAD MANAGED TO SAVE SEVERAL MEMBERS OF THE INSTITUTE'S STAFF, ALONG WITH A FEW PRICELESS ITEMS OF TEMPORAL TECHNOLOGY.
DUE TO THE HUGE RISKS INHERENT IN TIME MANIPULATION, THE INSTITUTE WAS THE U.P.'S ONLY LEGAL REPOSITORY OF SUCH DEVICES.
AN INSTITUTE SPOKESPERSON TOLD ME THAT SALVAGED ITEMS WOULD REMAIN IN THE LEGION'S CARE FOR THE TIME BEING.
IN A DRAMATIC DEVELOPMENT, THE LEGION TEAM WAS JOINED BY SOMEONE CLAIMING TO BE SUPERBOY.
SUPERBOY'S APPEARANCE PROVOKED STRONG REACTION FROM ALL QUARTERS.
THOUSANDS OF CITIZENS EXPRESSING A BELIEF IN THE SPIRIT OF THE LAST SON TOOK TO THE STREETS IN PEACEFUL CELEBRATION...
...BUT THE SCENES WERE MARRED BY VIOLENCE, AS THEY CLASHED WITH CATASTROPHISTS. THREE WERE KILLED AND FORTY-EIGHT INJURED IN THE WORST...

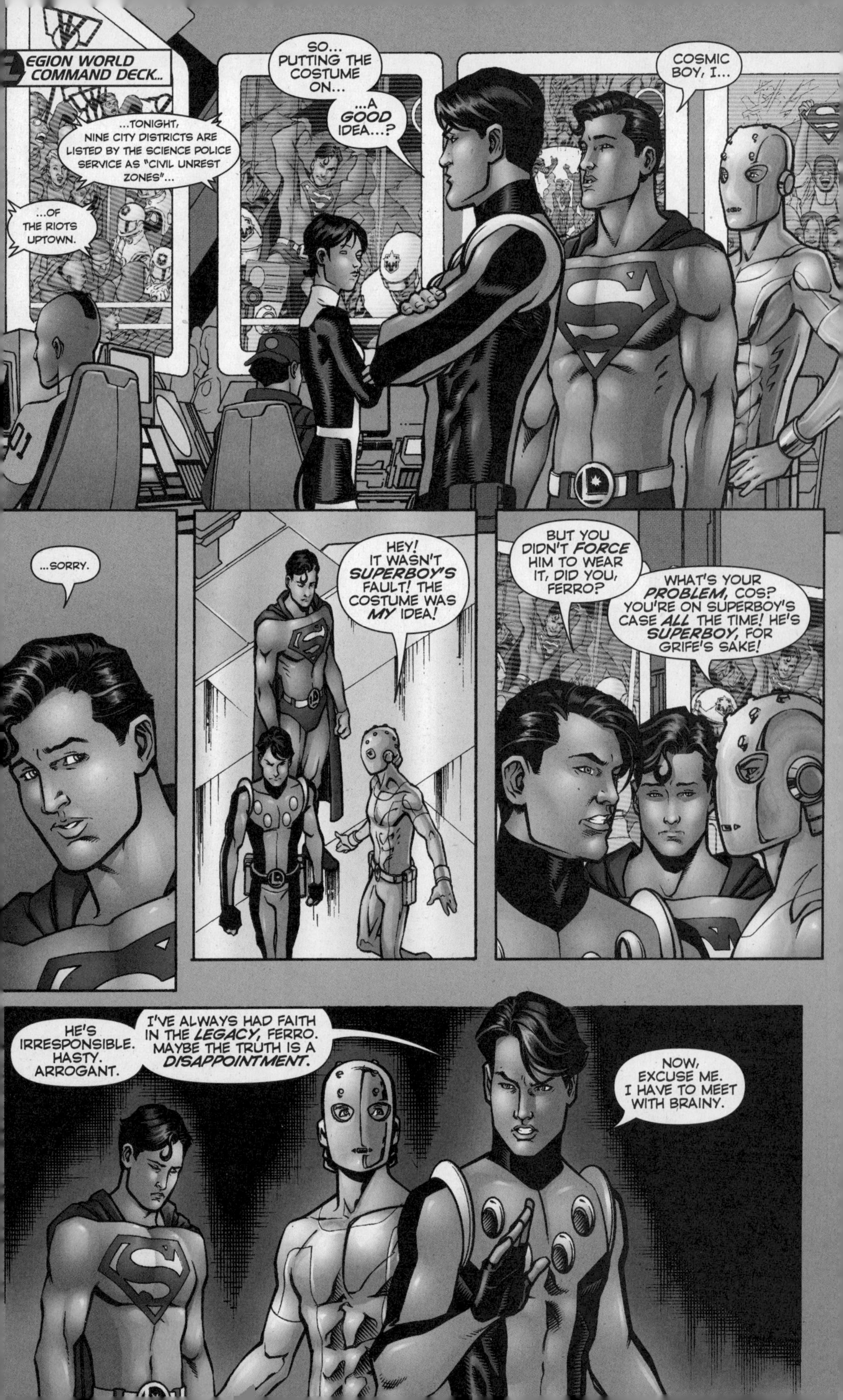

LEGION WORLD COMMAND DECK...
...TONIGHT, NINE CITY DISTRICTS ARE LISTED BY THE SCIENCE POLICE SERVICE AS "CIVIL UNREST ZONES"...
...OF THE RIOTS UPTOWN.
SO... PUTTING THE COSTUME ON...
...A GOOD IDEA...?
COSMIC BOY, I...
...SORRY.
HEY! IT WASN'T SUPERBOY'S FAULT! THE COSTUME WAS MY IDEA!
BUT YOU DIDN'T FORCE HIM TO WEAR IT, DID YOU, FERRO?
WHAT'S YOUR PROBLEM, COS? YOU'RE ON SUPERBOY'S CASE ALL THE TIME! HE'S SUPERBOY, FOR GRIFE'S SAKE!
HE'S IRRESPONSIBLE. HASTY. ARROGANT.
I'VE ALWAYS HAD FAITH IN THE LEGACY, FERRO. MAYBE THE TRUTH IS A DISAPPOINTMENT.
NOW, EXCUSE ME. I HAVE TO MEET WITH BRAINY.

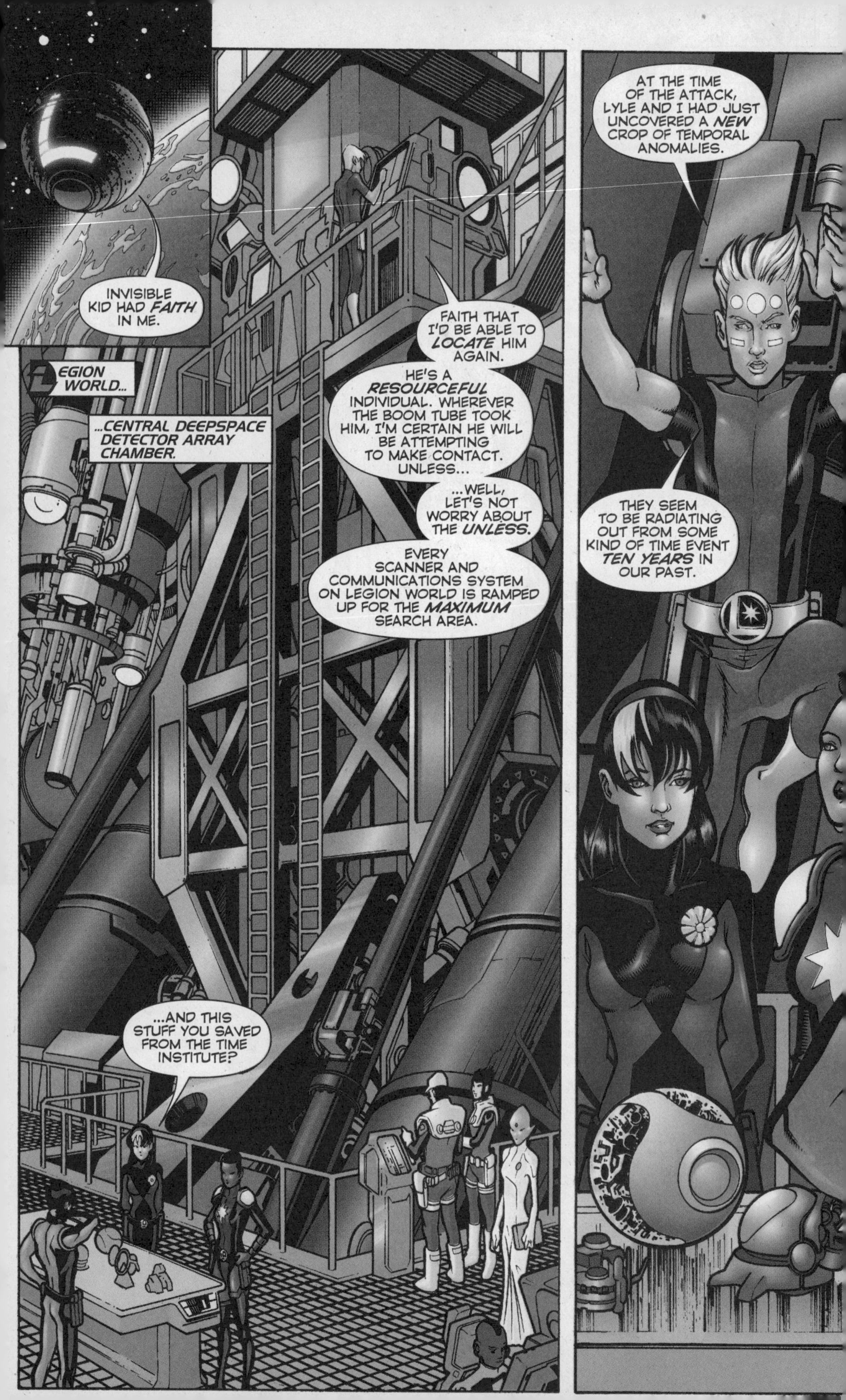
INVISIBLE KID HAD FAITH IN ME.
FAITH THAT I'D BE ABLE TO LOCATE HIM AGAIN.
LEGION WORLD...
...CENTRAL DEEPSPACE DETECTOR ARRAY CHAMBER.
HE'S A RESOURCEFUL INDIVIDUAL. WHEREVER THE BOOM TUBE TOOK HIM, I'M CERTAIN HE WILL BE ATTEMPTING TO MAKE CONTACT. UNLESS...
...WELL, LET'S NOT WORRY ABOUT THE UNLESS.
EVERY SCANNER AND COMMUNICATIONS SYSTEM ON LEGION WORLD IS RAMPED UP FOR THE MAXIMUM SEARCH AREA.
...AND THIS STUFF YOU SAVED FROM THE TIME INSTITUTE?
AT THE TIME OF THE ATTACK, LYLE AND I HAD JUST UNCOVERED A NEW CROP OF TEMPORAL ANOMALIES.
THEY SEEM TO BE RADIATING OUT FROM SOME KIND OF TIME EVENT TEN YEARS IN OUR PAST.

TELL ME *MORE* ABOUT THESE TEMPORAL ANOMALIES, BRAINY.

WELL, THEY--

BRAINIAC? THE SEARCH PATTERN RESULTS ARE...WELL, THEY'RE *OFF.*

LET ME SEE.

THAT'S... THAT'S NOT *POSSIBLE.* ADJUST THE SCALE AMPLITUDE, GEAR.

I *DID.* I'M RUNNING THE WHOLE *DATA LOAD* THROUGH MY OWN BIOSYSTEMS AS A SAFEGUARD.

CAN THIS BE RIGHT?

WHAT?

IN SCANNING FOR SIGNS OF LYLE, WE'RE NATURALLY ANALYZING THE FABRIC OF THE NEAR COSMOS *WHOLESALE.*

AND... THE UNIVERSE SEEMS TO BE *SHRINKING.*

IT *WHAT?*

SHRINKING.

THE QUANTIFIABLE MASS OF REALITY IS SIGNIFICANTLY *LESS* THAN LAST TIME IT WAS ASSAYED. BY A FACTOR OF *TWENTY-SEVEN PERCENT.*

IS IT JUST ME, OR IS THAT-- I DUNNO-- *IMPOSSIBLE?*

THE *INSTRUMENTS* MUST BE WRONG.

I *HOPE* THEY ARE. BECAUSE THAT WOULD ALSO EXPLAIN THE *SUPER-MASSIVE GRAVITATIONAL DISTORTION* THAT'S APPEARED ON THE FRINGES OF THE MILKY WAY.

DEFINE "SUPER-MASSIVE" IN THIS CONTEXT.

SOMETHING THE SIZE OF AN *INFANT GALAXY.* SOMETHING THAT SHOULD *NOT* BE THERE.

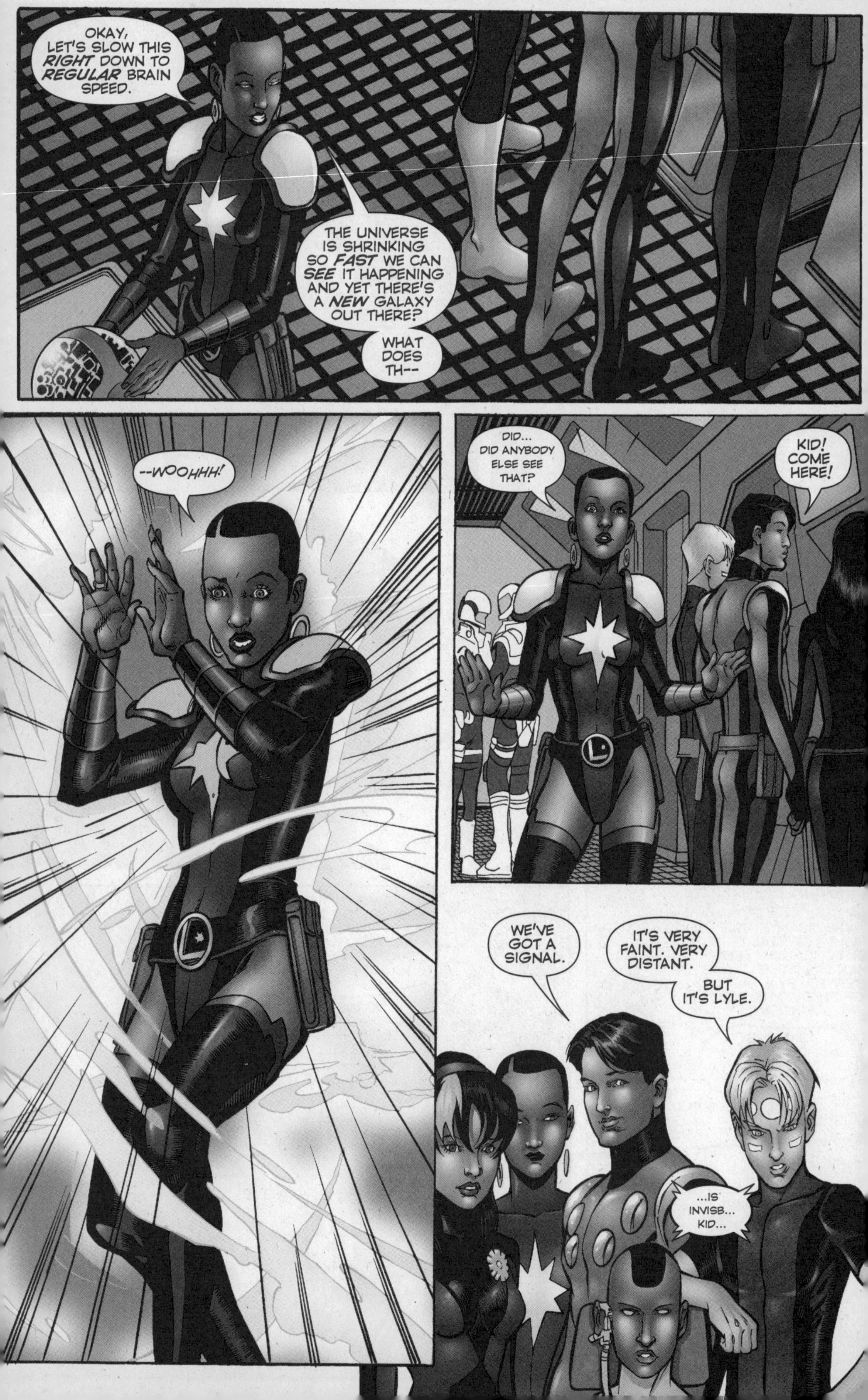
OKAY, LET'S SLOW THIS RIGHT DOWN TO REGULAR BRAIN SPEED.
THE UNIVERSE IS SHRINKING SO FAST WE CAN SEE IT HAPPENING AND YET THERE'S A NEW GALAXY OUT THERE?
WHAT DOES TH--
--WOOHHH!
DID... DID ANYBODY ELSE SEE THAT?
KID! COME HERE!
WE'VE GOT A SIGNAL.
IT'S VERY FAINT. VERY DISTANT.
BUT IT'S LYLE.
...IS INVISB... KID...

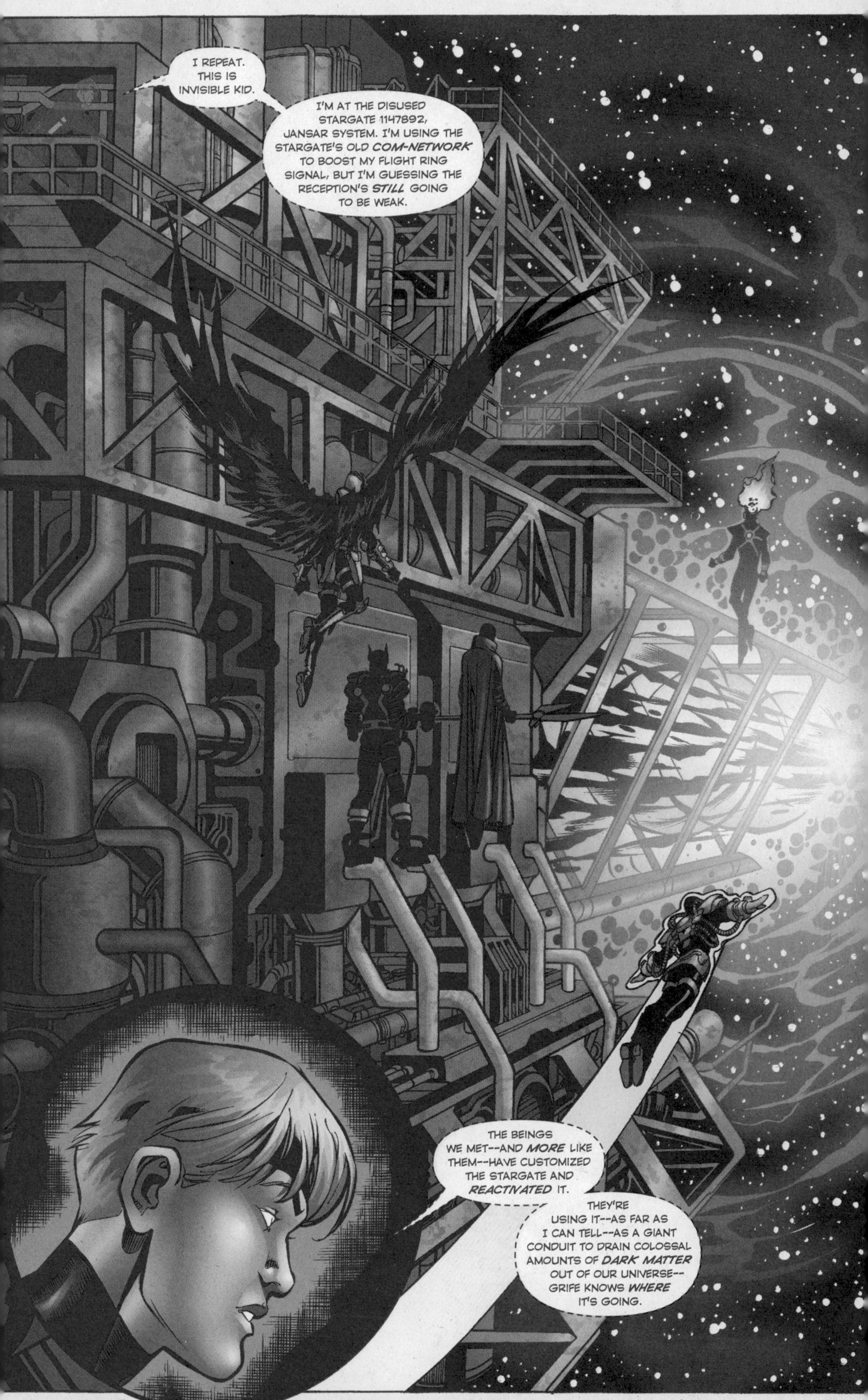
I REPEAT. THIS IS INVISIBLE KID.
I'M AT THE DISUSED STARGATE 1147892, JANSAR SYSTEM. I'M USING THE STARGATE'S OLD COM-NETWORK TO BOOST MY FLIGHT RING SIGNAL, BUT I'M GUESSING THE RECEPTION'S STILL GOING TO BE WEAK.
THE BEINGS WE MET--AND MORE LIKE THEM--HAVE CUSTOMIZED THE STARGATE AND REACTIVATED IT.
THEY'RE USING IT--AS FAR AS I CAN TELL--AS A GIANT CONDUIT TO DRAIN COLOSSAL AMOUNTS OF DARK MATTER OUT OF OUR UNIVERSE--GRIFE KNOWS WHERE IT'S GOING.

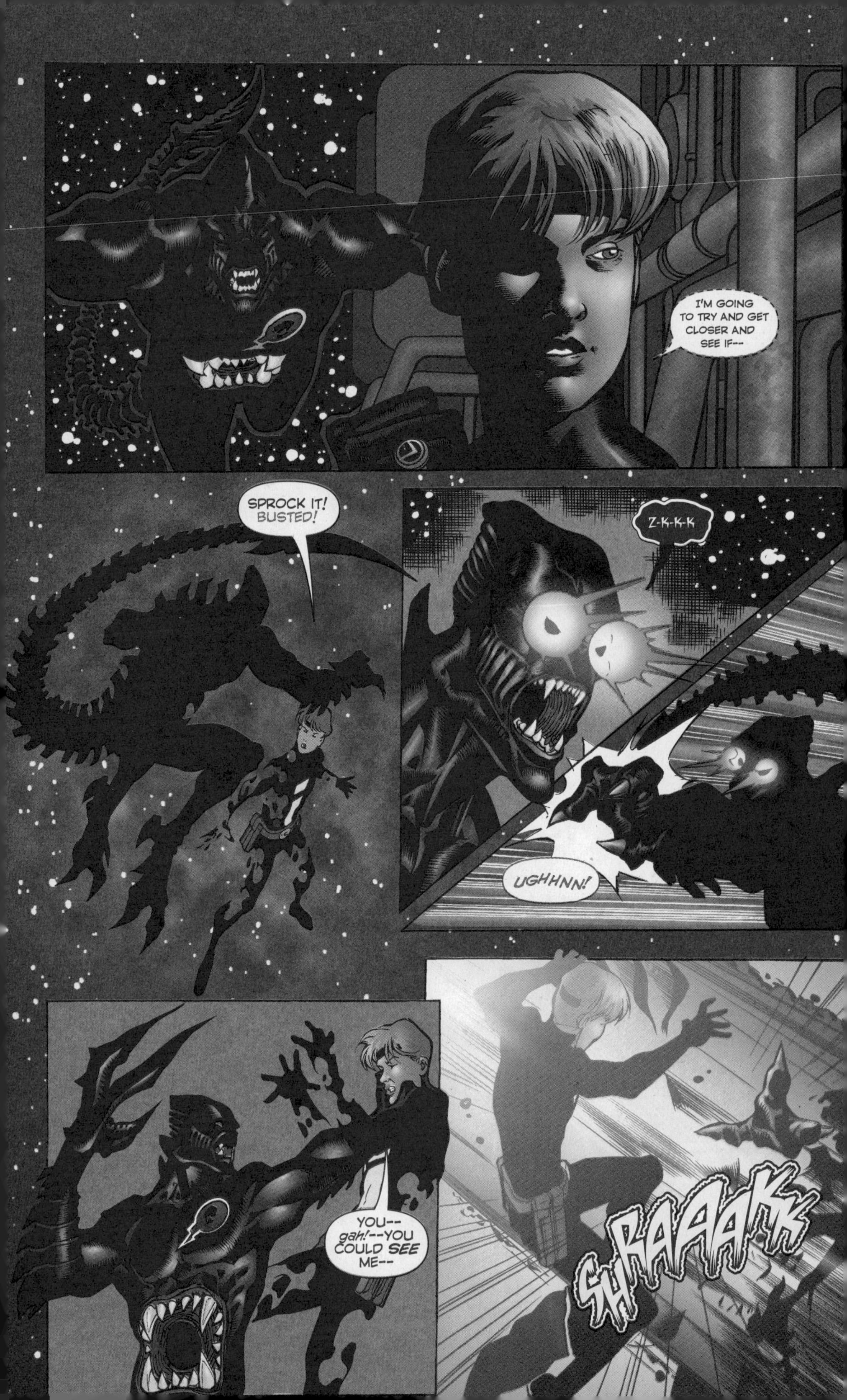
I'M GOING TO TRY AND GET CLOSER AND SEE IF--
SPROCK IT! BUSTED!
Z-K-K-K
UGHHNN!
YOU-- gah!--YOU COULD SEE ME--
SHRAAAAK

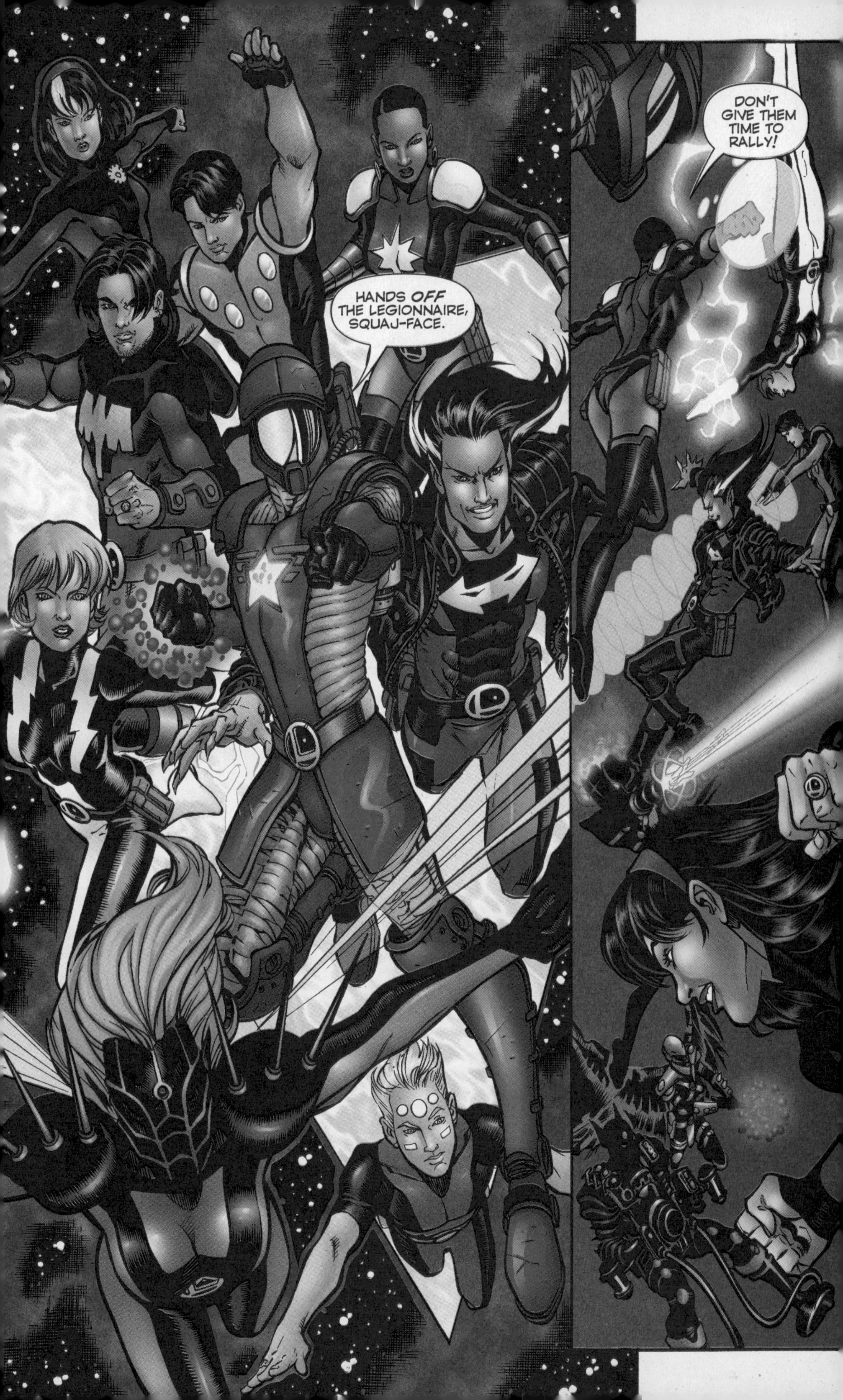
HANDS OFF THE LEGIONNAIRE, SQUAJ-FACE.
DON'T GIVE THEM TIME TO RALLY!

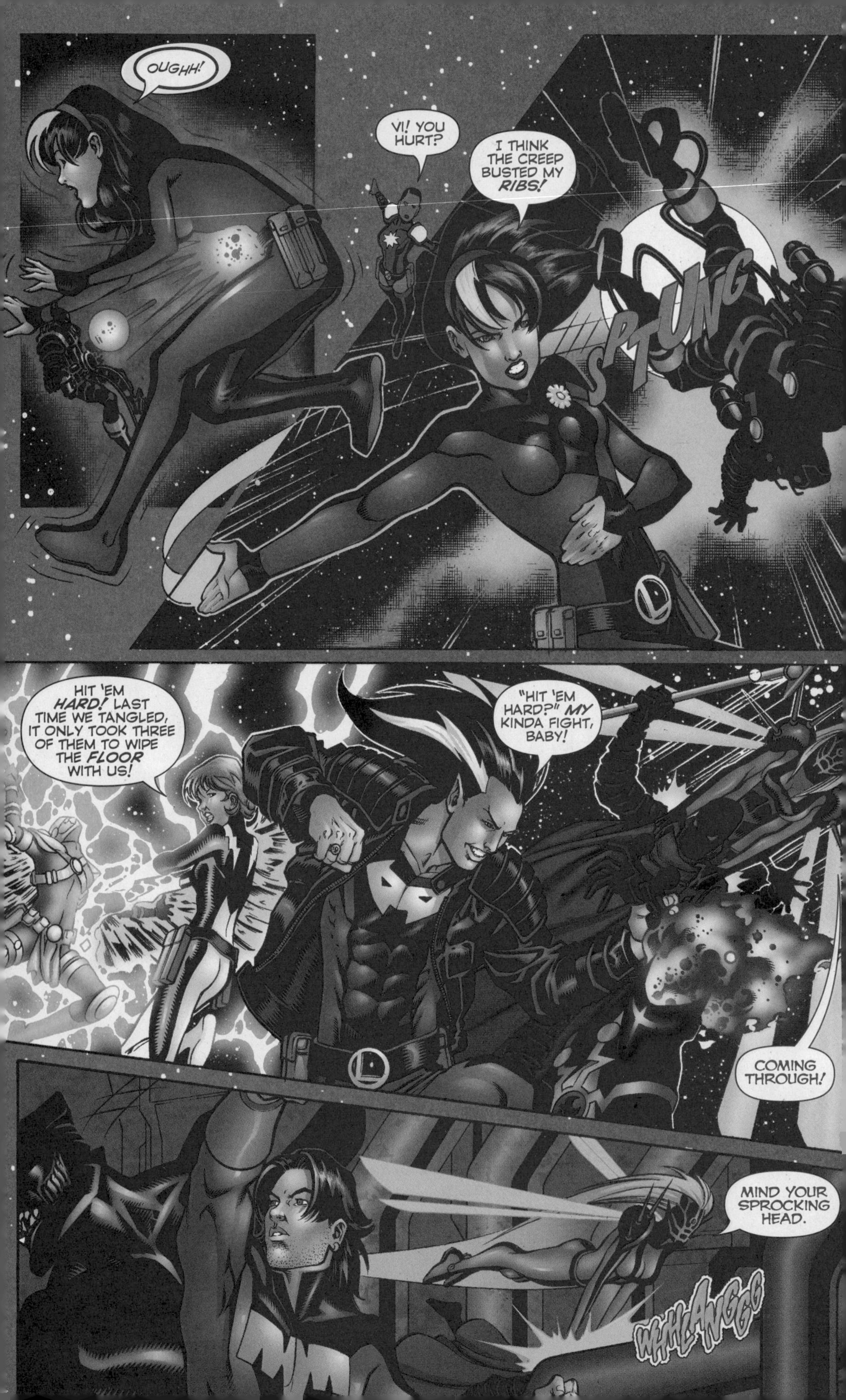
OUGHH!
VI! YOU HURT?
I THINK THE CREEP BUSTED MY RIBS!
SPTUNG
HIT 'EM HARD! LAST TIME WE TANGLED, IT ONLY TOOK THREE OF THEM TO WIPE THE FLOOR WITH US!
"HIT 'EM HARD?" MY KINDA FIGHT, BABY!
COMING THROUGH!
MIND YOUR SPROCKING HEAD.

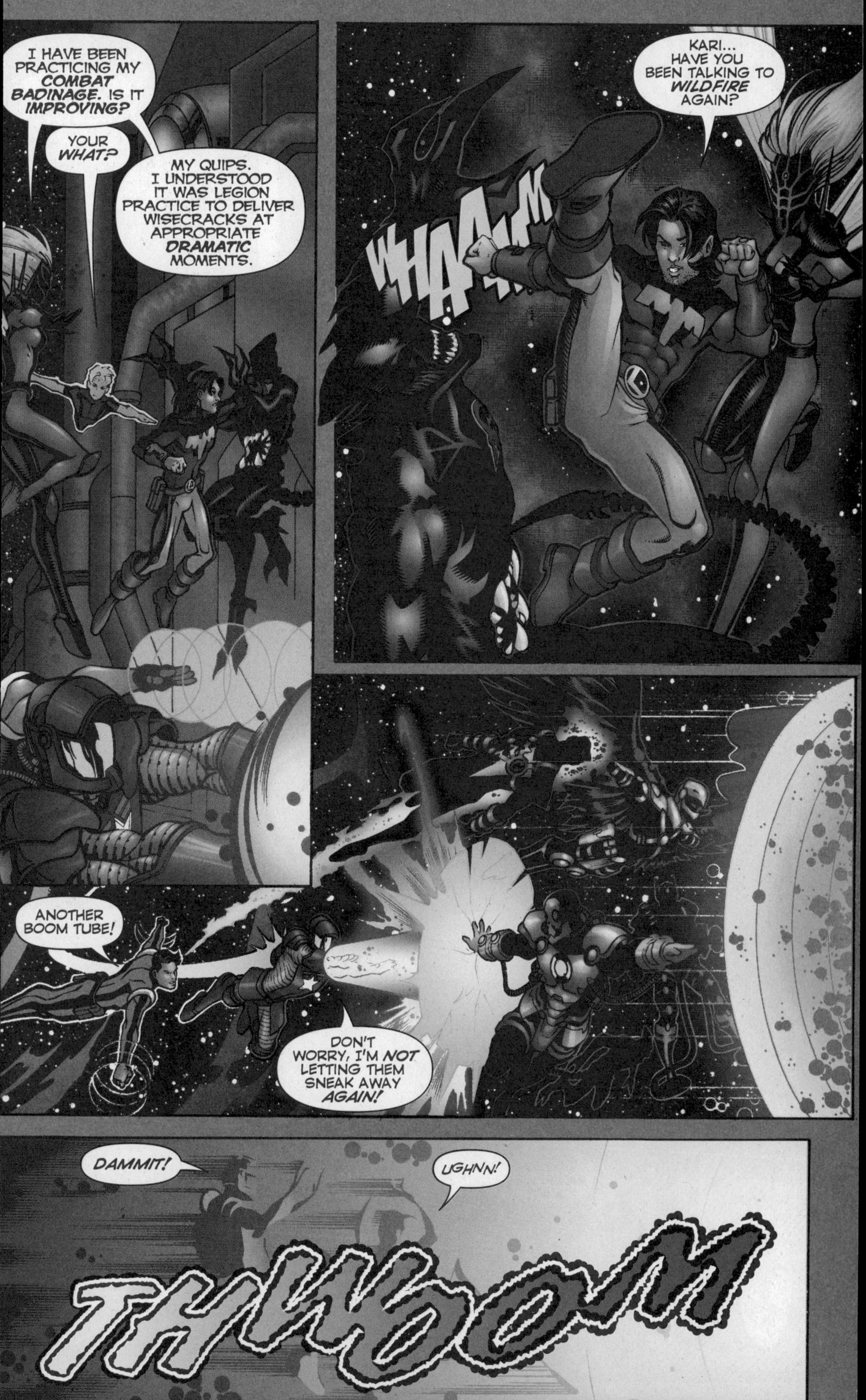
I HAVE BEEN PRACTICING MY COMBAT BADINAGE. IS IT IMPROVING?
YOUR WHAT?
MY QUIPS. I UNDERSTOOD IT WAS LEGION PRACTICE TO DELIVER WISECRACKS AT APPROPRIATE DRAMATIC MOMENTS.
KARI... HAVE YOU BEEN TALKING TO WILDFIRE AGAIN?
WHAAM
ANOTHER BOOM TUBE!
DON'T WORRY, I'M NOT LETTING THEM SNEAK AWAY AGAIN!
DAMMIT!
UGHNN!
THHBOOM

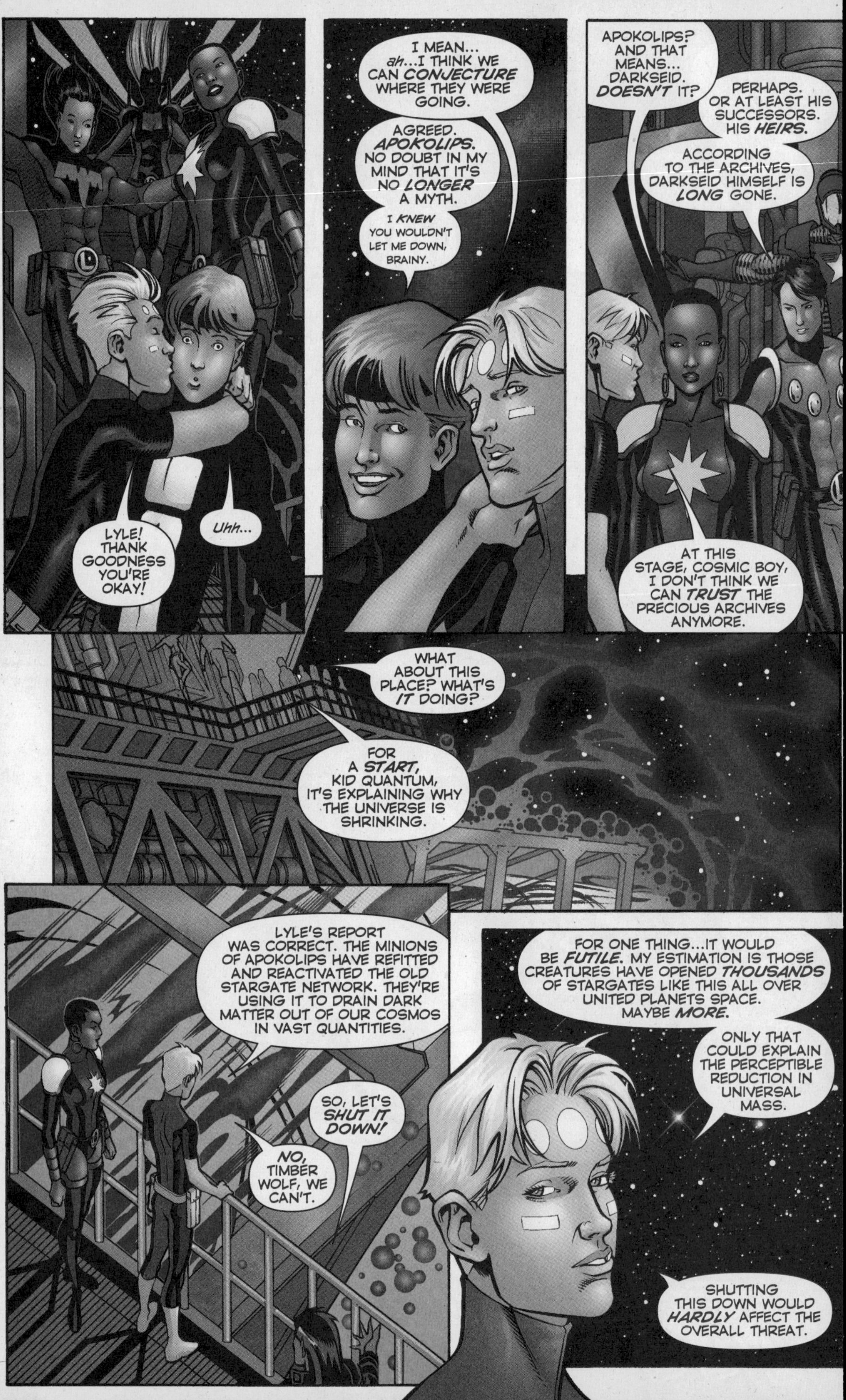
LYLE! THANK GOODNESS YOU'RE OKAY!
Uhh...
I MEAN... ah...I THINK WE CAN CONJECTURE WHERE THEY WERE GOING.
AGREED. APOKOLIPS. NO DOUBT IN MY MIND THAT IT'S NO LONGER A MYTH.
I KNEW YOU WOULDN'T LET ME DOWN, BRAINY.
APOKOLIPS? AND THAT MEANS... DARKSEID. DOESN'T IT?
PERHAPS. OR AT LEAST HIS SUCCESSORS. HIS HEIRS.
ACCORDING TO THE ARCHIVES, DARKSEID HIMSELF IS LONG GONE.
AT THIS STAGE, COSMIC BOY, I DON'T THINK WE CAN TRUST THE PRECIOUS ARCHIVES ANYMORE.
WHAT ABOUT THIS PLACE? WHAT'S IT DOING?
FOR A START, KID QUANTUM, IT'S EXPLAINING WHY THE UNIVERSE IS SHRINKING.
LYLE'S REPORT WAS CORRECT. THE MINIONS OF APOKOLIPS HAVE REFITTED AND REACTIVATED THE OLD STARGATE NETWORK. THEY'RE USING IT TO DRAIN DARK MATTER OUT OF OUR COSMOS IN VAST QUANTITIES.
SO, LET'S SHUT IT DOWN!
NO, TIMBER WOLF, WE CAN'T.
FOR ONE THING...IT WOULD BE FUTILE. MY ESTIMATION IS THOSE CREATURES HAVE OPENED THOUSANDS OF STARGATES LIKE THIS ALL OVER UNITED PLANETS SPACE. MAYBE MORE.
ONLY THAT COULD EXPLAIN THE PERCEPTIBLE REDUCTION IN UNIVERSAL MASS.
SHUTTING THIS DOWN WOULD HARDLY AFFECT THE OVERALL THREAT.

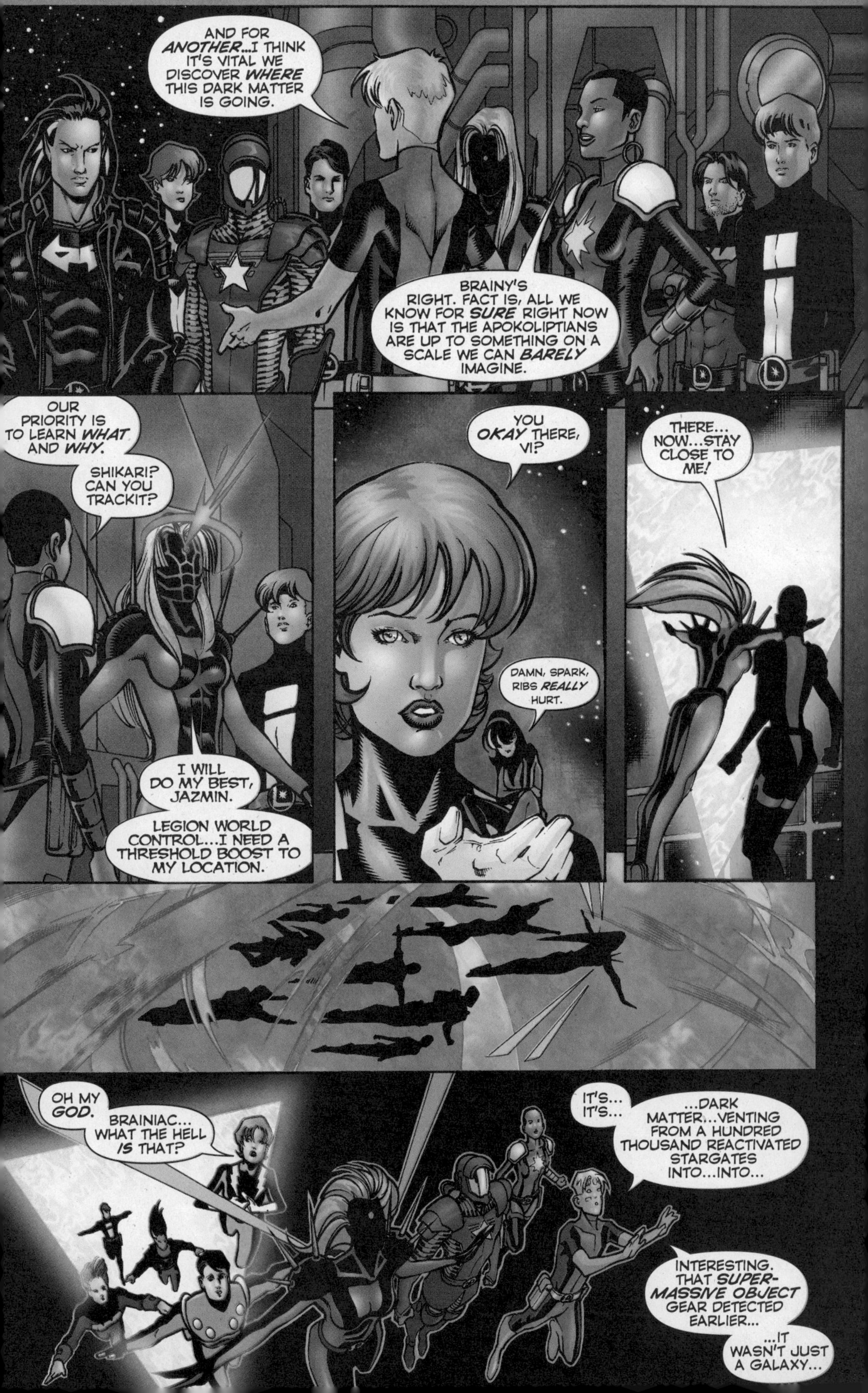
AND FOR ANOTHER...I THINK IT'S VITAL WE DISCOVER WHERE THIS DARK MATTER IS GOING.
BRAINY'S RIGHT. FACT IS, ALL WE KNOW FOR SURE RIGHT NOW IS THAT THE APOKOLIPTIANS ARE UP TO SOMETHING ON A SCALE WE CAN BARELY IMAGINE.
OUR PRIORITY IS TO LEARN WHAT AND WHY.
SHIKARI? CAN YOU TRACKIT?
I WILL DO MY BEST, JAZMIN.
LEGION WORLD CONTROL...I NEED A THRESHOLD BOOST TO MY LOCATION.
YOU OKAY THERE, VI?
DAMN, SPARK, RIBS REALLY HURT.
THERE... NOW...STAY CLOSE TO ME!
OH MY GOD.
BRAINIAC... WHAT THE HELL IS THAT?
IT'S... IT'S...
...DARK MATTER...VENTING FROM A HUNDRED THOUSAND REACTIVATED STARGATES INTO...INTO...
INTERESTING. THAT SUPER-MASSIVE OBJECT GEAR DETECTED EARLIER...
...IT WASN'T JUST A GALAXY...

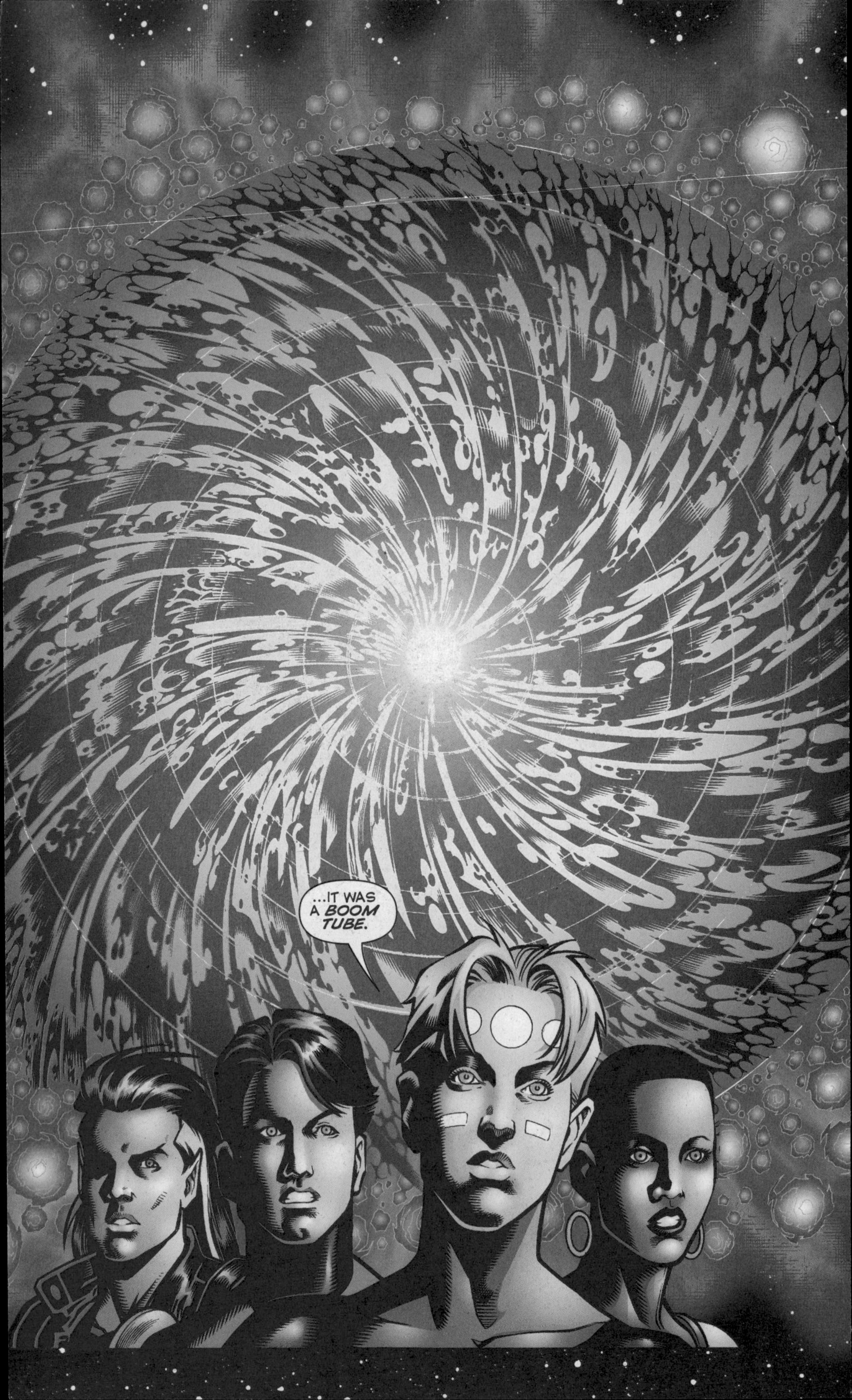
...IT WAS A BOOM TUBE.

B

WHA--?

OOM

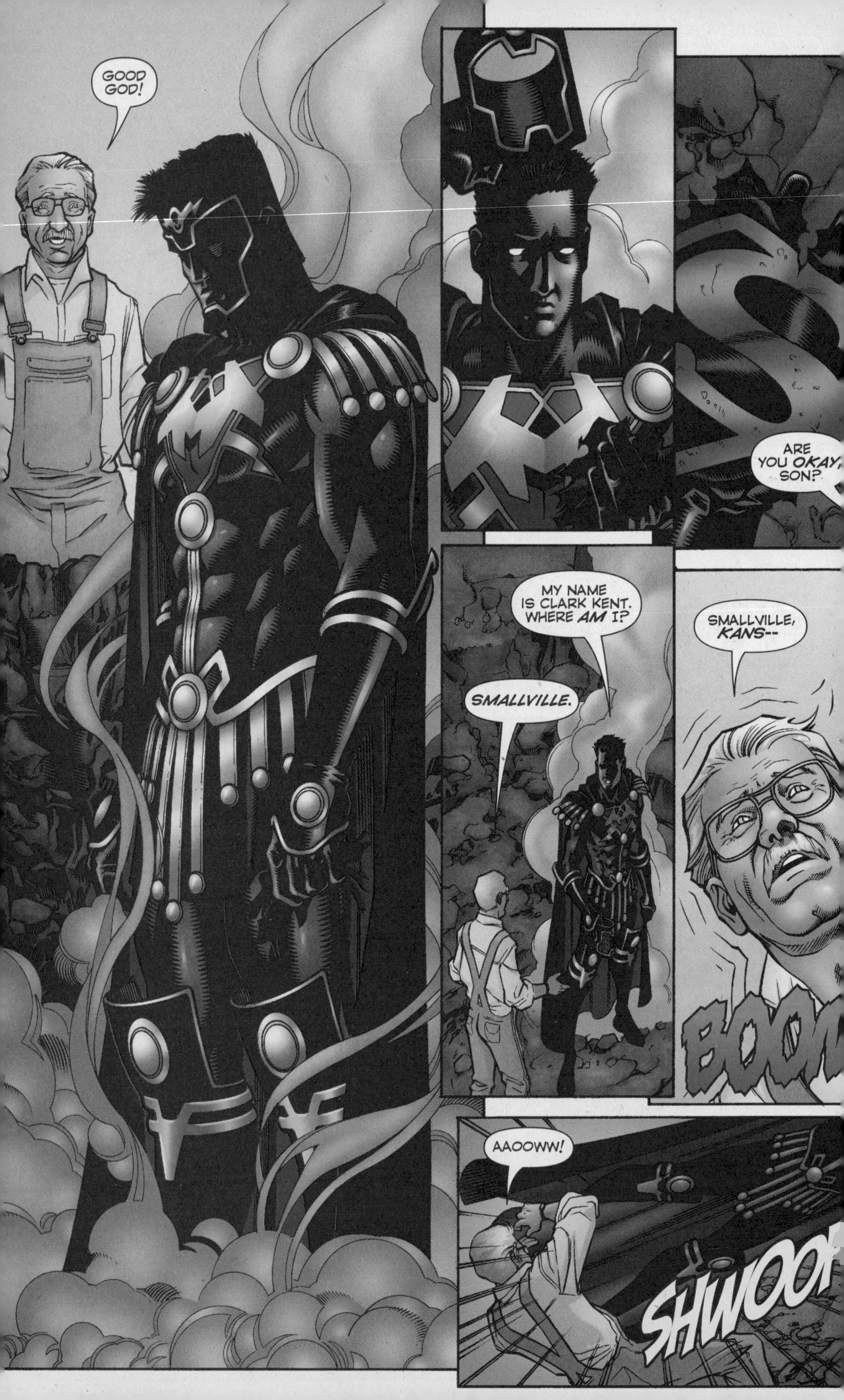
GOOD GOD!
ARE YOU OKAY, SON?
MY NAME IS CLARK KENT. WHERE AM I?
SMALLVILLE.
SMALLVILLE, KANS--
AAOOWW!

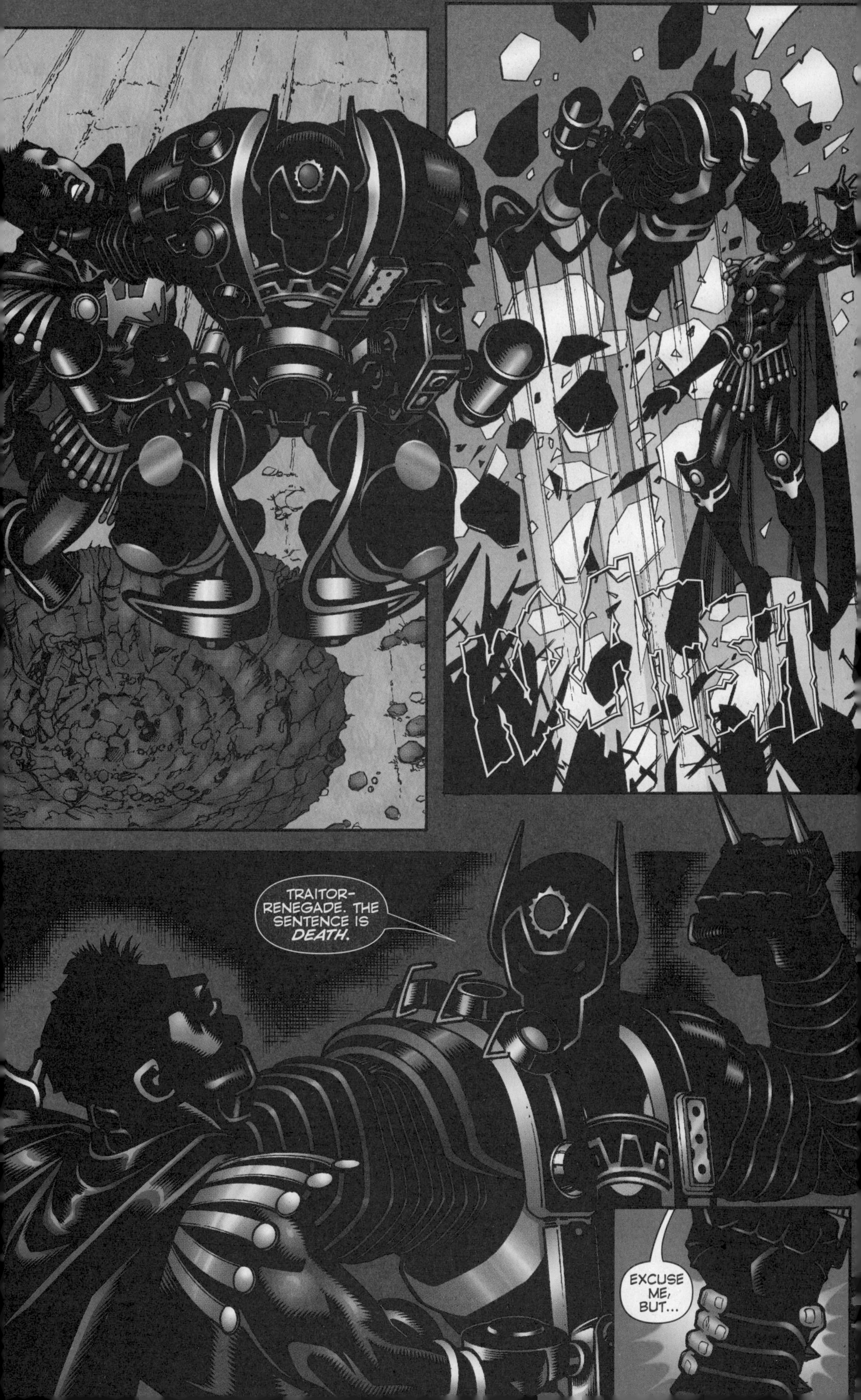
KRAASH
TRAITOR-RENEGADE. THE SENTENCE IS *DEATH*.
EXCUSE ME, BUT...

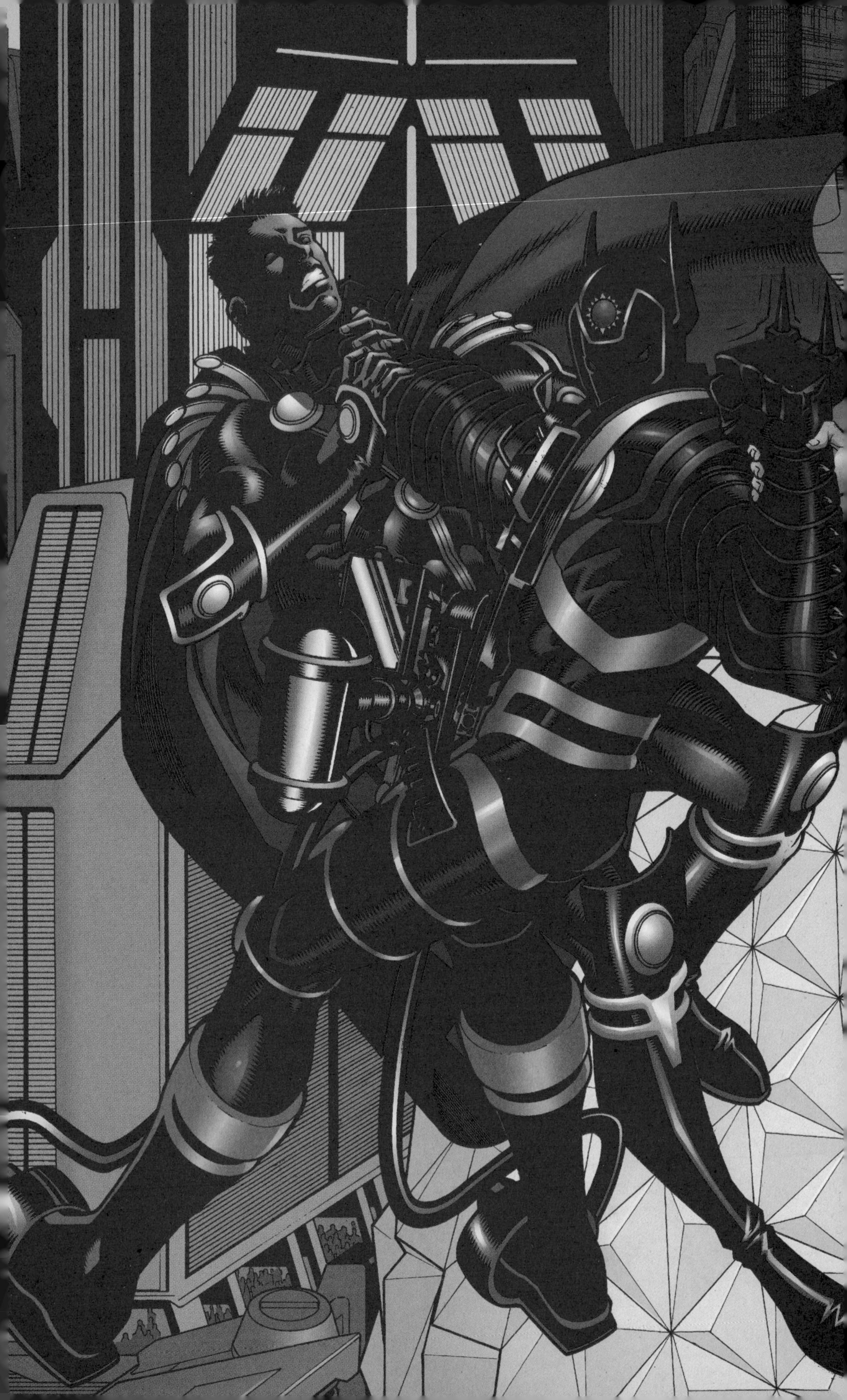

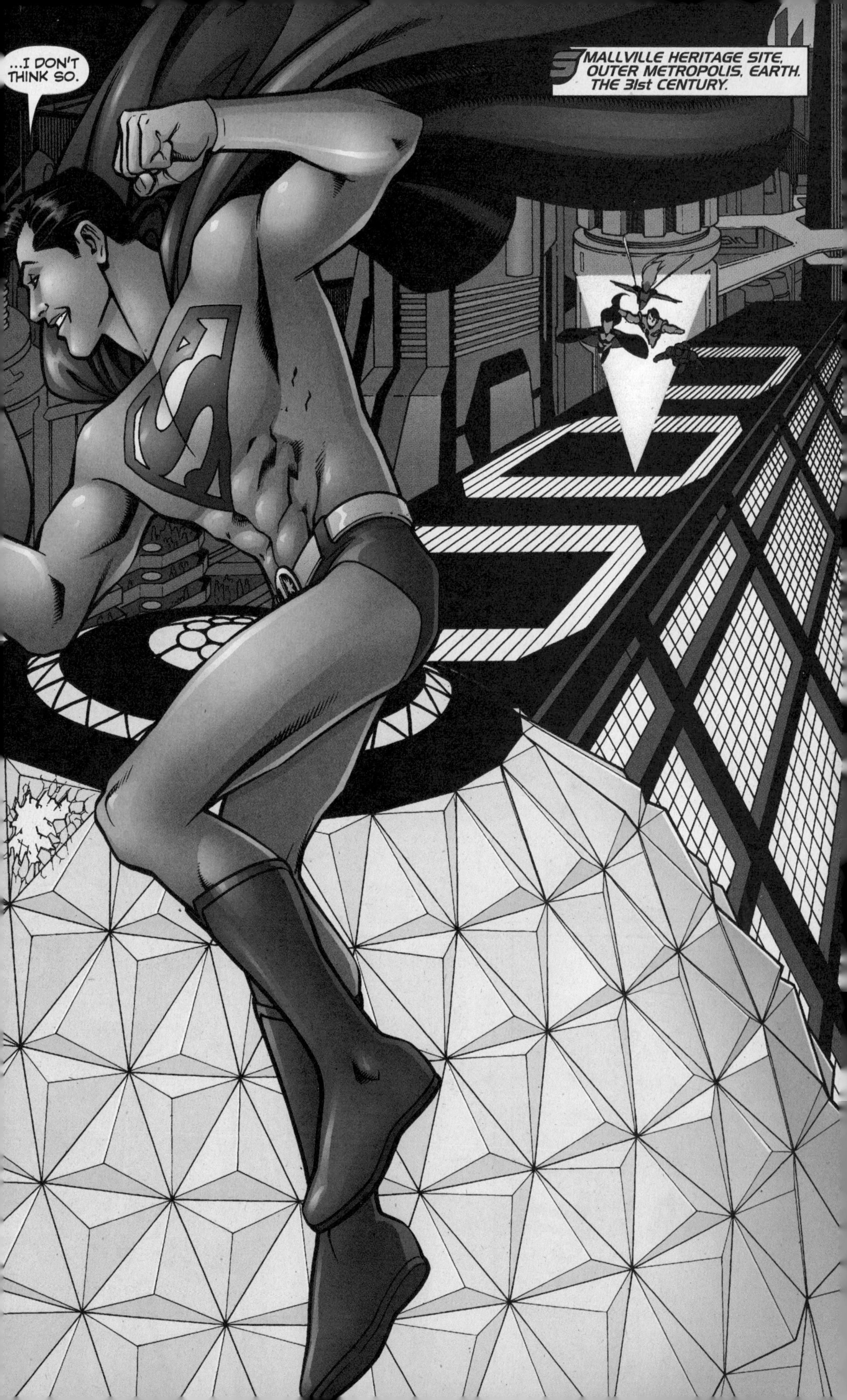
...I DON'T THINK SO.
SMALLVILLE HERITAGE SITE, OUTER METROPOLIS, EARTH. THE 31st CENTURY.

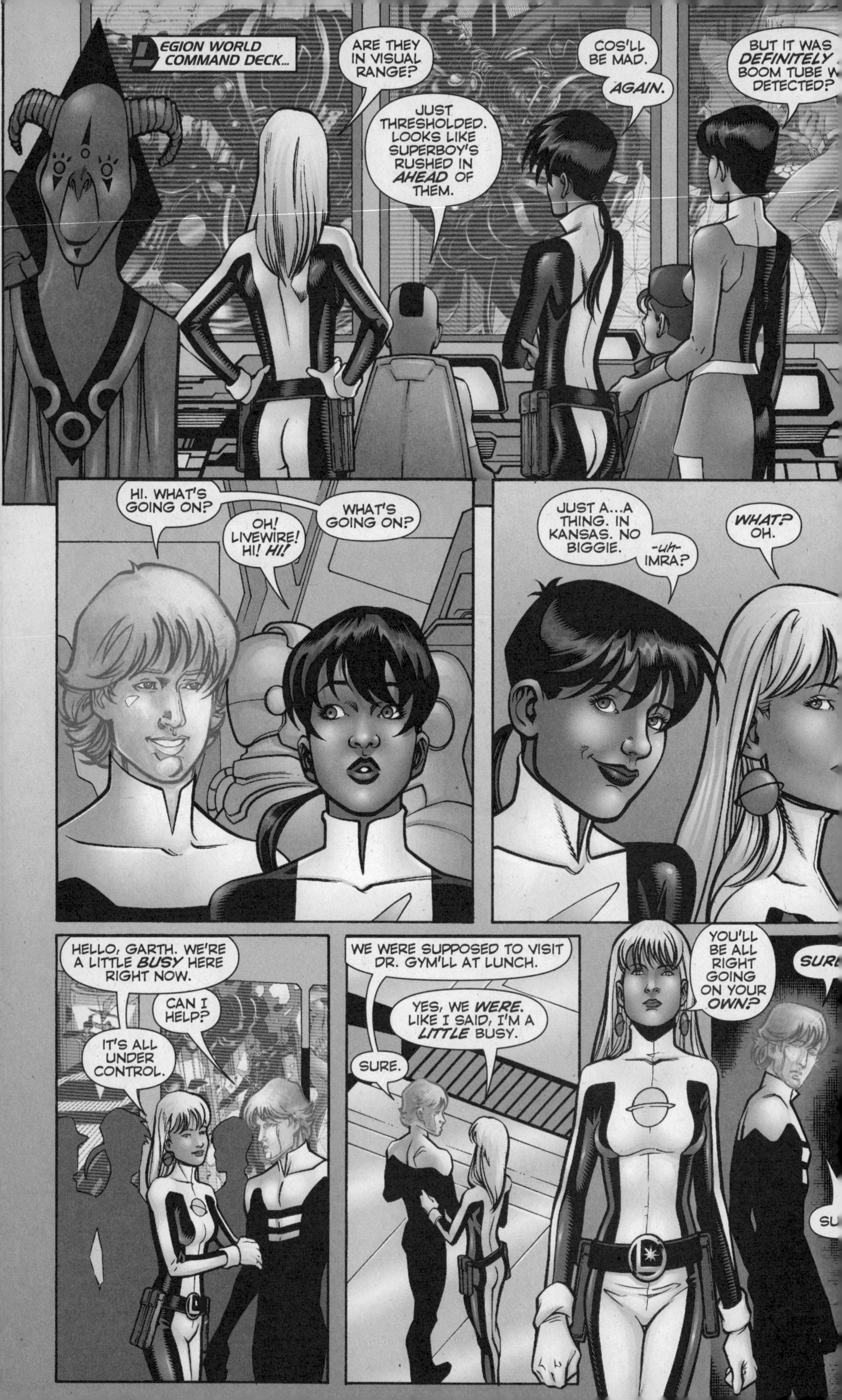
LEGION WORLD COMMAND DECK...
ARE THEY IN VISUAL RANGE?
JUST THRESHOLDED. LOOKS LIKE SUPERBOY'S RUSHED IN AHEAD OF THEM.
COS'LL BE MAD.
AGAIN.
BUT IT WAS DEFINITELY A BOOM TUBE W DETECTED?
HI. WHAT'S GOING ON?
OH! LIVEWIRE! HI! HI!
WHAT'S GOING ON?
JUST A...A THING. IN KANSAS. NO BIGGIE.
-uh- IMRA?
WHAT? OH.
HELLO, GARTH. WE'RE A LITTLE BUSY HERE RIGHT NOW.
CAN I HELP?
IT'S ALL UNDER CONTROL.
WE WERE SUPPOSED TO VISIT DR. GYM'LL AT LUNCH.
YES, WE WERE. LIKE I SAID, I'M A LITTLE BUSY.
SURE.
YOU'LL BE ALL RIGHT GOING ON YOUR OWN?
SUR
SU

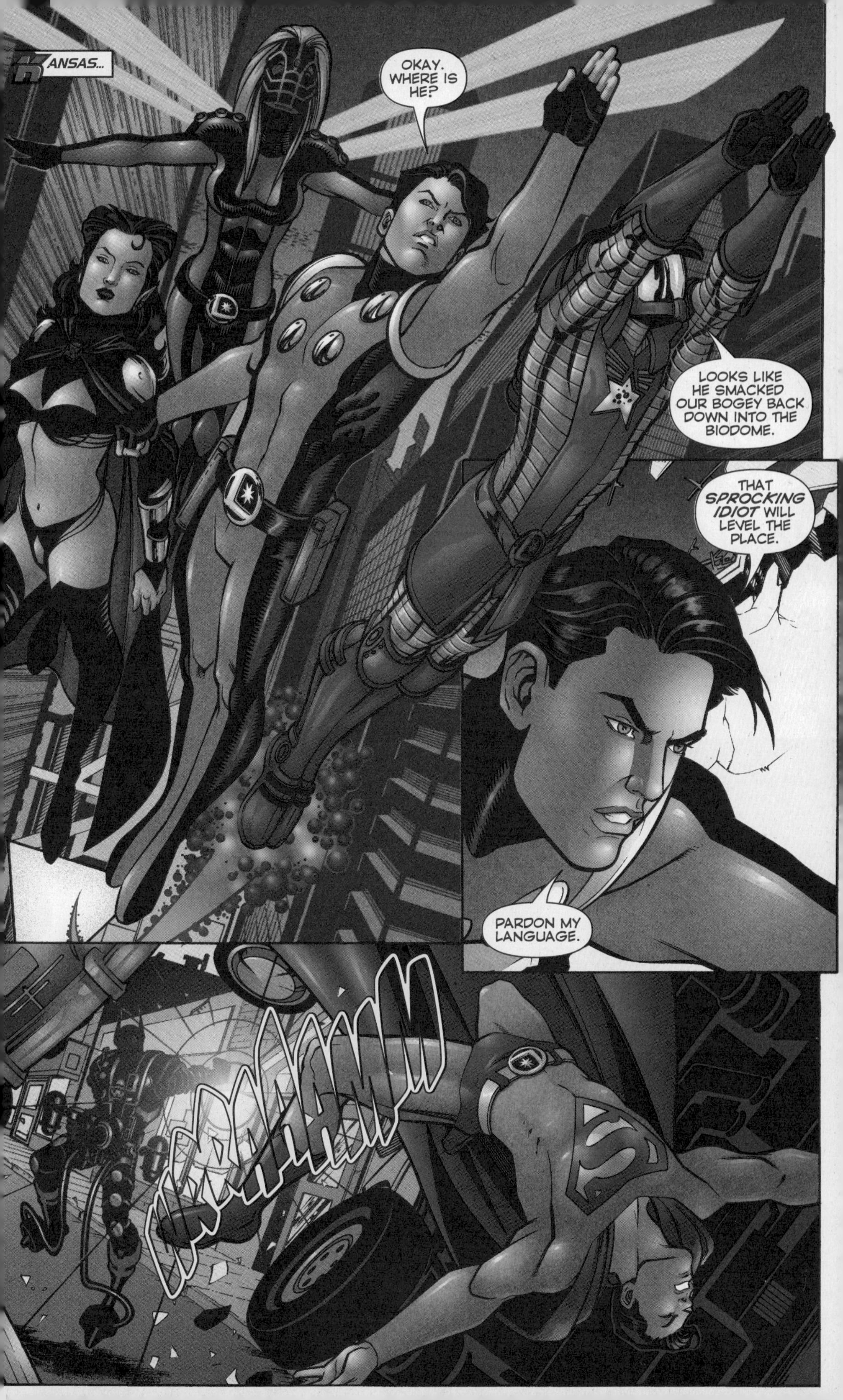
KANSAS...
OKAY. WHERE IS HE?
LOOKS LIKE HE SMACKED OUR BOGEY BACK DOWN INTO THE BIODOME.
THAT *SPROCKING IDIOT* WILL LEVEL THE PLACE.
PARDON MY LANGUAGE.

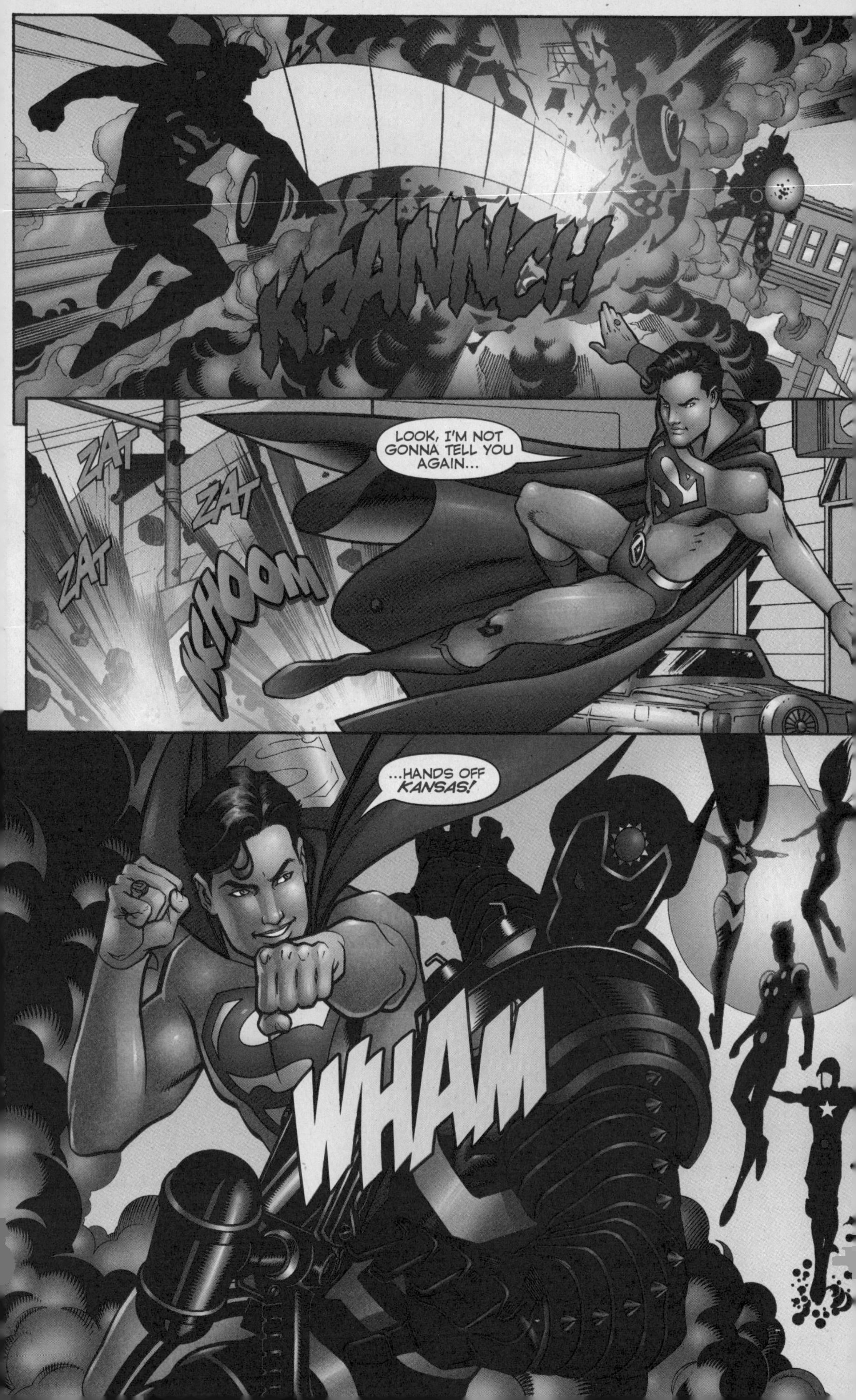
KRANNCH
ZAT
ZAT
ZAT
KKHOOM
LOOK, I'M NOT GONNA TELL YOU AGAIN...
...HANDS OFF *KANSAS!*
WHAM

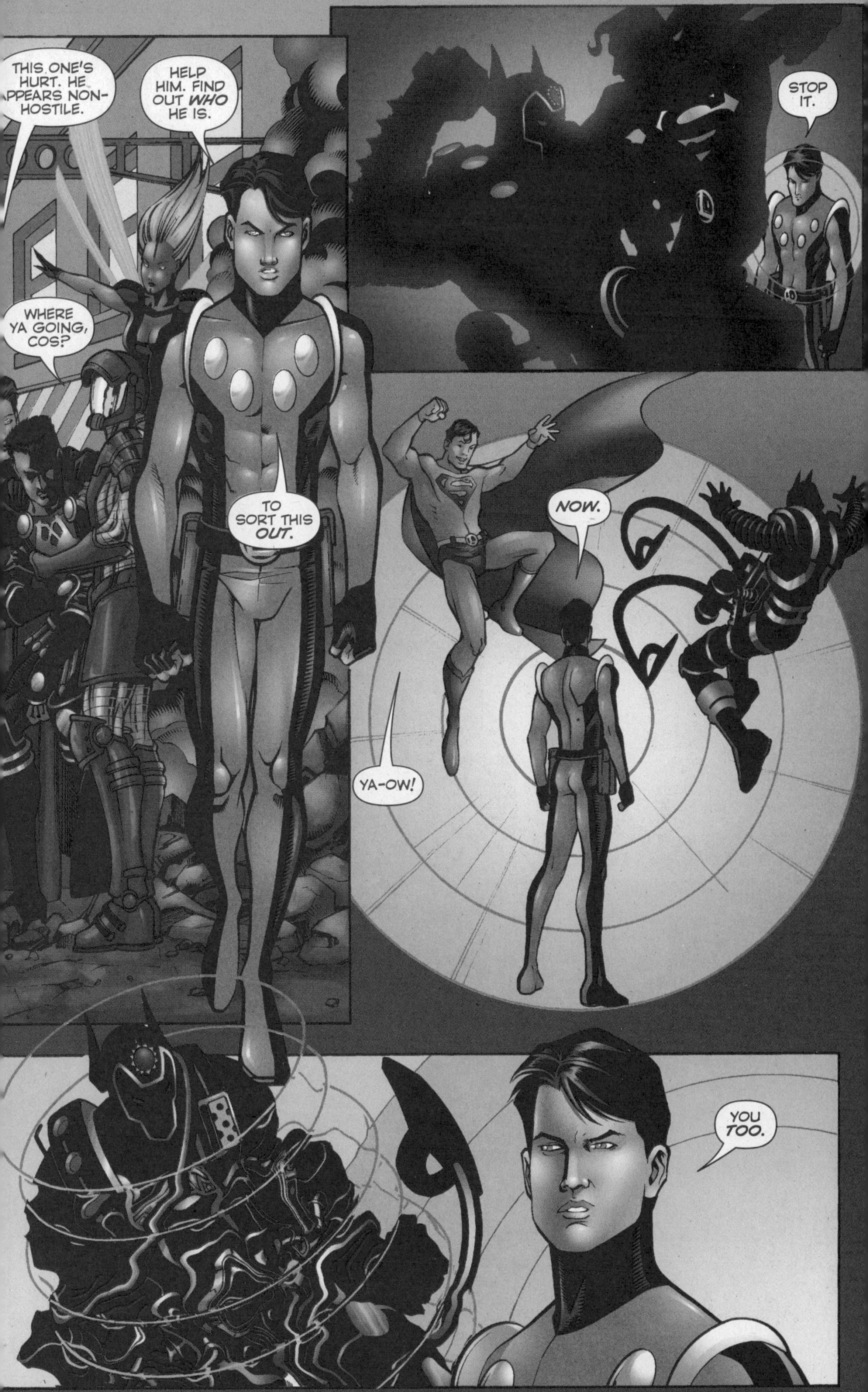
THIS ONE'S HURT. HE APPEARS NON-HOSTILE.
HELP HIM. FIND OUT WHO HE IS.
WHERE YA GOING, COS?
TO SORT THIS OUT.
STOP IT.
NOW.
YA-OW!
YOU TOO.

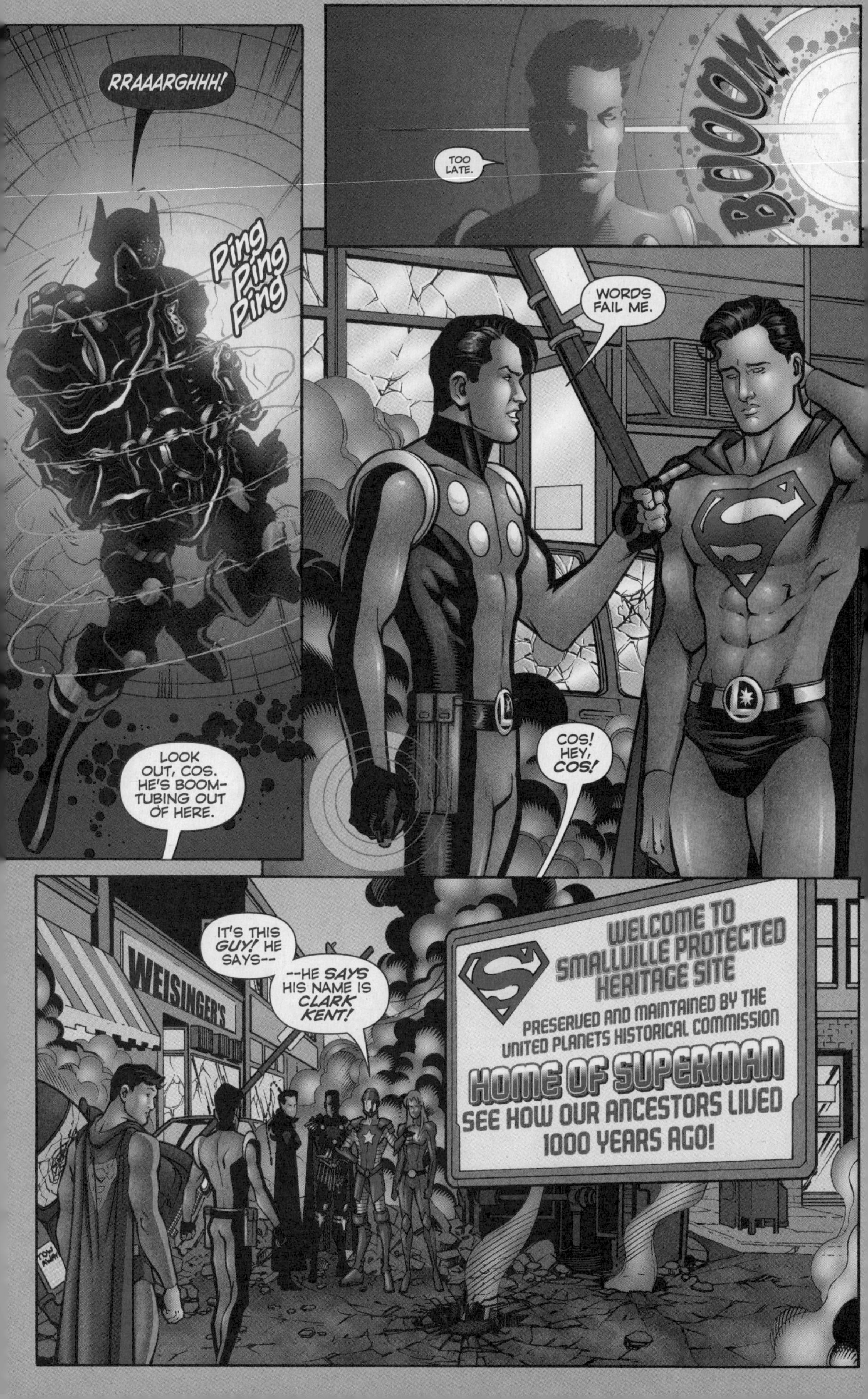
RRAAARGHHH!
Ping Ping Ping
TOO LATE.
BOOOM
LOOK OUT, COS. HE'S BOOM-TUBING OUT OF HERE.
WORDS FAIL ME.
COS! HEY, COS!
IT'S THIS GUY! HE SAYS--
--HE SAYS HIS NAME IS CLARK KENT!
WEISINGER'S
WELCOME TO SMALLVILLE PROTECTED HERITAGE SITE
PRESERVED AND MAINTAINED BY THE UNITED PLANETS HISTORICAL COMMISSION
HOME OF SUPERMAN
SEE HOW OUR ANCESTORS LIVED 1000 YEARS AGO!

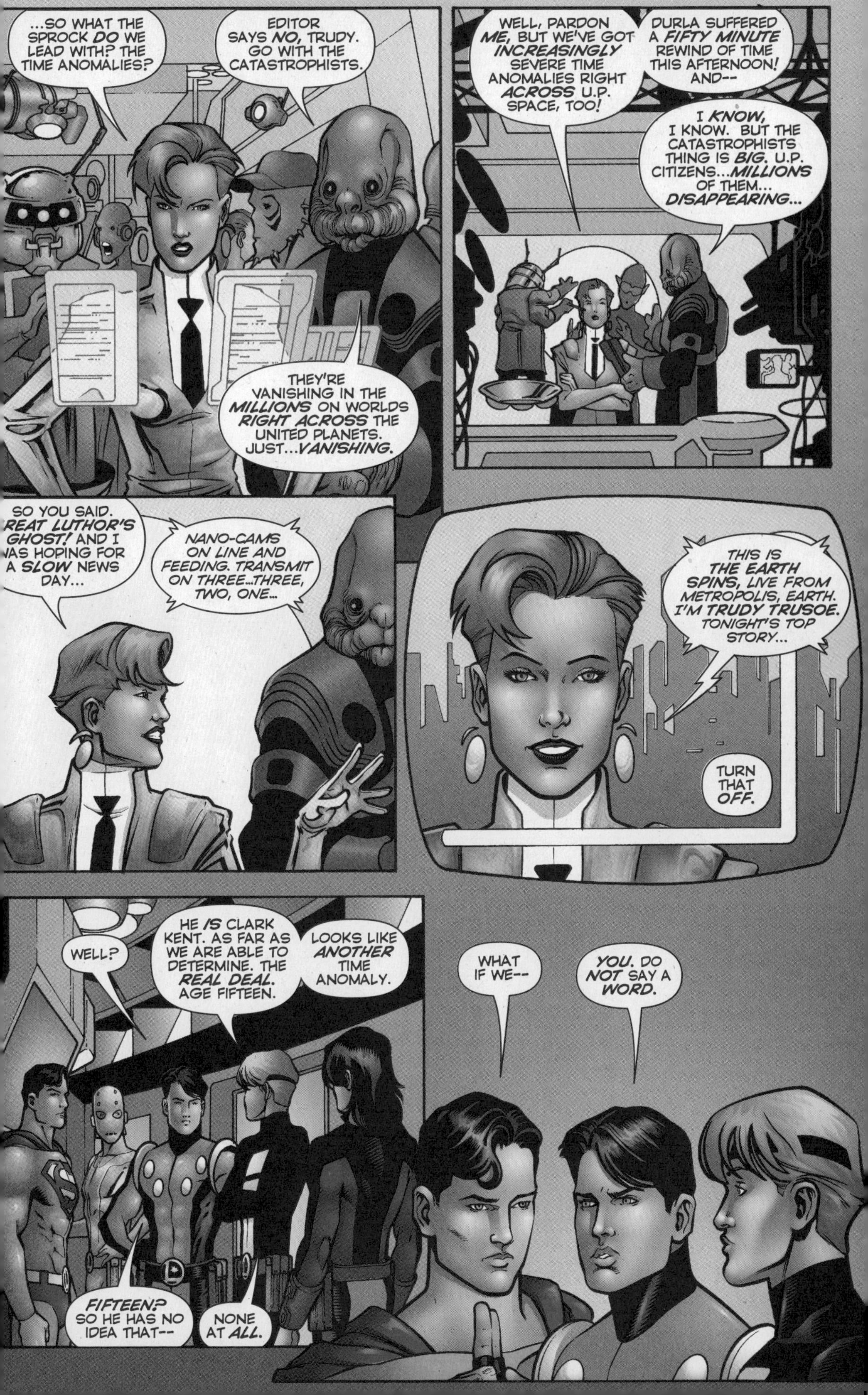
...SO WHAT THE SPROCK DO WE LEAD WITH? THE TIME ANOMALIES?
EDITOR SAYS NO, TRUDY. GO WITH THE CATASTROPHISTS.
THEY'RE VANISHING IN THE MILLIONS ON WORLDS RIGHT ACROSS THE UNITED PLANETS. JUST...VANISHING.
WELL, PARDON ME, BUT WE'VE GOT INCREASINGLY SEVERE TIME ANOMALIES RIGHT ACROSS U.P. SPACE, TOO!
DURLA SUFFERED A FIFTY MINUTE REWIND OF TIME THIS AFTERNOON! AND--
I KNOW, I KNOW. BUT THE CATASTROPHISTS THING IS BIG. U.P. CITIZENS...MILLIONS OF THEM... DISAPPEARING...
SO YOU SAID. REAT LUTHOR'S GHOST! AND I WAS HOPING FOR A SLOW NEWS DAY...
NANO-CAMS ON LINE AND FEEDING. TRANSMIT ON THREE...THREE, TWO, ONE...
THIS IS THE EARTH SPINS, LIVE FROM METROPOLIS, EARTH. I'M TRUDY TRUSOE. TONIGHT'S TOP STORY...
TURN THAT OFF.
WELL?
HE IS CLARK KENT. AS FAR AS WE ARE ABLE TO DETERMINE. THE REAL DEAL. AGE FIFTEEN.
LOOKS LIKE ANOTHER TIME ANOMALY.
WHAT IF WE--
YOU. DO NOT SAY A WORD.
FIFTEEN? SO HE HAS NO IDEA THAT--
NONE AT ALL.

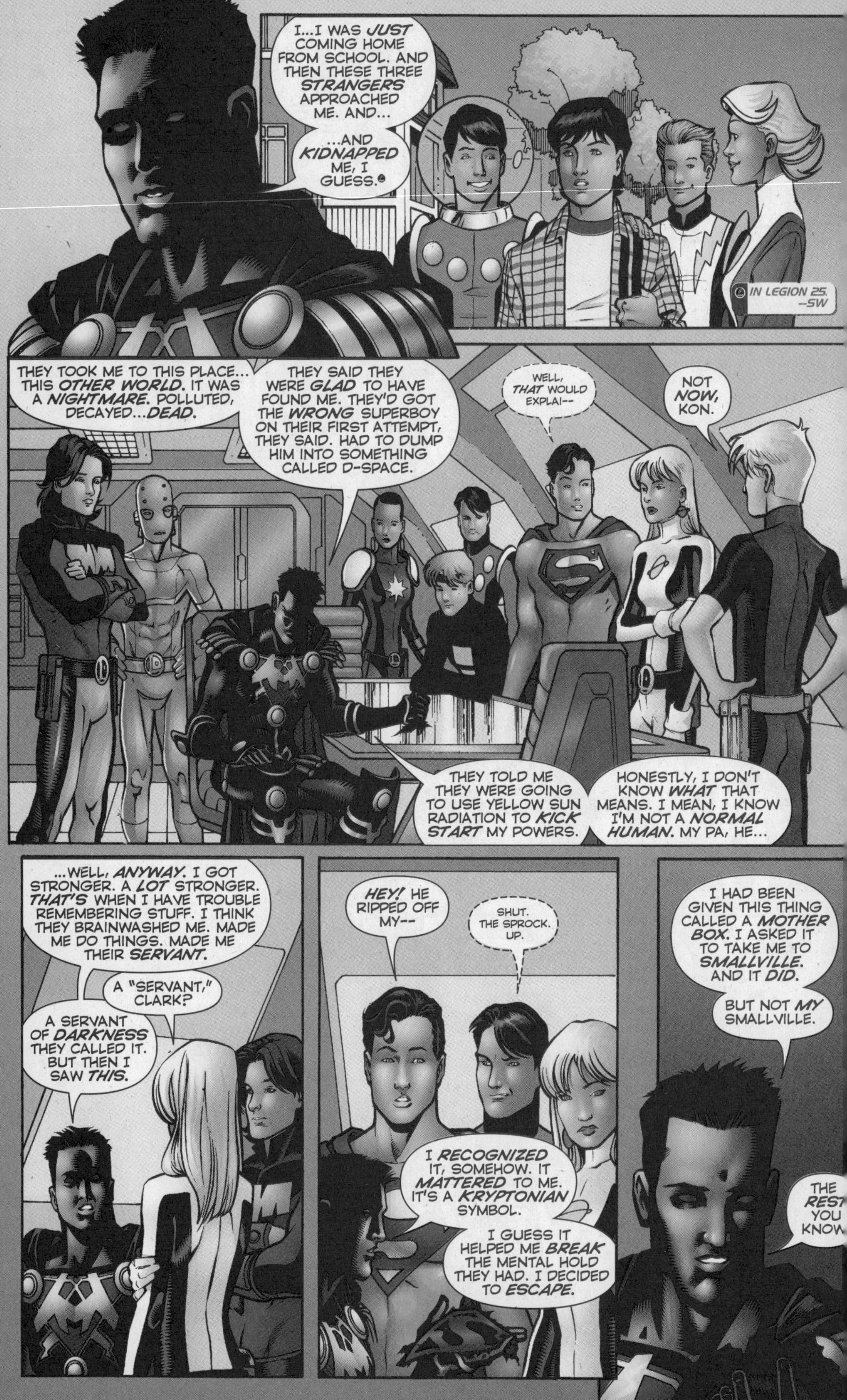

I...I WAS JUST COMING HOME FROM SCHOOL. AND THEN THESE THREE STRANGERS APPROACHED ME. AND...
...AND KIDNAPPED ME, I GUESS.
IN LEGION 25. --SW
THEY TOOK ME TO THIS PLACE... THIS OTHER WORLD. IT WAS A NIGHTMARE. POLLUTED, DECAYED...DEAD.
THEY SAID THEY WERE GLAD TO HAVE FOUND ME. THEY'D GOT THE WRONG SUPERBOY ON THEIR FIRST ATTEMPT, THEY SAID. HAD TO DUMP HIM INTO SOMETHING CALLED D-SPACE.
WELL, THAT WOULD EXPLAI--
NOT NOW, KON.
THEY TOLD ME THEY WERE GOING TO USE YELLOW SUN RADIATION TO KICK START MY POWERS.
HONESTLY, I DON'T KNOW WHAT THAT MEANS. I MEAN, I KNOW I'M NOT A NORMAL HUMAN. MY PA, HE...
...WELL, ANYWAY. I GOT STRONGER. A LOT STRONGER. THAT'S WHEN I HAVE TROUBLE REMEMBERING STUFF. I THINK THEY BRAINWASHED ME. MADE ME DO THINGS. MADE ME THEIR SERVANT.
A "SERVANT," CLARK?
A SERVANT OF DARKNESS THEY CALLED IT. BUT THEN I SAW THIS.
HEY! HE RIPPED OFF MY--
SHUT. THE SPROCK. UP.
I RECOGNIZED IT, SOMEHOW. IT MATTERED TO ME. IT'S A KRYPTONIAN SYMBOL.
I GUESS IT HELPED ME BREAK THE MENTAL HOLD THEY HAD. I DECIDED TO ESCAPE.
I HAD BEEN GIVEN THIS THING CALLED A MOTHER BOX. I ASKED IT TO TAKE ME TO SMALLVILLE. AND IT DID.
BUT NOT MY SMALLVILLE.
THE REST YOU KNOW

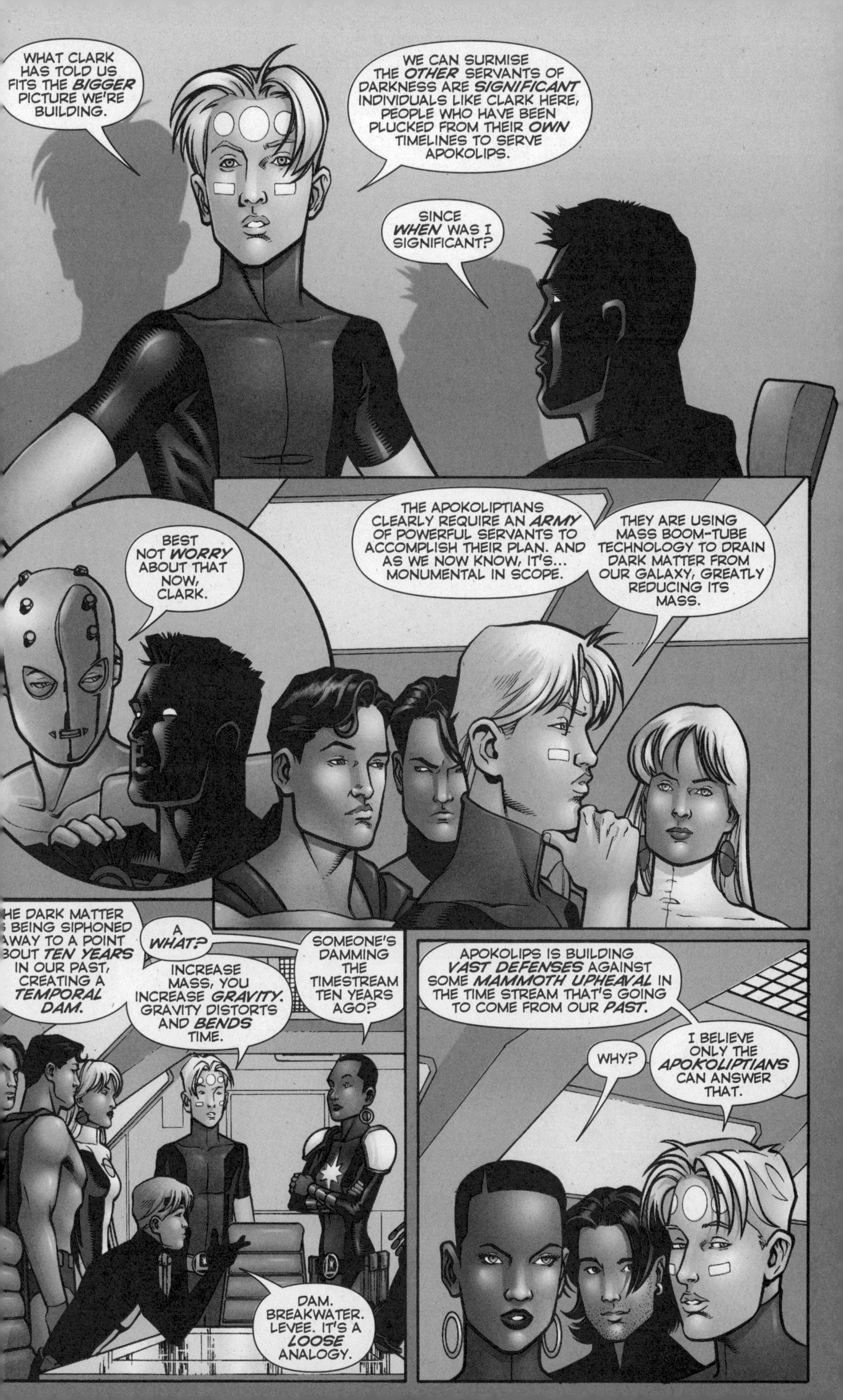
WHAT CLARK HAS TOLD US FITS THE BIGGER PICTURE WE'RE BUILDING.
WE CAN SURMISE THE OTHER SERVANTS OF DARKNESS ARE SIGNIFICANT INDIVIDUALS LIKE CLARK HERE, PEOPLE WHO HAVE BEEN PLUCKED FROM THEIR OWN TIMELINES TO SERVE APOKOLIPS.
SINCE WHEN WAS I SIGNIFICANT?
BEST NOT WORRY ABOUT THAT NOW, CLARK.
THE APOKOLIPTIANS CLEARLY REQUIRE AN ARMY OF POWERFUL SERVANTS TO ACCOMPLISH THEIR PLAN. AND AS WE NOW KNOW, IT'S... MONUMENTAL IN SCOPE.
THEY ARE USING MASS BOOM-TUBE TECHNOLOGY TO DRAIN DARK MATTER FROM OUR GALAXY, GREATLY REDUCING ITS MASS.
HE DARK MATTER S BEING SIPHONED AWAY TO A POINT BOUT TEN YEARS IN OUR PAST, CREATING A TEMPORAL DAM.
A WHAT?
INCREASE MASS, YOU INCREASE GRAVITY. GRAVITY DISTORTS AND BENDS TIME.
SOMEONE'S DAMMING THE TIMESTREAM TEN YEARS AGO?
DAM. BREAKWATER. LEVEE. IT'S A LOOSE ANALOGY.
APOKOLIPS IS BUILDING VAST DEFENSES AGAINST SOME MAMMOTH UPHEAVAL IN THE TIME STREAM THAT'S GOING TO COME FROM OUR PAST.
WHY?
I BELIEVE ONLY THE APOKOLIPTIANS CAN ANSWER THAT.

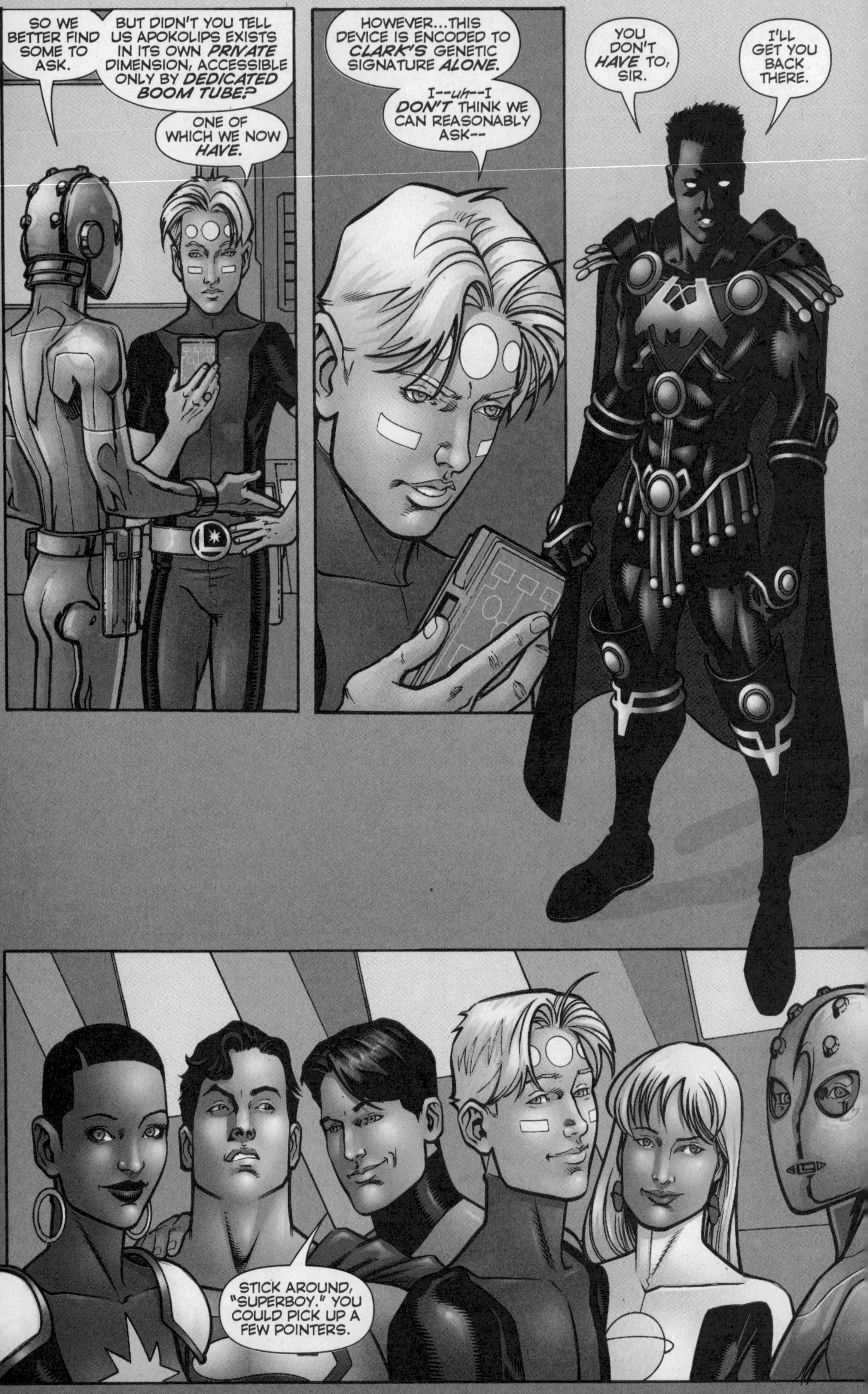
SO WE BETTER FIND SOME TO ASK.
BUT DIDN'T YOU TELL US APOKOLIPS EXISTS IN ITS OWN PRIVATE DIMENSION, ACCESSIBLE ONLY BY DEDICATED BOOM TUBE?
ONE OF WHICH WE NOW HAVE.
HOWEVER...THIS DEVICE IS ENCODED TO CLARK'S GENETIC SIGNATURE ALONE.
I--uh--I DON'T THINK WE CAN REASONABLY ASK--
YOU DON'T HAVE TO, SIR.
I'LL GET YOU BACK THERE.
STICK AROUND, "SUPERBOY." YOU COULD PICK UP A FEW POINTERS.

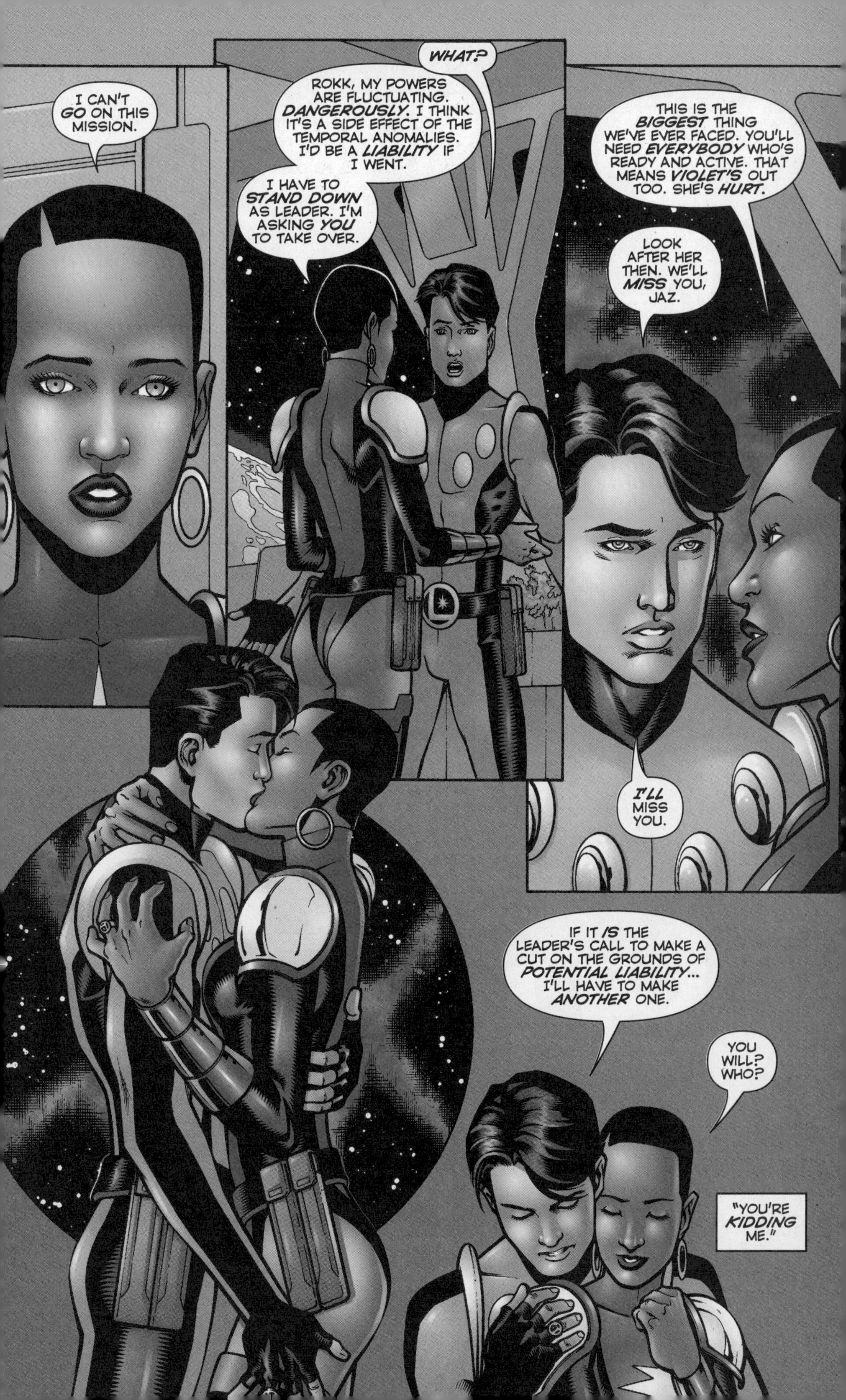
I CAN'T *GO* ON THIS MISSION.
WHAT?
ROKK, MY POWERS ARE FLUCTUATING. *DANGEROUSLY.* I THINK IT'S A SIDE EFFECT OF THE TEMPORAL ANOMALIES. I'D BE A *LIABILITY* IF I WENT.
I HAVE TO *STAND DOWN* AS LEADER. I'M ASKING *YOU* TO TAKE OVER.
THIS IS THE *BIGGEST* THING WE'VE EVER FACED. YOU'LL NEED *EVERYBODY* WHO'S READY AND ACTIVE. THAT MEANS *VIOLET'S* OUT TOO. SHE'S *HURT.*
LOOK AFTER HER THEN. WE'LL *MISS* YOU, JAZ.
I'LL MISS YOU.
IF IT *IS* THE LEADER'S CALL TO MAKE A CUT ON THE GROUNDS OF *POTENTIAL LIABILITY...* I'LL HAVE TO MAKE *ANOTHER* ONE.
YOU WILL? WHO?
"YOU'RE *KIDDING* ME."

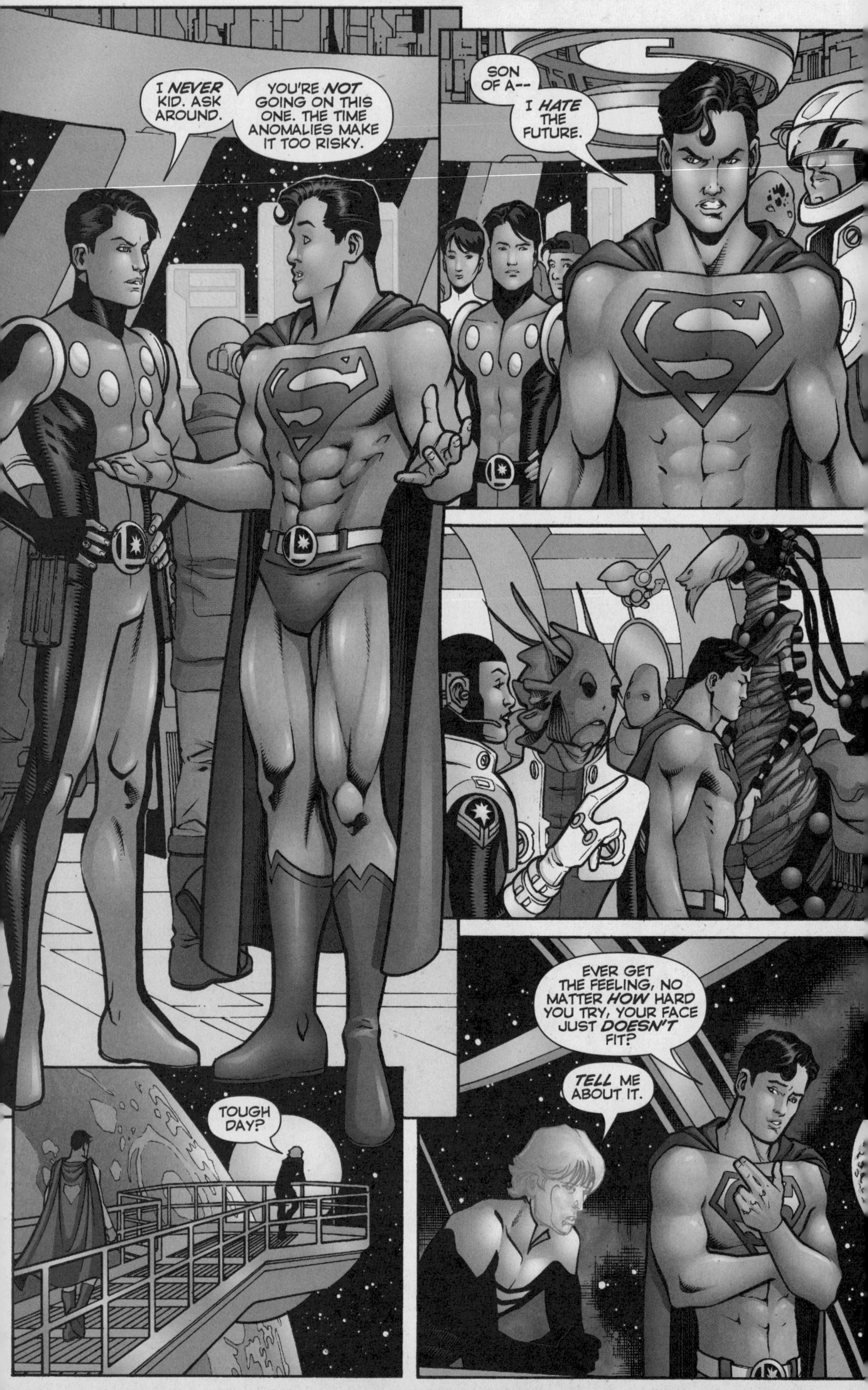
YOU'RE NOT GOING ON THIS ONE. THE TIME ANOMALIES MAKE IT TOO RISKY.
I NEVER KID. ASK AROUND.
SON OF A--
I HATE THE FUTURE.
TOUGH DAY?
EVER GET THE FEELING, NO MATTER HOW HARD YOU TRY, YOUR FACE JUST DOESN'T FIT?
TELL ME ABOUT IT.

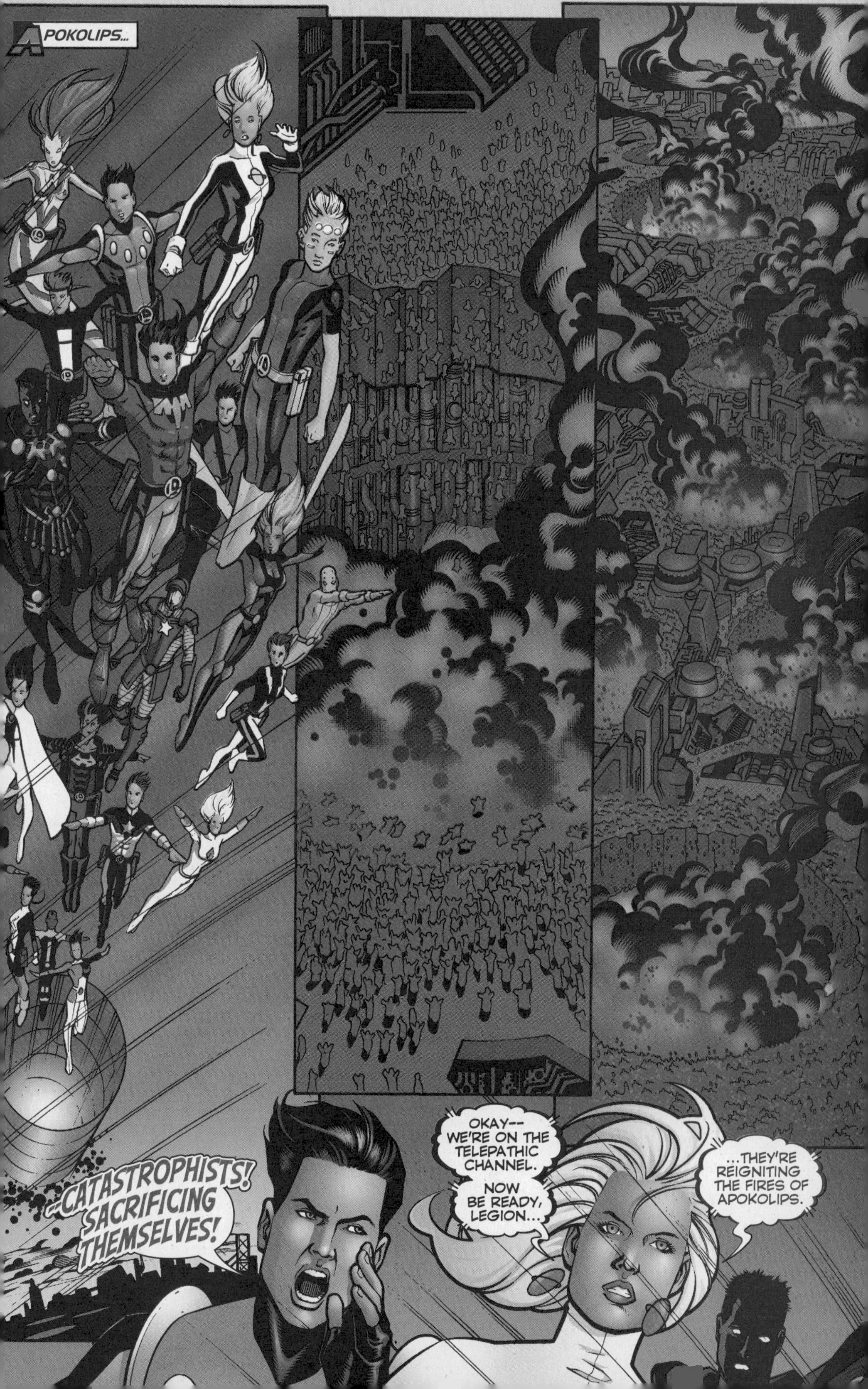
APOKOLIPS...
--CATASTROPHISTS! SACRIFICING THEMSELVES!
OKAY-- WE'RE ON THE TELEPATHIC CHANNEL.
NOW BE READY, LEGION...
...THEY'RE REIGNITING THE FIRES OF APOKOLIPS.

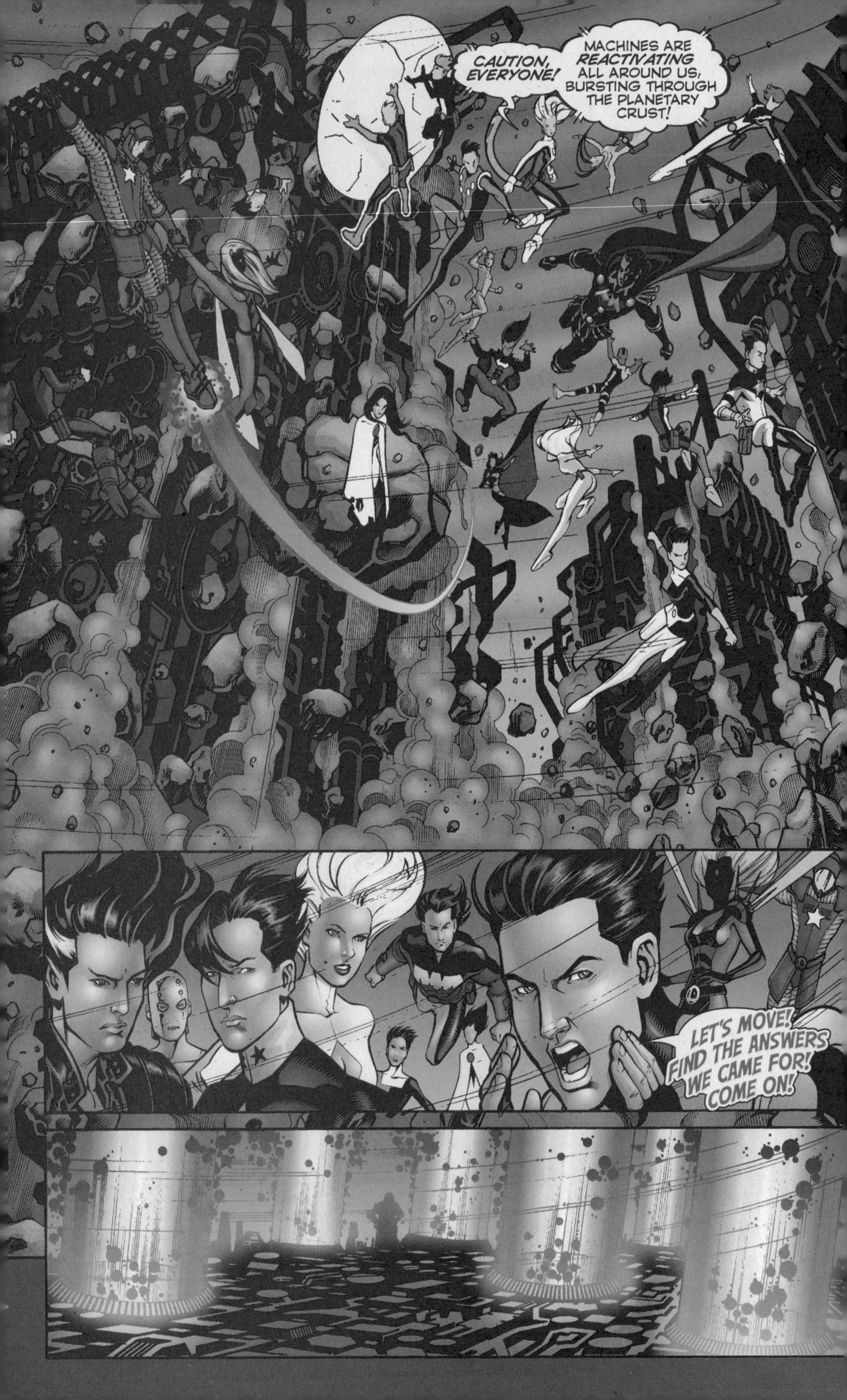
CAUTION, EVERYONE!
MACHINES ARE REACTIVATING ALL AROUND US, BURSTING THROUGH THE PLANETARY CRUST!
LET'S MOVE! FIND THE ANSWERS WE CAME FOR! COME ON!

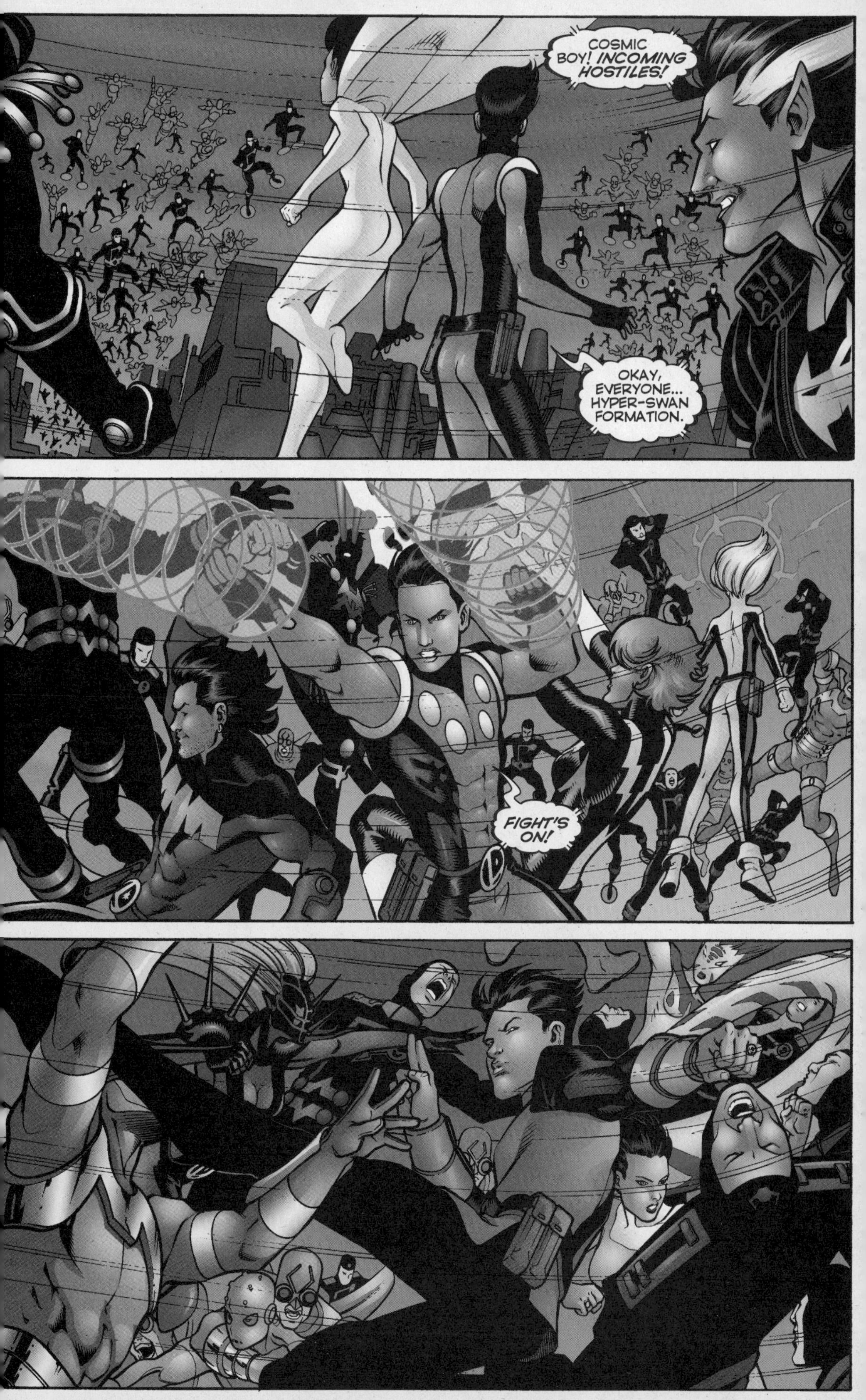
COSMIC BOY! INCOMING HOSTILES!
OKAY, EVERYONE... HYPER-SWAN FORMATION.
FIGHT'S ON!

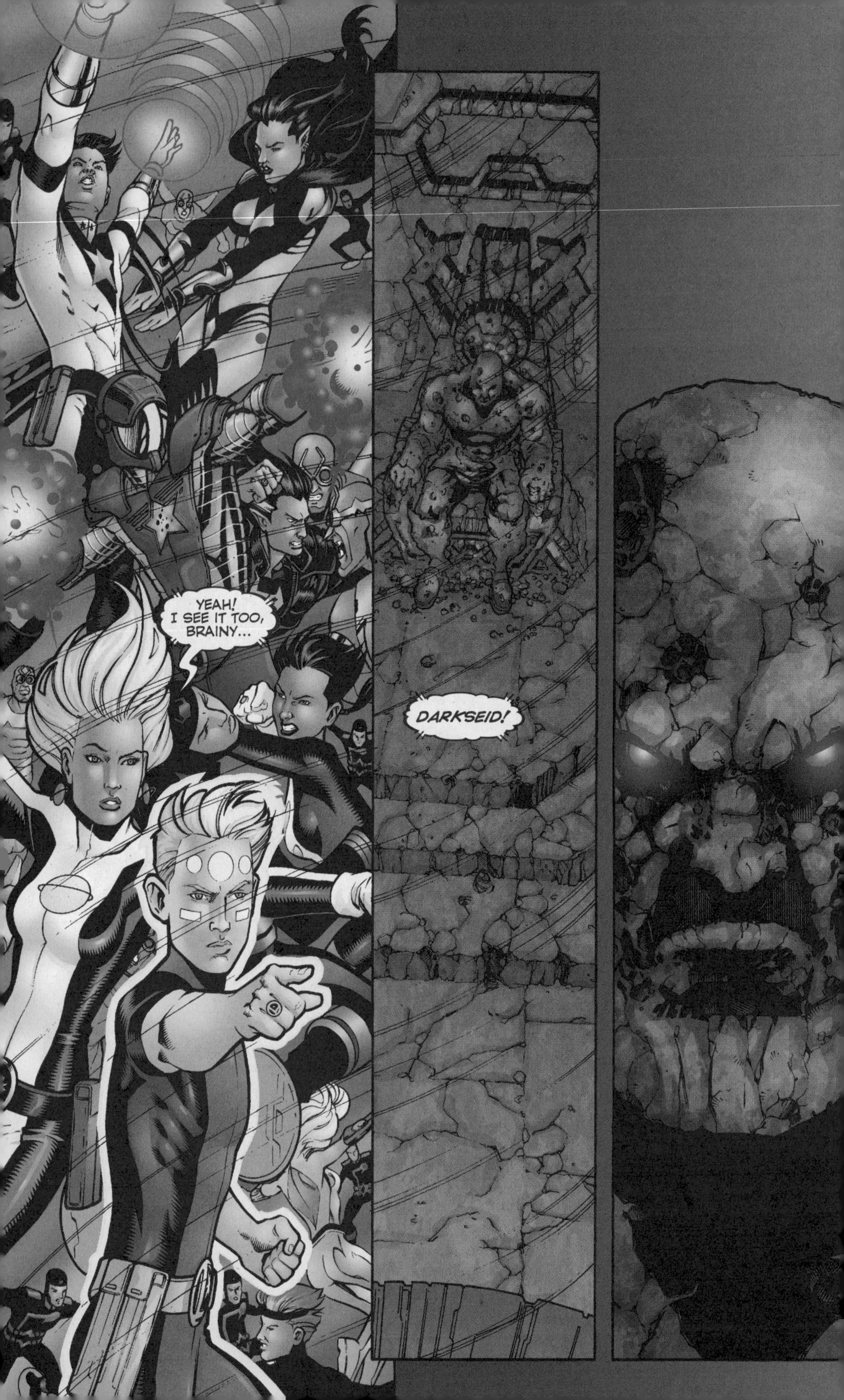
YEAH! I SEE IT TOO, BRAINY...
DARKSEID!

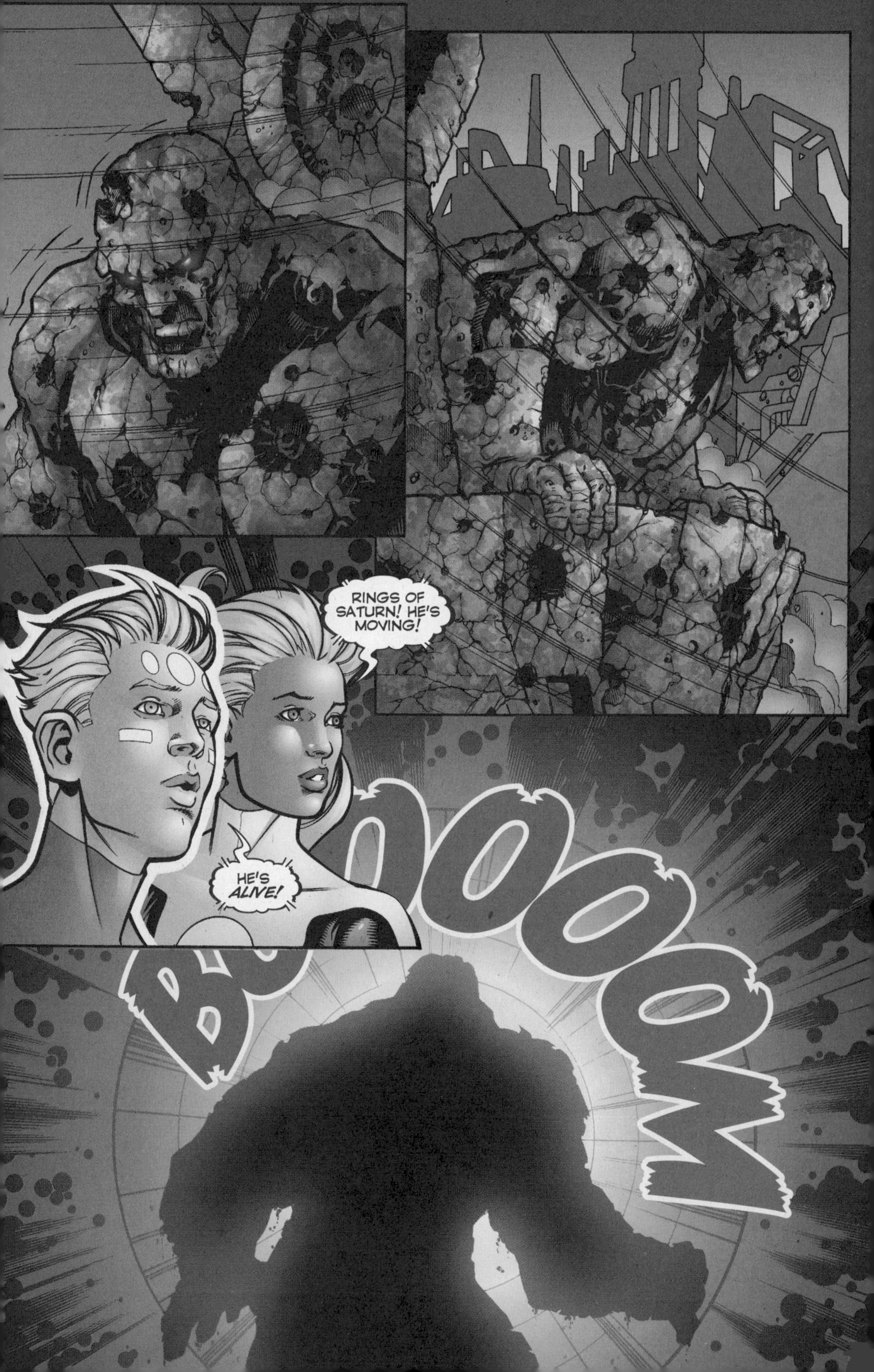
RINGS OF SATURN! HE'S MOVING!
HE'S ALIVE!
BOOOOOOM

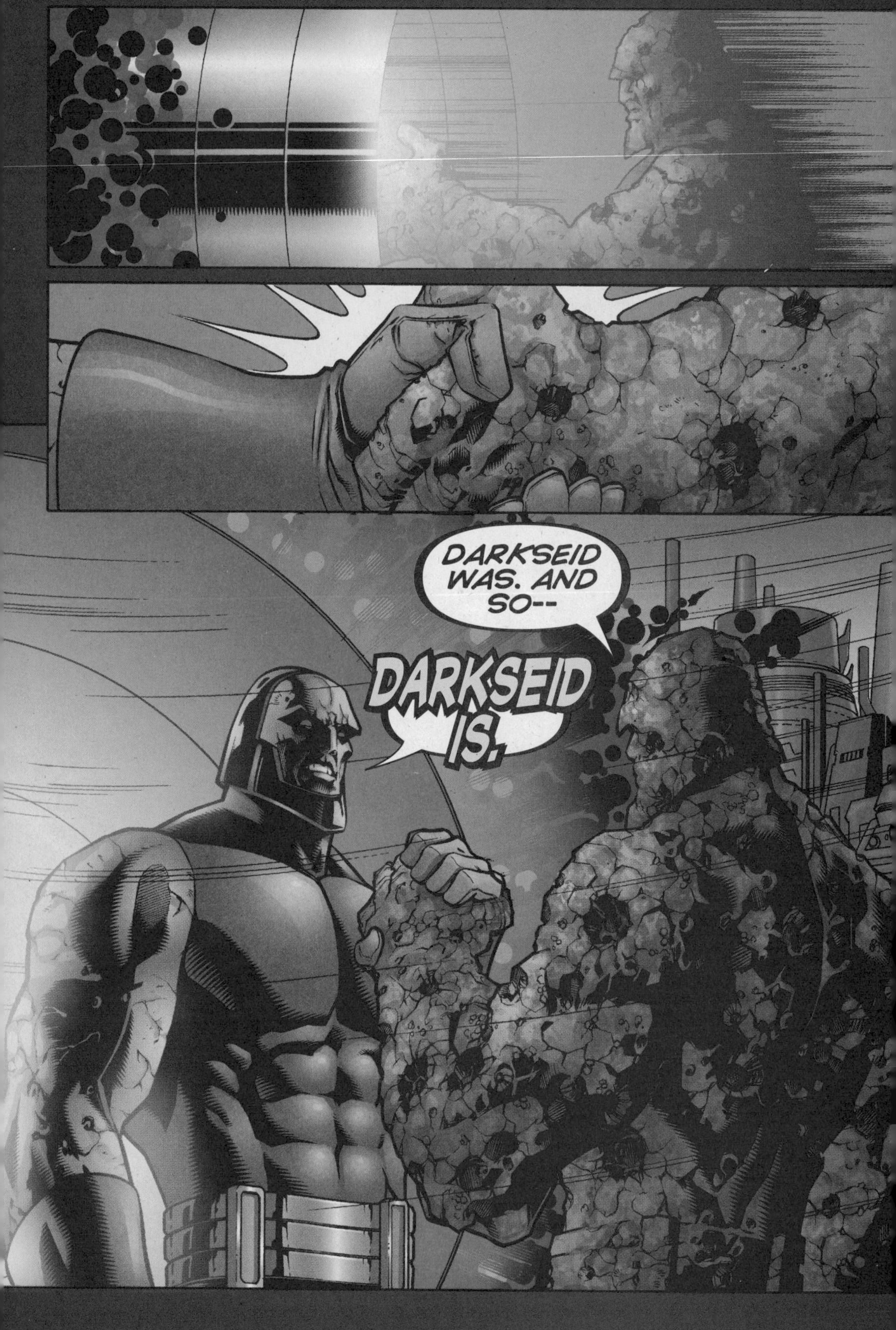
DARKSEID WAS. AND SO--
DARKSEID IS.

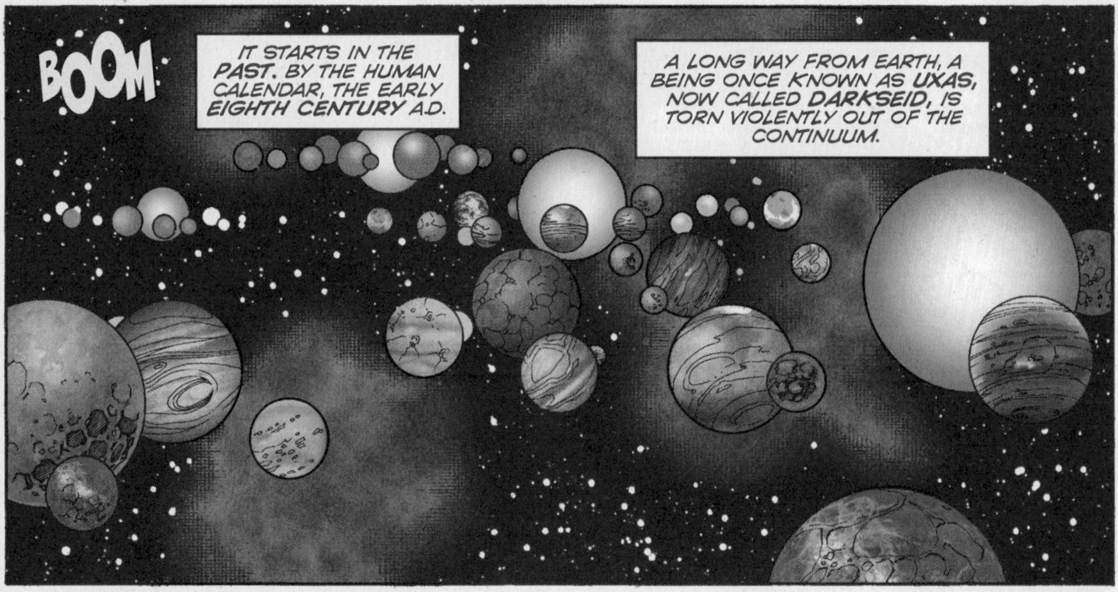
BOOM
IT STARTS IN THE PAST. BY THE HUMAN CALENDAR, THE EARLY EIGHTH CENTURY A.D.
A LONG WAY FROM EARTH, A BEING ONCE KNOWN AS UXAS, NOW CALLED DARKSEID, IS TORN VIOLENTLY OUT OF THE CONTINUUM.

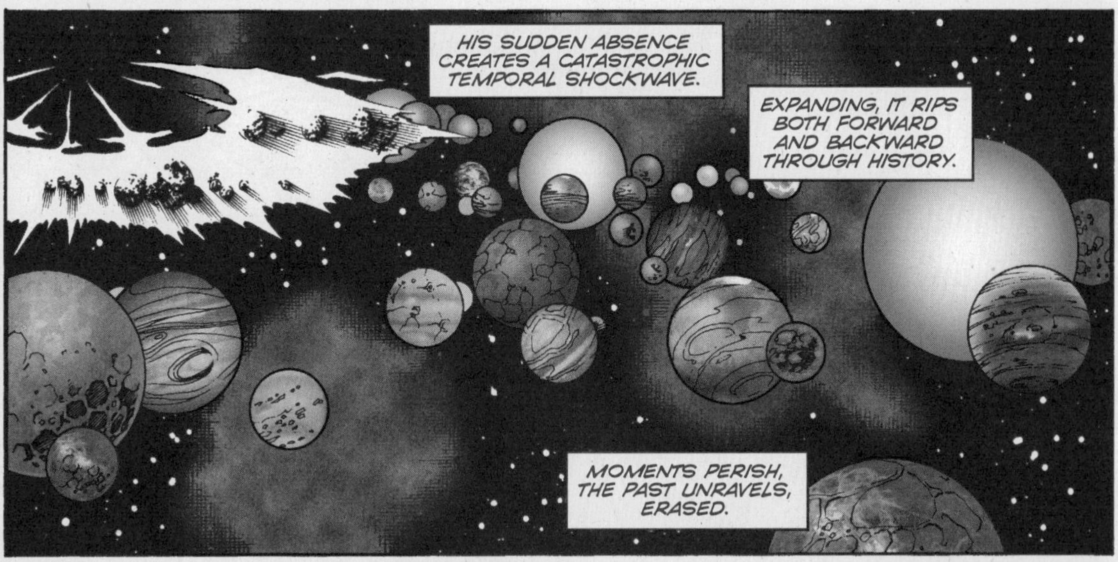
HIS SUDDEN ABSENCE CREATES A CATASTROPHIC TEMPORAL SHOCKWAVE.
EXPANDING, IT RIPS BOTH FORWARD AND BACKWARD THROUGH HISTORY.
MOMENTS PERISH, THE PAST UNRAVELS, ERASED.

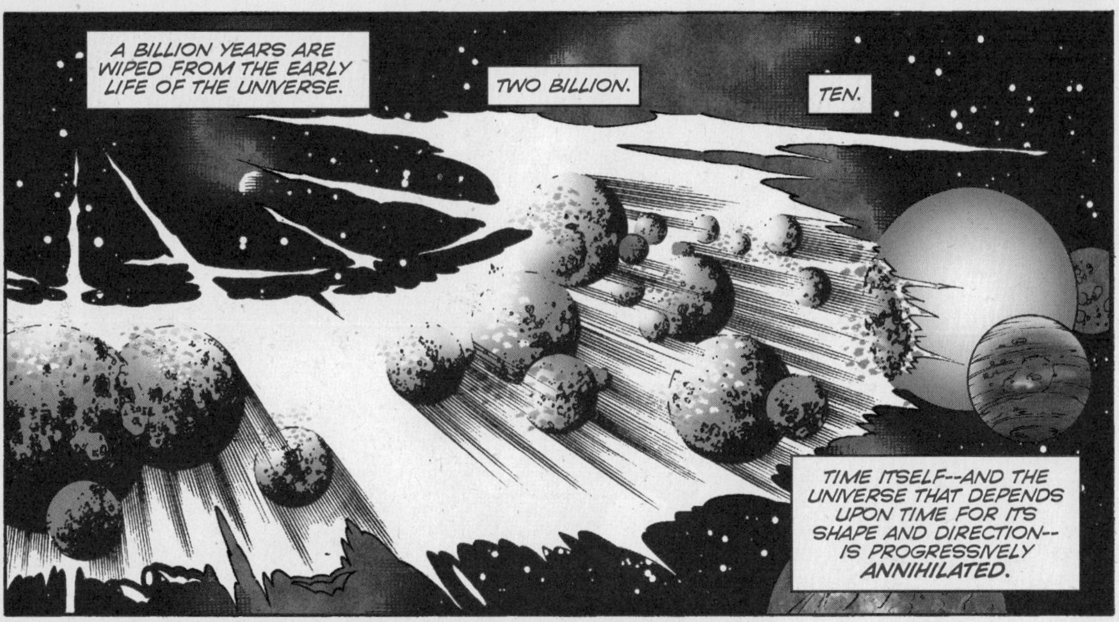
A BILLION YEARS ARE WIPED FROM THE EARLY LIFE OF THE UNIVERSE.
TWO BILLION.
TEN.
TIME ITSELF--AND THE UNIVERSE THAT DEPENDS UPON TIME FOR ITS SHAPE AND DIRECTION--IS PROGRESSIVELY ANNIHILATED.

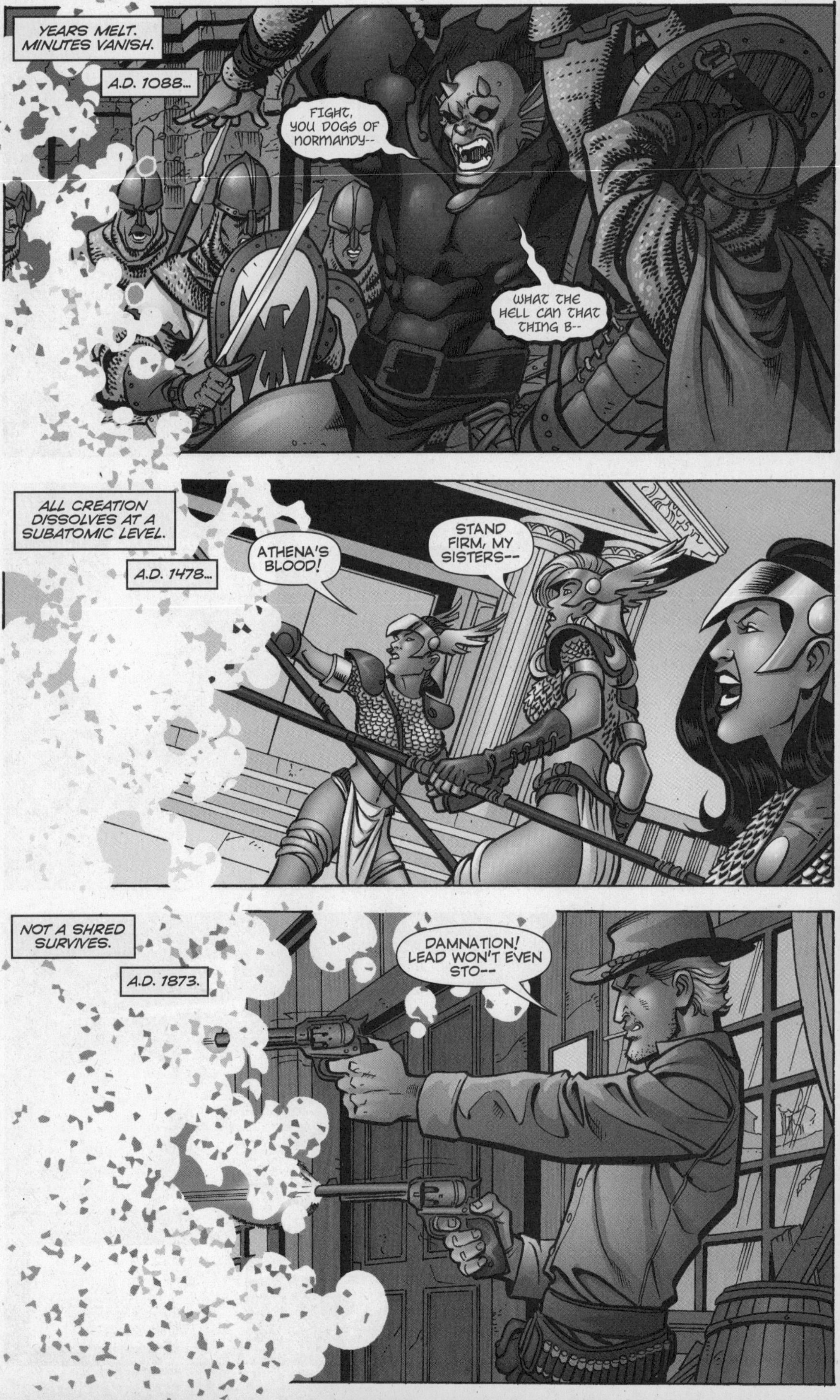
YEARS MELT. MINUTES VANISH.
A.D. 1088...
FIGHT, YOU DOGS OF NORMANDY--
WHAT THE HELL CAN THAT THING B--
ALL CREATION DISSOLVES AT A SUBATOMIC LEVEL.
A.D. 1478...
ATHENA'S BLOOD!
STAND FIRM, MY SISTERS--
NOT A SHRED SURVIVES.
A.D. 1873.
DAMNATION! LEAD WON'T EVEN STO--

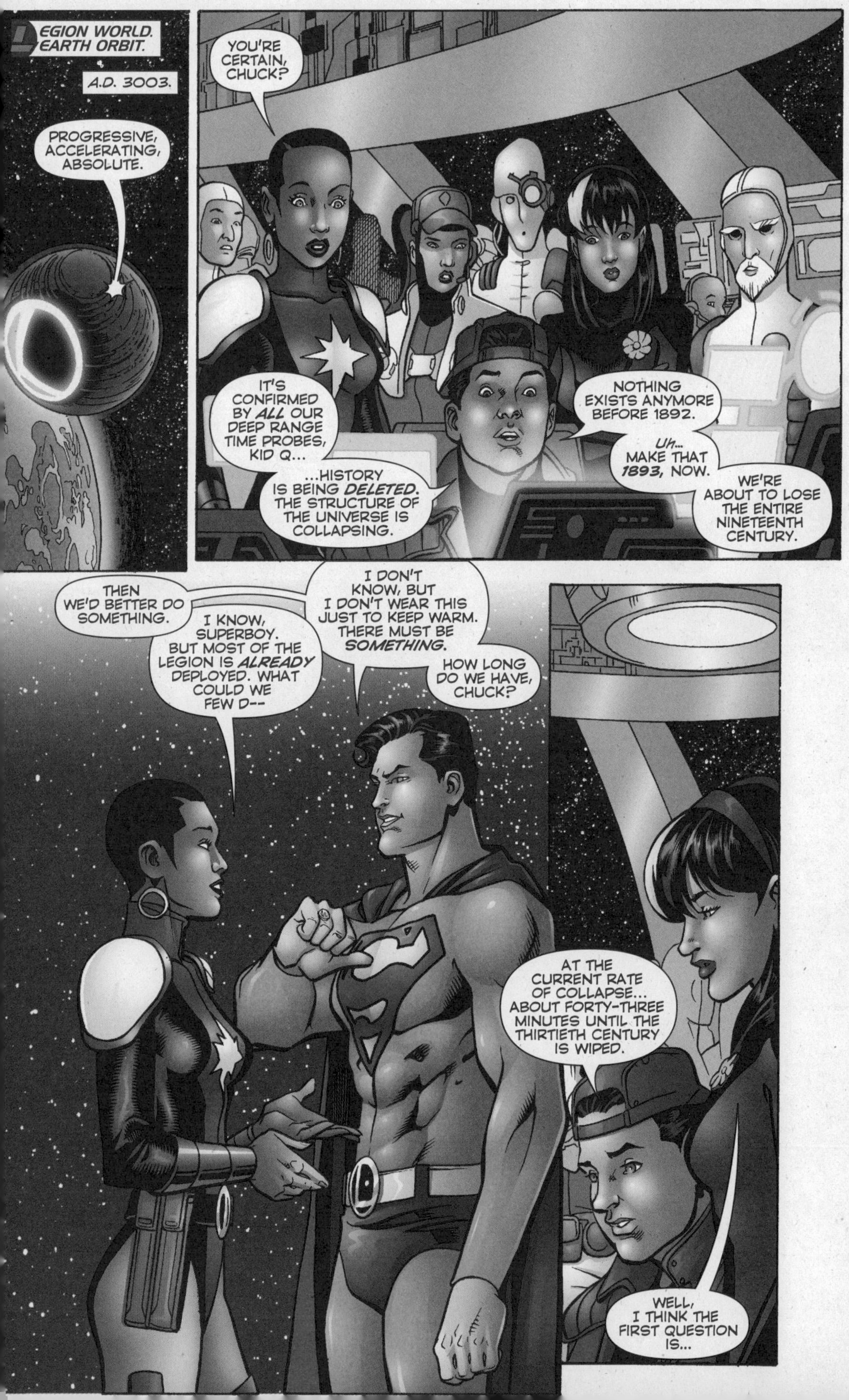
LEGION WORLD. EARTH ORBIT.
A.D. 3003.
PROGRESSIVE, ACCELERATING, ABSOLUTE.
YOU'RE CERTAIN, CHUCK?
IT'S CONFIRMED BY ALL OUR DEEP RANGE TIME PROBES, KID Q...
...HISTORY IS BEING DELETED. THE STRUCTURE OF THE UNIVERSE IS COLLAPSING.
NOTHING EXISTS ANYMORE BEFORE 1892.
Uh... MAKE THAT 1893, NOW.
WE'RE ABOUT TO LOSE THE ENTIRE NINETEENTH CENTURY.
THEN WE'D BETTER DO SOMETHING.
I KNOW, SUPERBOY. BUT MOST OF THE LEGION IS ALREADY DEPLOYED. WHAT COULD WE FEW D--
I DON'T KNOW, BUT I DON'T WEAR THIS JUST TO KEEP WARM. THERE MUST BE SOMETHING.
HOW LONG DO WE HAVE, CHUCK?
AT THE CURRENT RATE OF COLLAPSE... ABOUT FORTY-THREE MINUTES UNTIL THE THIRTIETH CENTURY IS WIPED.
WELL, I THINK THE FIRST QUESTION IS...

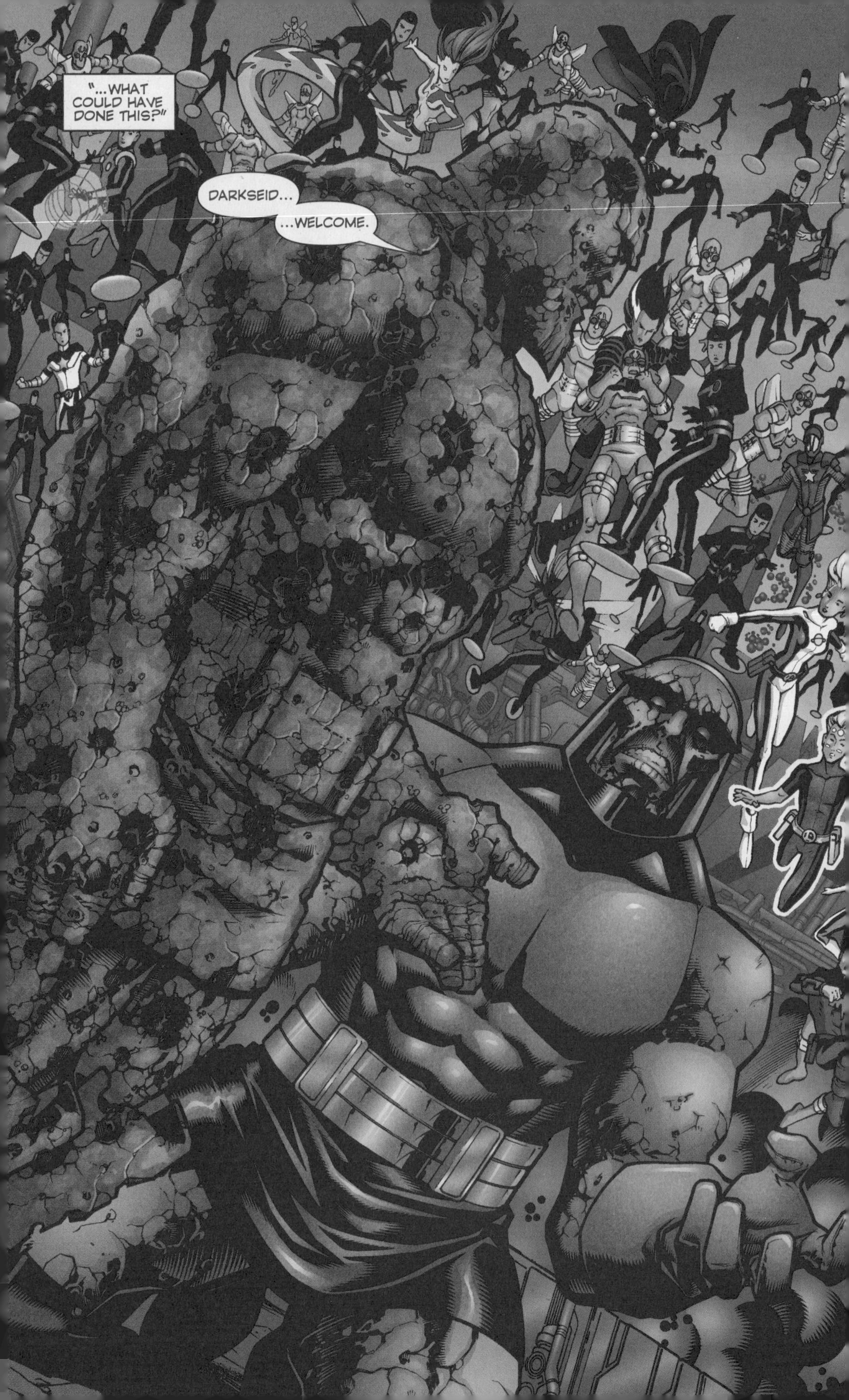
"...WHAT COULD HAVE DONE THIS?"
DARKSEID...
...WELCOME.

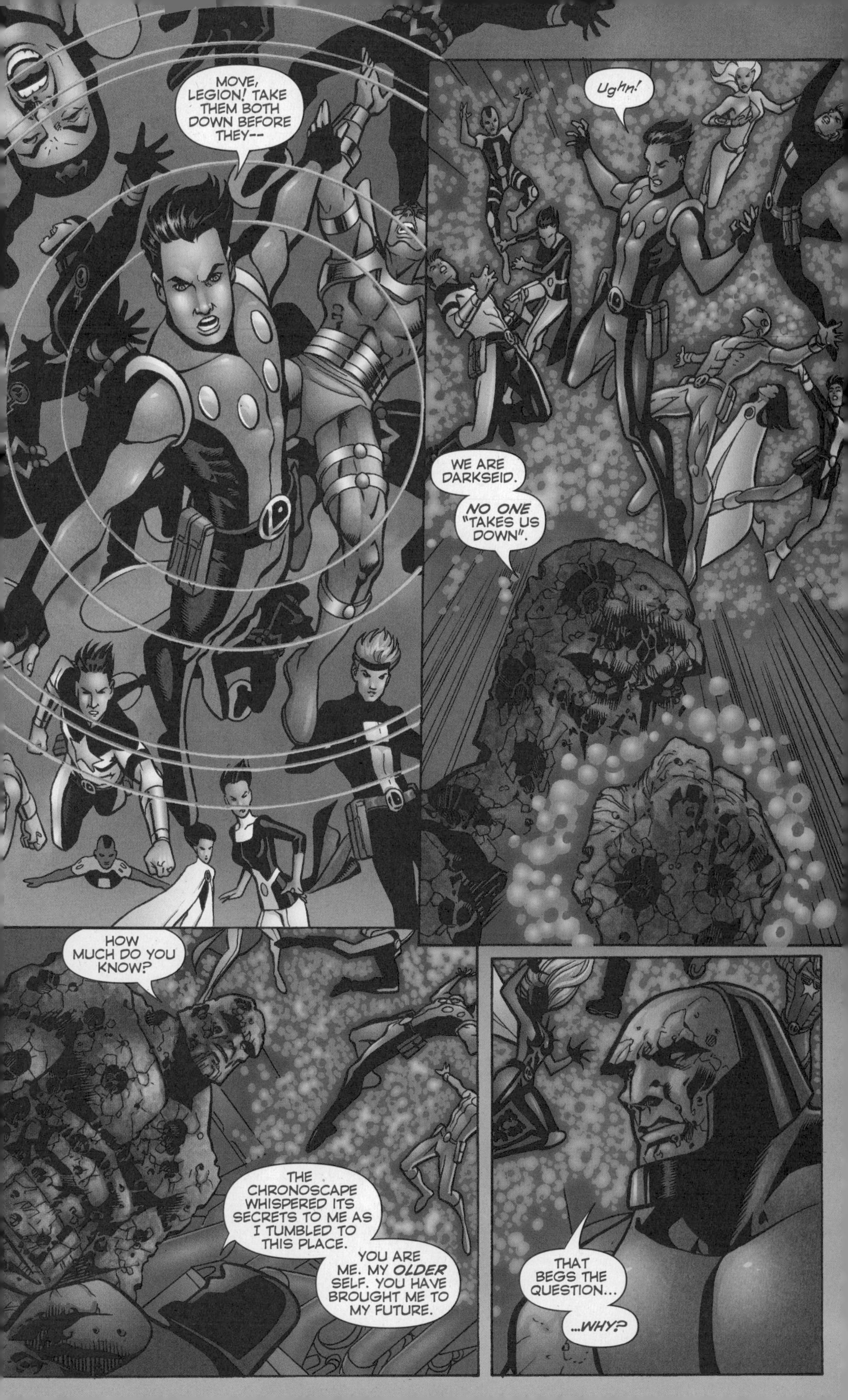
MOVE, LEGION! TAKE THEM BOTH DOWN BEFORE THEY--
Ughn!
WE ARE DARKSEID.
NO ONE "TAKES US DOWN".
HOW MUCH DO YOU KNOW?
THE CHRONOSCAPE WHISPERED ITS SECRETS TO ME AS I TUMBLED TO THIS PLACE.
YOU ARE ME. MY OLDER SELF. YOU HAVE BROUGHT ME TO MY FUTURE.
THAT BEGS THE QUESTION...
...WHY?

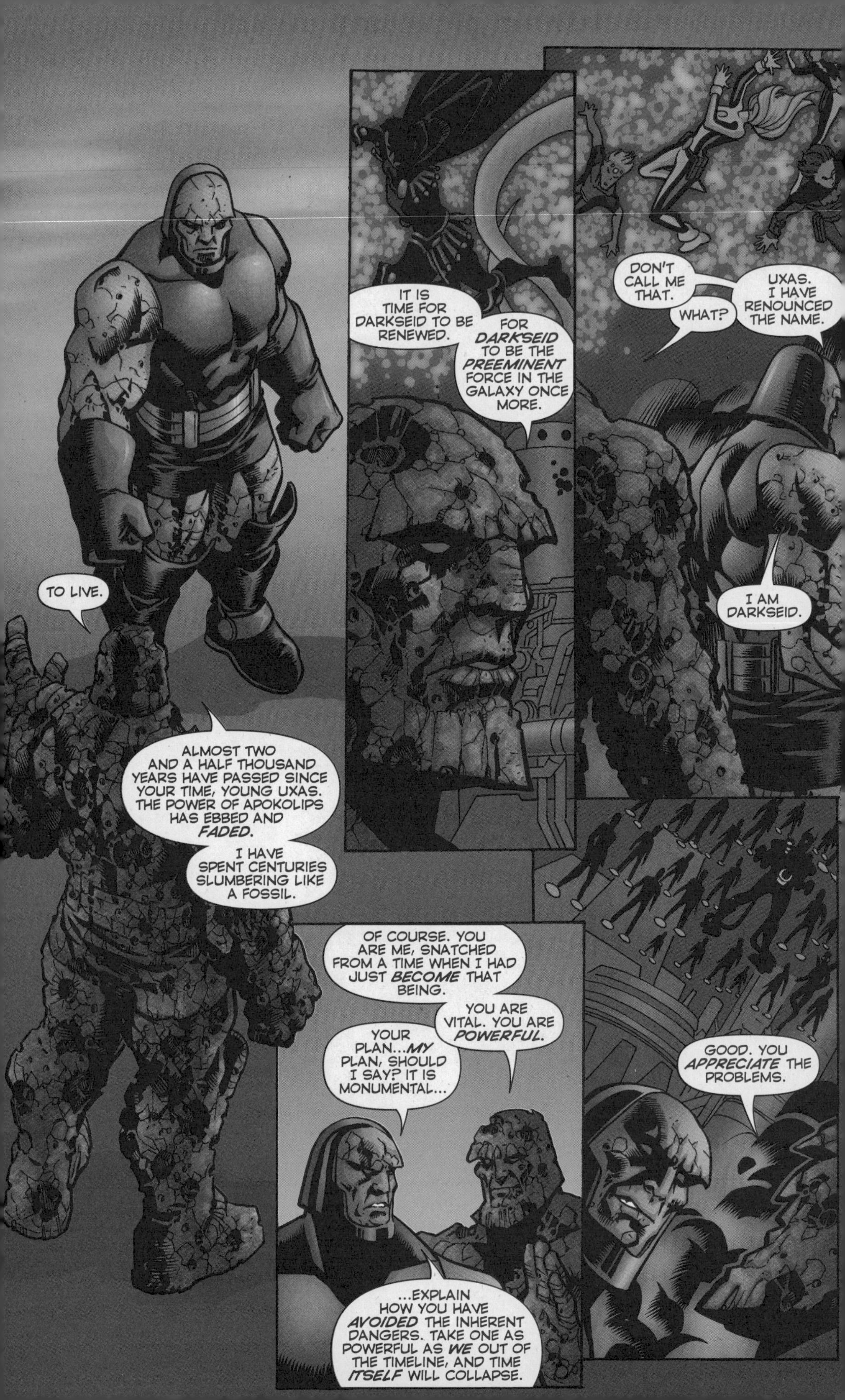
TO LIVE.
ALMOST TWO AND A HALF THOUSAND YEARS HAVE PASSED SINCE YOUR TIME, YOUNG UXAS. THE POWER OF APOKOLIPS HAS EBBED AND FADED.
I HAVE SPENT CENTURIES SLUMBERING LIKE A FOSSIL.
IT IS TIME FOR DARKSEID TO BE RENEWED.
FOR DARKSEID TO BE THE PREEMINENT FORCE IN THE GALAXY ONCE MORE.
UXAS. I HAVE RENOUNCED THE NAME.
WHAT?
DON'T CALL ME THAT.
I AM DARKSEID.
OF COURSE. YOU ARE ME, SNATCHED FROM A TIME WHEN I HAD JUST BECOME THAT BEING.
YOU ARE VITAL. YOU ARE POWERFUL.
YOUR PLAN...MY PLAN, SHOULD I SAY? IT IS MONUMENTAL...
...EXPLAIN HOW YOU HAVE AVOIDED THE INHERENT DANGERS. TAKE ONE AS POWERFUL AS WE OUT OF THE TIMELINE, AND TIME ITSELF WILL COLLAPSE.
GOOD. YOU APPRECIATE THE PROBLEMS.

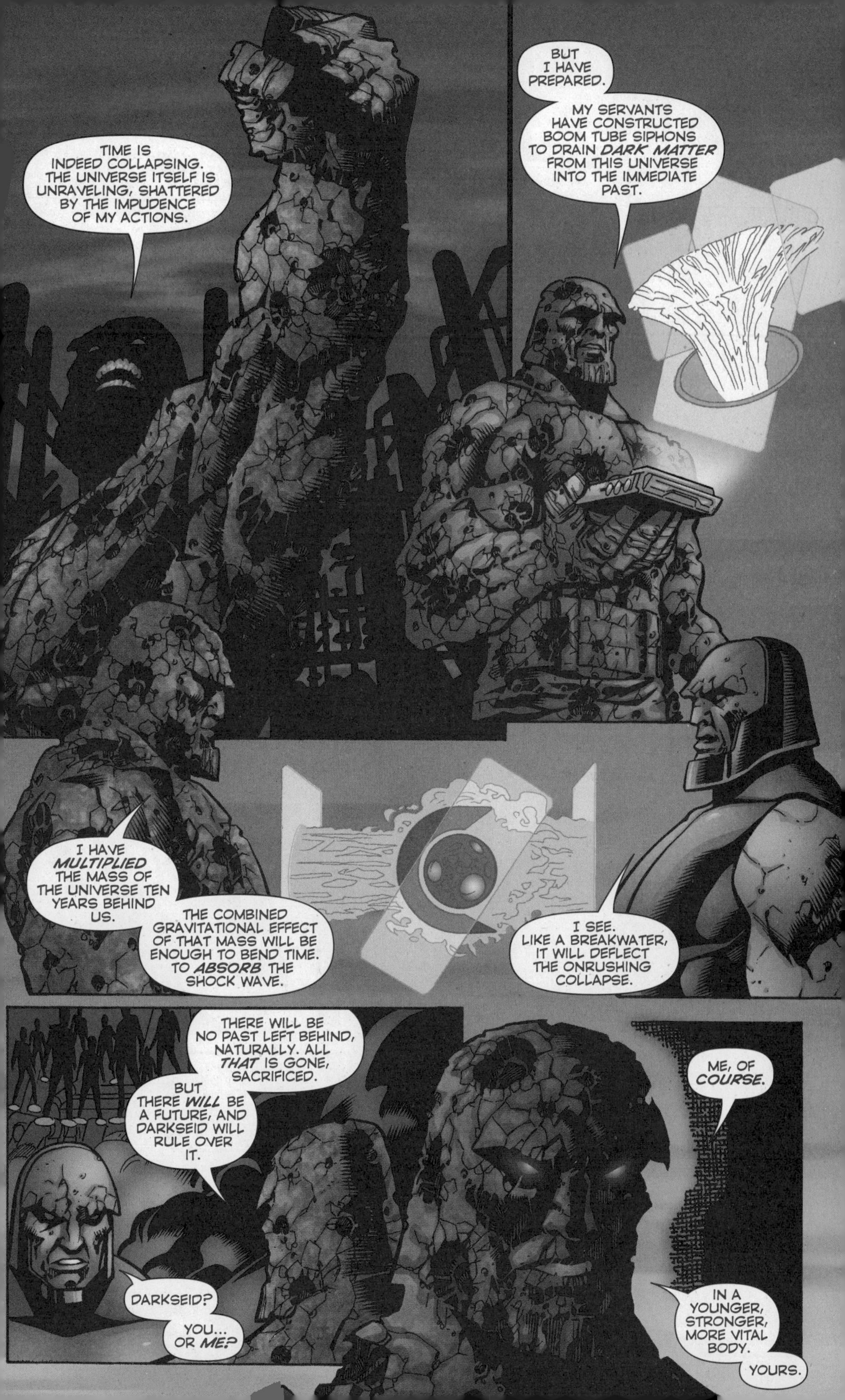
TIME IS INDEED COLLAPSING. THE UNIVERSE ITSELF IS UNRAVELING, SHATTERED BY THE IMPUDENCE OF MY ACTIONS.
BUT I HAVE PREPARED.
MY SERVANTS HAVE CONSTRUCTED BOOM TUBE SIPHONS TO DRAIN *DARK MATTER* FROM THIS UNIVERSE INTO THE IMMEDIATE PAST.
I HAVE *MULTIPLIED* THE MASS OF THE UNIVERSE TEN YEARS BEHIND US.
THE COMBINED GRAVITATIONAL EFFECT OF THAT MASS WILL BE ENOUGH TO BEND TIME. TO *ABSORB* THE SHOCK WAVE.
I SEE. LIKE A BREAKWATER, IT WILL DEFLECT THE ONRUSHING COLLAPSE.
THERE WILL BE NO PAST LEFT BEHIND, NATURALLY. ALL *THAT* IS GONE, SACRIFICED.
BUT THERE *WILL* BE A FUTURE, AND DARKSEID WILL RULE OVER IT.
DARKSEID?
YOU... OR *ME?*
ME, OF *COURSE.*
IN A YOUNGER, STRONGER, MORE VITAL BODY.
YOURS.

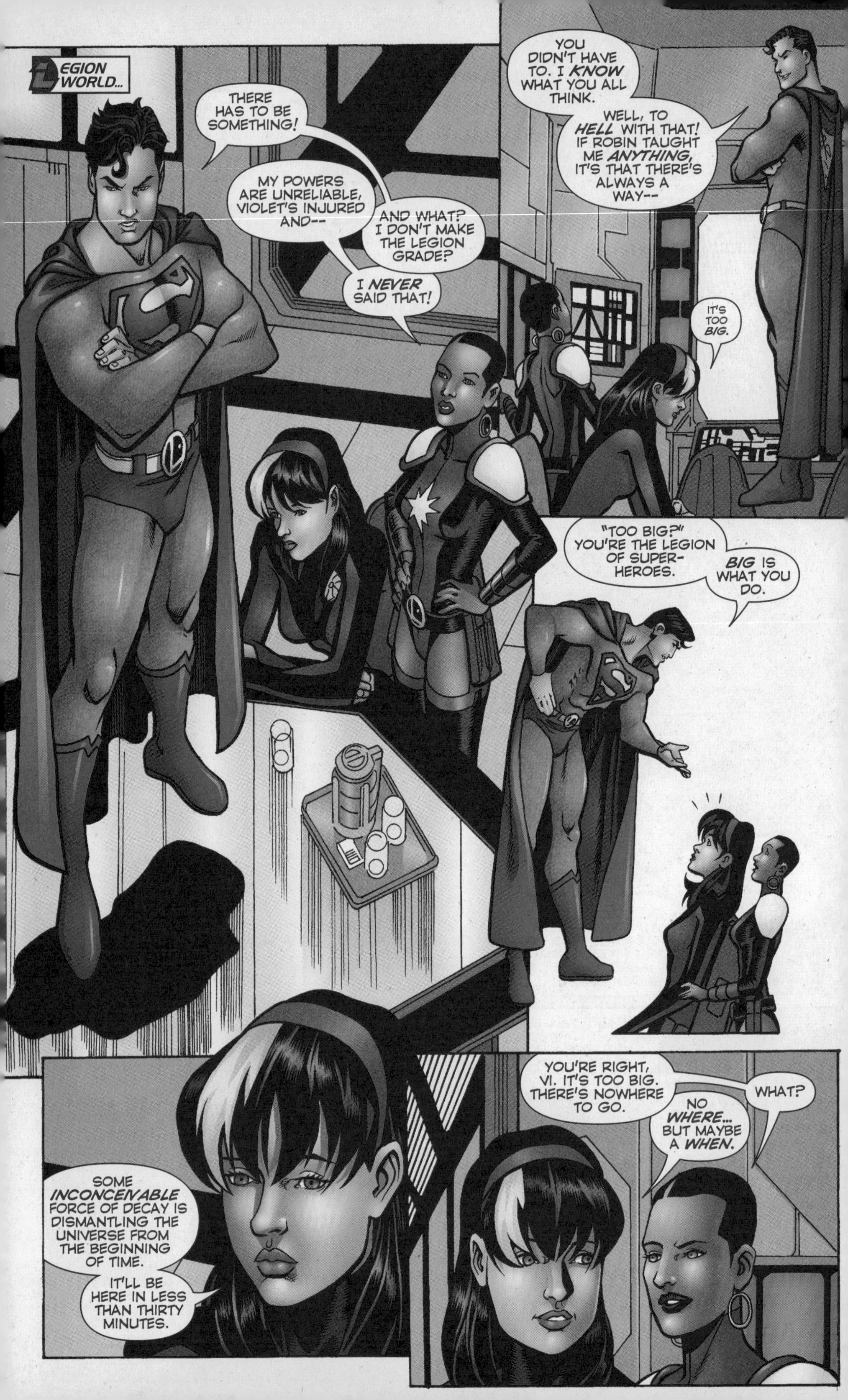
LEGION WORLD...
THERE HAS TO BE SOMETHING!
MY POWERS ARE UNRELIABLE, VIOLET'S INJURED AND--
AND WHAT? I DON'T MAKE THE LEGION GRADE?
I NEVER SAID THAT!
YOU DIDN'T HAVE TO. I KNOW WHAT YOU ALL THINK.
WELL, TO HELL WITH THAT! IF ROBIN TAUGHT ME ANYTHING, IT'S THAT THERE'S ALWAYS A WAY--
IT'S TOO BIG.
"TOO BIG?" YOU'RE THE LEGION OF SUPER-HEROES.
BIG IS WHAT YOU DO.
SOME INCONCEIVABLE FORCE OF DECAY IS DISMANTLING THE UNIVERSE FROM THE BEGINNING OF TIME.
IT'LL BE HERE IN LESS THAN THIRTY MINUTES.
YOU'RE RIGHT, VI. IT'S TOO BIG. THERE'S NOWHERE TO GO.
WHAT?
NO WHERE... BUT MAYBE A WHEN.

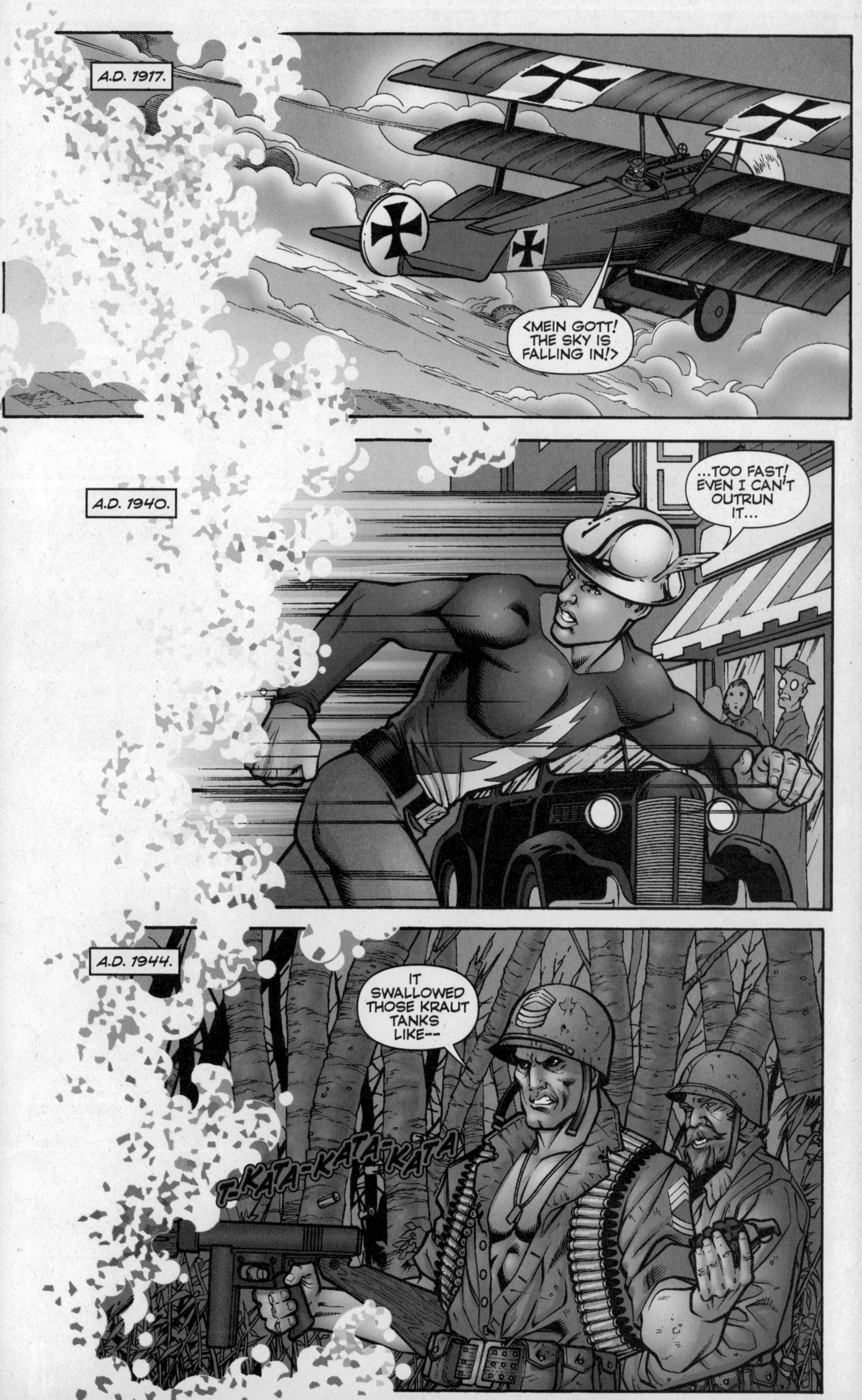
A.D. 1917.
<MEIN GOTT! THE SKY IS FALLING IN!>
A.D. 1940.
...TOO FAST! EVEN I CAN'T OUTRUN IT...
A.D. 1944.
IT SWALLOWED THOSE KRAUT TANKS LIKE--
T-KATA-KATA-KATA

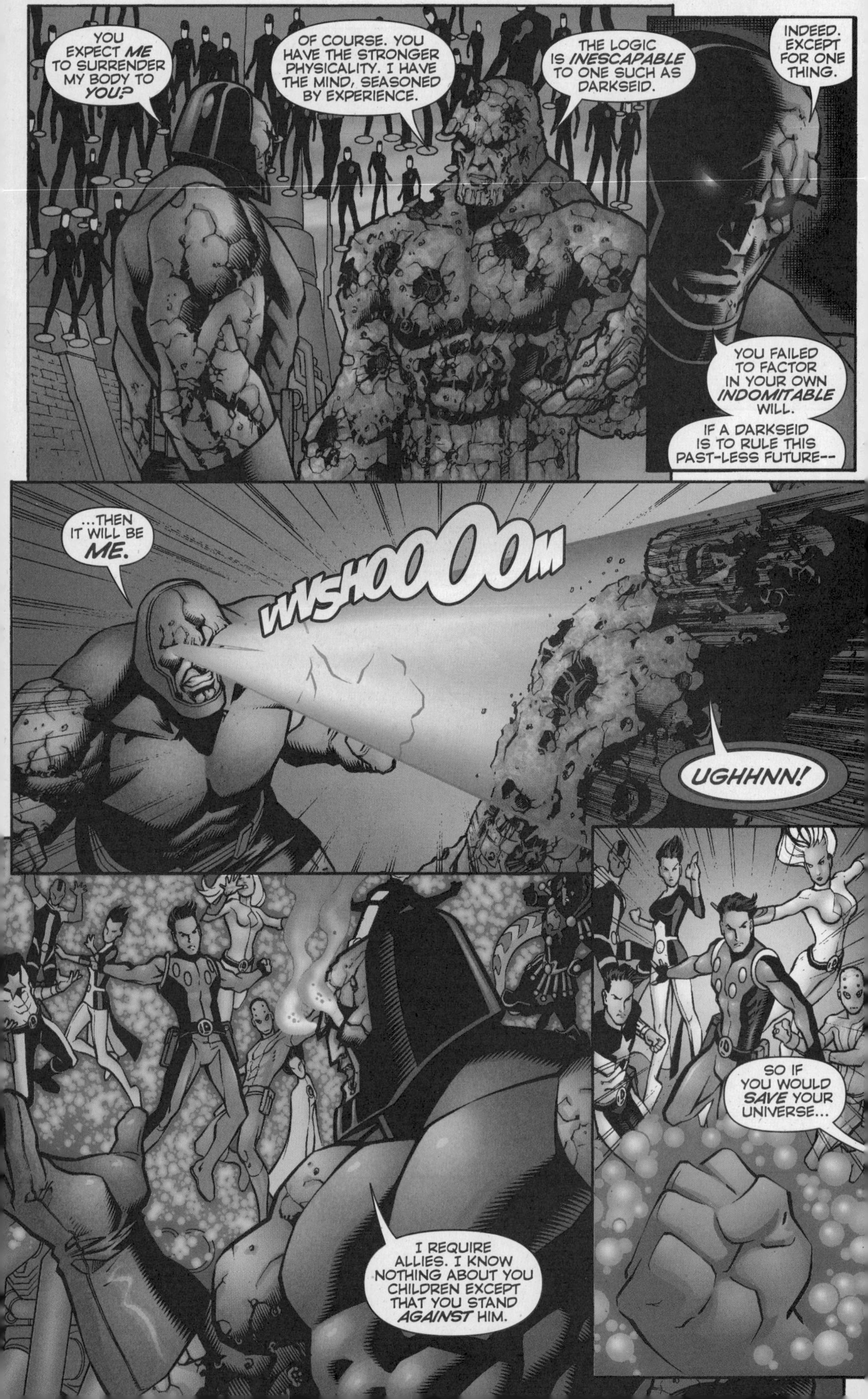
YOU EXPECT *ME* TO SURRENDER MY BODY TO *YOU?*
OF COURSE. YOU HAVE THE STRONGER PHYSICALITY. I HAVE THE MIND, SEASONED BY EXPERIENCE.
THE LOGIC IS *INESCAPABLE* TO ONE SUCH AS DARKSEID.
INDEED. EXCEPT FOR ONE THING.
YOU FAILED TO FACTOR IN YOUR OWN *INDOMITABLE* WILL.
IF A DARKSEID IS TO RULE THIS PAST-LESS FUTURE--
...THEN IT WILL BE *ME.*
VVVSHOOOOOM
UGHHNN!
SO IF YOU WOULD *SAVE* YOUR UNIVERSE...
I REQUIRE ALLIES. I KNOW NOTHING ABOUT YOU CHILDREN EXCEPT THAT YOU STAND *AGAINST* HIM.

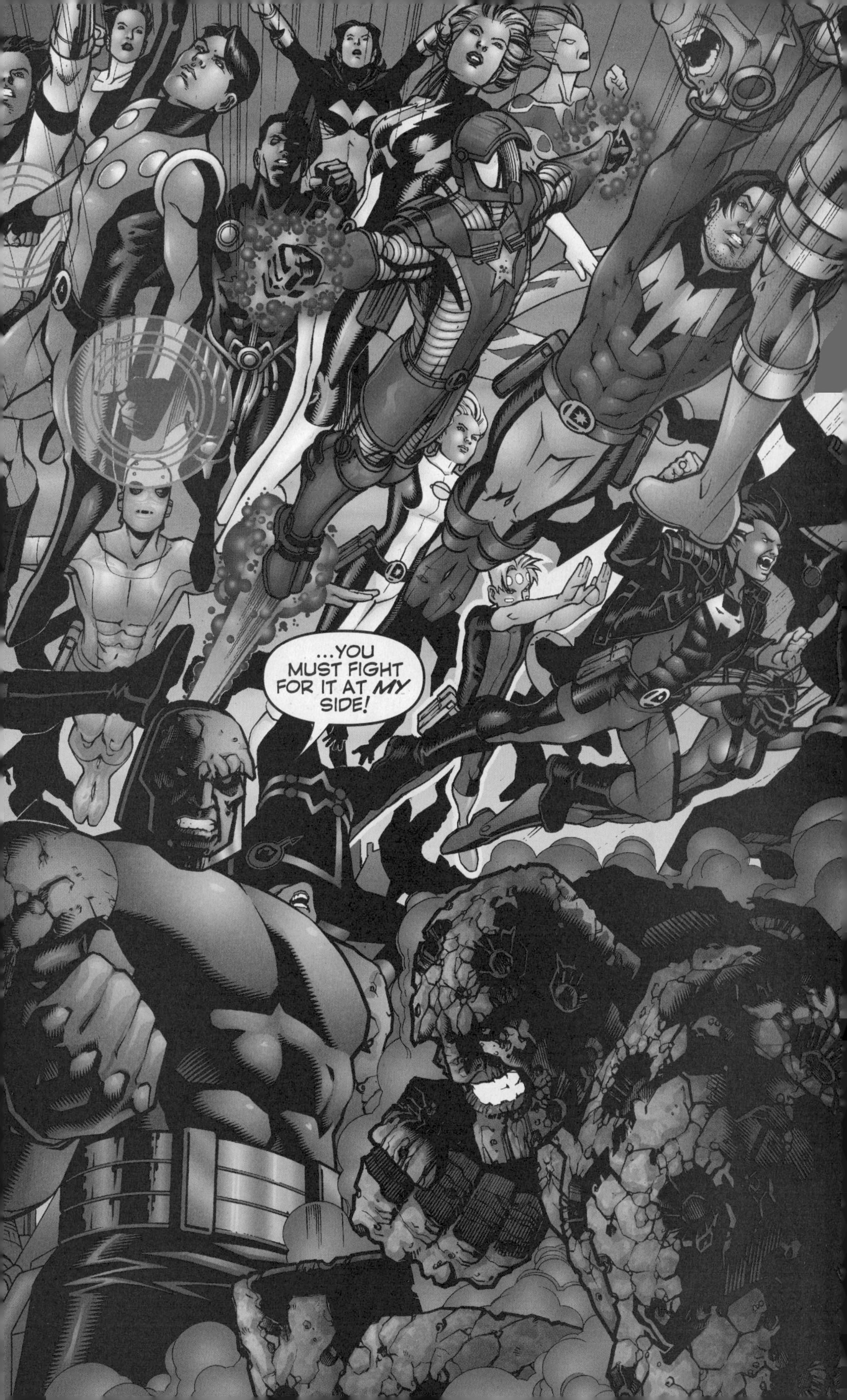
...YOU MUST FIGHT FOR IT AT *MY* SIDE!

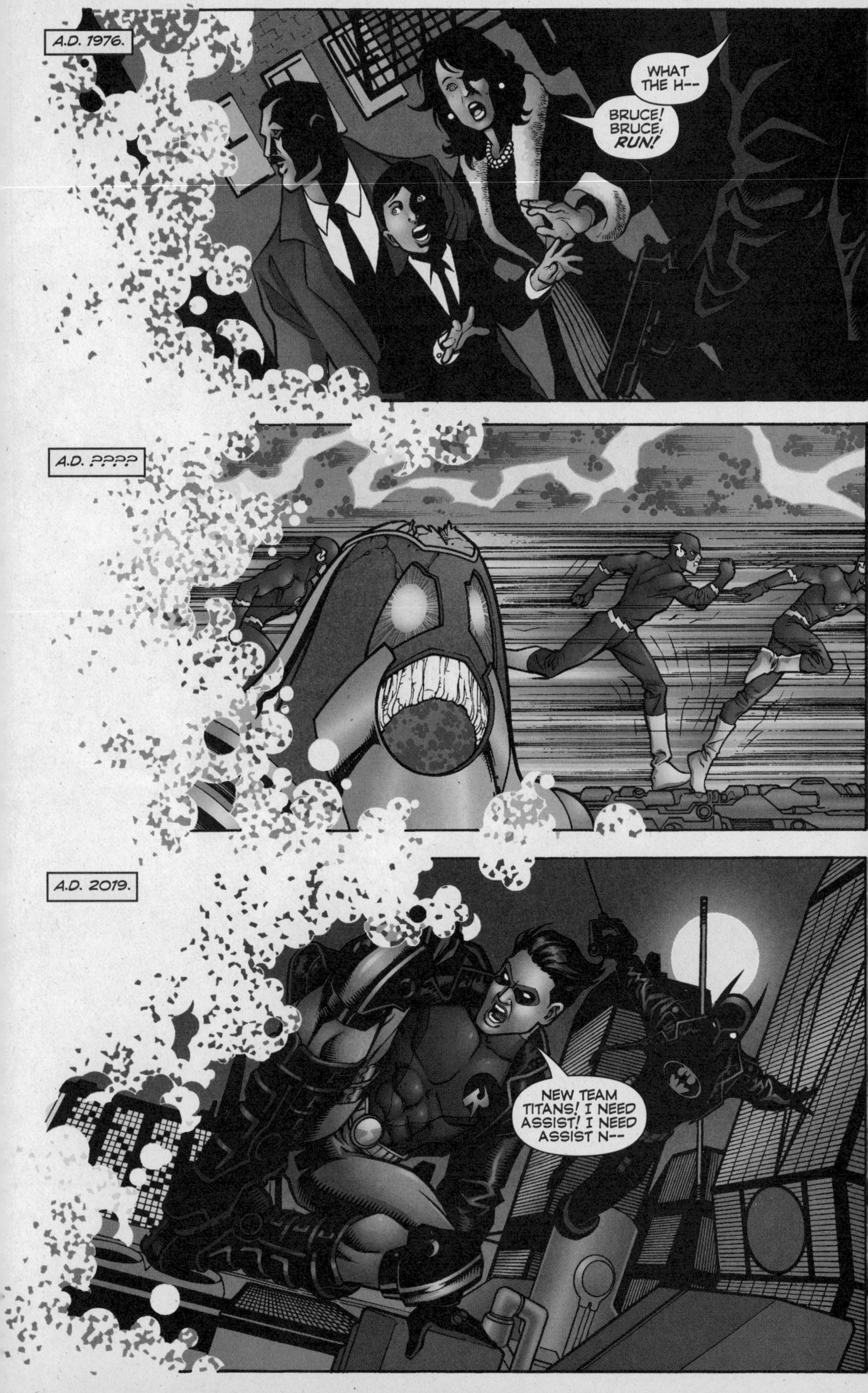
A.D. 1976.
WHAT THE H--
BRUCE! BRUCE, RUN!
A.D. ????
A.D. 2019.
NEW TEAM TITANS! I NEED ASSIST! I NEED ASSIST N--

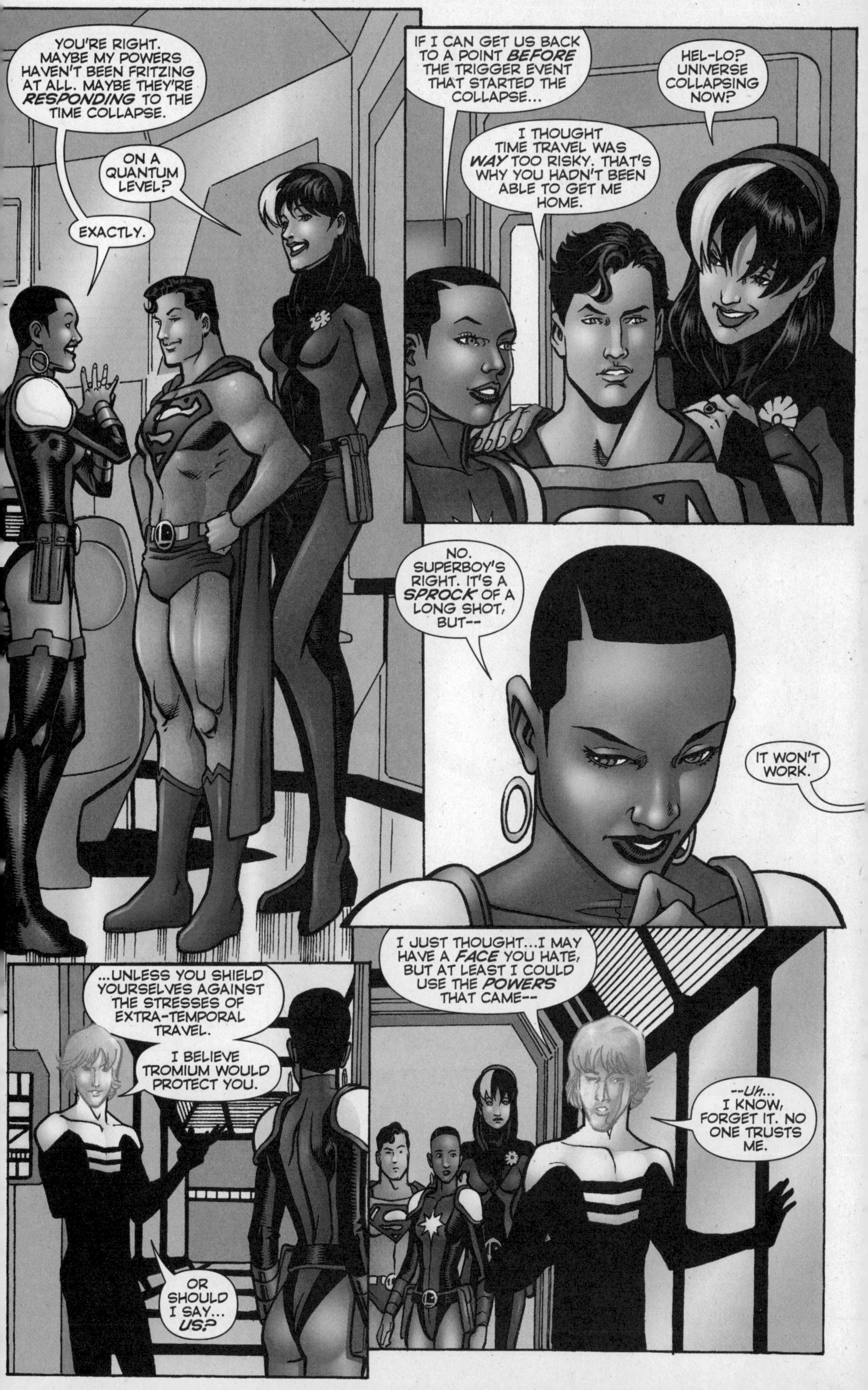
YOU'RE RIGHT. MAYBE MY POWERS HAVEN'T BEEN FRITZING AT ALL. MAYBE THEY'RE *RESPONDING* TO THE TIME COLLAPSE.
ON A QUANTUM LEVEL?
EXACTLY.
IF I CAN GET US BACK TO A POINT *BEFORE* THE TRIGGER EVENT THAT STARTED THE COLLAPSE...
HEL-LO? UNIVERSE COLLAPSING NOW?
I THOUGHT TIME TRAVEL WAS *WAY* TOO RISKY. THAT'S WHY YOU HADN'T BEEN ABLE TO GET ME HOME.
NO. SUPERBOY'S RIGHT. IT'S A *SPROCK* OF A LONG SHOT, BUT--
IT WON'T WORK.
...UNLESS YOU SHIELD YOURSELVES AGAINST THE STRESSES OF EXTRA-TEMPORAL TRAVEL.
I BELIEVE TROMIUM WOULD PROTECT YOU.
OR SHOULD I SAY... *US?*
I JUST THOUGHT...I MAY HAVE A *FACE* YOU HATE, BUT AT LEAST I COULD USE THE *POWERS* THAT CAME--
--*Uh*... I KNOW, FORGET IT. NO ONE TRUSTS ME.

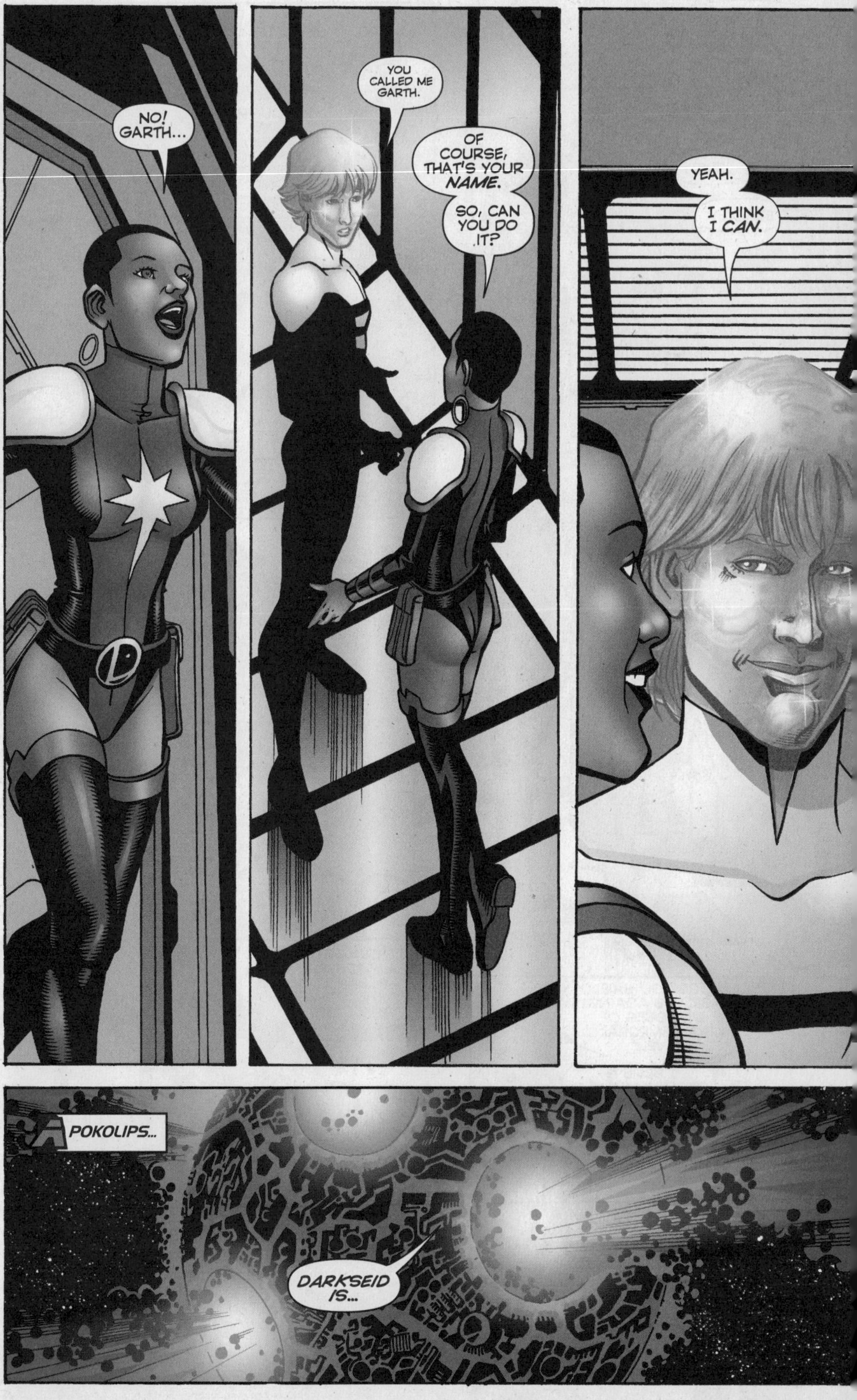
NO! GARTH...
YOU CALLED ME GARTH.
OF COURSE, THAT'S YOUR *NAME.*
SO, CAN YOU DO IT?
YEAH.
I THINK I *CAN.*
APOKOLIPS...
DARKSEID IS...

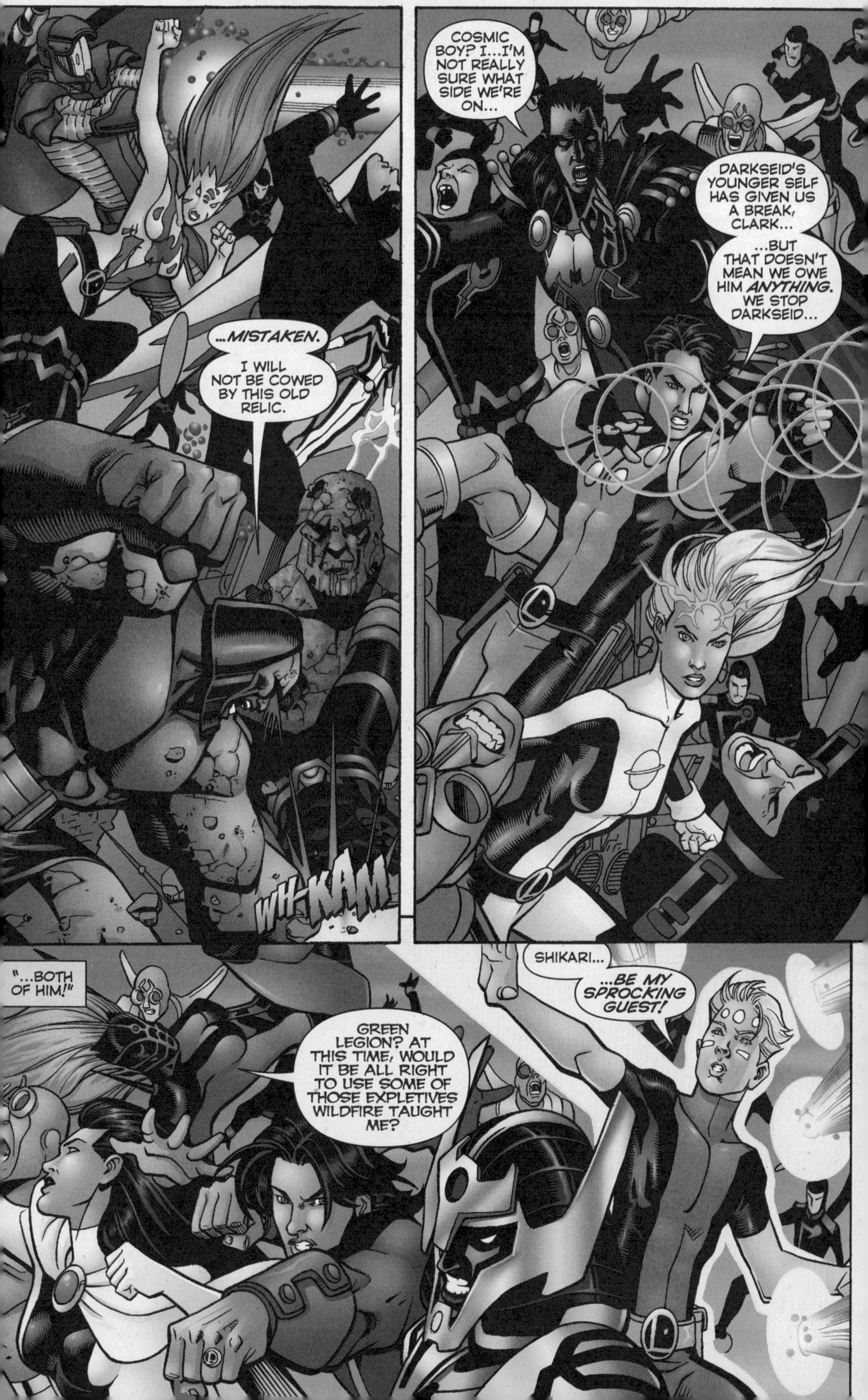
...MISTAKEN.
I WILL NOT BE COWED BY THIS OLD RELIC.
WH-KAM
COSMIC BOY? I...I'M NOT REALLY SURE WHAT SIDE WE'RE ON...
DARKSEID'S YOUNGER SELF HAS GIVEN US A BREAK, CLARK...
...BUT THAT DOESN'T MEAN WE OWE HIM ANYTHING. WE STOP DARKSEID...
"...BOTH OF HIM!"
GREEN LEGION? AT THIS TIME, WOULD IT BE ALL RIGHT TO USE SOME OF THOSE EXPLETIVES WILDFIRE TAUGHT ME?
SHIKARI...
...BE MY SPROCKING GUEST!

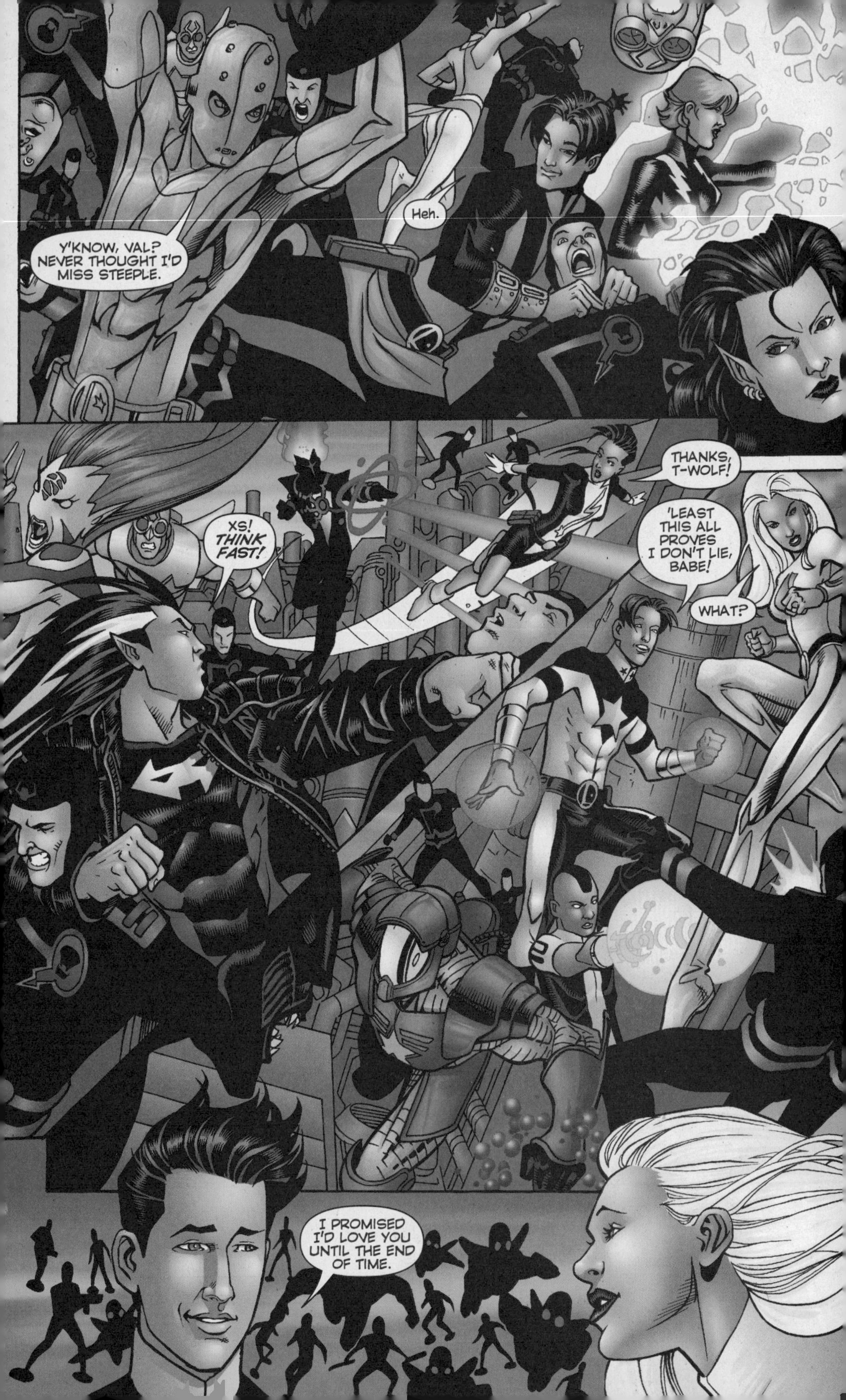
Heh.
Y'KNOW, VAL? NEVER THOUGHT I'D MISS STEEPLE.
THANKS, T-WOLF!
XS! THINK FAST!
'LEAST THIS ALL PROVES I DON'T LIE, BABE!
WHAT?
I PROMISED I'D LOVE YOU UNTIL THE END OF TIME.

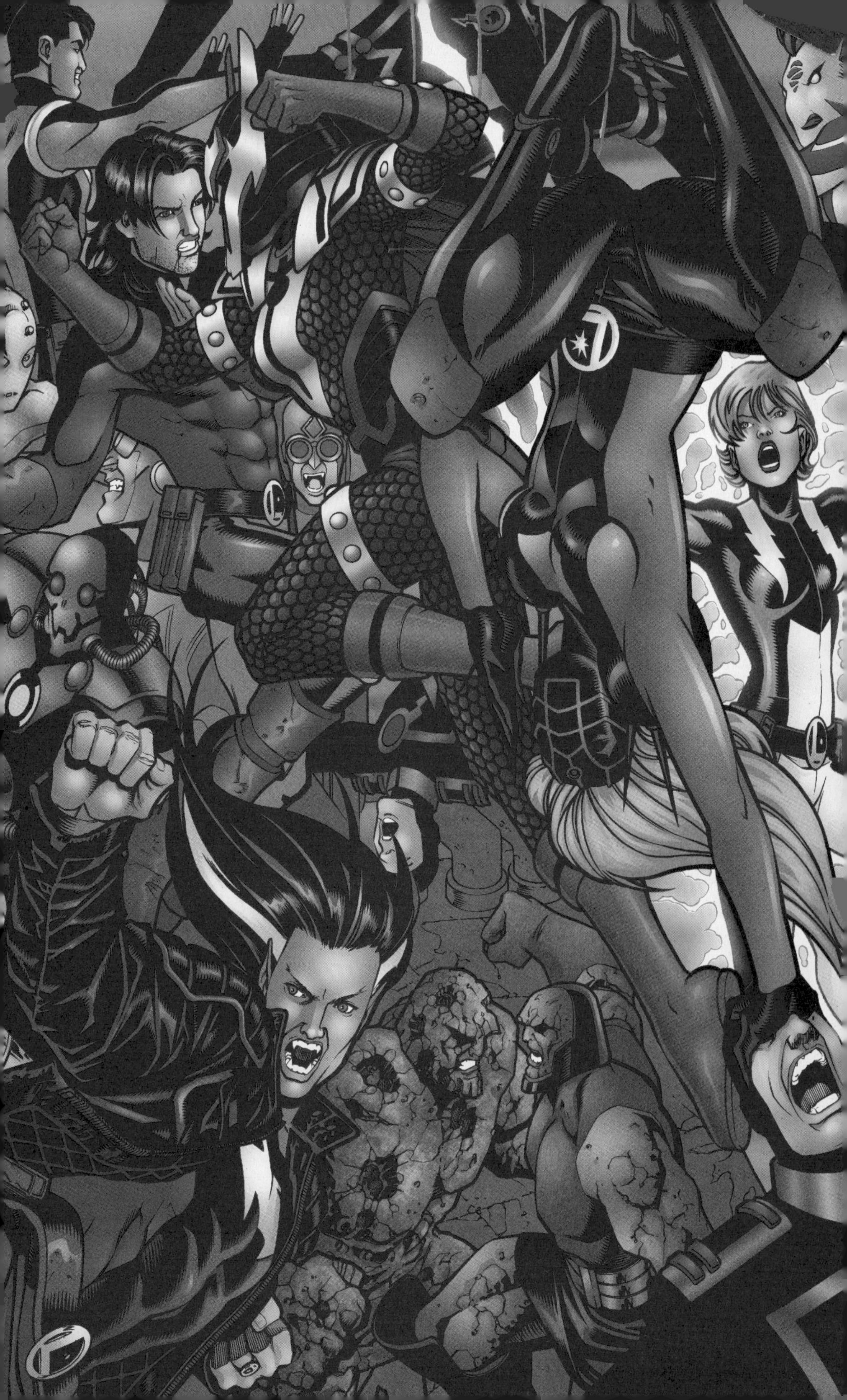

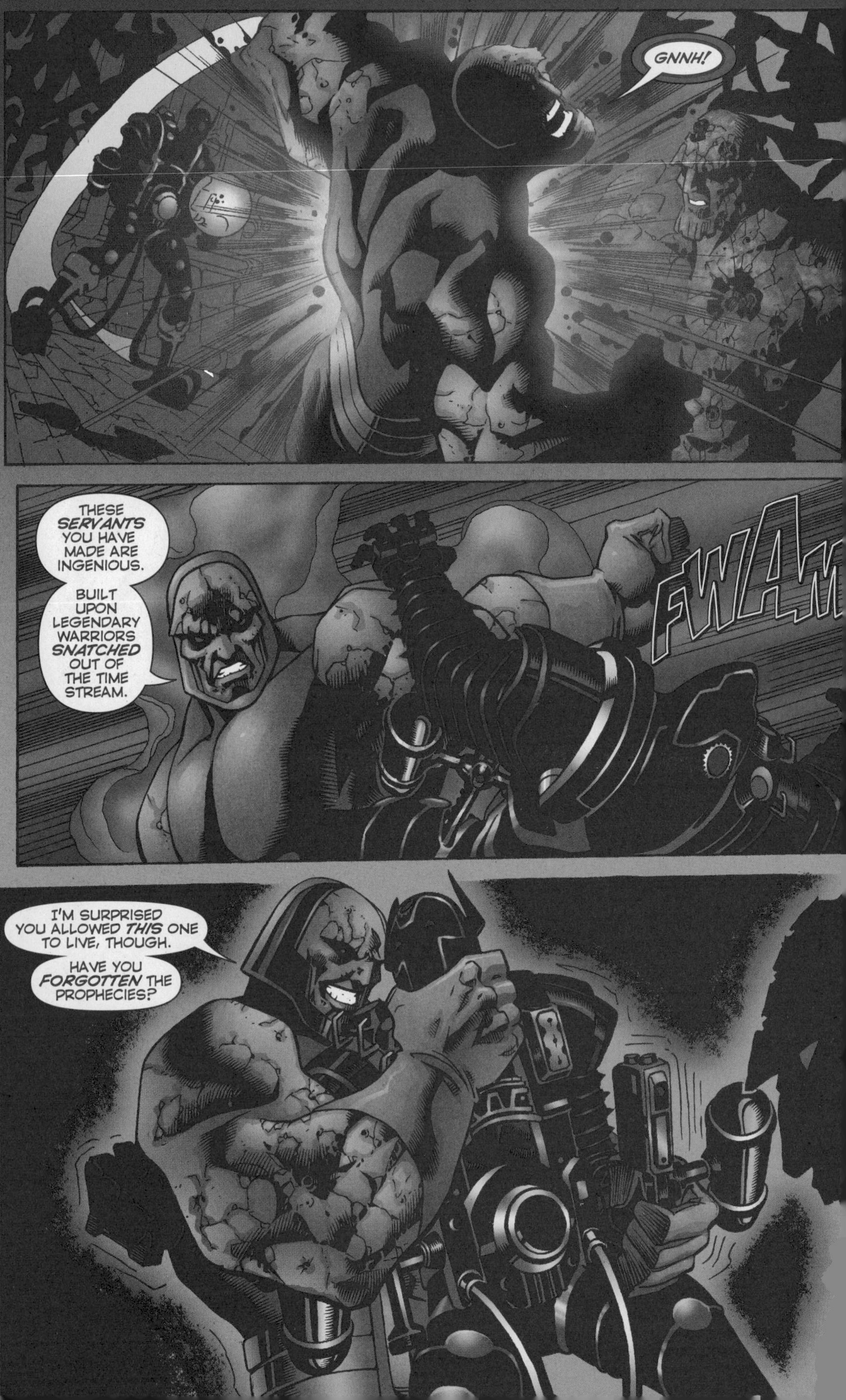

GNNH!
THESE SERVANTS YOU HAVE MADE ARE INGENIOUS.
BUILT UPON LEGENDARY WARRIORS SNATCHED OUT OF THE TIME STREAM.
FWAM
I'M SURPRISED YOU ALLOWED THIS ONE TO LIVE, THOUGH.
HAVE YOU FORGOTTEN THE PROPHECIES?

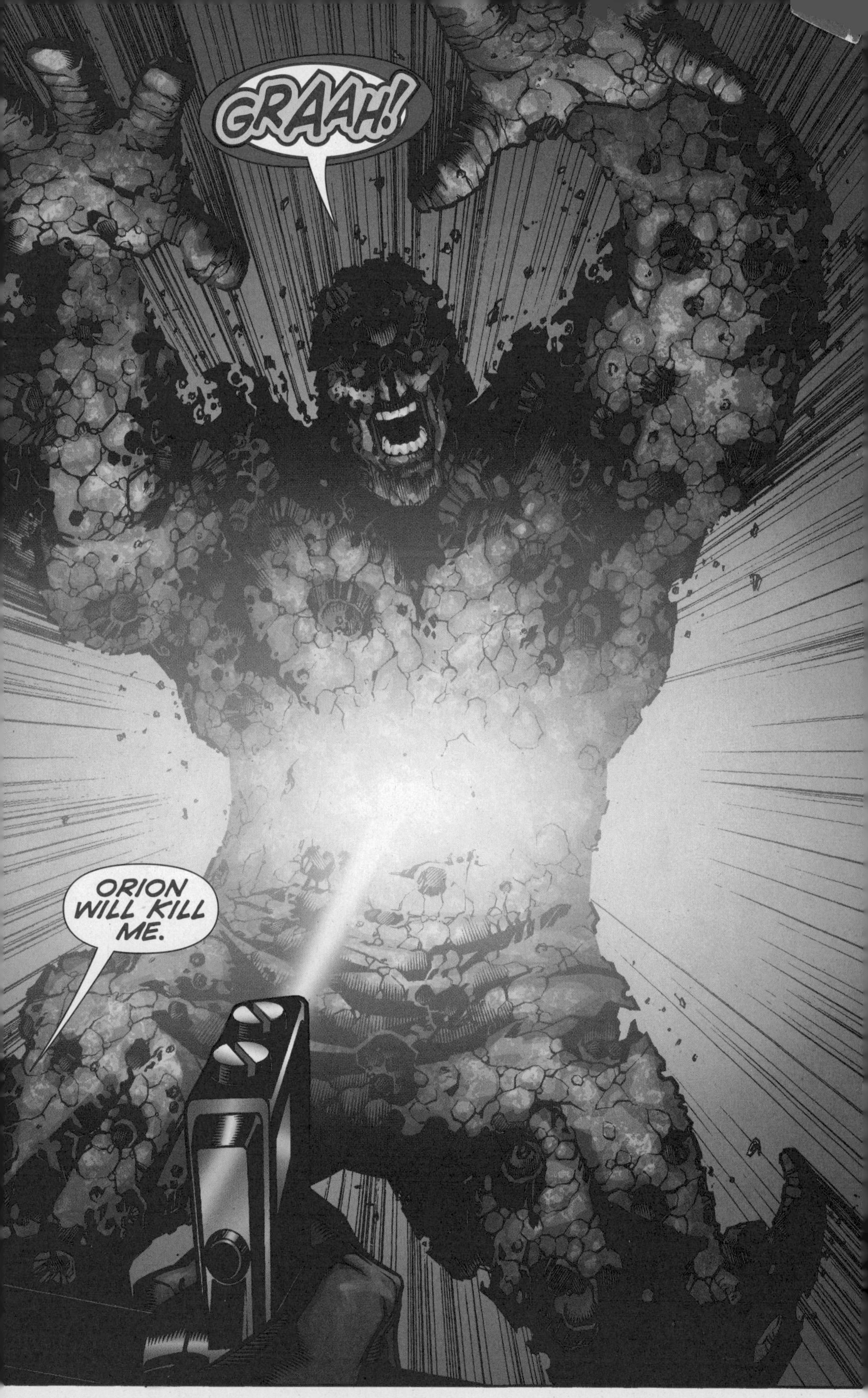
GRAAH!
ORION WILL KILL ME.

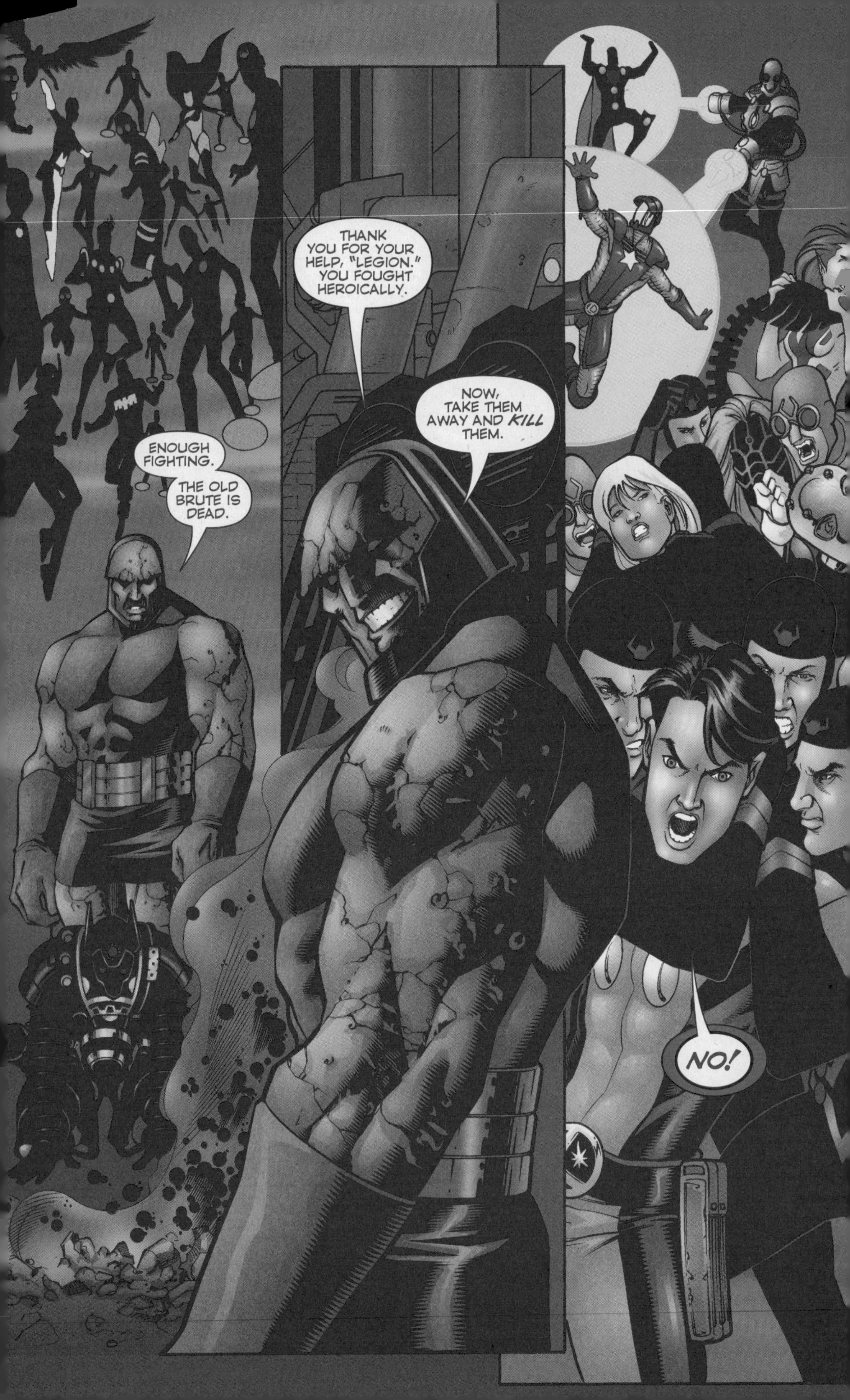
ENOUGH FIGHTING.
THE OLD BRUTE IS DEAD.
THANK YOU FOR YOUR HELP, "LEGION." YOU FOUGHT HEROICALLY.
NOW, TAKE THEM AWAY AND *KILL* THEM.
NO!

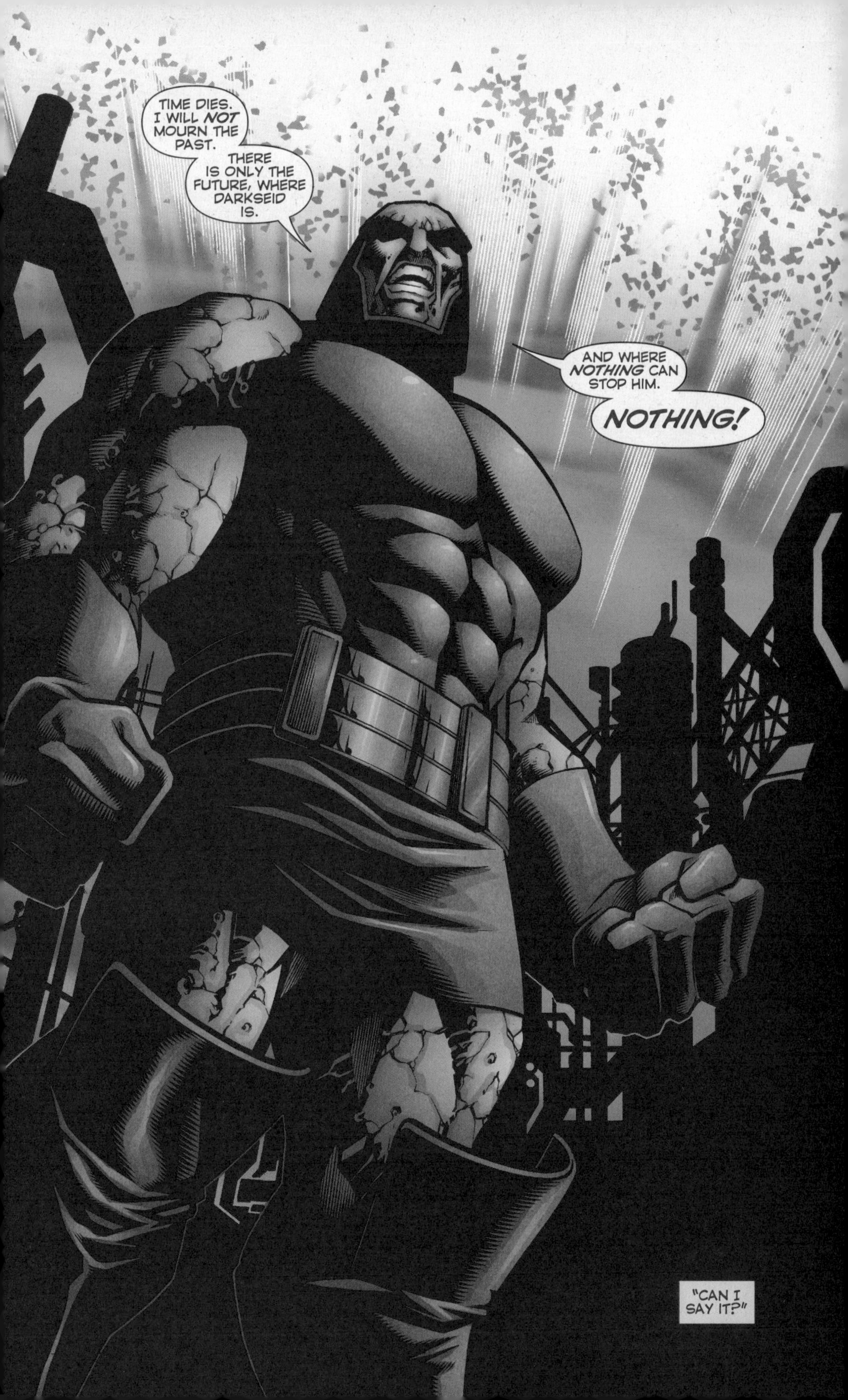
TIME DIES. I WILL *NOT* MOURN THE PAST.
THERE IS ONLY THE FUTURE, WHERE DARKSEID IS.
AND WHERE *NOTHING* CAN STOP HIM.
NOTHING!
"CAN I SAY IT?"

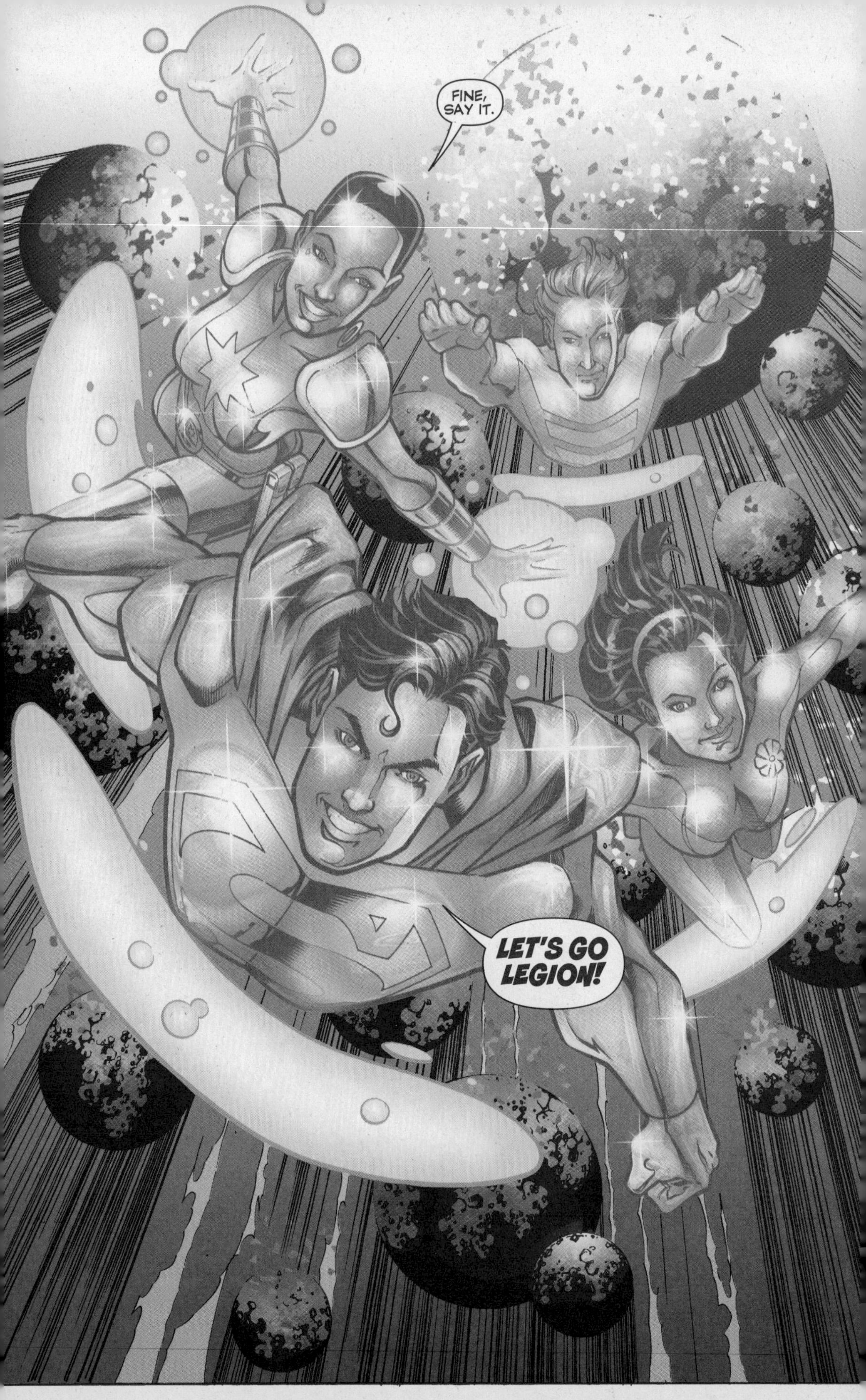
FINE, SAY IT.
LET'S GO LEGION!

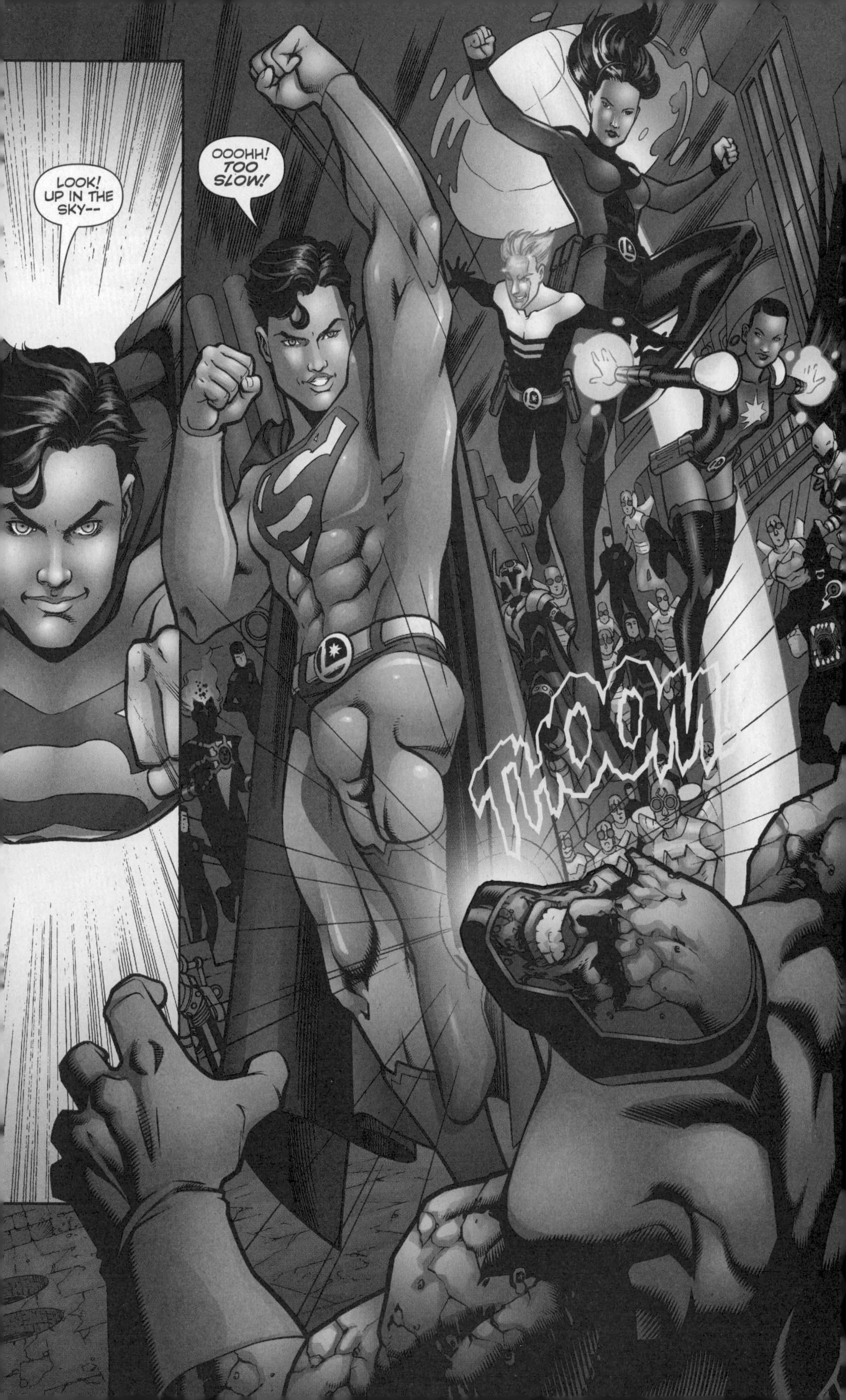
LOOK! UP IN THE SKY--
OOOHH! TOO SLOW!
THOOM!

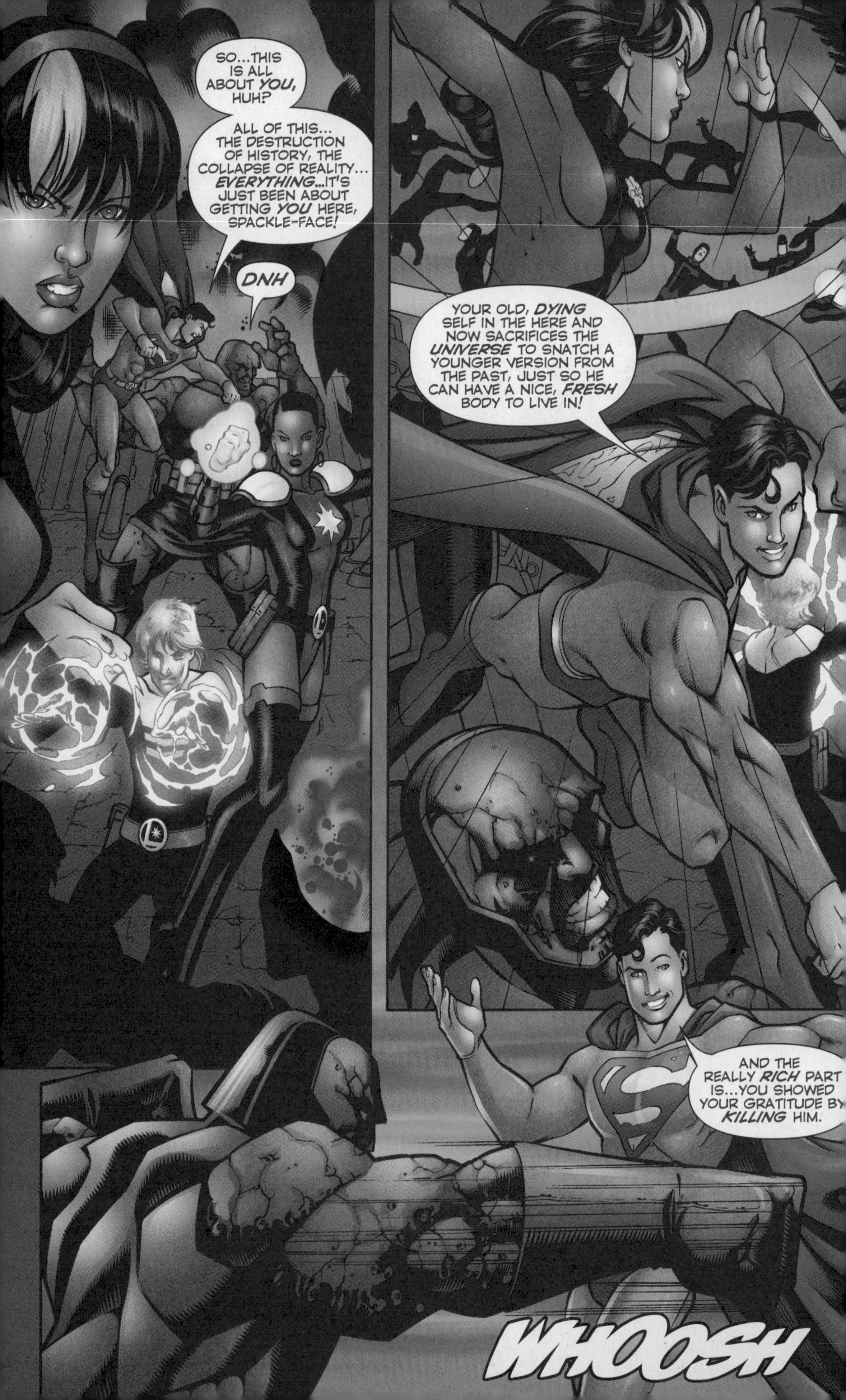
SO...THIS IS ALL ABOUT YOU, HUH?
ALL OF THIS... THE DESTRUCTION OF HISTORY, THE COLLAPSE OF REALITY... EVERYTHING...IT'S JUST BEEN ABOUT GETTING YOU HERE, SPACKLE-FACE!
DNH
YOUR OLD, DYING SELF IN THE HERE AND NOW SACRIFICES THE UNIVERSE TO SNATCH A YOUNGER VERSION FROM THE PAST, JUST SO HE CAN HAVE A NICE, FRESH BODY TO LIVE IN!
AND THE REALLY RICH PART IS...YOU SHOWED YOUR GRATITUDE BY KILLING HIM.
WHOOSH

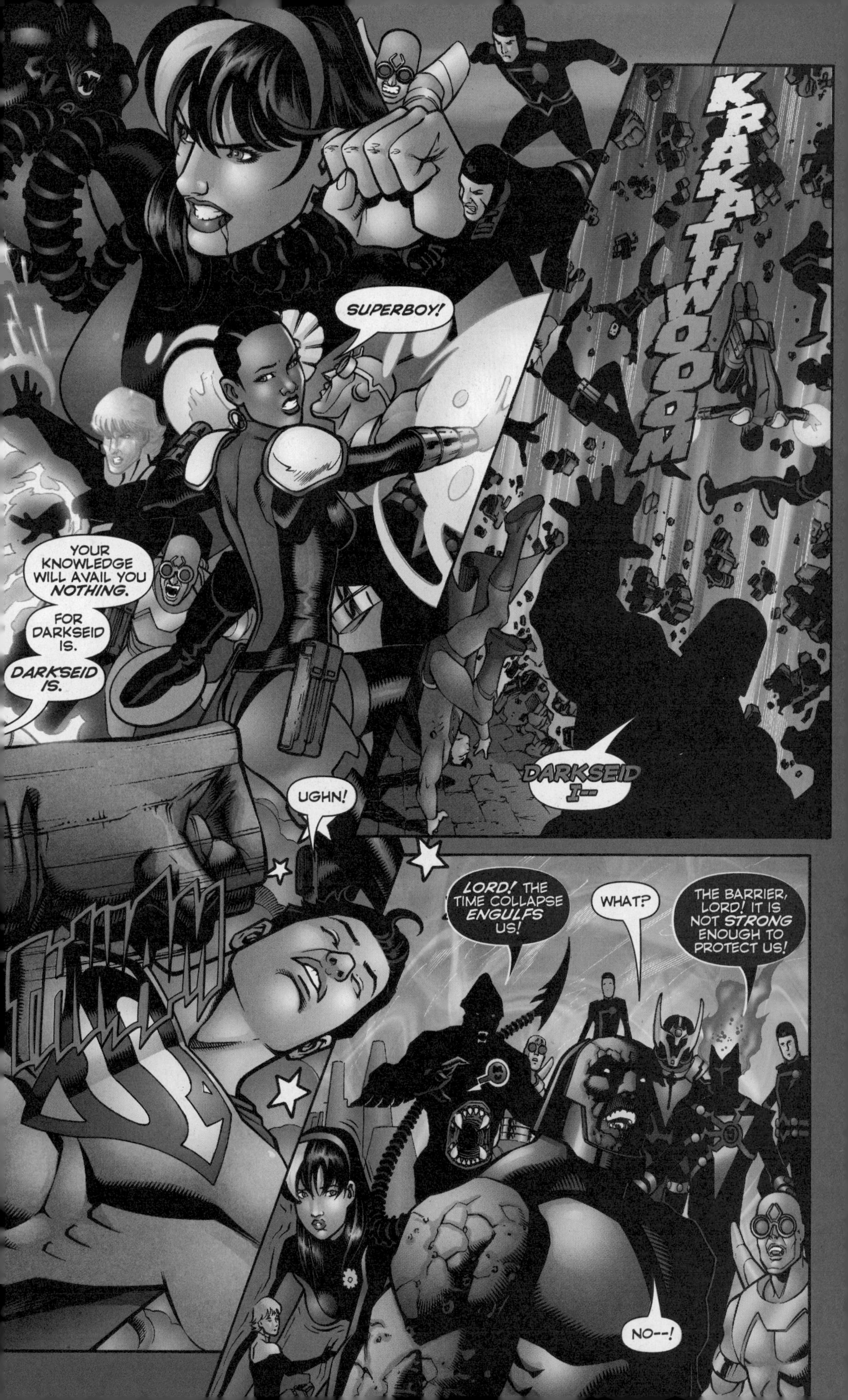
KRAKATHWOOM
SUPERBOY!
YOUR KNOWLEDGE WILL AVAIL YOU NOTHING.
FOR DARKSEID IS.
DARKSEID IS.
DARKSEID I--
UGHN!
LORD! THE TIME COLLAPSE ENGULFS US!
WHAT?
THE BARRIER, LORD! IT IS NOT STRONG ENOUGH TO PROTECT US!
NO--!

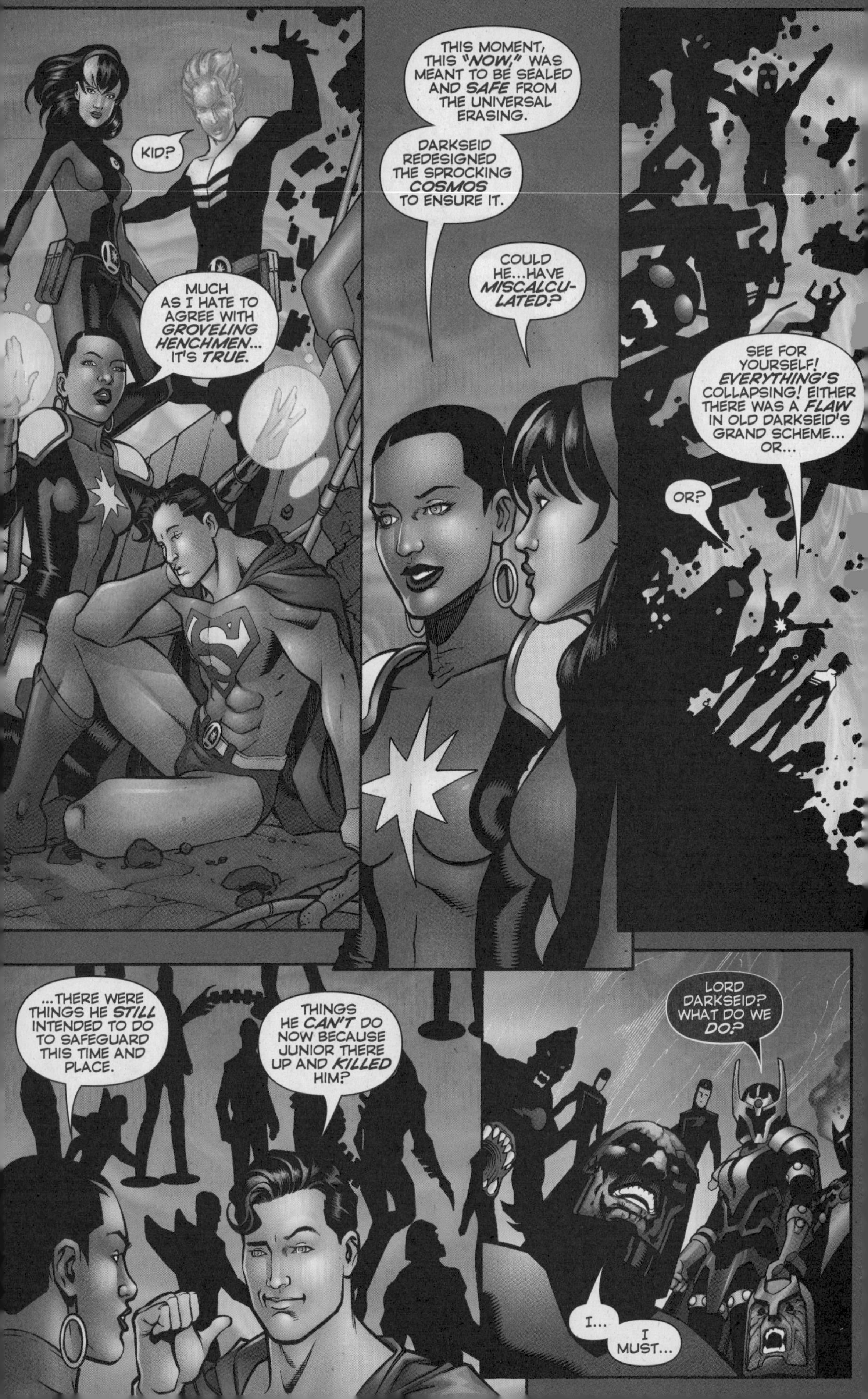
KID?
MUCH AS I HATE TO AGREE WITH GROVELING HENCHMEN... IT'S TRUE.
THIS MOMENT, THIS "NOW," WAS MEANT TO BE SEALED AND SAFE FROM THE UNIVERSAL ERASING.
DARKSEID REDESIGNED THE SPROCKING COSMOS TO ENSURE IT.
COULD HE...HAVE MISCALCU-LATED?
SEE FOR YOURSELF! EVERYTHING'S COLLAPSING! EITHER THERE WAS A FLAW IN OLD DARKSEID'S GRAND SCHEME... OR...
OR?
...THERE WERE THINGS HE STILL INTENDED TO DO TO SAFEGUARD THIS TIME AND PLACE.
THINGS HE CAN'T DO NOW BECAUSE JUNIOR THERE UP AND KILLED HIM?
LORD DARKSEID? WHAT DO WE DO?
I...
I MUST...

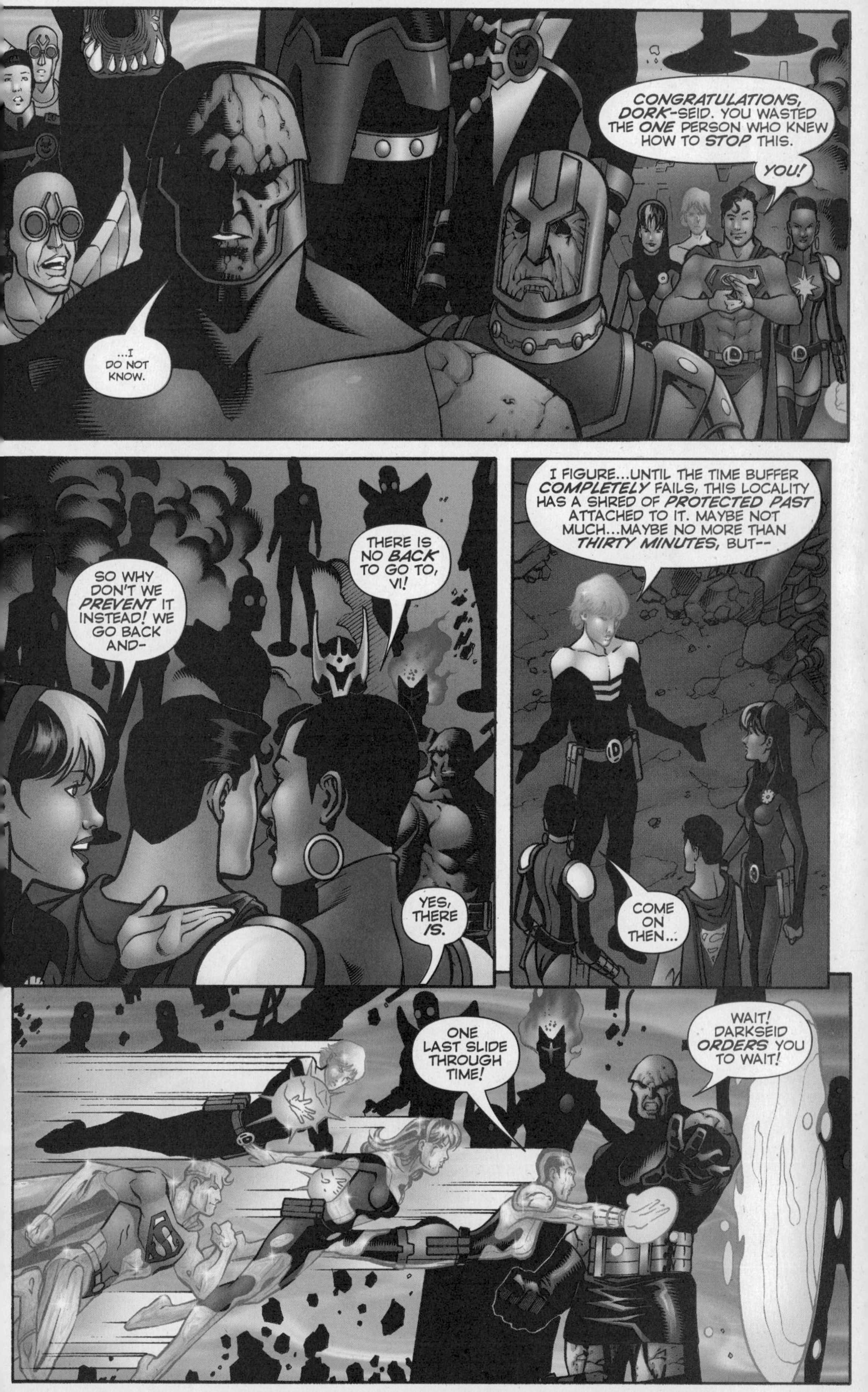
CONGRATULATIONS, DORK-SEID. YOU WASTED THE ONE PERSON WHO KNEW HOW TO STOP THIS.
YOU!
...I DO NOT KNOW.
SO WHY DON'T WE PREVENT IT INSTEAD! WE GO BACK AND-
THERE IS NO BACK TO GO TO, VI!
YES, THERE IS.
I FIGURE...UNTIL THE TIME BUFFER COMPLETELY FAILS, THIS LOCALITY HAS A SHRED OF PROTECTED PAST ATTACHED TO IT. MAYBE NOT MUCH...MAYBE NO MORE THAN THIRTY MINUTES, BUT--
COME ON THEN...
ONE LAST SLIDE THROUGH TIME!
WAIT! DARKSEID ORDERS YOU TO WAIT!

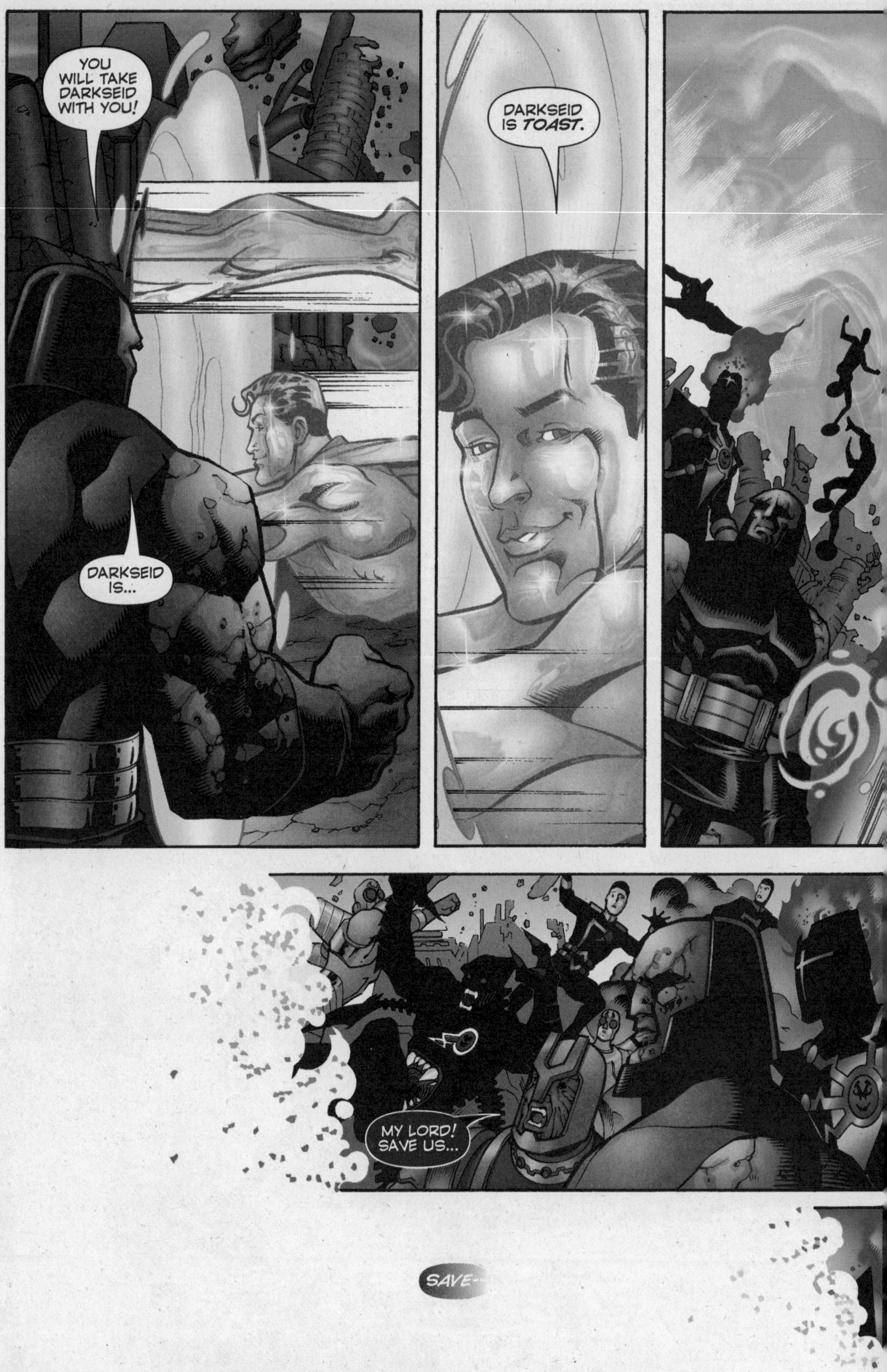
YOU WILL TAKE DARKSEID WITH YOU!
DARKSEID IS...
DARKSEID IS *TOAST*.
MY LORD! SAVE US...
SAVE--

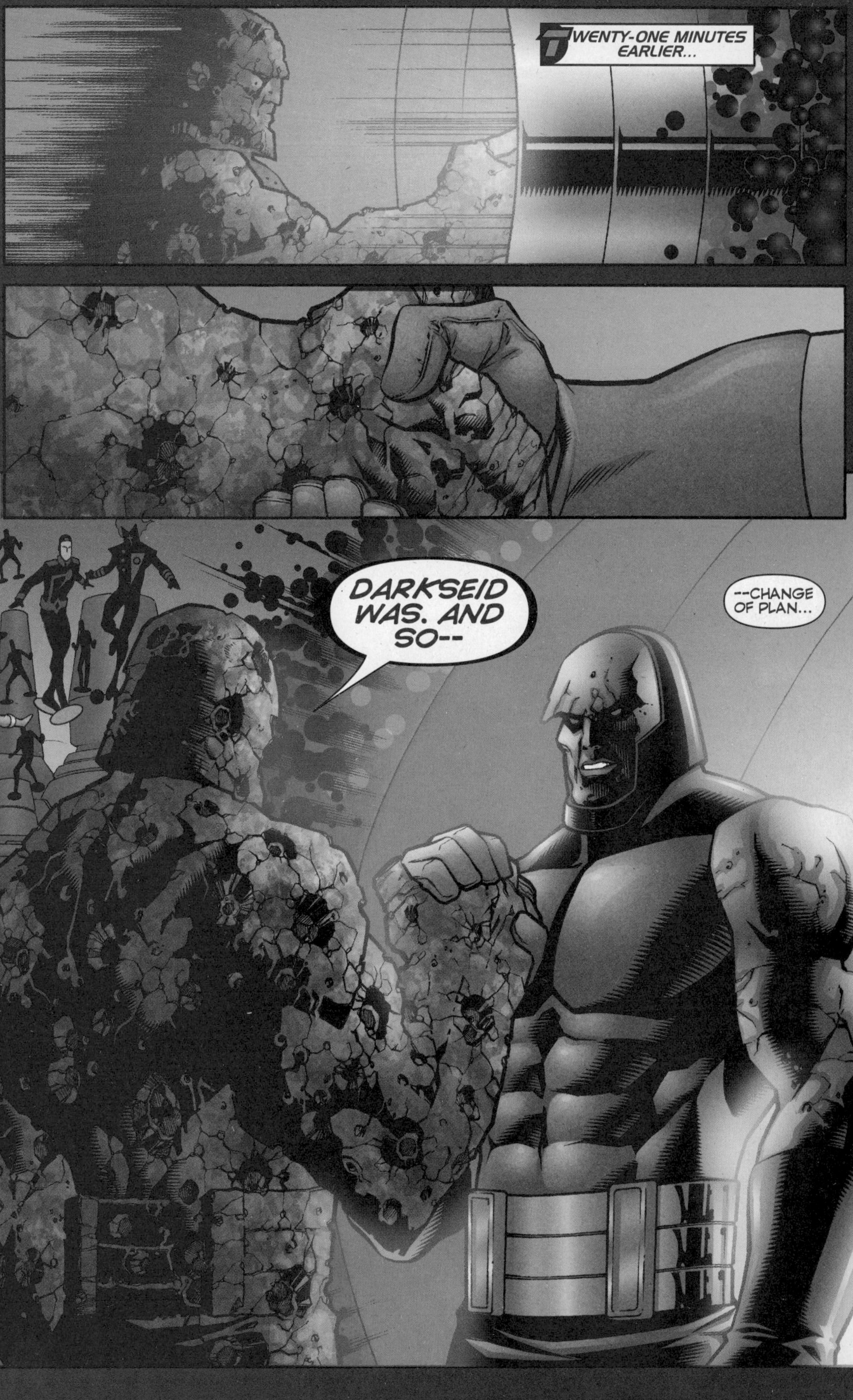
TWENTY-ONE MINUTES EARLIER...
DARKSEID WAS. AND SO--
--CHANGE OF PLAN...

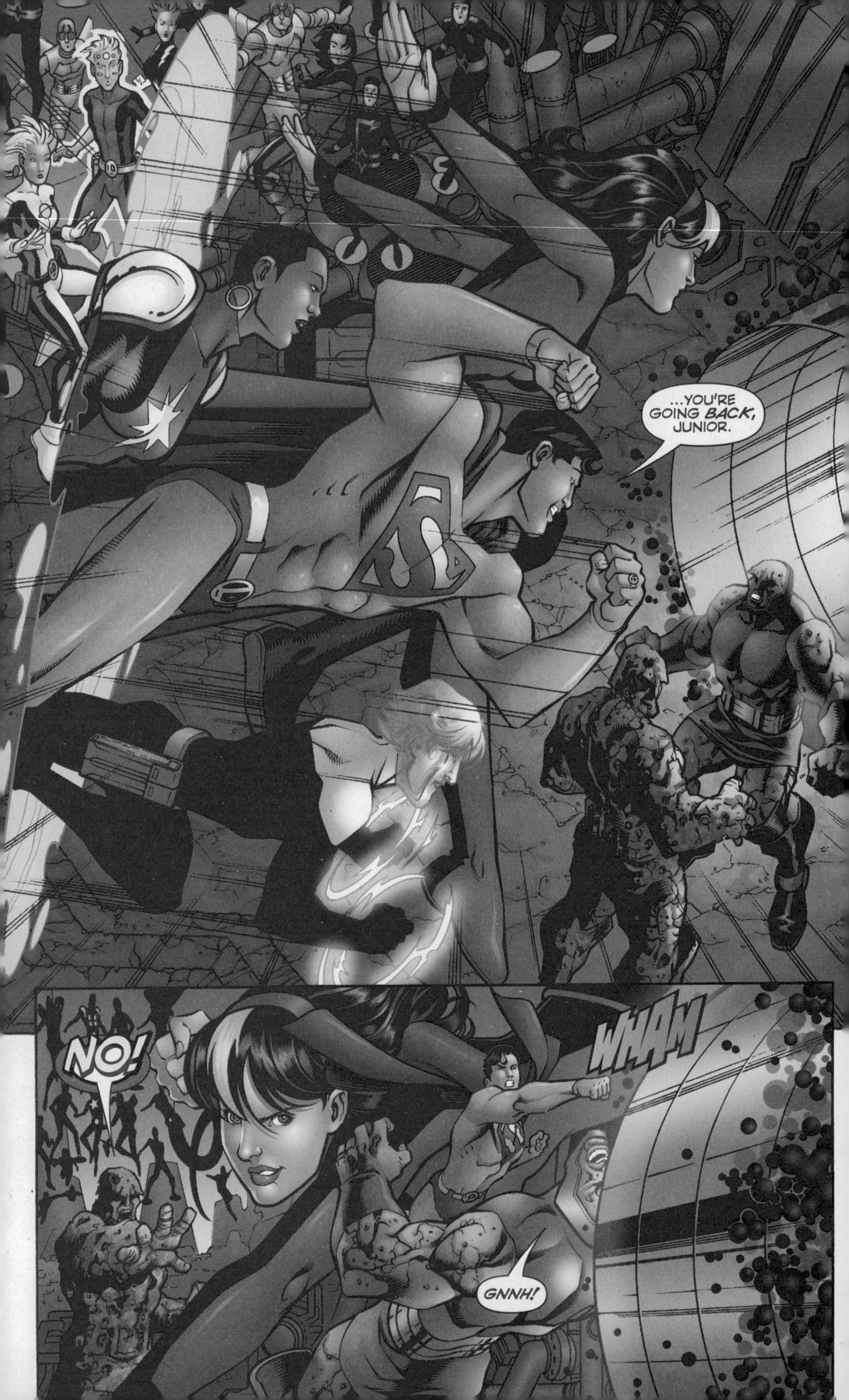
...YOU'RE GOING BACK, JUNIOR.
NO!
WHAM
GNNH!

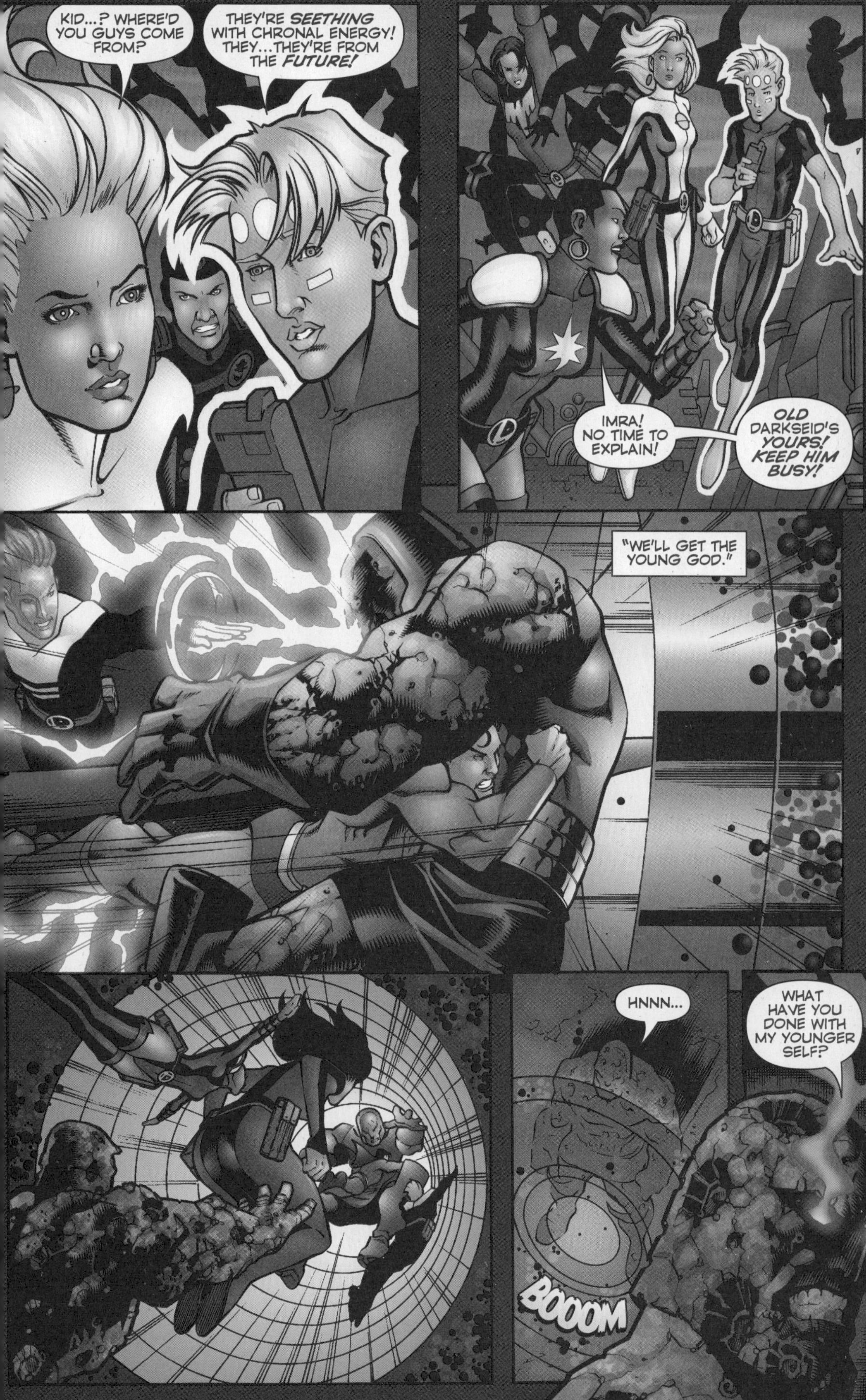
KID...? WHERE'D YOU GUYS COME FROM?
THEY'RE SEETHING WITH CHRONAL ENERGY! THEY...THEY'RE FROM THE FUTURE!
IMRA! NO TIME TO EXPLAIN!
OLD DARKSEID'S YOURS! KEEP HIM BUSY!
"WE'LL GET THE YOUNG GOD."
HNNN...
WHAT HAVE YOU DONE WITH MY YOUNGER SELF?
BOOOM

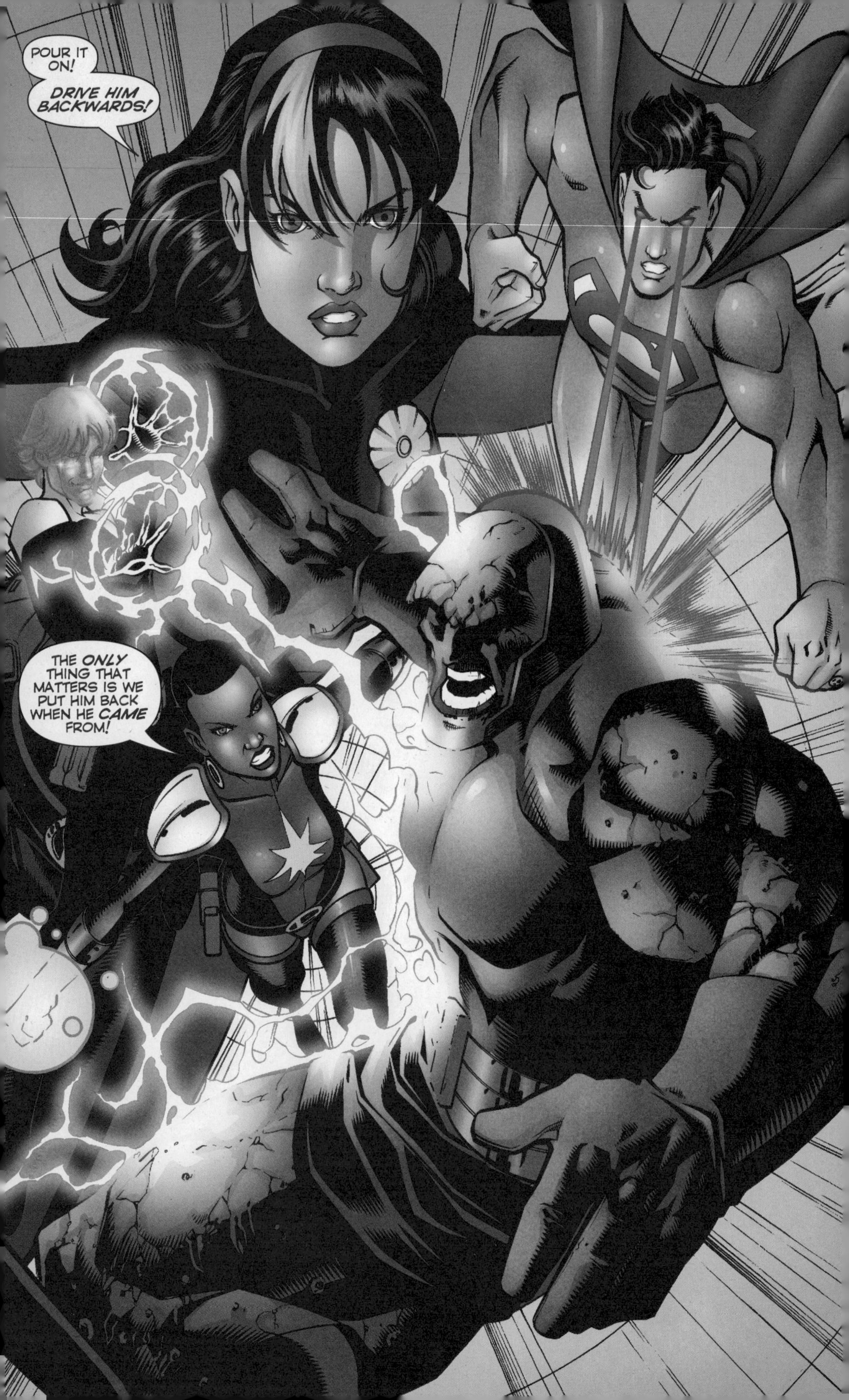
POUR IT ON! DRIVE HIM BACKWARDS!
THE ONLY THING THAT MATTERS IS WE PUT HIM BACK WHEN HE CAME FROM!

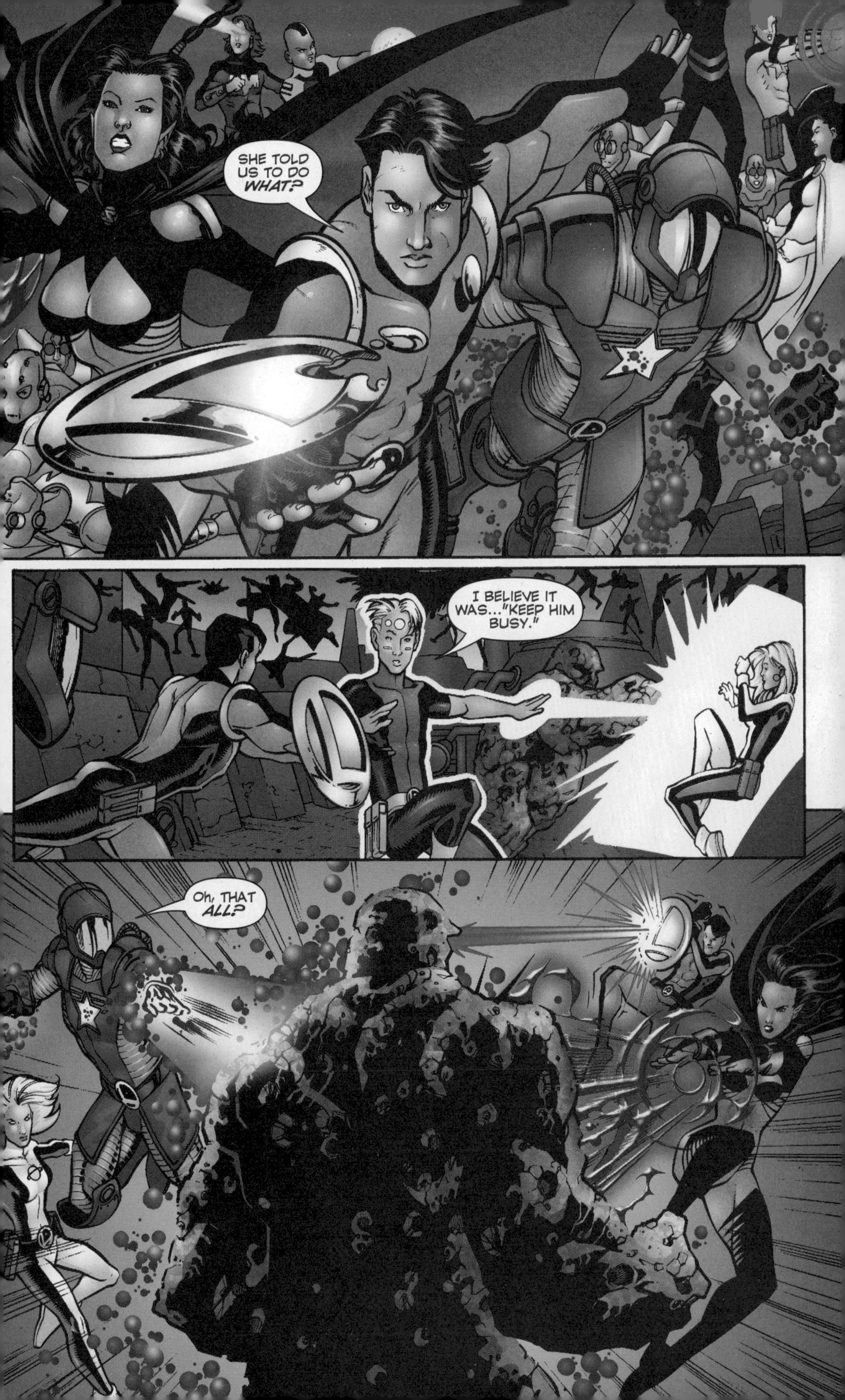
SHE TOLD US TO DO *WHAT?*
I BELIEVE IT WAS..."KEEP HIM BUSY."
Oh, THAT *ALL?*

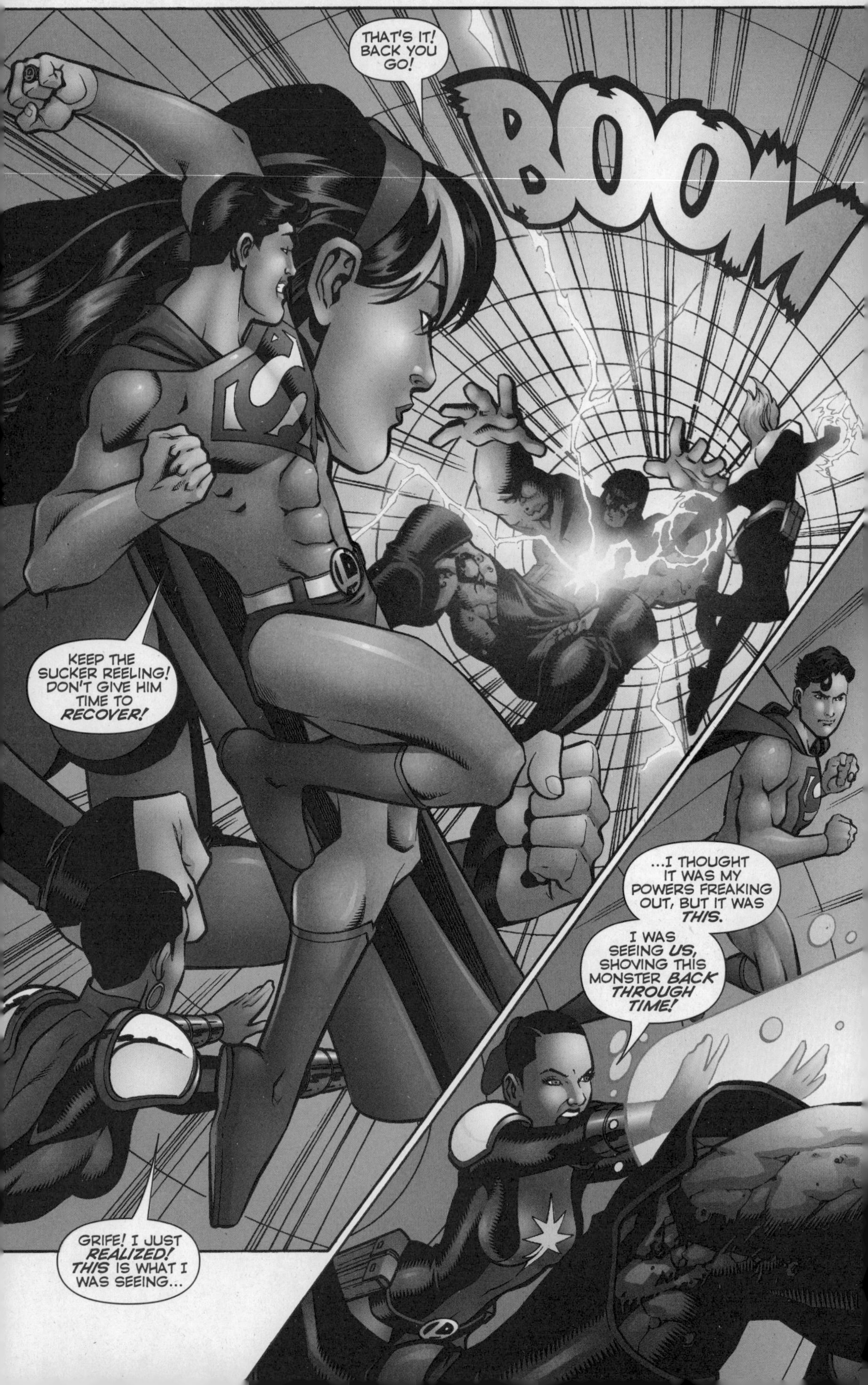
THAT'S IT! BACK YOU GO!
BOOM
KEEP THE SUCKER REELING! DON'T GIVE HIM TIME TO RECOVER!
GRIFE! I JUST REALIZED! THIS IS WHAT I WAS SEEING...
...I THOUGHT IT WAS MY POWERS FREAKING OUT, BUT IT WAS THIS.
I WAS SEEING US, SHOVING THIS MONSTER BACK THROUGH TIME!

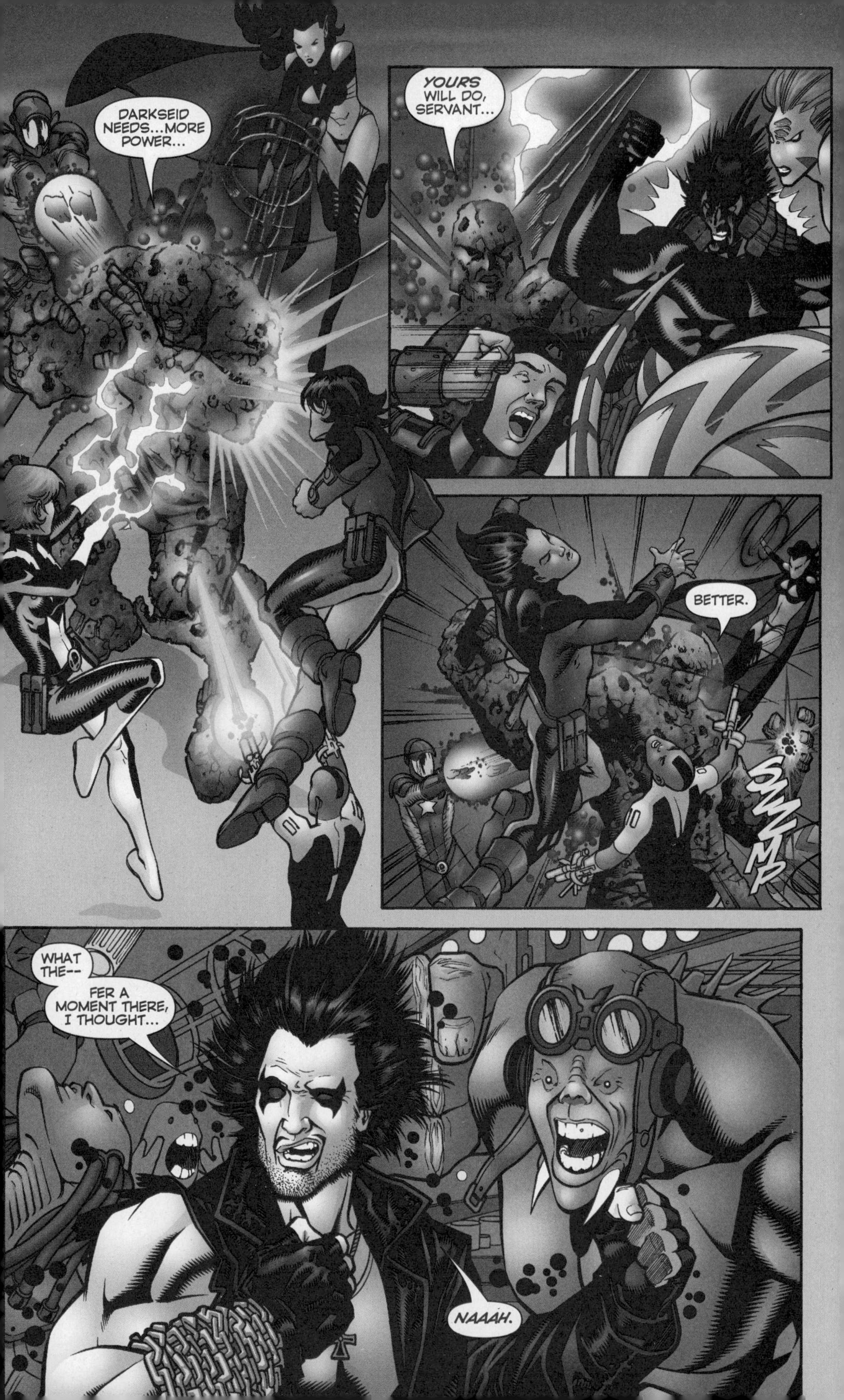
DARKSEID NEEDS...MORE POWER...
YOURS WILL DO, SERVANT...
BETTER.
SWUMP
WHAT THE--
FER A MOMENT THERE, I THOUGHT...
NAAAH.

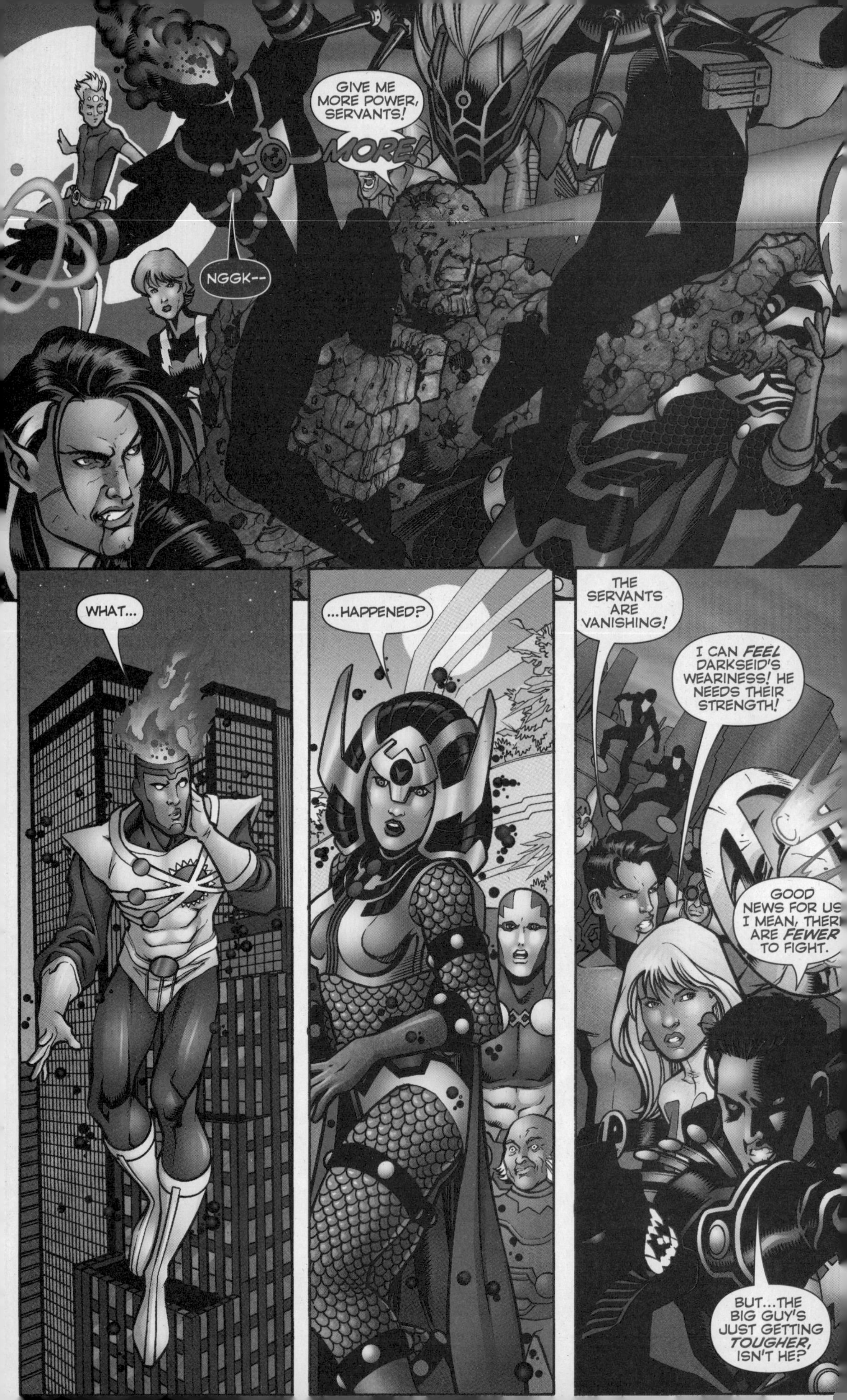
GIVE ME MORE POWER, SERVANTS!
MORE!
NGGK--
WHAT...
...HAPPENED?
THE SERVANTS ARE VANISHING!
I CAN FEEL DARKSEID'S WEARINESS! HE NEEDS THEIR STRENGTH!
GOOD NEWS FOR US I MEAN, THERE ARE FEWER TO FIGHT.
BUT...THE BIG GUY'S JUST GETTING TOUGHER, ISN'T HE?

A-ALMOST THERE!

I SEE THE END OF THE TUBE!

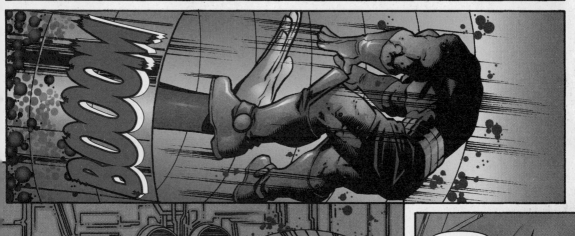

BOOOM

MY LORD! MY LORD! ARE YOU ALL RIGHT?!?

YOU *VANISHED*...AND THEN REAPPEARED A MOMENT LATER IN A BLAZE OF FIRE!

MY LORD DARKSEID?

LEGION...

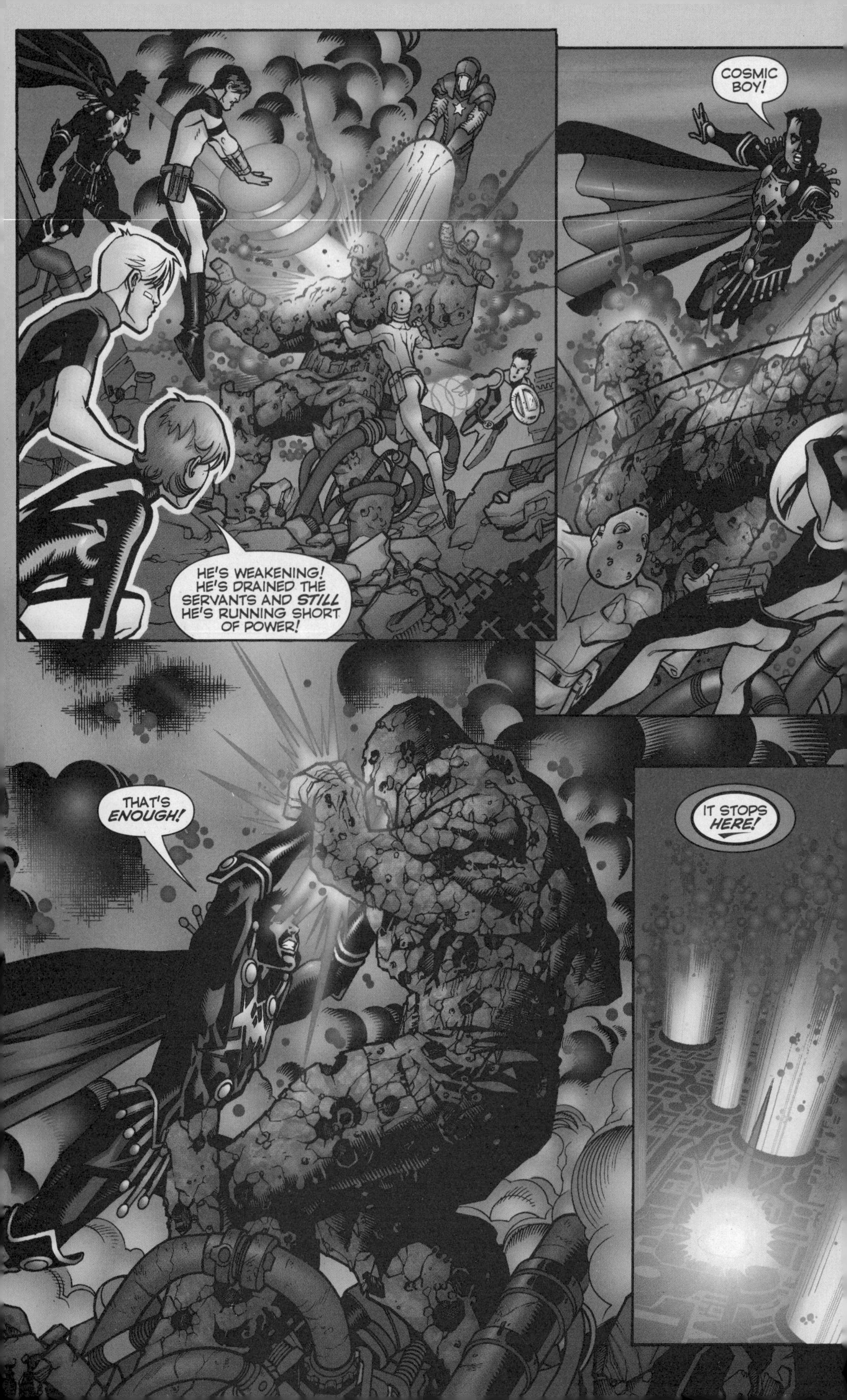

HE'S WEAKENING! HE'S DRAINED THE SERVANTS AND STILL HE'S RUNNING SHORT OF POWER!
COSMIC BOY!
THAT'S ENOUGH!
IT STOPS HERE!

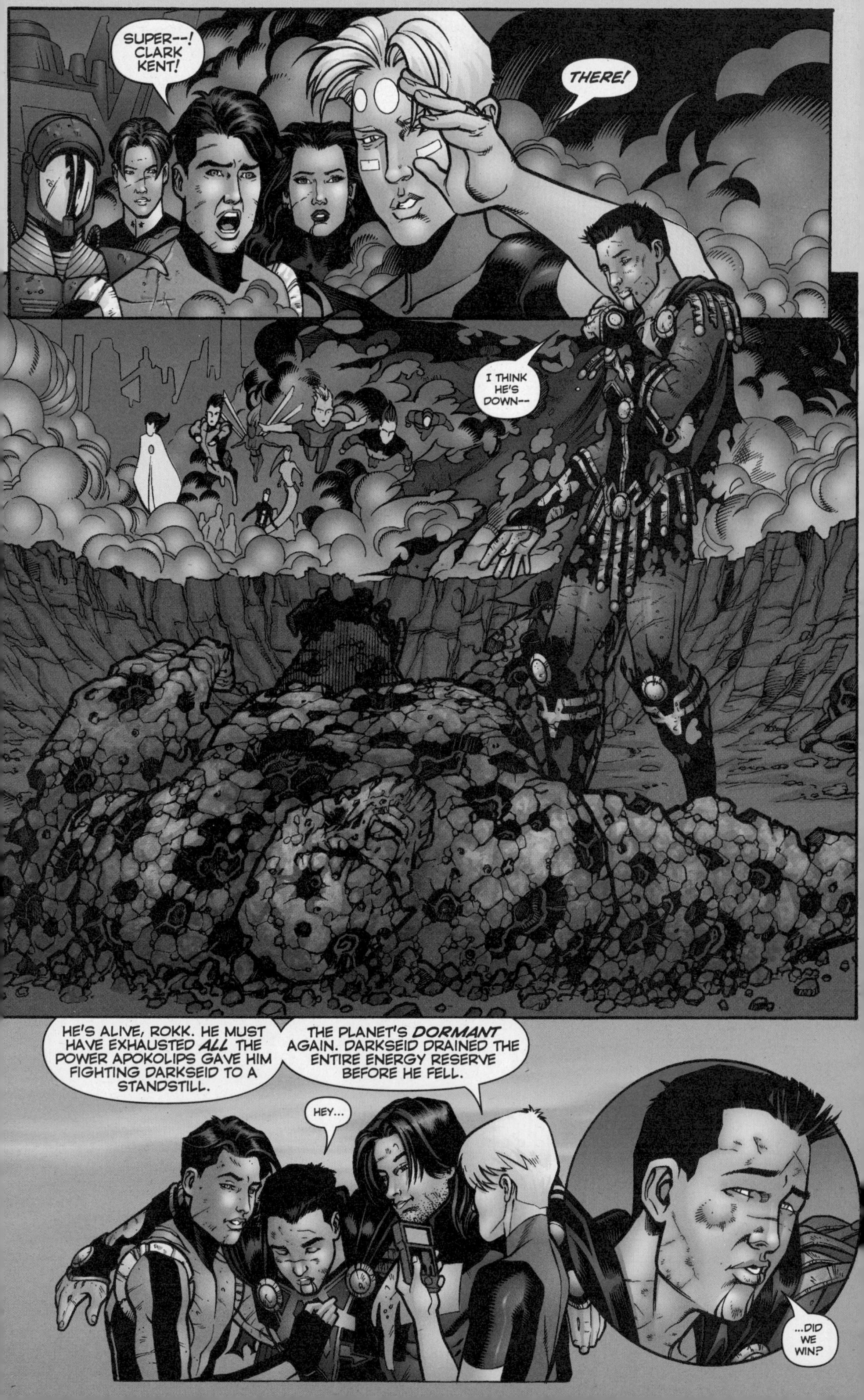
SUPER--! CLARK KENT!
THERE!
I THINK HE'S DOWN--
HE'S ALIVE, ROKK. HE MUST HAVE EXHAUSTED ALL THE POWER APOKOLIPS GAVE HIM FIGHTING DARKSEID TO A STANDSTILL.
THE PLANET'S DORMANT AGAIN. DARKSEID DRAINED THE ENTIRE ENERGY RESERVE BEFORE HE FELL.
HEY...
...DID WE WIN?

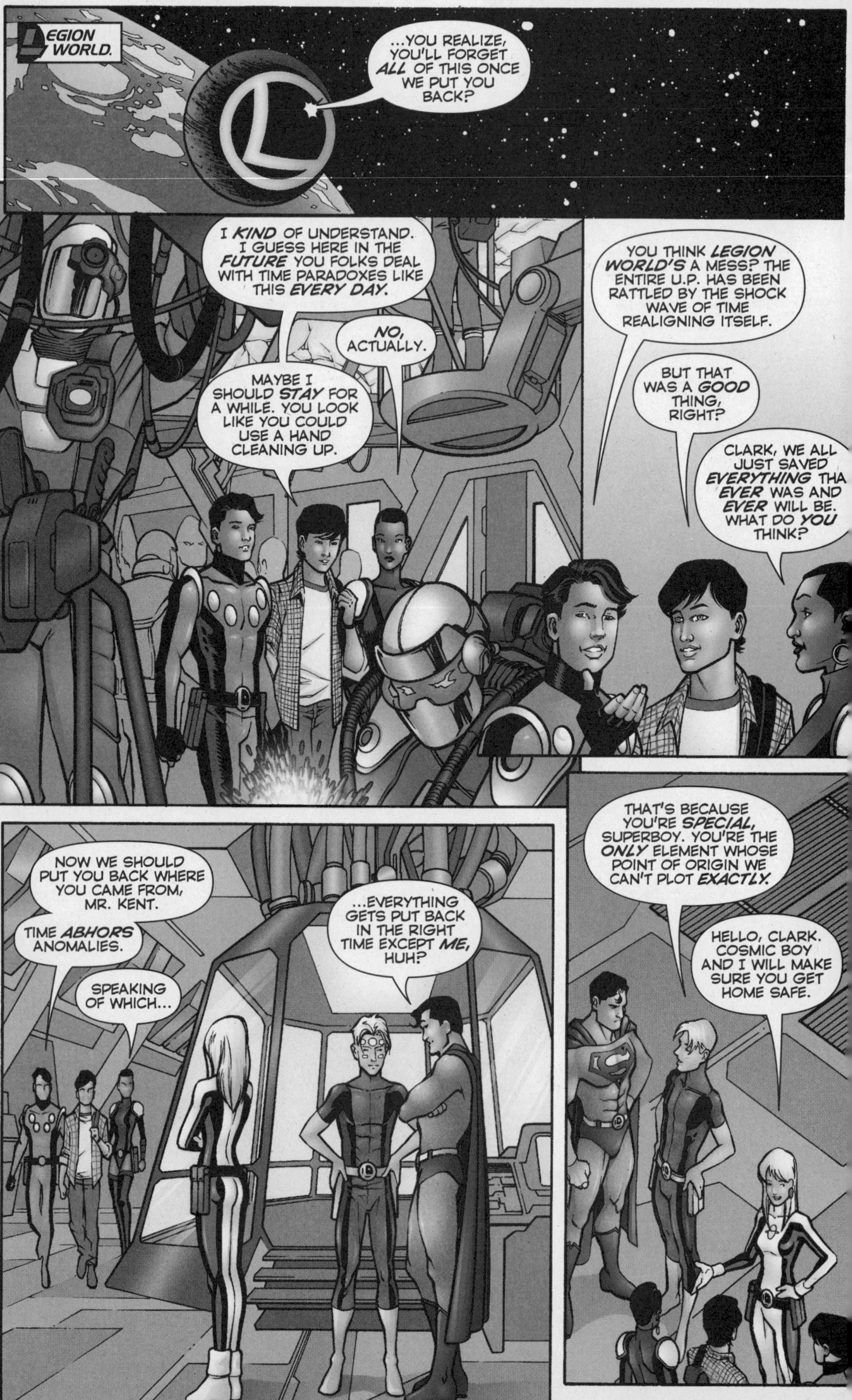
LEGION WORLD.
...YOU REALIZE, YOU'LL FORGET ALL OF THIS ONCE WE PUT YOU BACK?
I KIND OF UNDERSTAND. I GUESS HERE IN THE FUTURE YOU FOLKS DEAL WITH TIME PARADOXES LIKE THIS EVERY DAY.
NO, ACTUALLY.
MAYBE I SHOULD STAY FOR A WHILE. YOU LOOK LIKE YOU COULD USE A HAND CLEANING UP.
YOU THINK LEGION WORLD'S A MESS? THE ENTIRE U.P. HAS BEEN RATTLED BY THE SHOCK WAVE OF TIME REALIGNING ITSELF.
BUT THAT WAS A GOOD THING, RIGHT?
CLARK, WE ALL JUST SAVED EVERYTHING THA EVER WAS AND EVER WILL BE. WHAT DO YOU THINK?
NOW WE SHOULD PUT YOU BACK WHERE YOU CAME FROM, MR. KENT.
TIME ABHORS ANOMALIES.
SPEAKING OF WHICH...
...EVERYTHING GETS PUT BACK IN THE RIGHT TIME EXCEPT ME, HUH?
THAT'S BECAUSE YOU'RE SPECIAL, SUPERBOY. YOU'RE THE ONLY ELEMENT WHOSE POINT OF ORIGIN WE CAN'T PLOT EXACTLY.
HELLO, CLARK. COSMIC BOY AND I WILL MAKE SURE YOU GET HOME SAFE.

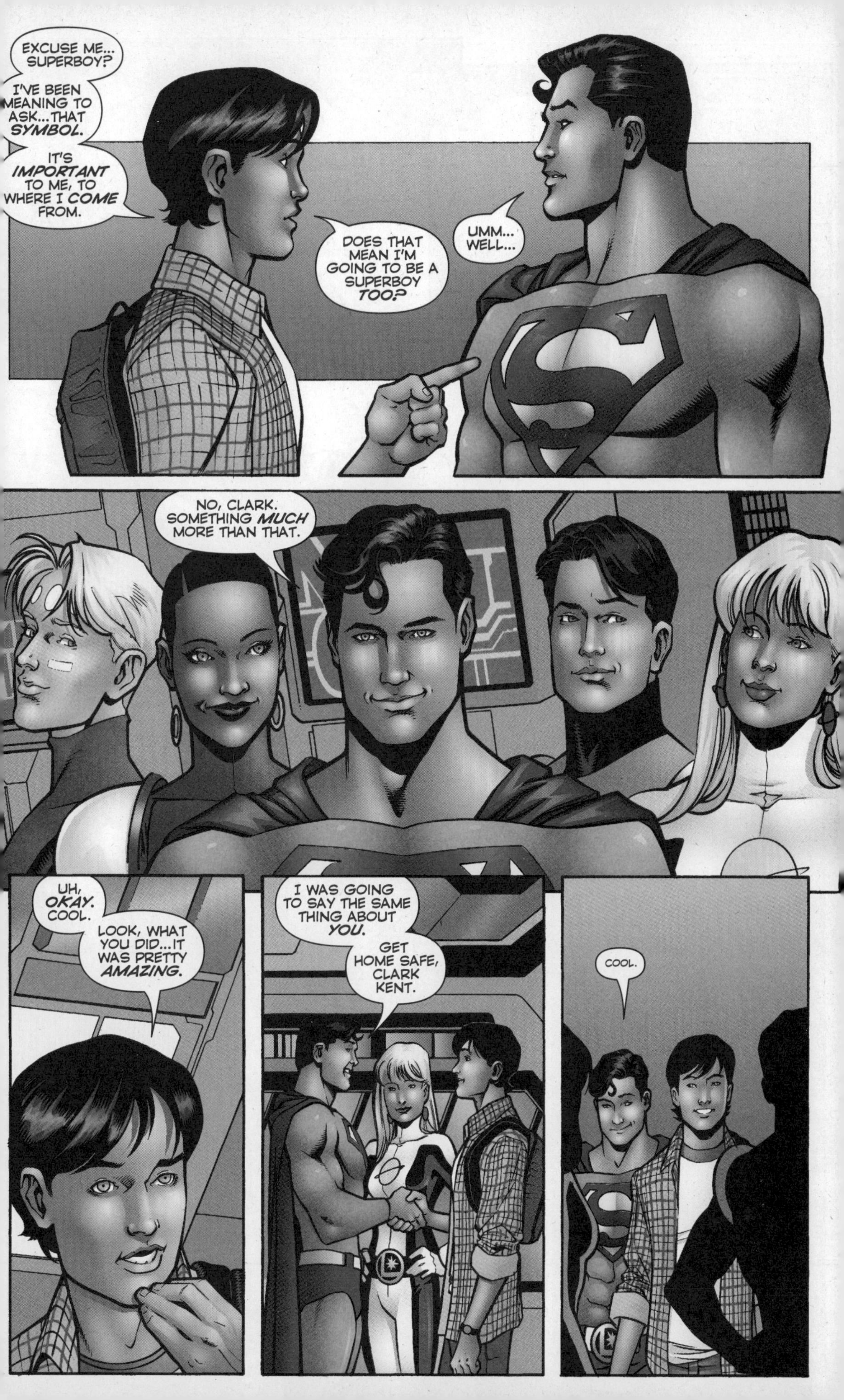
EXCUSE ME... SUPERBOY?
I'VE BEEN MEANING TO ASK...THAT SYMBOL.
IT'S IMPORTANT TO ME, TO WHERE I COME FROM.
DOES THAT MEAN I'M GOING TO BE A SUPERBOY TOO?
UMM... WELL...
NO, CLARK. SOMETHING MUCH MORE THAN THAT.
UH, OKAY. COOL.
LOOK, WHAT YOU DID...IT WAS PRETTY AMAZING.
I WAS GOING TO SAY THE SAME THING ABOUT YOU.
GET HOME SAFE, CLARK KENT.
COOL.

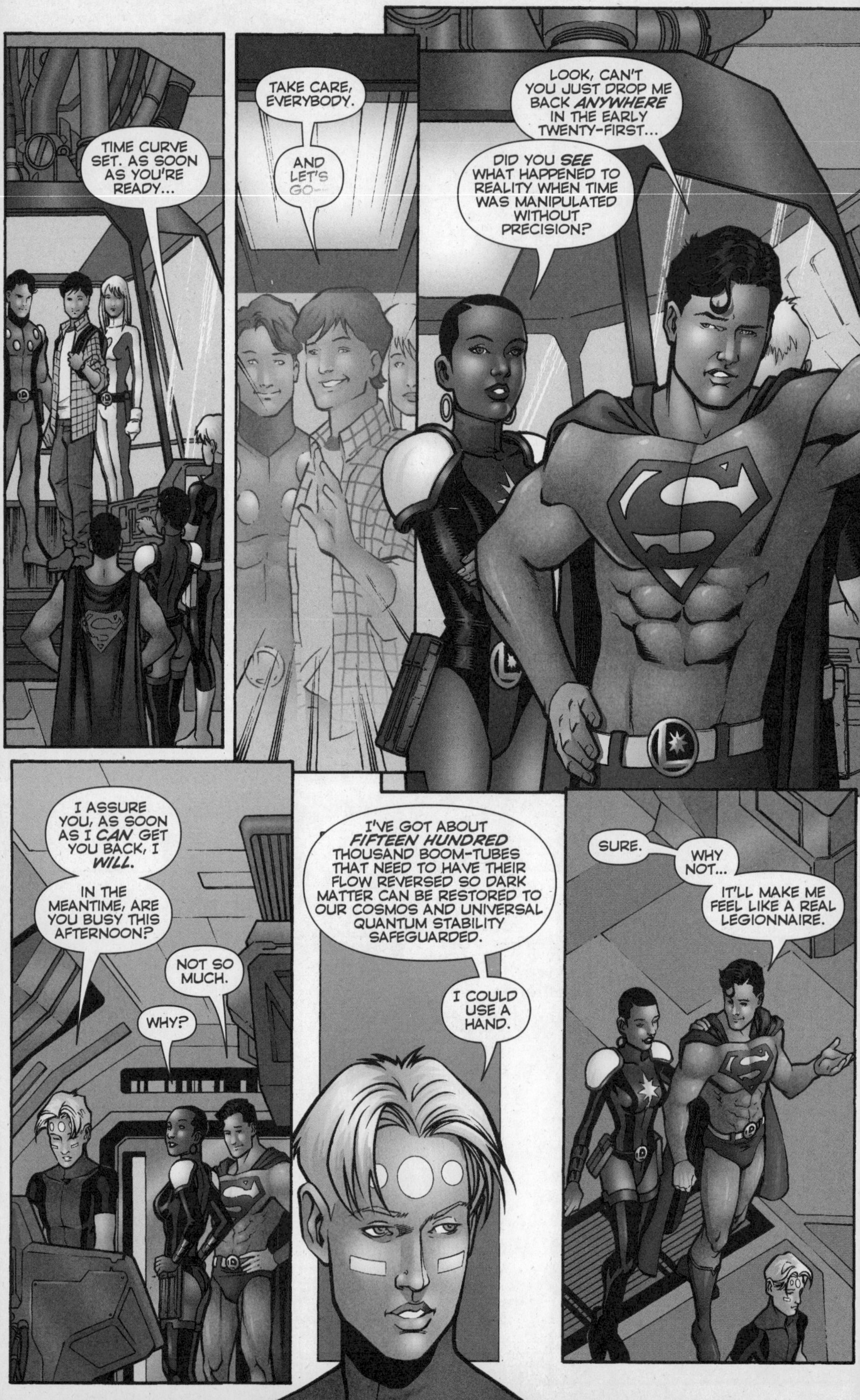
TIME CURVE SET. AS SOON AS YOU'RE READY...
TAKE CARE, EVERYBODY.
AND LET'S GO--
LOOK, CAN'T YOU JUST DROP ME BACK ANYWHERE IN THE EARLY TWENTY-FIRST...
DID YOU SEE WHAT HAPPENED TO REALITY WHEN TIME WAS MANIPULATED WITHOUT PRECISION?
I ASSURE YOU, AS SOON AS I CAN GET YOU BACK, I WILL.
IN THE MEANTIME, ARE YOU BUSY THIS AFTERNOON?
NOT SO MUCH.
WHY?
I'VE GOT ABOUT FIFTEEN HUNDRED THOUSAND BOOM-TUBES THAT NEED TO HAVE THEIR FLOW REVERSED SO DARK MATTER CAN BE RESTORED TO OUR COSMOS AND UNIVERSAL QUANTUM STABILITY SAFEGUARDED.
I COULD USE A HAND.
SURE.
WHY NOT...
IT'LL MAKE ME FEEL LIKE A REAL LEGIONNAIRE.

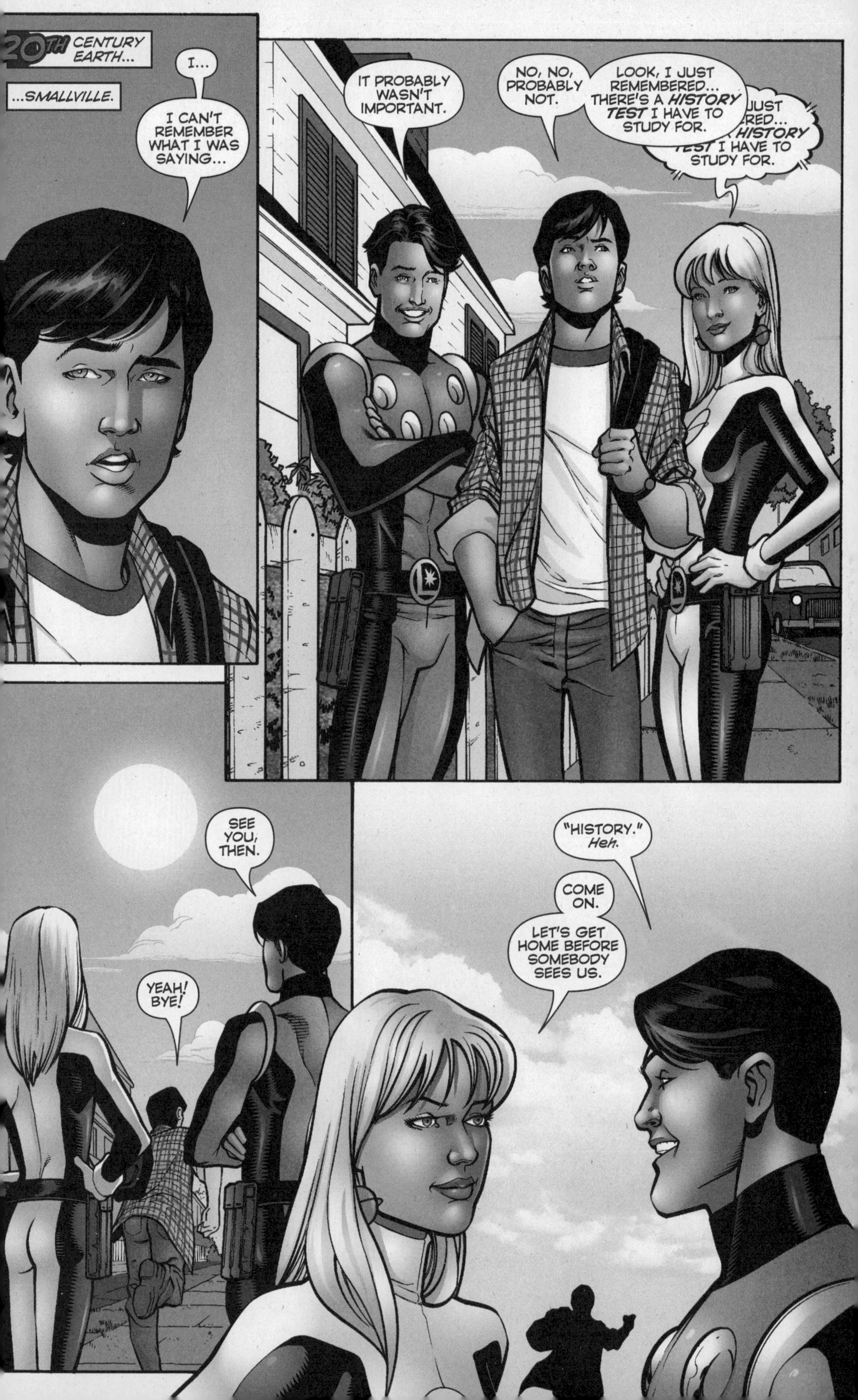
20TH CENTURY EARTH...
...SMALLVILLE.
I...
I CAN'T REMEMBER WHAT I WAS SAYING...
IT PROBABLY WASN'T IMPORTANT.
NO, NO, PROBABLY NOT.
LOOK, I JUST REMEMBERED... THERE'S A *HISTORY TEST* I HAVE TO STUDY FOR.
SEE YOU, THEN.
YEAH! BYE!
"HISTORY." *Heh.*
COME ON.
LET'S GET HOME BEFORE SOMEBODY SEES US.

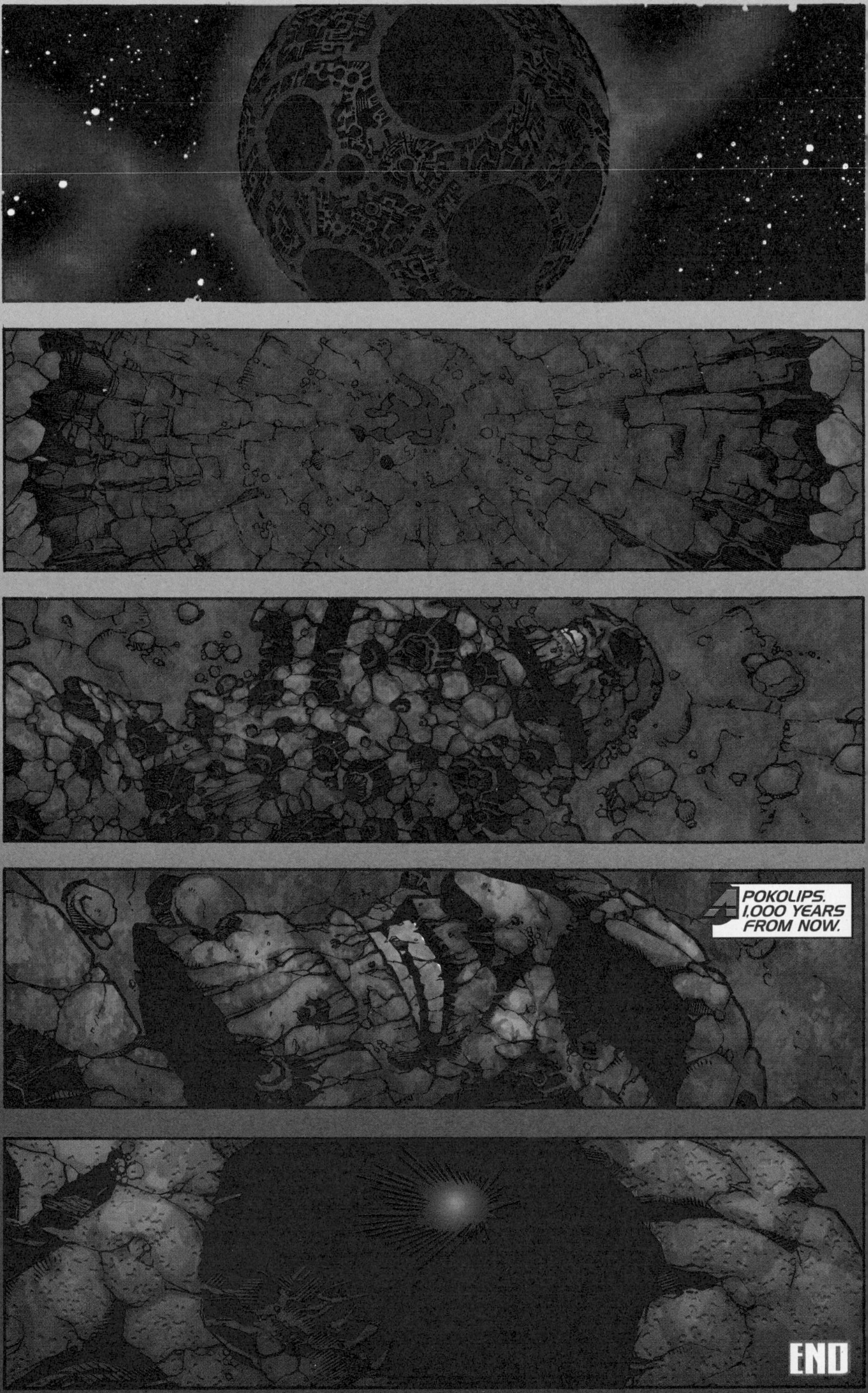
POKOLIPS.
1,000 YEARS
FROM NOW.
END

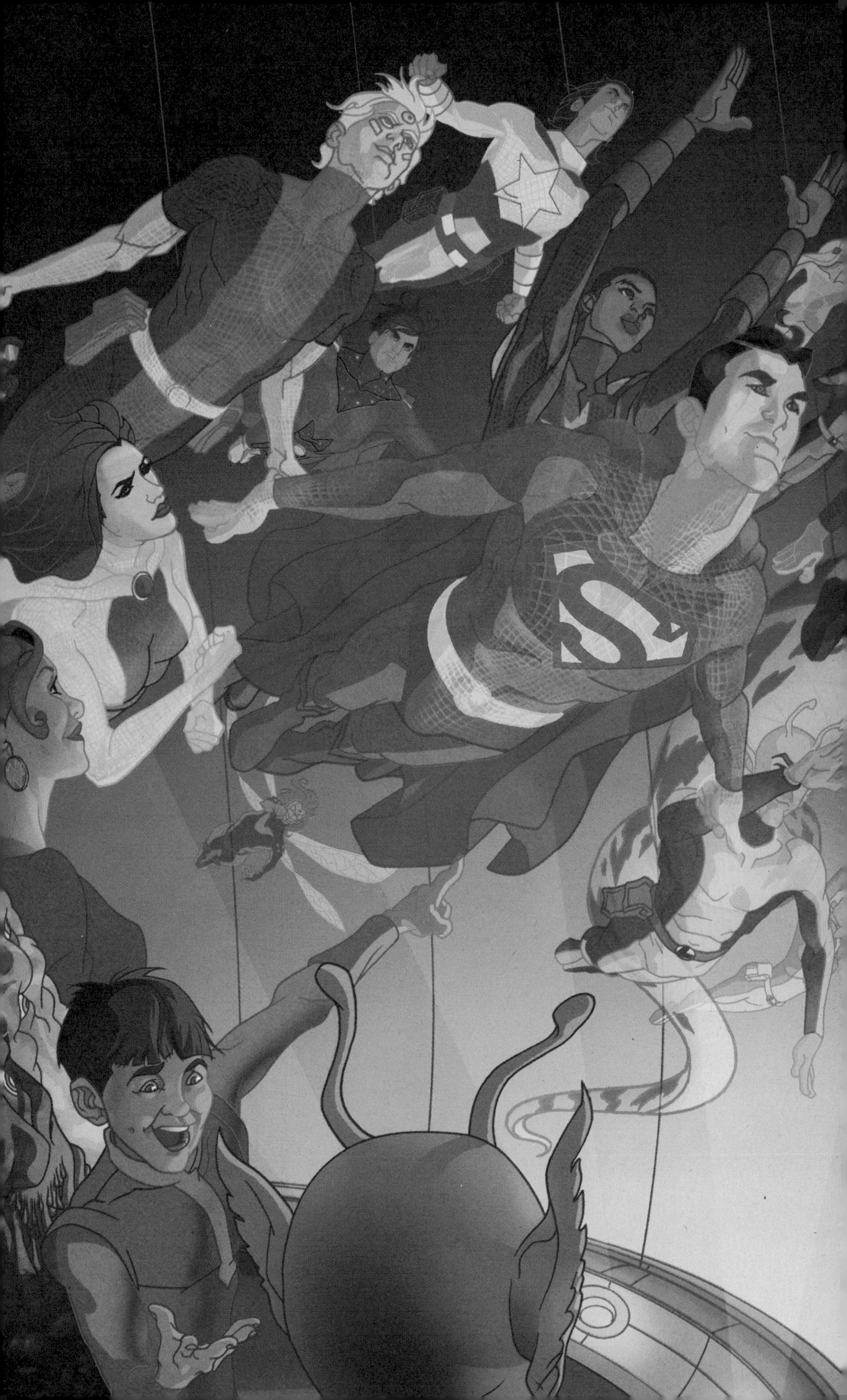

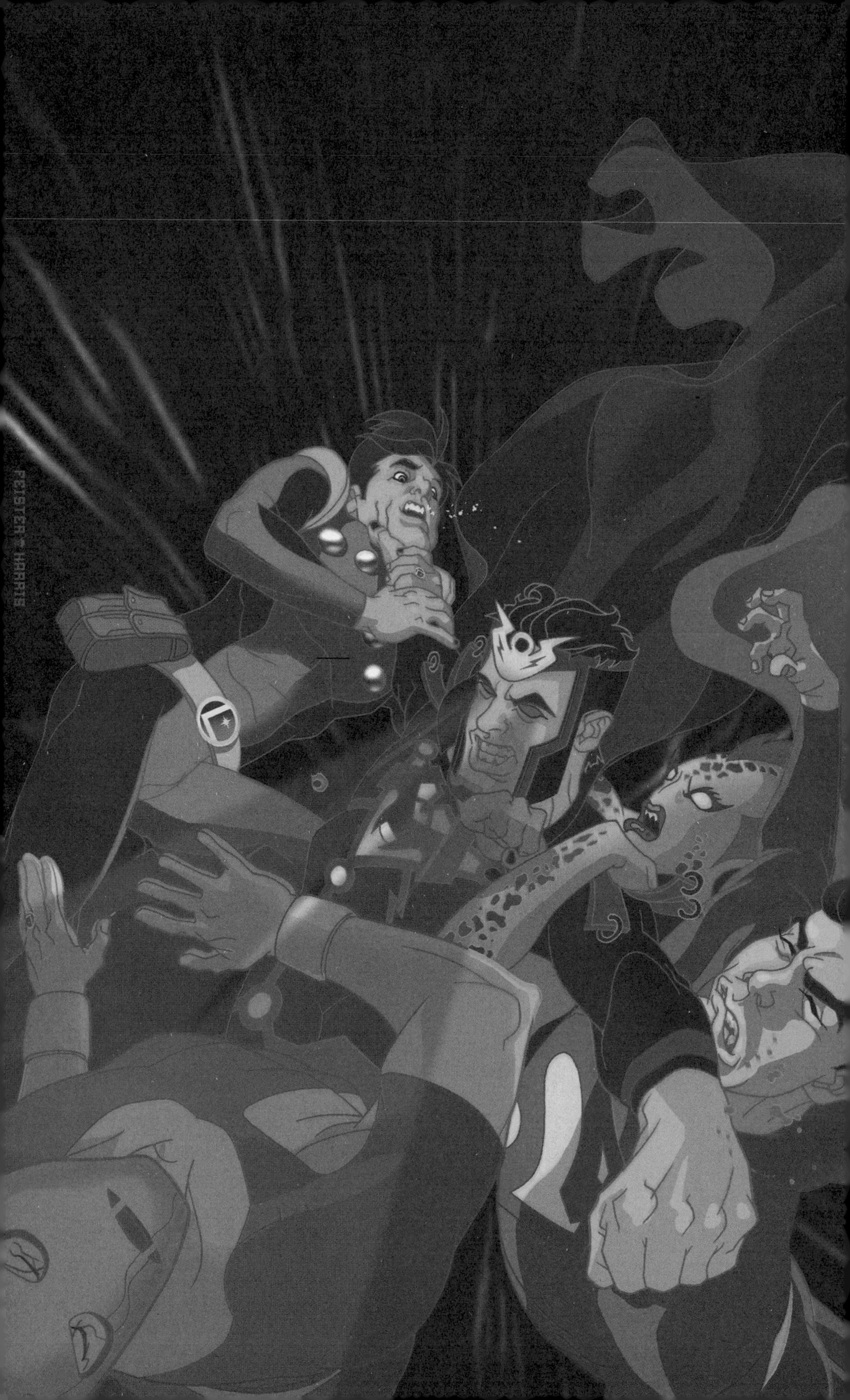
FEISTER HARRIS

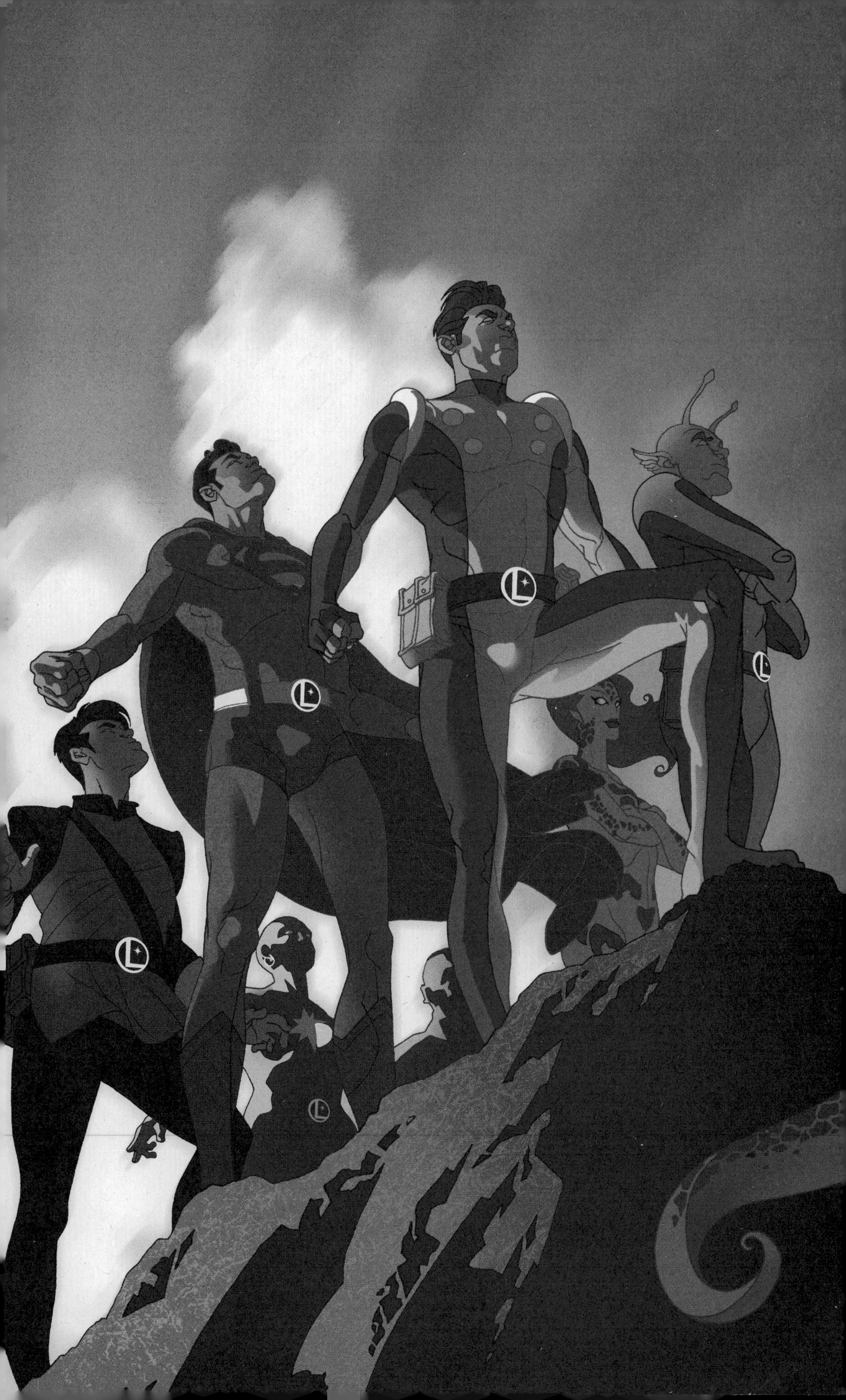

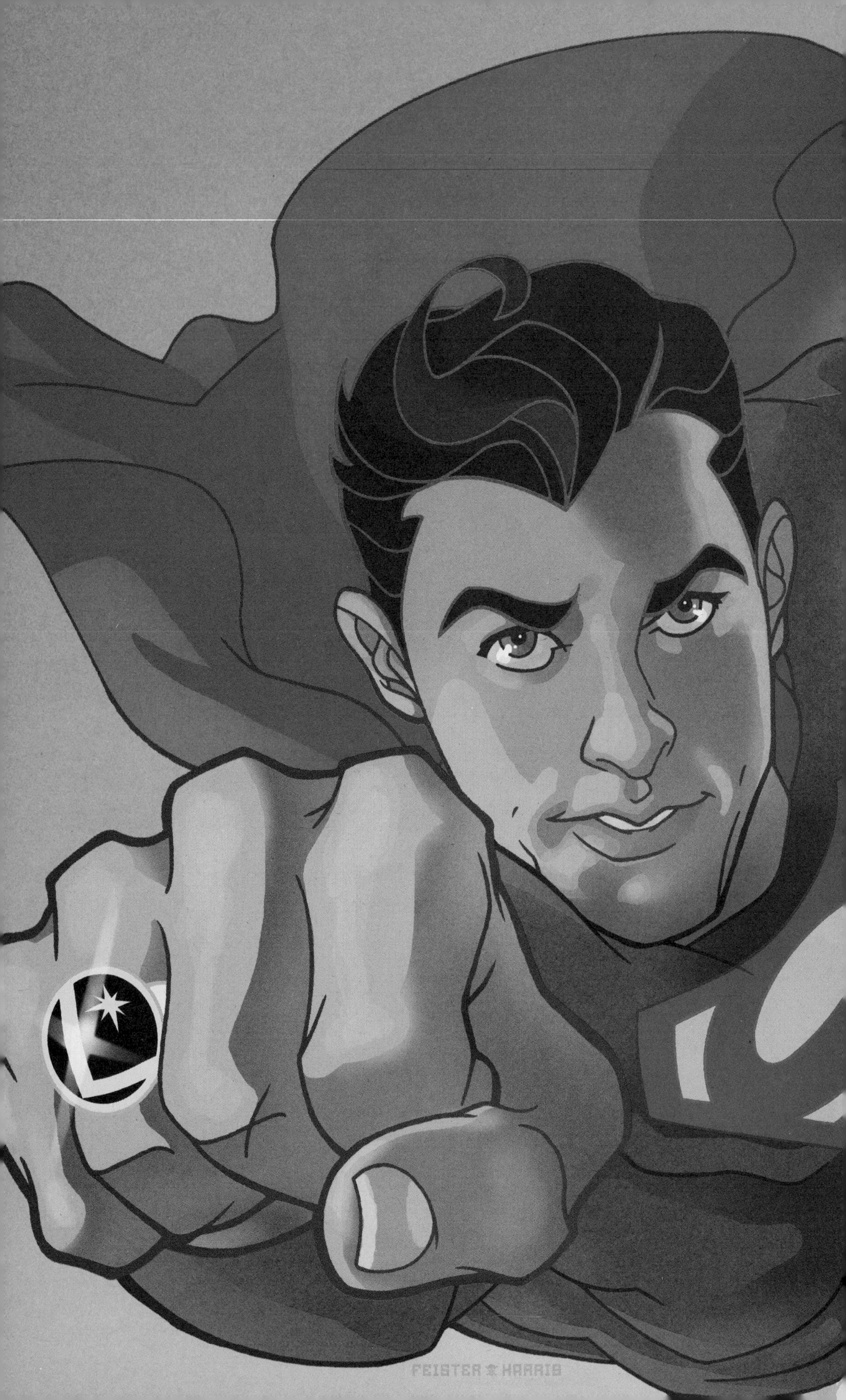
FEISTER HARRIS

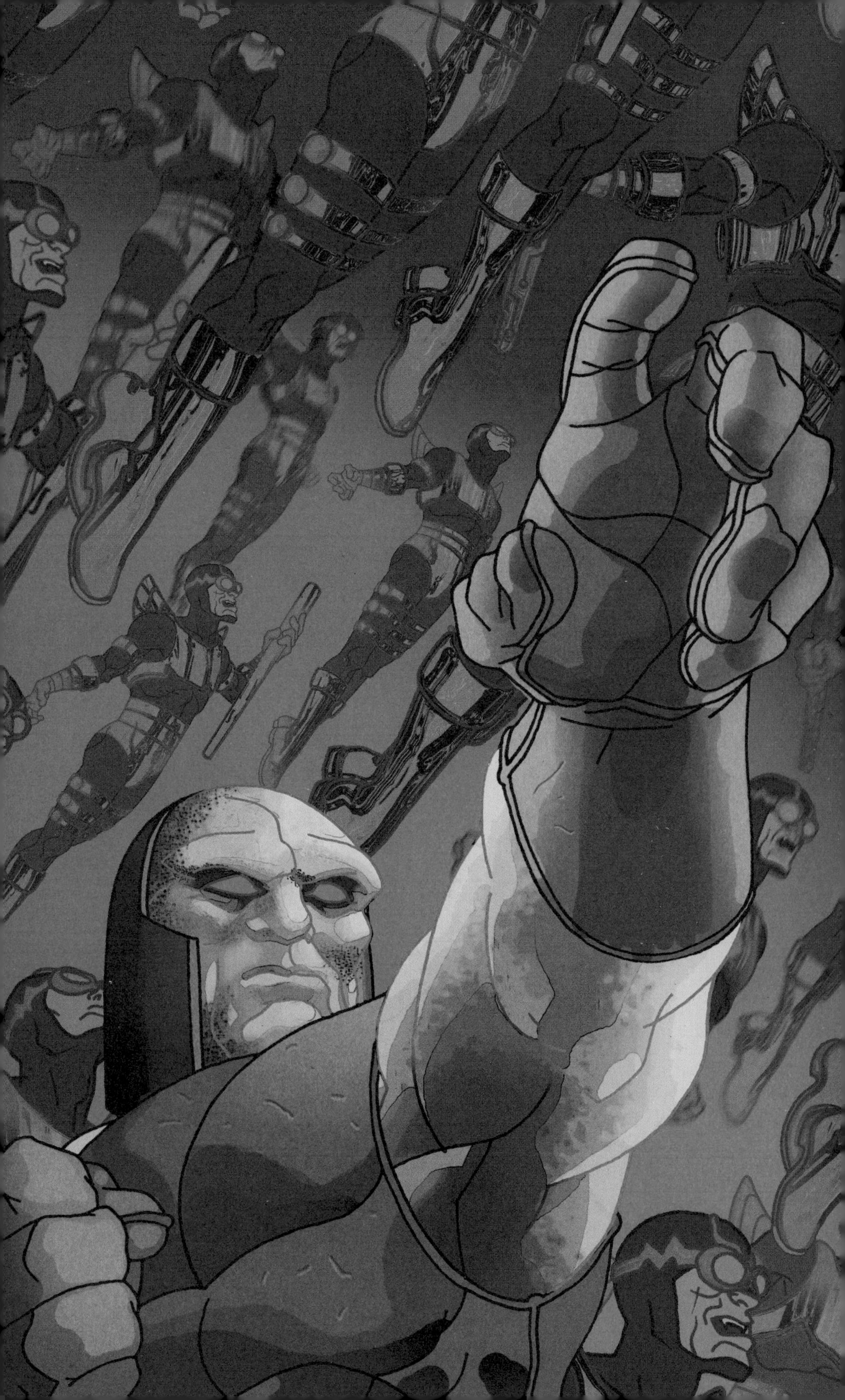

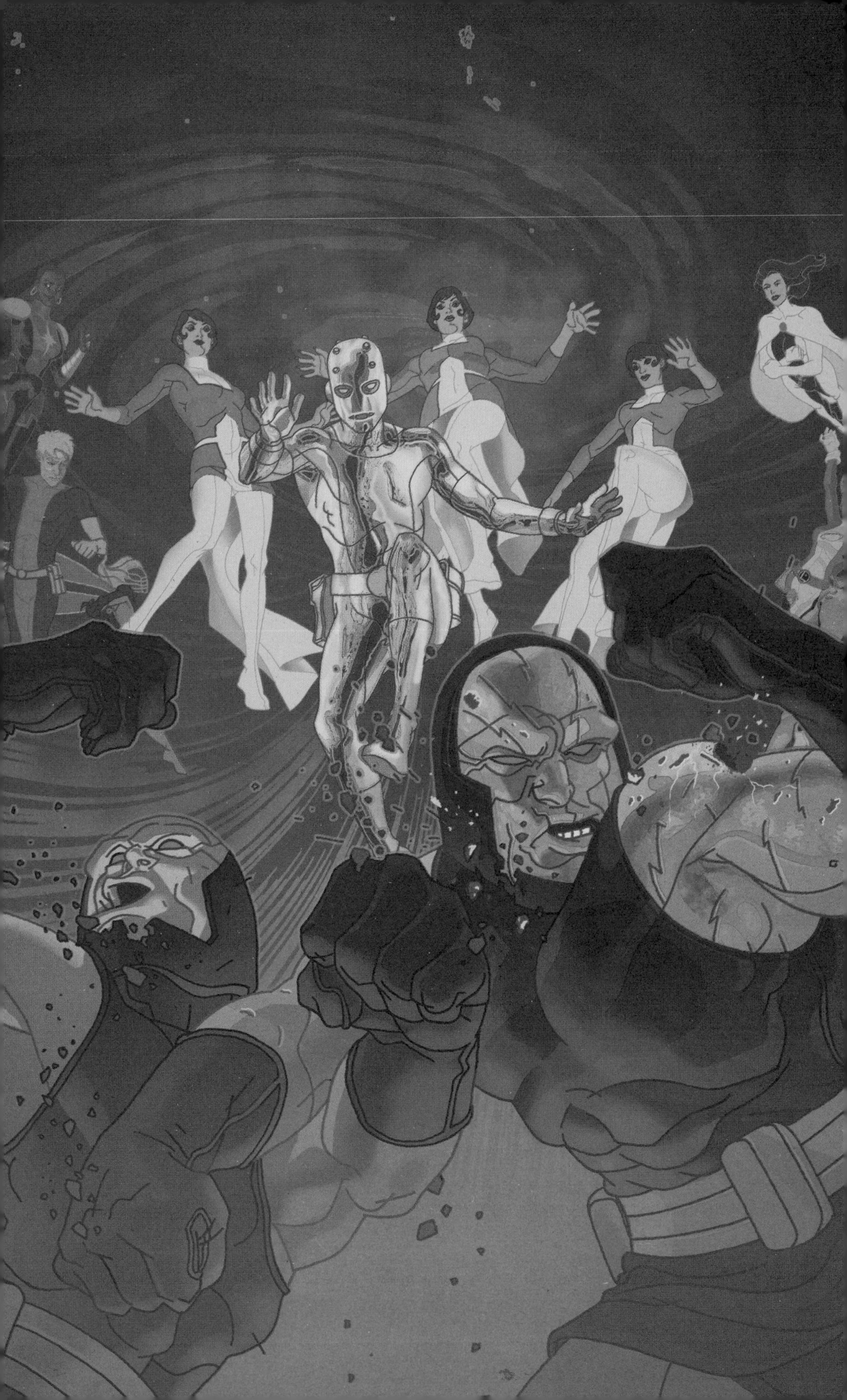

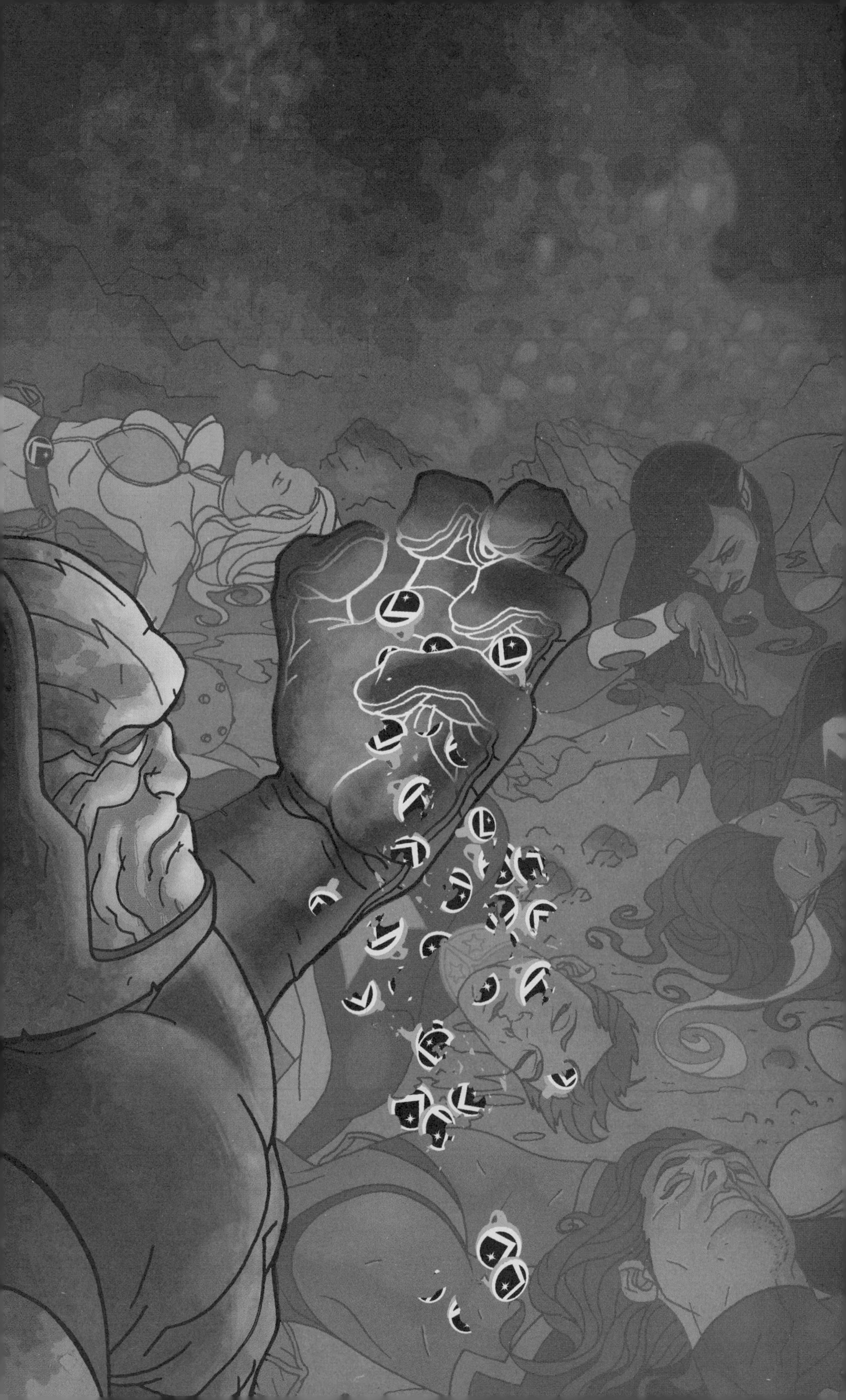

THE STARS OF THE
DC UNIVERSE
CAN ALSO BE FOUND IN THESE BOOKS:

TO FIND MORE COLLECTED EDITIONS AND MONTHLY COMIC BOOKS FROM DC COMICS,
CALL 1-888-COMIC BOOK FOR THE NEAREST COMICS SHOP OR GO TO YOUR LOCAL BOOK STORE.

Visit us at www.dccomics.com

DCU0011